# PENNSYLVANIA DUTCH COOKING

Books of similar interest from
Random House Value Publishing, Inc.

*Amish Cooking*

*The Amish: A Photographic Tour*

*As American As Apple Pie*

*Christmas Memories with Recipes*

*The 1896 Boston Cooking-School Cookbook*

*The Fannie Farmer Baking Book*

*The Pioneer Lady's Country Christmas*

# PENNSYLVANIA DUTCH COOKING

## A Mennonite Community Cookbook

# Mary Emma Showalter

Drawings by Naomi Nissley

Gramercy Books
New York

This 2000 edition is published by Gramercy Books ™, an imprint of Random House Value
Publishing, Inc. 201 East 50<sup>th</sup> Street, New York, N.Y. 10022 by arrangement
with Herald Press, Scottdale, Pa.

Gramercy Books™ and design are trademarks of Random House Value Publishing, Inc.
(Originally published as *Mennonite Community Cookbook*)

Random House
New York • Toronto • London • Sydney • Auckland
http://www.randomhouse.com/

Printed and bound in the United States of America.

Library of Congress Cataloging-in-Publication Data

Showalter, Mary Emma, 1913–
[Mennonite community cookbook]
Pennsylvania Dutch cooking : a Mennonite community cookbook / Mary Emma Showalter.
   p. cm.
Originally published: Mennonite community cookbook. Philadelphia : Winston, 1950.
  ISBN 0-517-16213-X (hc)
  1. Cookery, Mennonite. I. Title.

TX721 .S5414   2000
641.5'66—dc21
                                                        .  99-058320

9  8  7  6  5  4  3  2  1

DEDICATED TO

The memory of my grandmothers

MARY HEATWOLE SHOWALTER

and

EMMA CRAIG GROVE

for whom I was named and who, in
my early childhood, taught me by
example the worth of good cooking

# ACKNOWLEDGMENTS

The author wishes to acknowledge the whole-hearted coöperation on the part of many who have made this collection of recipes possible.

Those deserving special thanks are:

1. The one hundred and twenty-five women located in Mennonite communities throughout the United States and Canada, each of whom canvassed her community and collected recipes.

2. My advisers and professors at the University of Tennessee, BERNADINE MEYER, Ph.D., Professor of Foods, and RUTH BUCKLEY, Professor of Foods and Institution Management, who assisted me in setting up plans for the book and in testing recipes as a part of the requirement for my Master's thesis.

3. The photographer, M. T. BRACKBILL, professor at Eastern Mennonite College, Harrisonburg, Virginia, who took the colored photographs.

4. The typists, MERNA and ROSALYN BRENNEMAN, Harrisonburg, Virginia, who typed the manuscript.

5. My family and friends, who encouraged me during the months and years of work required in producing this book.

# CONTENTS

# CONTENTS

# INTRODUCTION

AMONG THE COOKBOOKS ON THE PANTRY SHELF AT HOME THERE HAS always been the little hand-written notebook of recipes. As a child I learned that this blue notebook, which contained a collection of my mother's favorite recipes, was her favorite cookbook.

Not only were all the pages of this notebook filled with recipes, but inserted between the pages were loose sheets of paper on which were written other favorites. These were copied by friends and relatives whom Mother had visited at some time and whose specialty she had admired. The recipes were usually named for the donor and thus the book contained many queer names, such as "Grandmother's Ginger Cakes" and "Aunt Emma's Fat Cakes."

As a child I occasionally visited my grandmother and an aunt in an adjoining county. They always had such delicious things to eat, and I noticed that they too frequently referred to quaint little hand-written notebooks similar to my mother's.

As a student in high school I took home economics and was delighted to learn of many new and beautifully illustrated cookbooks. The time had come when I felt I had outgrown that old-time notebook; so I pushed it aside while I tried out new recipes.

Then came college days and frequent visits to my roommate's home in Lancaster County, Pennsylvania. In the heart of that region, where Pennsylvania Dutch cookery abounds, I suddenly became aware of the fact that hand-written notebooks of recipes were still in use.

My first position after finishing college took me throughout the United States. En route I chanced to visit numerous Mennonite communities. I soon began to observe that wherever I went, to California or Colorado, to Iowa or Ohio, our cooking was much the same. Some of the recipes that my mother had recorded in her little book were being used even in the Far West.

Since a cookbook of the favorite recipes of Mennonite families had never been published, I now began to sense that the handwritten recipe books were responsible. I asked to see them wherever I went and was astonished to learn how many of them had been destroyed in recent years. The daughters of today were guilty of pushing them aside in favor of the new, just as I had done one day. It is true that many of our mothers were still using the old favorite recipes, but were doing so by memory. When I found them, the little notebooks were usually at the bottom of a stack of modern cookbooks and were kept only for memory's sake. Through the years many had become so worn and soiled that in places they were no longer legible.

By now these old books with their recipes had become like cherished pieces of old china, each telling a story of the days when Grandmother was queen of the kitchen. Two factors were responsible for my desire to collect these old recipes and have them published. The first was the realization that in many instances our mothers would be the last generation to use them. The second was the realization, on my own part, of how much I had learned to appreciate many of these fine old recipes. I was challenged with the thought that now is the time to preserve them. So this book is an attempt to preserve for posterity our own peculiar type of cookery that has been handed down for many generations.

In order to make this book more inclusive than it would be if only Grandmother's recipes were recorded, it also includes favorite recipes of our own day. Grandmother recorded no salad recipes or casserole dishes or numerous other dishes that our present appetites call for.

Many of the old recipes came in a form that would not be much help to the modern homemaker. In order to make each recipe usable today, all these have been tested, and ingredients have been measured by standard measuring equipment. Details for procedure in carrying out the recipe have also been added.

Most of the stories recorded in chapter introductions came from my grandmother, known to everyone outside the family as "Aunt Mary." At ninety years of age, she still entertained us with these stories from the good old days.

This collection is a compilation of over 1,100 recipes, chosen from more than 5,000 recipes sent in. They come to you from most of the Mennonite communities in the United States and Canada.

# GENERAL INFORMATION

Every possible effort has been made to present to the users of this book recipes that are properly balanced and those which can be easily followed. This fact alone, however, is not enough to assure one success in carrying them out. In order to obtain excellent results and thus give each recipe a chance to prove itself, the following things must be remembered:

1. All measurements are level.

2. There is a wrong and a right way of measuring each ingredient. (Details are given later.)

3. Standard measuring utensils must be used, a cup does not mean a tea or coffee cup. It refers to the standard measuring cup that holds 16 tablespoons.

4. Ingredients must be combined according to procedure given in the recipe. If the recipe states that the cake is to be made by the conventional method, one cannot expect to get the same results by using the quick method of mixing. The proportion of ingredients varies according to the method of mixing used.

5. The technique used in mixing a product is important. If the recipe states that one ingredient be folded into another, good results will not be obtained if these are beaten together.

6. The amount of mixing is important. If a cake is overmixed, the result is a decrease in volume. If undermixed, the texture is bread-like and the walls are coarse and thick.

7. Substitutions should not be made unless these are of such nature that good results can be assured.

8. The size of the baking pan is also important. The most satisfactory tins for layer cakes should be not more than 1½ inches deep. Straight-sided pans result in better textures than sloped ones. For fine, velvety texture, the batter should be at least one inch in depth when poured into pan.

9. Correct temperatures must be used. If the oven is too hot, a hard crust forms, which does not allow the batter to rise sufficiently. If

this occurs, the inside pressure causes the crust to break and a ridge will result. If too high temperature is used in meat cookery, a great amount of shrinkage results. If too high temperature is used in baking milk and egg products, the finished dish will be watery.

10. When a recipe calls for flour, it means all-purpose flour unless otherwise stated.

11. When a recipe calls for sugar, it means granulated sugar unless otherwise stated.

12. When a recipe calls for shortening, part lard or vegetable shortening may be used for economy and part butter or margarine for flavor.

## To Measure Dry Ingredients

Fill the cup or spoon to overflowing, then level it off with a straight-sided knife or spatula. Do not tap or shake cup in leveling, as this tends to pack ingredients. Flour should always be sifted before measuring.

To measure brown sugar, pack it firmly into a cup.

To measure confectioner's or powdered sugar, sift and pile it lightly into a cup.

## To Measure Liquids

Use a glass measuring cup on which the 1-cup mark does not come to the top of the cup. Otherwise it will be difficult to pour the liquid from the cup. Keep cup on a flat surface and check contents at eye level. Empty completely.

## To Measure Shortenings

If fat is hard, measure it by the water-displacement method. Fill cup with water to the 1-cup level. Then pour out as much water as shortening called for. Add shortening until the cup mark is again reached. If shortening is pliable, press it firmly into spoon or cup in order to remove air spaces. Level off with the straight edge of a knife or spatula.

## Equivalent Measurements

| | |
|---|---|
| 3 teaspoons = 1 tablespoon | 2 pints = 1 quart |
| 4 tablespoons = ¼ cup | 4 quarts = 1 gallon |
| 16 tablespoons = 1 cup | 16 ounces = 1 pound |
| 2 cups = 1 pint | |

## Common Food Equivalents

1 pound butter = 2 cups

1 pound corn meal = 3 cups

1 pound flour
    (all-purpose) = 4 cups

1 pound raisins = 3 cups

1 pound rice = 2 cups

1 pound sugar
    (granulated) = 2 cups

## Substitutions

1 ounce square chocolate...¼ cup cocoa plus 1½ teaspoons shortening

1 cup cake flour.........................⅞ cup all-purpose flour

1 tablespoon cornstarch for thickening.........2 tablespoons flour

## Oven Temperatures

Slow  .  .  .  250° to 300°F.

Moderate  .  325° to 375°F.

Hot  .  .  .  400° to 450°F.

Very hot .  .  above 475°F.

# DEFINITIONS OF COMMON COOKING TERMS

*Au gratin* ..... Food creamed, covered with bread or cracker crumbs and cheese or butter and browned in an oven.

*Bake* ......... To cook by dry heat as in an oven.

*Baste* ......... To moisten roasting meat or fowl with melted fat, milk, water, etc., to prevent burning.

*Beat* ......... To mix with a brisk rotary or up-and-over motion.

*Boil* .......... To cook in liquid (usually water) at a temperature above the boiling point.

*Blend* ........ To combine two or more ingredients thoroughly.

*Braise* ........ To cook by searing and browning in fat, and then simmering in a covered dish with little moisture.

*Broil* ......... To cook by direct heat under a flame or over hot coals.

*Brush* ........ To spread with a thin coat of butter, egg, etc., by means of a brush, paper or cloth.

*Caramelize* ... To heat sugar in a skillet until it melts and turns brown; to heat foods containing sugar until light brown and they have a caramel flavor.

*Chop* ........ To cut into very small pieces.

*Consommé* .... A highly seasoned clear soup made from meat and vegetables.

*Condiments* ... Food seasonings, such as salt, pepper, vinegar, spices and herbs.

*Coat* ......... To dip food into flour, bread or cracker crumbs, then into beaten egg and again into crumbs.

*Cream* ....... To mix one or more foods together until soft and fluffy.

*Croquette* .... A combination of previously cooked meat, fish, fowl, rice, etc., seasoned and held together with eggs or a thick sauce, shaped, then dipped in egg and crumbs and fried.

*Cube* ......... To cut into small squares.

*Cut* .......... To separate foods with a knife or scissors.

*Cut in* ........ To mix shortening and dry ingredients, with cutting motion of knives or spatulas or pastry blender.

| | |
|---|---|
| *Dice* ......... | To cut into small cubes, but not so small that the food loses its identity. |
| *Dot* .......... | To put small pieces of butter, cheese, etc., on the top of food. |
| *Drain* ........ | To pour off the liquid, as from meat or vegetables. |
| *Dredge* ....... | To coat well, usually with flour. |
| *Drippings* .... | The fat from roasted meat or cooked bacon. |
| *Dust* ......... | To sprinkle lightly with flour or sugar. |
| | |
| *Fat* .......... | Shortening, lard, butter, suet, etc., rendered; also oils. |
| *Fillet* ........ | A boneless piece of meat or fish. |
| *Flake* ........ | To separate into small pieces. |
| *Fold in* ....... | To blend two ingredients together by a down-over-up and across motion; used in adding beaten egg whites or whipped cream mixture. |
| *Fricassee* ..... | A stew, or to stew meat, poultry, etc., and serve with gravy or sauce. |
| *Fritter* ........ | A small amount of batter, often containing fruit, vegetables, etc., and fried in deep fat. |
| *Frosting* ...... | A coating for cakes, either cooked or uncooked, containing sugar and water or milk, egg white and flavoring. |
| *Fry* .......... | To cook in hot fat. To pan fry, a small amount of fat is used. For deep-fat frying, use enough fat to cover the food. |
| *Fryings* ....... | The fat from fried meat. |
| | |
| *Garnish* ...... | To adorn food with parsley, lemon, etc., to add to the attractiveness of its appearance. |
| *Giblets* ....... | The heart, liver and gizzard of poultry. |
| *Glaze* ........ | To coat with crystallized sugar. |
| *Grate* ........ | To rub into small particles by means of a grater. |
| *Grease* ....... | Any kind of fat with a buttery consistency; to coat a pan or dish with soft shortening to prevent ingredients from sticking to dish. |
| | |
| *Icing* ......... | See Frosting. |
| | |
| *Knead* ........ | To work dough with a pressing motion of the hands, stretching, then folding it over itself. |
| | |
| *Lard* ......... | To enrich by the insertion of strips of pork or bacon before roasting. |

**Liquor** ....... The liquid in which meat or other food has been boiled, or the natural liquid of oysters.

**Melt** ........ To change to a liquid by heating.
**Meringue** ..... An icing made of beaten white of egg and sugar.
**Mince** ........ To cut or chop into very small pieces.
**Mix** .......... To blend by beating or stirring.

**Panbroil** ...... To cook, with very little fat, in a hot frying pan or skillet.
**Parbroil** ...... To cook partially by boiling.
**Pare** ........ To cut away the outside covering on fruits or vegetables, such as potatoes and apples.
**Peel** .......... To strip or tear off the skin or rind of a fruit or vegetable, as an onion or orange.
**Poach** ........ To cook an egg by dropping it into boiling water and continuing the cooking process with water under boiling point until the white is set.

**Render** ....... To purify or separate fat from connective tissue by heating slowly until fat melts and can be poured off.
**Roll** .......... To flatten dough with a rolling pin.
**Roast** ........ To cook by dry heat, usually in an oven.

**Sauté** ........ To fry quickly and lightly in a pan containing little grease.
**Scald** ......... To bring a liquid, such as milk, just below the boiling point, at which bubbles appear around the sides of the pan.
**Score** ........ To mark light lines or notches on a surface.
**Sear** ......... To brown the surface of meat quickly, usually in a hot oven or pan.
**Shred** ........ To cut or tear into thin strips.
**Shortening** .... Butter, lard, etc.; any fat suitable for baking.
**Sift** .......... To put dry ingredients through a sifter or sieve.
**Simmer** ....... To cook in water just below the boiling point.
**Skewer** ....... A long pin of wood or metal, used to fasten meat, fowl, etc.
**Sliver** ........ To cut or shred into lengths.
**Soak** ......... To steep in liquid for a time.
**Soufflé** ....... A baked dish of eggs, milk, cheese, made fluffy with beaten egg whites.

*Steam* ........ To cook with the heat of boiling water, usually by means of a double boiler or steamer.

*Steep* ........ To cover with boiling water and allow to stand, as in making tea.

*Sterilize* ...... To destroy germs or bacteria by means of heat.

*Stew* ......... To cook slowly in liquid held just below the boiling point.

*Stir* .......... To blend ingredients with a circular or rotary motion.

*Stock* ........ Liquid in which meat or vegetables have been cooked.

*Toast* ........ To brown by direct heat or in an oven.

*Truss* ........ To bind or fasten a fowl or other meat with skewers or string to retain its shape.

*Whip* ........ To beat rapidly so as to incorporate air and increase volume, as in whipping cream and egg whites.

# Breads

## Chapter I

B READ IS THE STAFF OF LIFE," GRANDPA USED TO SAY WHEN HE CAME IN for dinner and smelled Grandma's freshly baked bread. But Grandma must have sometimes wished that baking day would not come so often. She always baked twice each week as regularly as she served three meals a day.

One of the essential pieces of equipment in the old-fashioned kitchen was the dough tray. In this boxy type of cabinet Grandma kept her flour and made up her bread. It was about four feet long and one and a half feet wide and deep. This stood on legs that were a comfortable height for Grandmother. The lid that slipped off was smooth on the underneath side and was used as a dough board.

1

Each Tuesday and Thursday evening Grandmother brought from the cellar or springhouse the can of liquid yeast that she had saved from the preceding bake day. She mixed into this some salt, sugar and fat and added enough warm water to make a gallon crock full of liquid. She then took the lid off the dough tray and at one end sifted a large amount of flour. Her next step was to make a well in the sifted flour and pour in the liquid. She worked the dough with her hands, adding more flour until she had a smooth, round ball of dough that no longer stuck to her fingers. Then she covered this with a clean cloth, put the lid on the tray, added another log to the fire, and went to bed.

In the morning she was up bright and early. As soon as breakfast had been started, she hurried to the outdoor oven in the back yard and made a fire. While the stones or bricks heated on the inside, she worked "out" the loaves of bread. She usually had twelve to fourteen loaves each baking. When the oven had heated to the correct temperature, she raked all the coals and ashes outside and slipped in the pans of dough.

There are many families who still make all their own bread, but I know of none who continue to use the dough tray and outdoor oven. The dough tray has moved from the lowly corner in the kitchen to a place of distinction in someone's colonial-furnished living room. The outdoor oven, when seen at all, is covered with ivy and kept only for memory's sake.

Grandmother had other favorites that she made for holiday occasions or just to have variety. There was salt rising bread, which many of us still enjoy. It was made by setting a sponge of sliced potatoes, corn meal and hot water. This was allowed to stand overnight, and then flour was added. Cheese rolls, zwieback and Portzelky (yeast fritters) are favorites among the Russian Mennonites. The latter were always made at New Year's time.

Fried corn-meal mush for breakfast or a big dish of cooked mush and milk for supper was a good substitute for bread. Recently I learned a new way of making mush from an old recipe. It said, "Add enough meal and flour to the boiling water until it becomes sufficiently thick to say 'pouff' when it cooks!"

## YEAST BREADS
### Starter for Liquid Yeast

| | |
|---|---|
| 4 medium-sized potatoes | 2 teaspoons salt |
| 3 pints boiling water | 1 small yeast cake |
| ½ cup sugar | ½ cup lukewarm water |

Pare and slice the potatoes and cook in hot water until soft.

Force potatoes through a ricer or colander and add to potato water.

There should be 1 quart of this mixture.

Add to this the sugar and salt.

When mixture has cooled to lukewarm temperature, add the yeast that has been dissolved in ½ cup warm water.

Keep at room temperature for 24 hours and then pour into sterilized jars and keep in refrigerator or cool cellar.

To make up bread, use 1 cup of starter in place of 1 compressed yeast cake.

To 3 cups starter add:

    3 quarts lukewarm water
    I cup sugar
    ¾ cup lard
    2 tablespoons salt

Before adding flour to make a sponge, remove 3 cups of liquid for next baking.

This may be kept in refrigerator for three weeks.

## Basic White Bread Recipe

| | |
|---|---|
| 4 cups scalded milk or | 2 tablespoons salt |
| 2 cups milk and 2 cups water | 3 tablespoons shortening |
| 2 cakes compressed yeast | 12 cups sifted flour |
| 2 tablespoons sugar | |

Dissolve yeast in ½ cup warm water.

Add fat, sugar and salt to scalded milk or boiling water.

Add softened yeast to milk that has cooled to lukewarm temperature.

Add flour gradually, making a dough stiff enough so that it can be easily handled.

Knead dough quickly and lightly until it is smooth and elastic.

Place in greased bowl, cover and set in a warm place to rise.

Let rise until double in bulk (about 2 hours).

Shape into loaves, brush with melted fat and allow to rise again until double in bulk.

Bake at 350-375° for approximately 1 hour or at 425° for 15 minutes and then reduce to 375° for 30 minutes.

When done, bread will shrink from the sides of the pan and should have a hollow sound when tapped.

When baked, remove bread from pans.

Do not cover while cooling if a crusty bread is desired.

Makes 3 large or 4 medium loaves.

Mrs. Paul Godshall, *Harleysville, Pa.*; Mrs. Aaron Stauffer, *Adamstown, Pa.*

## Basic Roll Recipe

2 cups milk
5 tablespoons sugar
5-6 cups flour
1½ teaspoons salt

¼ cup shortening
1 yeast cake softened in ½ cup warm water
1 egg (optional)

Scald the milk and add shortening and sugar.

When liquid is cooled to lukewarm temperature, add yeast that has been dissolved in ½ cup lukewarm water.

Add 3 cups of flour and beat thoroughly.

Set sponge in a warm place for 30 minutes, or until light.

Beat egg and salt and add to sponge along with the remaining flour.

Knead until dough no longer sticks to the board or fingers.

When dough is light, cut into small pieces and shape into rolls.

Brush with fat and let rise until light.

Bake at 400-425° until a golden brown (15 to 20 minutes).

Makes approximately 2 dozen medium-sized rolls.

MRS. JOHN W. GINGERICH, *Wellman, Iowa*

## "Bubbat"
### *A Favorite of the Russian Mennonites*

1 yeast cake
1 egg
1½ cups milk
1 tablespoon salt

3 tablespoons sugar
1 pound smoked sausage
Flour enough to make stiff dough (approximately 3½-4 cups)

Scald milk and then cool it to lukewarm temperature.

Add dissolved yeast and sugar.

Then add beaten egg, salt and enough flour to make a soft dough that can barely be stirred with a spoon.

Let dough rise and then pour into a greased pan 10 x 14 x 2 inches.

Into this press 3 inch lengths of sausage at 3 inch intervals.

Let rise again; the dough will almost cover sausages.

Bake at 375-400° for approximately 45 minutes.

Serve hot.

Serves 6-8.

ESTHER BARGEN, *North Newton, Kan.*

# VARIATIONS FOR ROLLS
## Butter Horns

1 cake compressed yeast dissolved in
½ cup warm water
1 cup scalded milk
½ cup sugar

½ cup shortening
3 eggs
1½ teaspoons salt
4½-5 cups flour

Scald milk. When cooled to lukewarm temperature, add yeast that has
been dissolved in warm water.

Add salt, sugar and beaten eggs.

Beat thoroughly.

Stir in flour gradually, adding enough so that dough no longer sticks to
fingers.

Cover, set in a warm place and let rise until light.

Roll out dough ⅜ inches thick into circular shapes the size of a dinner
plate.

Cut into pie-shape wedges and brush with melted butter.

Start rolling at wide end and roll toward center.

Place on greased sheet or pan and let rise again until double in size.

Bake at 425° for 20 minutes.

Makes 3½ dozen small rolls.

MRS. EVA COOPRIDER, *Hesston, Kan.*; MRS. KATIE JANTZ, *Haviland, Kan.*
MRS. HARVEY STAHLY, *Nappanee, Ind.*

## Clover-Leaf Rolls

¾ cup scalded milk
¼ cup sugar
3 tablespoons shortening
1½ teaspoons salt

1 cake compressed yeast
¼ cup lukewarm water
1 egg, beaten
3½ cups flour

Pour scalded milk over sugar, salt and shortening.

Soften yeast in lukewarm water.

Add beaten egg.

Add yeast mixture to milk that has cooled to lukewarm temperature.

Add flour gradually, mixing well after each addition.

Knead lightly for several minutes.

Place in greased bowl, cover and let rise in a warm place until double
in bulk.

Pinch off pieces of dough the size of a marble, roll into round balls,
and place 3 of these in greased muffin tin.

Let rise until double in bulk.

Bake at 425° for 20 minutes.

Makes 15-18 rolls.

MRS. RHEDA KEIM, *Holsopple, Pa*

## Parker House Rolls

1 cake compressed yeast
2 cups milk
3 tablespoons sugar

1¼ teaspoons salt
4 tablespoons shortening
6 cups flour

Scald milk. When cooled to lukewarm temperature, add sugar, salt and
shortening.

Add yeast which has been softened in ¼ cup warm water.

Stir into the mixture 3 cups of flour and beat thoroughly.

Cover and let rise in a warm place for 45 minutes.

Add the remainder of flour and knead for 5 minutes.

Place in greased bowl and allow to rise again until double in bulk.

Roll out ¼ inch thick and cut with biscuit cutter.

Crease through center with dull side of knife, brush with melted butter
and fold over as a half-moon.

Pinch at center of outer edge to hold together.

Let rise until light.

Bake at 425° for 15 minutes.

Yields about 3 dozen rolls.

MARY BRUBAKER, *Harrisonburg, Va.;* MRS. J. T. SCHROCK, *Hutchinson, Kan.*

## Refrigerator Rolls

| | |
|---|---|
| 2 cups boiling water | 2 yeast cakes |
| ¼ cup sugar | ¼ cup warm water |
| 1/3 cup shortening | 2 eggs, beaten |
| 1 teaspoon salt | 8 cups flour |

Mix together the sugar, salt, shortening and boiling water. Let cool.

Dissolve yeast in ¼ cup warm water and add to above cooled mixture.

Add beaten eggs.

Add 4 cups flour and beat thoroughly.

Add the remaining 4 cups and beat. Do not knead.

Cover tightly and store in refrigerator until ready to use.

Remove from refrigerator 1½ hours before serving time and shape as
desired.

This dough may be kept in refrigerator for 7 days.

Follow directions for baking given in basic roll recipe (page 4).

MIRIAM SHAFFER, *Martinsburg, Pa.;* MRS. MOSES H. YODER, *Hartville, Ohio*
EMMA WITMER, *Columbiana, Ohio*

## Cheese Rolls

To basic roll recipe (page 4) add:

2 cups grated cheese to flour and work into dough.

## Fruit Rolls

To basic roll recipe (page 4) add:

2 cups of finely chopped or ground dried fruit
½ cup each of raisins, figs, dates and nuts makes a good combination.

## Toasted Oats or Grape Nut Rolls

To basic roll recipe (page 4) add:

2 cups grape nuts or
2 cups of rolled oats that have been toasted in the oven.

For these, less flour than usual should be added to basic roll recipe.

ANNA MUSSER, *Mohnton, Pa.*

## Foundation Sweet Dough Recipe
### *An Old Tried Recipe!*

I cup scalded milk
I cup lukewarm water
2 cakes compressed yeast
½ cup shortening
½ cup sugar

1½ teaspoons salt
2 eggs, beaten
7 cups flour
½ teaspoon nutmeg or
½ lemon, rind and juice may be added

Scald milk and pour it over sugar, salt and shortening.

Dissolve yeast in lukewarm water.

Add beaten eggs.

When milk has cooled to lukewarm temperature, add the yeast and beaten eggs.

Beat well.

Add flour gradually, beating well.

Knead lightly, working in just enough flour so that dough can be handled.

Place dough in a greased bowl, cover and let stand in a warm place.

Let rise until double in bulk (about 2 hours).

Make into cinnamon, butterscotch or pecan rolls in following recipes.

MRS. JOHN RIEHL, *Leetonia, Ohio*

## Cinnamon Rolls

One recipe of foundation sweet dough (preceding recipe).

6 tablespoons melted butter
1½ cups brown sugar

I tablespoon cinnamon
I cup raisins (optional)

When dough is light, divide into 2 portions.

Roll into oblong pieces ¼ inch thick.

Brush with melted butter and sprinkle with brown sugar and raisins.

Roll like a jelly roll and cut slices ½ inch thick, using a sharp knife.

Place slices 1 inch apart on greased tin with cut side down.

Let rise in a warm place until light (about 1 hour).

Bake at 400° for 20-25 minutes.

These may be spread with plain butter frosting while still warm.

They are also delicious if baked in 2 cups of syrup that is poured into the bottom of the pan before dough is added.

Mrs. Raymond Tice, *Grantsville, Md.*

Another variation is to cut roll into ½ inch strips, but do not cut all the way through.

Then twine roll in a ring around the inside of a round pan and pour syrup over top to bake.

## Butterscotch Rolls

Make 1 recipe of foundation sweet dough (page 7).

Roll out as a jelly roll.

Cut into pieces ½ inch thick.

Place rolls in a greased pan and let rise until double in size.

Bake at 375° for approximately 20 minutes.

Just before baking, pour over them a syrup made of:

    ½ cup brown sugar
    I cup water
    I cup of pecans or other nut meats may be added

Mrs. Henry Sola, *Holsopple, Pa.*

## Oatmeal Yeast Bread

| | |
|---|---|
| I cup rolled oats | I cup milk, scalded |
| 2 tablespoons sugar | I compressed yeast cake |
| I tablespoon shortening | ¼ cup warm water |
| I teaspoon salt | 2½ cups flour |

Mix together the oats, sugar, salt and shortening.

Pour over this the scalded milk.

When cooled to lukewarm, add yeast that has been softened in ¼ cup warm water.

Stir in flour and knead until dough no longer sticks to fingers.

Shape into a loaf of bread or into rolls.

Let rise until double in bulk.

Bake at 400° for rolls for 20 minutes and at 375° for 40-45 minutes for a loaf.

Mrs. Herman Rinkenberger, *Bradford, Ill.*

## Orange Bowknots

| | |
|---|---|
| I¼ cups milk, scalded | 2 eggs, beaten |
| ½ cup shortening | ¼ cup orange juice |

1/3 cup sugar
1 teaspoon salt
1 cake compressed yeast

2 tablespoons grated orange peel
5 cups flour

Combine sugar, salt, shortening and scalded milk.

Cool to lukewarm temperature and crumble yeast cake in this mixture.

Add beaten eggs, orange juice and grated rind.

Beat mixture thoroughly.

Add flour gradually, mixing to a soft dough.

Cover and let stand 10 minutes.

Knead and then let rise until double its bulk.

Roll dough ½ inch thick.

Cut in 10 inch strips ½ inch wide.

Tie each strip into a knot.

Place on baking sheet and let rise again until double in size.

Bake at 400° for 15 minutes.

Spread with topping made of:

2 tablespoons orange juice
1 teaspoon grated orange rind
1 cup confectioners' sugar

This amount makes 2 dozen rolls.

FLORENCE STRONG, *Mechanicsburg, Pa.*

## Russian Easter Bread

### *Paska*

2 cups flour
1 cup cream
1 cup milk
1½ cups sugar

10 eggs
1 cup butter
1 teaspoon lemon extract
1½ yeast cakes

Dissolve yeast and 1 tablespoon sugar in ½ cup warm water.

Scald milk and cream; while hot pour over the 2 cups flour.

When flour mixture has cooled, add beaten egg yolks that have been
    mixed with sugar.

Add dissolved yeast and beaten egg whites.

Beat thoroughly and put in a warm place to rise overnight.

In the morning add butter and enough flour to make a dough that no
    longer sticks to the fingers.

Let rise.

At noon divide dough into 3 parts, putting each part into a gallon tin
    can (this gives the Paska the traditional shape).

Let rise 2 hours and bake at 350° for 1 hour.

## Cheese Spread for Paska

4 cups cottage cheese
Yolks of 10 hard-cooked eggs
1 cup cream

1 cup butter
1 cup sugar
1 teaspoon grated lemon rind

Press cheese and egg yolks through a sieve.
Bring cream to a boil and then cool.
Cream together the butter and sugar and add the other ingredients.
Mix thoroughly.
This is now ready to use as a spread when serving Paska.

MRS. H. J. FAST, *Mountain Lake, Minn.*

## Sally Lunn

### Old Virginia

This recipe was brought to Virginia by colonial settlers from England
and has become a favorite American recipe.

2 cups milk
¼ cup fat
1½ yeast cakes
3 eggs, beaten

2 tablespoons sugar
2 teaspoons salt
6 cups flour

Scald milk, add sugar, salt and shortening.
Cool to lukewarm and crumble in the yeast.
Stir in beaten eggs.
Add flour and beat thoroughly.
Cover and let rise until double in bulk.
Beat down and pour into greased bundt pan.
Let rise again until double in bulk.
Bake at 350° for 45 to 50 minutes.
Yields 16 large servings.

KATE BEACHY, *Grantsville, Md.*

## Soy Bean Bread

2 cups boiling water or milk
2 cups soy bean flour
1 tablespoon shortening
1 teaspoon salt

1 tablespoon sugar
1 compressed yeast cake
Enough white flour to make a dough
that can be handled easily

Mix as for white bread (page 3).
Let rise until double in bulk.
Knead and shape into loaves.
Bake at 375° for 1 hour.

## Milk Bread
### *Stretzel*

| | |
|---|---|
| 4 cups scalded milk | ½ cup lukewarm water |
| 1½ cups shortening | 1½-2 yeast cakes |
| 3 tablespoons salt | 11-12 cups flour |
| 1 tablespoon sugar | |

Mix as for standard bread recipe (page 3).

Let rise until double in bulk.

Bake at 350° for 1 hour.

Yields 3 large or 4 medium-sized loaves.

For variation: 1 cup raisins may be added for each cup of milk used.

MRS. JOHN J. BECKER, *Mountain Lake, Minn.*

## Vegetable Bread

| | |
|---|---|
| 1 cup carrots | 3 sprigs parsley |
| 1 cup canned peas | 2 yeast cakes |
| 1 potato | ½ cup shortening |
| 1 quart tomato juice | ¼ cup sugar |
| 1 cup green beans | 3 tablespoons salt |
| 1 onion | 12½ cups flour, approximately |

Cook vegetables together until tender.

Force vegetables through a sieve. There should be 1½ quarts juice and pulp.

Dissolve yeast in 1 cup lukewarm water.

Add yeast to vegetable pulp and add sugar, salt and shortening.

Add 5 cups flour and stir until well blended.

Let batter work until light and full of bubbles (about 1 hour).

Add remaining flour and let rise until double in bulk.

Knead and shape into loaves.

Rub each loaf with melted butter; let rise again until double in bulk.

Bake at 350° for 45 to 50 minutes.

Makes 4 loaves.

MRS. RALPH D. MILLER, *Nampa, Idaho*

## Whole Wheat Bread

| | |
|---|---|
| 1 cup scalded milk | ¼ cup honey or syrup |
| 1 cup hot water | 3 tablespoons shortening |
| 1 compressed yeast cake | 2 cups white flour |
| 1 tablespoon salt | 4 cups whole wheat flour |

Follow directions for yeast breads in basic recipe (page 3).

Shape into loaves.

Bake at 350° for 50-60 minutes.

Makes 2 small-medium loaves.

MRS. EARL MARTIN, *Hagerstown, Md.;* EMMA WITMER, *Columbiana, Ohio*

## Zwieback

| | |
|---|---|
| 2 cups scalded milk | I cup shortening |
| I cup warm water | 2 eggs (optional) |
| 2 teaspoons sugar | I yeast cake |
| 2 teaspoons salt | 8-10 cups sifted flour |
| 4 tablespoons sugar | |

Scald milk, add shortening, salt and 4 tablespoons sugar.

Crumble yeast in a small bowl, add 2 teaspoons sugar and 1 cup lukewarm water. Set in a warm place until spongy.

Add yeast mixture and beaten eggs to lukewarm milk.

Mix well and stir in flour gradually.

Knead dough until very soft and smooth.

Cover and let rise in a warm place until double in bulk.

Pinch off small balls of dough the size of a small egg.

Place these 1 inch apart on greased pan.

Put a similar ball, but slightly smaller, on top of bottom ball.

Press down with thumb.

Let rise until double in bulk (about 1 hour).

Bake at 400-425° for 15-20 minutes.

Yields approximately 4 dozen.

Mrs. J. J. Voth, *North Newton, Kan.*
Mrs. Dietrich Warkentin, *Mountain Lake, Minn.*

# QUICK BREADS
## Banana Tea Bread

| | |
|---|---|
| 1¾ cups sifted flour | 1/3 cup fat |
| ¾ teaspoon soda | 2/3 cup sugar |
| 1¼ teaspoon cream of tartar | 2 eggs well beaten |
| ½ teaspoon salt | I cup mashed bananas |

Sift the flour, salt, soda and cream of tartar together.

Beat the fat until creamy and then add sugar gradually.

Add eggs and beat well.

Add dry ingredients alternately with crushed bananas.

When well blended, pour batter into a greased loaf pan 8 x 4 x 3 inches.

Bake at 350° for 1 hour and 10 minutes.

Cut in squares and serve cold.

Mrs. Frank Raber, *Detroit, Mich.*

## Biscuits

| | |
|---|---|
| 2 cups flour | 3 tablespoons fat |
| 4 teaspoons baking powder | ¾ to I cup milk |
| ½ teaspoon salt | |

Sift flour, baking powder and salt together.
Cut in fat, this may be lard or vegetable shortening.
When the mixture is in lumps the size of peas, add the milk all at once.
Mix well together and turn dough out onto a floured board.
Knead 20 to 30 strokes.
Roll ⅝ inch thick and cut with biscuit cutter.
Bake at 450° for 12 minutes.
Makes 16-18 biscuits.

GRANDMOTHER SENSENIG, *Oley, Pa.*

Drop biscuits may be made by adding ¼ cup milk to preceding recipe and dropping dough from a spoon onto cookie sheet or into muffin pans.

## Buttermilk Biscuits

| | |
|---|---|
| 2 cups flour | ½ teaspoon soda |
| ½ teaspoon salt | 3 tablespoons fat |
| 3 teaspoons baking powder | I cup sour milk or buttermilk |

Sift dry ingredients together.
Cut in shortening until mixture resembles coarse crumbs.
Add sour milk all at once.
Stir until dough follows fork or spoon around the bowl.
Turn out on floured board and knead ½ minute.
Roll ⅝ inch thick and cut with biscuit cutter.
Bake on ungreased sheet at 450° for 12 minutes.
This makes 2 dozen biscuits 1 inch in diameter.

MRS. B. L. BUCHER, *Dallastown, Pa.;* MRS. MARY FLORY, *Stuarts Draft, Va.*

## Chicken Biscuits

Make biscuit dough from one of the two preceding recipes.
Roll out the entire amount in a round sheet ¼ inch thick.
Cover generously with chopped, cooked chicken.
Roll as a jelly roll and slice in pieces 1 inch thick.
Place on greased sheet, 1 inch apart and bake at 425° for 15 minutes.
Serve with chicken broth thickened to make gravy.

MRS. JOHN KOPPENHAVER, *Perkasie, Pa.*

## Finger Biscuits
### Schnetki

| | |
|---|---|
| 2 cups flour | ½ cup shortening |
| 3 teaspoons baking powder | I cup milk |
| ½ teaspoon salt | I cup cream |

Sift dry ingredients together.

Cut in shortening as in pastry.

Add cream and milk and blend together well.

Turn out on floured bowl and knead 20 strokes.

Roll out to ¼ inch thickness.

At one edge lap dough over to 1 inch width.

Cut off this double strip.

Lap dough over again and cut.

Repeat until entire strip has been cut.

Cut long double strips in 3 inch lengths.

Bake at 425° for 15 minutes or until golden brown.

Makes 16-18 biscuits.

HELEN LOHRENZ, *Mountain Lake, Minn.*

## Butterscotch Rolls

2½ cups sifted pastry flour
3½ teaspoons baking powder
1 teaspoon salt
¼ cup granulated sugar
5 tablespoons shortening

½ cup milk
1 egg, well beaten
For bottom of tins:
½ cup melted butter or margarine
1¼ cups brown sugar

Put 1 teaspoon of melted butter and 1 teaspoon of brown sugar in bottom of each muffin tin.

Sift flour, baking powder, salt and sugar together.

Cut in shortening and blend well.

Add beaten egg to milk, and pour into flour mixture.

Mix together and turn out on floured surface, knead 20 strokes.

Roll in oblong shape ¼ inch thick.

Spread with remainder of the melted butter and sprinkle with brown sugar.

Roll like a jelly roll.

Slice in pieces ½ inch thick and place in muffin tins.

Bake at 400° for 20 to 30 minutes.

Makes 24 rolls.

GRACE GLICK, *Sugar Creek, Ohio*

## Corn Bread

¾ cup yellow corn meal
1 cup white flour
2 tablespoons sugar
2 tablespoons melted shortening

1 teaspoon salt
3½ teaspoons baking powder
2 eggs
1 cup sweet milk

Sift flour and corn meal; measure and add baking powder, salt and
sugar. Sift again.

Add beaten eggs and melted shortening (half fat and half butter).

Beat thoroughly.

Pour into well-greased shallow pan, 8 x 10 inches.

Bake at 425° for 25 minutes.

MRS. PAUL FETROW, *Camp Hill, Pa.*

## Sour Cream Corn Bread
### An Old Recipe

¾ cup corn meal
1 cup flour
1 teaspoon soda
1 teaspoon cream of tartar
1 teaspoon salt

2½ tablespoons sugar
1 egg, well beaten
2 tablespoons melted butter
1 cup thick sour cream
4 tablespoons milk

Sift flour and corn meal; measure and add soda, cream of tartar, salt
and sugar. Sift again.

Add beaten egg, cream, milk and melted shortening.

Beat thoroughly.

Pour into a greased pan 9 inches square.

Bake at 425° for 20 minutes.

MRS. JOHN SALTZMAN, *Shickley, Neb.*

## Apple Corn Bread

¾ cup corn meal
¾ cup flour
3 teaspoons baking powder
½ teaspoon salt
2 tablespoons melted shortening

2 tablespoons sugar
1 egg, slightly beaten
¾ cup diced apples
¾ cup sweet milk

Sift flour and corn meal; measure and add baking powder, salt, and
sugar. Sift again.

Add beaten egg and milk.

Stir until well blended.

Add apples and melted shortening.

Mix thoroughly.

Pour butter into greased shallow pan 9 inches square.

Bake at 400° for 25 minutes.

MRS. L. J. POWELL, *South English, Iowa*

## Cinnamon Rolls from Pastry Dough

This is an excellent way to use leftover scraps of pastry.

Children are very fond of these rolls.

Roll out pastry into an oblong shape.

Spread with melted butter and sprinkle generously with sugar and cinnamon (brown sugar preferred).

Roll as a jelly roll and slice in ½ inch pieces.

Place in shallow pan with cut side down and bake 20 minutes at 400°.

Mrs. Lloyd Lefever, *East Petersburg, Pa.*

## Dutch Apple Bread

| | |
|---|---|
| 2 cups flour | I egg |
| 3 teaspoons baking powder | I cup milk |
| 2 tablespoons sugar | 2 tablespoons butter |
| I teaspoon salt | 5 tart apples, pared and sliced |

Sift flour; measure and add baking powder, salt and sugar. Sift again.

Cut shortening into dry ingredients as for pastry.

Add beaten egg and milk.

Beat thoroughly until well blended.

Spread in a greased shallow pan, 8 x 12 inches.

Press apple slices over the top and sprinkle with sugar and cinnamon.

Bake at 400° for 25-30 minutes.

Serve with milk.

Mrs. P. L. Buckwalter, *Atglen, Pa.*

## Plain Muffins

| | |
|---|---|
| 2½ cups flour | 3 tablespoons melted fat |
| 4 teaspoons baking powder | I or 2 eggs |
| ½ teaspoon salt | I cup milk |
| 2 tablespoons sugar | |

Sift flour; measure and add baking powder, salt and sugar. Sift again.

Beat eggs and add to milk; pour this into flour mixture.

Stir only enough to blend ingredients together, batter should appear slightly lumpy.

Drop by spoonfuls into greased muffin tins, filling tin ⅔ full.

Bake at 400° for 20-25 minutes.

Yields 12 to 15 muffins.

Mrs. Ed Umble, *Gap, Pa.*

## Apple Sugar Muffins

| | |
|---|---|
| 4 tablespoons shortening | I cup milk |
| ½ cup sugar | I cup apples, peeled and chopped |
| I egg, beaten | I teaspoon cinnamon |

2 cups sifted flour  
3½ teaspoons baking powder  
½ teaspoon salt  
2 tablespoons sugar  
1 cup crushed corn flakes

Cream shortening and sugar.

Add well-beaten egg.

Sift flour; measure and add baking powder, salt, and ½ teaspoon cinnamon. Sift again.

Add dry ingredients to first mixture alternately with milk.

Stir only enough to mix ingredients.

Fold in chopped apples and corn flakes.

Drop by spoonfuls into greased muffin tins, filling each ⅔ full.

Mix 2 tablespoons of sugar and ½ teaspoon cinnamon together and sprinkle on top.

Bake at 400° for 25 minutes.

Serve while hot.

Makes 12-15 muffins.

MRS. LOYAL KAUFFMAN, *Tofield, Alta., Can.*

## Bran Muffins

1 cup all bran  
1 cup milk  
2 tablespoons shortening  
¼ cup sugar  
1 egg, well beaten  
1 cup sifted flour  
3 teaspoons baking powder  
½ teaspoon salt

Add bran to milk and let soak 5 minutes.

Cream shortening and sugar together.

Add beaten egg and beat until smooth.

Add bran mixture.

Measure and sift dry ingredients together and add to mixture, stirring only enough to blend.

Drop from a spoon in greased muffin tins, filling each ⅔ full.

Bake at 400° for 25 minutes.

Makes 10 muffins.

NAOMI YODER, *Hartville, Ohio*

## Corn Meal Muffins

¾ cup corn meal  
1¼ cups flour  
4 teaspoons baking powder  
½ teaspoon salt  
2 tablespoons sugar  
1 cup milk  
2 tablespoons shortening  
1 egg

Sift flour and corn meal. Measure and add baking powder, salt and sugar. Sift again.

Add beaten egg to milk.

Pour liquid into dry ingredients all at once.
Stir only enough to blend together.
Add melted shortening.
Drop batter into greased muffin tins, filling each ⅔ full.
Bake at 425° for 20-25 minutes.
Yields 12 muffins.

ANNA MARY ZIMMERMAN, *Mechanicsburg, Pa.*

## Date or Raisin Muffins

| | |
|---|---|
| 2 cups flour | 4 tablespoons shortening |
| 4 teaspoons baking powder | I egg |
| ½ teaspoon salt | ¾ cup milk |
| 4 tablespoons sugar | ¾ cup chopped dates or raisins |

Sift flour; measure and add baking powder and salt. Sift again.
Cream shortening, add sugar and blend well.
Add beaten egg and chopped dates, or raisins.
Add sifted dry ingredients alternately with milk.
Stir only enough to mix ingredients together.
Drop by spoonfuls into greased muffin tins, filling them ⅔ full.
Bake at 400° for 20-25 minutes.
Yields 12-15 muffins.

MRS. AMOS KREIDER, *East Petersburg, Pa.*

## Graham Muffins

| | |
|---|---|
| I cup graham flour | I egg |
| I cup white flour | ¾ cup milk |
| 4 teaspoons baking powder | 4 tablespoons brown sugar |
| I teaspoon salt | 4 tablespoons melted shortening |

Measure and sift dry ingredients together.
Beat egg.
Add sugar, milk and melted butter.
Combine with dry ingredients and pour into greased muffin tins.
Bake at 425° for 25 minutes.
Yields 10-12 muffins.

GENEVIEVE FRIESEN, *Drug C.P., India*

## Graham Nut Muffins

| | |
|---|---|
| I cup graham flour | I egg |
| I cup white flour | 4 tablespoons sugar |
| 3 teaspoons baking powder | ½ cup chopped nuts |
| ½ teaspoon salt | I cup milk |

Sift white and graham flour; measure and add baking powder and salt. Sift again.

Add beaten egg and mix slightly.

Add chopped nuts.

Combine milk and melted shortening and add to mixture.

Stir only until ingredients are combined.

Drop by spoonfuls into greased muffin tins, filling each ⅔ full.

Bake at 400° for 25 minutes.

Yields 15 muffins.

ANNIE BEACHY, *Salisbury, Pa.;* MRS. C. A. GRAYBILL, *Martinsburg, Pa.*

## Graham Raisin or Prune Muffins

| | |
|---|---|
| 3 tablespoons sugar | ¾ cup graham flour |
| 3 tablespoons shortening | 2 teaspoons baking powder |
| I egg | ½ teaspoon soda |
| I cup sour milk | ½ teaspoon salt |
| I cup white flour | ¾ cup raisins or dried prunes |

Sift white and graham flour; measure and add baking powder, soda and salt. Sift again.

Cream shortening and sugar together.

Add beaten egg.

Add flour mixture alternately with milk.

Add stewed chopped raisins or prunes.

Pour into greased muffin tins and bake at 400° for 25 minutes.

Makes 12-15 muffins.

MRS. PAUL HEGE, *Dayton, Va.;* MRS. E. M. GLICK, *Parkesburg, Pa.*

## Blueberry Muffins

| | |
|---|---|
| 2 cups flour | 2 tablespoons melted butter |
| 4 teaspoons baking powder | I egg |
| ½ teaspoon salt | I cup milk |
| 4 tablespoons sugar | I cup blueberries |

Sift flour; measure and reserve 3 tablespoons to dust berries. To remaining flour add baking powder, salt and sugar. Sift again.

Add beaten egg and melted butter to milk and combine with dry ingredients.

Fold in berries.

Drop by spoonfuls into greased muffin tins.

Bake at 400° for 25 minutes.

Yields 12-15 muffins.

MRS. HUBERT PELLMAN, *Harrisonburg, Va.*

## Whole Wheat Muffins

| | |
|---|---|
| 2 cups whole wheat flour | 1 cup sour cream or |
| 1/2 teaspoon baking soda | 1 cup sour milk plus |
| 1/2 teaspoon salt | 3 tablespoons butter |
| 3 tablespoons sugar or syrup | |

Sift flour; measure and add soda, salt and sugar. Sift again.

Add sour cream.

Stir only enough to mix ingredients.

Drop by spoonfuls into greased muffin tins.

Bake at 400° for 25 minutes.

Yields 12 muffins.

MRS. E. N. SWARTZENDRUBER, *Wellman, Iowa*

## Nut Bread

| | |
|---|---|
| 3 cups flour | 1 1/2 cups milk |
| 4 teaspoons baking powder | 1 egg, well beaten |
| 1/2 cup sugar | 1 cup chopped nuts |
| 1/2 teaspoon salt | |

Sift flour; measure and add baking powder, salt and sugar. Sift again.

Beat egg and add to milk.

Combine liquid with dry ingredients.

Fold in floured nuts.

Let stand in loaf pan (5¼ x 9¼ inches) for 20 minutes.

Bake at 375° for 1 hour.

Makes 1 loaf.

BETTY SCHULTZ, *Milverton, Ont., Can.;* MRS. E. S. GARBER, *Nampa, Idaho*

## Orange Nut Bread

| | |
|---|---|
| 3 cups flour | 1 1/2 cups milk |
| 1 teaspoon salt | 1 teaspoon grated orange peel |
| 4 teaspoons baking powder | 2 tablespoons melted shortening |
| 3/4 cup sugar | 1/2 cup nuts, chopped |
| 1 egg, beaten | |

Sift flour; measure and add baking powder, salt and sugar. Sift again.

Combine milk, beaten eggs and shortening and add to flour mixture.

Fold in orange peel and nuts.

Stir until mixed but do not beat.

Pour into a greased pan 4 x 8 inches.

Bake at 375° for 1 hour.

This makes delicious sandwiches when slices are spread with a filling
made by adding chopped olives and pimiento to cream cheese.

MRS. RACHEL POWELL, *South English, Iowa*

## Carrot Nut Bread

| | |
|---|---|
| I cup grated carrots | I cup warm water or milk |
| ¾ cup brown sugar | 2 eggs |
| I teaspoon baking soda | 1½ cups flour |
| 2½ teaspoons baking powder | I cup whole wheat flour |
| 2 tablespoons shortening | ½ cup nuts, chopped |
| I teaspoon salt | |

Sift flour; measure and add baking powder, soda, salt and sugar. Mix thoroughly.

Add to the liquid the beaten eggs and melted shortening.

Combine liquid with dry ingredients.

Fold in floured, chopped nuts and grated carrots.

Pour batter into greased loaf pan 4 x 8 inches.

Let stand 5 minutes.

Bake at 375° for 1 hour.

Delicious for school lunches.

EMMA KAUFMAN, *Davidsville, Pa.*


## Popovers

| | |
|---|---|
| 2 cups flour | I 2/3 cups milk |
| 3 eggs | 2 tablespoons melted butter |
| ½ teaspoon salt | |

Sift flour; measure and add salt. Sift again.

Beat eggs until light and add milk and melted butter.

Add liquid slowly to dry ingredients, beating thoroughly with electric beater or rotary egg beater (about 2 minutes).

Grease custard cups or muffin tins. Heat these in oven before filling with batter.

Fill tins half full of batter.

Bake at 450° for 20 minutes, then reduce heat to 350° for last 20 to 25 minutes.

This makes 14-16 popovers.

MRS. ISHMEIL MARTIN, *Conestoga, Ont., Can.*


## Salt Rising Bread

| | |
|---|---|
| 2½ cups potatoes, sliced | I teaspoon baking soda |
| 2 tablespoons corn meal | I cup warm milk |
| 1½ tablespoons salt | I tablespoon shortening, melted |
| I quart boiling water | II cups flour |
| 1½ teaspoons sugar | |

Sprinkle 1 tablespoon salt and the corn meal over potatoes.

Add boiling water and stir until salt has dissolved.

Cover and keep warm from noon to the following morning.

Then drain off liquid. Add to it the soda, 1½ teaspoons sugar, and 5 cups flour.

Stir until ingredients are well blended; this sponge should be the consistency of cake batter.

Set mixture in a warm place and let rise until light and full of bubbles. This requires about 1½ hours.

Scald milk and cool to lukewarm; add shortening.

Add milk and remaining flour to sponge.

Knead for 10 to 12 minutes and shape into loaves.

Makes 3 medium-sized loaves.

Let rise until light, about 1½ hours.

Bake at 350° for 1 hour. Delicious!

MAGGIE DRIVER, *Waynesboro, Va.;* MRS. G. H. BRUNK, *Elida,* **Ohio**

## Southern Spoon Bread

| | |
|---|---|
| 2½ cups milk | I cup yellow corn meal |
| 2 teaspoons sugar | 3 eggs, separated |
| I teaspoon salt | 3 tablespoons butter |

Place milk in top of double boiler and heat to boiling point.

Add salt and corn meal, stirring constantly to prevent lumps.

Cook 4 minutes and pour slowly over beaten yolks.

Add butter and beat until it is melted.

Fold in stiffly beaten whites and pour in greased casserole.

Bake at 400° for 45 minutes.

Serves 8.

MARY C. SHENK, *Denbigh,* **Va.**

# DOUGHNUTS

If a fat frying thermometer is not available, test temperature of fat by dropping a ½ inch cube of bread into it.

It should brown in 1 minute.

## Potato Doughnuts

| | |
|---|---|
| 1½ cups sugar | 5 cups flour |
| 3 eggs | 3 tablespoons melted shortening |
| 2 cups mashed potatoes | I teaspoon salt |
| I cup sweet milk | ¼ teaspoon nutmeg |
| 5 teaspoons baking powder | |

Beat mashed potatoes, add melted fat, beaten eggs and milk.
Sift dry ingredients together and add to liquid.
Dough should be soft yet firm enough to roll.
Divide dough into four parts.
Roll out one part at a time to ¾ inch thickness.
Cut with doughnut cutter and drop into deep fat (375°).
Fry until a golden brown on both sides.
Drain on absorbent paper.
Shake in a paper bag containing a mixture of sugar and cinnamon or
    powdered sugar.
This makes approximately 4½ dozen doughnuts.

MRS. SUSIE HOCHSTETLER, *Shanesville, Ohio*

## Sweet Cream Doughnuts

1¼ cups sweet cream
½ cup brown sugar
2 eggs

½ teaspoon salt
3 teaspoons baking powder
3⅛ cups flour

Beat eggs, add sugar and sweet cream.
Combine with sifted dry ingredients.
Mix well and roll out ⅜ inch thick.
Cut with doughnut cutter and let stand 1 hour.
Fry in deep fat at 375° until brown on both sides.
Roll in sugar.
Makes about 3½ dozen.

## Puffball or Quick Tea Doughnuts

3 eggs
1 cup sugar
2 cups milk
2 tablespoons melted fat

½ teaspoon salt
2 teaspoons baking powder
2 cups flour

Beat eggs.
Add sugar and milk.
Sift dry ingredients together and add to liquid.
Beat thoroughly and add melted fat.
Add more flour to make a batter stiff enough to hold a spoon in a
    standing position.
Drop by spoonfuls into deep fat at 375°.
Remove when brown and drain on absorbent paper.
This makes approximately 4 dozen.

MRS. HERMAN A. SOMMERFELD, *Canton, Kan.*

## Crullers
### *Roll Kuchen*

½ cup cream, sweet or sour
½ cup milk
2 eggs
1 teaspoon baking soda

1 teaspoon salt
1 teaspoon sugar
3½ to 4 cups flour

Beat eggs, add cream and milk.

Sift dry ingredients together and add to liquid.

Use just enough flour so that dough can be rolled but is still soft.

When well mixed, let stand 2 hours.

Roll out ⅜ inch thick and cut into oblong strips 2 x 7 inches.

Cut 2 slashes through strip crosswise to aid in frying.

Fry in deep fat (375°) until light brown on both sides.

Makes 3½ dozen crullers.

If a sweet cruller is preferred, add ½ cup of sugar.

MRS. HERBERT R. SCHMIDT, *Newton, Kan.;* MRS. G. G. FAST, *Mountain Lake, Minn.*
MRS. C. H. WEDEL, *Newton, Kan.*

## Fastnachts or Raised Doughnuts

1¼ cups milk
¼ cup shortening
1 teaspoon salt
1 small yeast cake

3 eggs, beaten
¾ cup sugar
¼ teaspoon nutmeg
4½ to 5 cups sifted flour

Scald the milk, add shortening and salt.

Cool milk until it is lukewarm; then add crumbled yeast cake and stir.

Gradually add 2⅝ cups sifted flour, beating batter thoroughly.

Put in a warm place and allow to stand until full of bubbles.

Mix sugar with nutmeg and combine with beaten eggs.

Stir into first mixture and add remaining flour.

Knead well, cover and let rise in a warm place for about 1 hour.

Turn out lightly on floured board and roll ⅜ inch thick.

Cut with doughnut cutter or biscuit cutter shaping into a ball, or make into twists.

Cover with a thin cloth and let rise on board until top is springy to touch of finger.

Drop into hot fat (375°) with the raised side down, so the top side will rise while under side cooks.

Drain on absorbent paper.

Yields 3 dozen.

MRS. PAUL H. HORST, *Millersburg, Ind.;* MRS. HARRY RHODES, *Salem, Ohio*

Raised doughnuts are delicious if dipped in a syrup made by boiling
together for 5 minutes the following:

I cup sugar
¾ cup water
I tablespoon white syrup

Mrs. O. D. Brunk, *Hyattsville, Md.*

## Dewey Buns

I½ pints lukewarm water
½ cup shortening
I cup sugar

I large yeast cake
2 tablespoons salt
Flour (approximately 8 cups)

Dissolve yeast in lukewarm water.

Add salt, sugar and melted shortening.

Work in enough flour so that dough can be kneaded without sticking
to the hands.

Place in greased bowl, cover and let rise until light or doubled in bulk.

Roll dough on board to ½ inch thickness.

Cut into strips ¾ inch wide and 3 inches long.

Place these strips on greased sheets.

Brush with melted fat.

Let rise again until light.

Fry in deep hot fat as you do doughnuts (375°), until brown on both
sides.

Roll in powdered sugar.

These are delicious when served warm.

Nannie Showalter and Mary Suter, *Harrisonburg, Va.*
Barbara Moyer, *Telford, Pa.*

## COFFEE CAKES
### Coffee Cake

Filling and topping:

½ cup brown sugar
2 teaspoons cinnamon
2 tablespoons flour

2 tablespoons melted butter
½ cup chopped nuts
¼ cup dates or raisins

Blend these ingredients together well before mixing coffee cake batter.

Coffee cake batter:

I½ cups sifted flour
3 teaspoons baking powder
¼ teaspoon salt
¾ cup sugar

¼ cup shortening
I egg
½ cup milk

Sift dry ingredients together and cut in shortening.

Beat eggs well and add milk.

Combine liquid with dry ingredients.
Spread half the batter in a greased flat pan 8 x 8 inches or 6 x 10 inches.
Sprinkle with half of the filling.
Add the other half of the batter and sprinkle remaining filling on top.
Bake at 375° for 25 minutes.
Cut in squares.

MRS. HIRAM L. GROSS, *Kulpsville, Pa.*

## Coffee Crumb Cake

| | |
|---|---|
| 1½ cups sifted flour | 3 teaspoons baking powder |
| ½ cup soya flour | ⅛ teaspoon baking soda |
| ¾ cup brown sugar | 1 egg |
| ½ teaspoon salt | ½ cup cold coffee |
| 1/3 cup shortening | 1/3 cup chopped nuts |
| 1 teaspoon cinnamon | |

Sift all dry ingredients together, except soda and baking powder.
Cut in shortening until mixture resembles coarse corn meal.
Reserve ½ cup of this mixture for topping.
To remainder, add soda and baking powder and mix thoroughly with
a fork.
Beat egg, add coffee and combine with flour mixture.
Pour into a 9 inch greased pie plate and sprinkle with the ½ cup of
crumbs and chopped nuts.
Bake at 400° for 30 minutes.
This is excellent when served with coffee for breakfast or lunch.

MRS. CLAYTON ROHRER, *Wadsworth, Ohio*

## Spice Filled Coffee Cake

| | |
|---|---|
| 3 cups flour | ¼ teaspoon nutmeg |
| ¾ cup sugar | ½ teaspoon cinnamon |
| 2 eggs beaten | ¼ cup shortening |
| 4 teaspoons baking powder | 1 cup milk |
| ½ teaspoon salt | |

Sift together the flour, baking powder, salt, spices and sugar.
Cut in shortening.
Beat eggs and add to them the milk.
Combine liquid and dry ingredients.
Pour into two round greased cake pans.
Bake at 400° for 35 minutes.
When cool, spread with the following topping:

| | |
|---|---|
| 3 tablespoons butter | ⅛ teaspoon salt |
| 1 cup brown sugar | ½ teaspoon cinnamon |
| 3 tablespoons flour | |

Cream butter, add sugar, cinnamon, salt and flour.

Mix together well and spread on top of the cake.

This cake is delicious when served with whipped cream.

Mrs. Paul Martin, *Campbell, Ohio*

## "Streusel Kuchen"
### *Raised Coffee Cake*

| | |
|---|---|
| 2 cups milk | 6½ cups flour |
| ½ cup shortening | I yeast cake (small) |
| I cup sugar | 1/3 cup lukewarm water |
| ½ teaspoon salt | I egg white |
| I egg yolk | |

Heat milk to boiling in top of double boiler and let it cool until lukewarm.

Cream together the butter, sugar, salt and egg yolk.

Add the yeast, which has been softened in ⅓ cup of lukewarm water.

Add milk and flour alternately to above mixture.

Beat egg white until stiff and add to batter.

Allow to rise in a covered bowl overnight or until light.

Divide into 4 parts and pat each into a pie pan.

Let rise 1½ hours.

Sprinkle with streusel crumbs made with the following:

| | |
|---|---|
| ½ cup sugar | 3 tablespoons soft butter |
| I teaspoon cinnamon | ½ teaspoon vanilla |
| ¼ cup sifted flour | 3 tablespoons chopped nuts |

Bake at 425° for 20 minutes.

Stella Huber Stauffer, *Tofield, Alta., Can.;* Mrs. Leo Brandt, *Newton, Kan.*

## GRIDDLE CAKES, WAFFLES, FRIED MUSH
### Plain Pancakes

| | |
|---|---|
| I teaspoon sugar | 2 cups milk |
| I teaspoon salt | 2 cups flour |
| I tablespoon shortening | 3 teaspoons baking powder |
| 2 egg yolks | 2 egg whites |

Measure and sift the dry ingredients together.

Add the milk gradually, beating to make a smooth batter.

Add the beaten egg yolks and the melted fat.

Fold in stiffly beaten egg whites.

Bake on a hot griddle.

Makes 8 medium-sized cakes.

Mrs. David A. Bontrager, *Haven, Kan.*

## Buckwheat Griddle Cakes (With Yeast)

¼ yeast cake
¾ cup lukewarm water
1½ cups scalded milk
½ teaspoon salt

1¾ cups buckwheat flour
1 teaspoon baking soda
1 tablespoon molasses
1 egg

Soften yeast in ¼ cup water.
Scald milk and cool to lukewarm.
Stir in salt, yeast and flour.
Beat well.
Cover and let stand in a warm place overnight.
In the morning, dissolve soda in ½ cup warm water and add to sponge.
Add molasses and beaten egg.
Bake on hot griddle.
Turn cakes only once.
Makes approximately 6-8 medium-sized cakes.

MRS. MARK RHODES, *Columbiana, Ohio*

## Sour Milk Buckwheat Cakes

2 cups buckwheat flour
¾ cup white bread flour
2 teaspoons baking powder
1 teaspoon soda

1 teaspoon salt
2 cups sour milk or buttermilk
1¼ cups sweet milk
1 tablespoon shortening

Measure and sift dry ingredients together.
Add milk gradually, stirring constantly to make a smooth batter.
Add melted shortening.
Bake on a hot griddle.
Makes 8 medium-sized cakes.

CATHERINE J. MILLER, *Grantsville, Md.*

## Century Griddle Cakes

2 cups flour
2 teaspoons baking powder
1 teaspoon salt
2 tablespoons melted butter

3 tablespoons sugar
2 eggs
1 cup sweet milk

Measure and sift dry ingredients together.
Beat eggs until light and add milk.
Add dry ingredients to milk and eggs.
Beat thoroughly.
Add melted shortening.
Bake on a hot griddle.
Makes about 8 medium-sized cakes.

## Syrup for Griddle Cakes

2 cups water  
1 cup brown sugar

1 teaspoon vanilla

Cook water and sugar together until slightly thickened.
Remove from heat and add vanilla.

MRS. CHESTER WENGER, *Fentress, Va.*

## Corn Meal Griddle Cakes

2 cups buttermilk  
2 egg yolks  
1½ teaspoons salt  
2 tablespoons melted shortening  
1 teaspoon baking powder

1 teaspoon soda  
1 cup corn meal  
1 cup white flour  
2 egg whites

Sift flour; measure and add baking powder, soda and salt. Sift again.
Beat yolks, add buttermilk.
Then add dry ingredients.
Beat until smooth and add melted butter.
Fold in stiffly beaten egg whites.
Bake on a hot griddle.
Yields approximately 8 medium-sized cakes.

MRS. MARTHA KREIDER, *Wadsworth, Ohio*

## Corn Meal Pancakes with Raisins

To the above corn meal griddle cake recipe add:

½ cup chopped raisins

My favorite breakfast dish!

RITA RAE EBERSOLE (AGED 5), *Sterling, Ill.*

## Coconut and Corn Griddle Cakes

1½ cups corn meal  
½ cup flour  
4 teaspoons baking powder  
½ teaspoon salt  
1 tablespoon sugar

1 egg  
¾ cup milk  
¾ cup water  
1 tablespoon melted butter  
1 cup grated coconut

Measure and sift dry ingredients together.
Beat egg, add milk and water and mix with dry ingredients.
Add melted butter and then the coconut.
Bake on hot griddle and serve with honey or syrup.
Yields about 8 medium-sized cakes.

ESTHER HISTAND, *Cottage City, Md.*

## Fried Corn Meal Mush

3 cups yellow corn meal
2 quarts boiling water

1 teaspoon salt
½ cup white flour

Bring water to a boil.

Sift together corn meal, white flour and salt.

Slowly add dry ingredients to boiling water, stirring constantly to prevent lumps.

When well blended, cover and cook slowly in a double boiler for two hours or in a heavy pan on slow heat for 1 hour.

Pour into flat pans to mold.

Set in refrigerator to chill thoroughly.

Cut in slices ¼ inch thick and fry on griddle or in skillet until a golden brown on both sides.

Delicious with hot maple syrup or apple butter!

GERALDINE GINGERICH, *Lowville, N. Y.;* MRS. JAMES BAUMAN, *Oyster Point, Va.*

## Flannel Cakes

3 cups flour
4 teaspoons baking powder
1 teaspoon salt

3 cups sweet milk
2 eggs, separated
2 tablespoons melted butter

Measure and sift dry ingredients together.

Beat egg yolks and add milk.

Pour milk mixture slowly into dry ingredients and beat thoroughly.

Add melted butter and then fold in stiffly beaten egg whites.

Bake on hot griddle.

Yields about 12 medium-sized cakes.

MRS. LIZZIE ANDERS, *Telford, Pa.*

## Fried Bread Cakes

2½ cups stale bread crumbs
2 cups milk
3 eggs
1 teaspoon salt

3 teaspoons baking powder
3 tablespoons flour
2 tablespoons shortening

Soak the bread crumbs in the milk until soft.

Add well-beaten eggs and the sifted dry ingredients.

Drop from a spoon on a hot greased griddle.

Turn carefully, as these cakes are very tender.

Serve with syrup.

Yields about 8-10 cakes.

MRS. AARON GROFF, *Bareville, Pa.*

## Hominy Cakes

| | |
|---|---|
| 2 cups cooked hominy | 2 cups milk |
| 2 eggs | ¾ teaspoon salt |
| 1 cup flour | |

Cook hominy in salt water until soft. Drain.
Add beaten eggs, flour, salt and milk.
Drop batter from a spoon onto a hot griddle.
Fry until brown on both sides.
Serve as griddle cakes.
Will make about 12-15 cakes.

Mrs. William Reiff, *Hagerstown, Md.*

## Potato Pancakes

| | |
|---|---|
| 1 cup mashed potatoes | 2 eggs, separated |
| 1 cup milk | 2 teaspoons baking powder |
| ½ cup flour | |

Add egg yolks to mashed potatoes and beat.
Stir in flour and baking powder alternately with milk.
Fold in stiffly beaten egg whites.
Drop from a spoon onto a hot greased griddle and bake.
Makes about 12 cakes.

Mrs. William H. Nafziger, *Archbold, Ohio*

## German Potato Pancakes

| | |
|---|---|
| 4 medium-sized potatoes | 1 teaspoon baking powder |
| 3 eggs | ½ cup flour |
| ½ cup milk | 1 teaspoon salt |

Pare the potatoes and grate them.
Add beaten eggs and sifted dry ingredients.
Drop from a spoon into a hot, greased frying pan.
Bake until a golden brown on both sides.
Makes 10-12 cakes.

Mrs. Fred Lavers, *Detroit, Mich.;* Mary Keffer, *Waterloo, Ont., Can.*

## Rice Cakes

| | |
|---|---|
| 1 cup cooked rice | 1 teaspoon baking powder |
| 3 eggs, separated | 1 cup flour |
| 1 cup milk | ½ teaspoon salt |
| 1 tablespoon sugar | 1 tablespoon melted butter |

Add beaten egg yolks to warm cooked rice and beat.
Add all the other ingredients and mix together.

Fold in the stiffly beaten egg whites.

Drop from a spoon onto a hot griddle and brown on both sides.

Serve with syrup.

Makes about 10 cakes.

MRS. AMOS SHOWALTER, *Paramount, Md.*

## Russian Pancakes

| | |
|---|---|
| I egg | I cup flour |
| ½ teaspoon salt | I cup milk |

Beat egg until light.

Measure and sift flour and salt together. Add to beaten egg.

Add milk gradually and beat until batter is smooth.

This is a very thin batter.

Pour some pancake batter into hot, greased frying pan, allowing it to run over the entire surface of the pan in a thin layer.

When edges are golden brown, turn and fry on the other side.

These may be rolled like crêpes Suzette or served with butter and sugar, syrup or jam.

Makes about 8 cakes.

MRS. GEORGE P. EITZEN, *Mountain Lake, Minn.*

## Sour Milk Griddle Cakes

| | |
|---|---|
| 2 cups flour | ½ teaspoon soda |
| I teaspoon salt | 2 eggs |
| 2 tablespoons sugar | 2 cups sour milk |
| 2 teaspoons baking powder | 2 tablespoons melted fat |

Measure and sift dry ingredients together.

Beat eggs, add milk and stir into dry ingredients.

Add melted fat and stir only enough to blend ingredients.

Bake on hot griddle.

These are very good.

Makes 10-12 cakes.

RUTH FLISHER, *Nampa, Idaho;* MRS. QUINTUS LEATHERMAN, *Souderton, Pa.*

## Whole Wheat Pancakes

| | |
|---|---|
| 2 eggs | 2 teaspoons baking powder |
| I cup brown sugar | I cup milk |
| I tablespoon butter | 2 cups whole wheat flour |
| ½ teaspoon salt | |

Beat eggs, add sugar and milk.

Sift dry ingredients together and add to liquid.

Add melted shortening and blend together.
Bake on hot griddle.
Makes 8-10 cakes.

MRS. AMOS LEIS, *Wellesley, Ont., Can.*

## Waffles

| | |
|---|---|
| 2 cups flour | 6 tablespoons melted butter |
| 1 teaspoon salt | 2 eggs, separated |
| 4 teaspoons baking powder | 1½ cups milk |
| 2 tablespoons sugar | |

Sift dry ingredients into a mixing bowl.
Beat egg yolks and add milk.
Combine with flour mixture.
Add melted butter.
Fold in stiffly beaten egg whites.
Bake in hot waffle iron.
Makes 6 waffles.

MRS. BERNICE HOBBS, *Iowa City, Iowa;* GRACE EASH, *Jerome, Pa.*

## Apple Waffles

| | |
|---|---|
| 1¼ cups pastry flour | 2 teaspoons baking powder |
| 1 tablespoon sugar | 2 eggs, separated |
| ¼ teaspoon salt | 1 cup milk |
| ½ teaspoon cinnamon | 1¾ cups finely chopped apples |
| 6 tablespoons melted fat | |

Sift dry ingredients together.
Beat egg yolks.
Add milk.
Combine with flour mixture.
Beat until smooth.
Add chopped apples and melted butter.
Fold in stiffly beaten egg whites.
Makes 6 waffles.

ANNA HORST, *Blue Ball, Pa.*

## Cream Waffles

| | |
|---|---|
| 2 cups flour | 1 teaspoon sugar |
| ½ cup thick sour cream | 2 teaspoons baking powder |
| 1½ cups sweet milk | 2 eggs, separated |
| ½ teaspoon salt | |

Sift dry ingredients together.
Beat egg yolks and add milk and cream.

Combine with dry ingredients.
Fold in stiffly beaten egg whites.
Makes 6 waffles.

Mrs. Richard Martin, *Elida, Ohio*

## Gingerbread Waffles

2¼ cups sifted flour
½ teaspoon salt
1¼ teaspoons soda
2 teaspoons ginger

1 cup dark molasses
½ cup milk
1 egg, separated
1/3 cup butter

Sift dry ingredients together.
Beat egg yolk, add molasses and milk.
Combine egg and flour mixtures.
Add melted butter and fold in stiffly beaten egg whites.
Bake in waffle iron and serve with ice cream, or lemon or orange sauce.
Makes 6-8 waffles.

Mrs. William Hunsberger, *Spring City, Pa.*

# Soups

## Chapter II

Gone with the years is that old soup kettle that always stood
on the back of the stove. It was no problem to Grandma to know what
to do with the liquid in which vegetables had cooked, for in that soup
pot she placed all her meat scraps and vegetable broths. She did not
serve soup every day, but when she needed it to fill out a meal that
was a little more lean than usual, she was prepared.

As soon as you mention soup to the Pennsylvania Dutchman he
immediately smacks his lips with the thought of chicken corn soup. To
those of Russian background nothing is more delicious, in the way of
soups, than borsch. This is a type of vegetable soup to which sour cream
is added just before serving. Another soup that is a universal favorite

among our people is bean soup, seasoned with ham bone or salt pork. This is delicious, as someone suggested, when served with green garden onions.

Besides soups containing meat stock, there are numerous types of milk and cream soups thickened with rivels (tiny balls of dough no larger than a cherry stone) or cubes of toasted bread. Equally as good as the bean soup cooked with meat is the one prepared by adding rich milk, butter and slices of toasted bread to the beans before serving. A favorite of my grandmother was her milk and rivel soup. It was one of her few dishes I never learned to appreciate. There was another in the same category, which she called "Pap." This was made by adding sugar and flour paste to hot milk, and it had the reputation of being able to get anyone on his feet after any kind of illness!

"Chilly Day Soup" had just the right name, for it touched the spot on those chilly days during the "sheep rains," or on dreary days in fall and winter. The old recipe says to "add four chopped onions to a kettle half full of water, then add diced potatoes, cabbage," etc. It is a vegetable soup without a meat stock.

There is yet another type of soup made in some Mennonite communities and known as "Cold Soup" or "Farmer's Summer Supper Dish." It is made by adding crushed fruit or berries to cold milk. This is then poured over a dish of broken-up bread and allowed to stand until all the milk is absorbed. In this same class of soaked bread soups is the very old "Vinegar Soup" or "Black Strap," which was popular in eastern Pennsylvania during the early days. The fact that these have not survived to any extent is proof enough that they are no longer considered palatable.

## VEGETABLE SOUPS AND CHOWDERS

### Bean Soup with Pork

| | |
|---|---|
| 1½ pounds ham butt | 2 cups strained tomatoes or tomato |
| 1 pound soup beans | juice |
| 1 cup diced celery | 2 teaspoons minced parsley |
| 2 onions, chopped | Salt and pepper |

Soak beans overnight in enough water to cover.

In the morning drain and add 2 quarts of fresh water, cook until almost tender.

Wash ham, cover with cold water and cook until tender.

Skim fat from the broth and add beans.

Add other ingredients, season, and cook until vegetables are soft.
Serves 8.

Mrs. Hartley Rhines, *Souderton, Pa.*
Mrs. Florence C. Friesen, *Greensburg, Kan.*

## Bean Soup

| | |
|---|---|
| 2 cups navy beans | 1 pound salt pork |
| 2 quarts water | Salt and pepper |

Soak beans overnight in enough water to cover.
Drain in the morning and add 2 quarts of water and salt pork.
Cook slowly for approximately 3 hours or until beans are soft.
Strain or mash through a colander. Season.
Serve with green garden onions.
Serves 6.

Kate Beachy, *Grantsville, Md.*

## Old-fashioned Bean Soup

| | |
|---|---|
| 1½ cups navy beans | 2 quarts milk |
| Salt and pepper | 3 tablespoons butter |
| 3 cups toasted bread cubes | ¼ cup cream |

Soak beans and cook until soft.
Add milk and butter, salt and pepper.
Bring almost to a boil; and just before serving add cream and pour over
   bread cubes.
Serves 8.

Mrs. Samuel N. Schultz, *Wellesley, Ont., Can.*
Erma M. Bender, *Grantsville, Md.*

## Borsch

### Russian Vegetable Soup

| | |
|---|---|
| 2 pounds beef (with soup bone) | 6 whole pepper kernels |
| 2 carrots | 1 bay leaf |
| 1 medium-sized head of cabbage | A few sprigs of parsley or dill |
| 2 medium-sized onions | ½ cup sour cream |
| 2 cups fresh or canned tomatoes | 1 cup chopped beets (optional) |
| 6 medium-sized potatoes | |

Cover meat with cold water and bring to a boil.
Let simmer until almost tender, adding water if necessary to keep meat
   covered.
One hour before serving, add chopped vegetables and seasonings.
Potatoes may be cooked separately and added just before serving.
When ready to serve, remove from heat and add sour cream.

This is a delicious thick soup.
Serves 8.

MRS. JOHN WARKENTIN, *Mountain Lake, Minn.*

## Celery Chowder

3 cups chopped celery (outside
   stems and leaves)
1 cup diced potatoes
1 onion, minced

1 quart milk
2 hard-cooked eggs, chopped
Salt and pepper

Brown onion in 1 tablespoon fat.
Add chopped celery and potatoes.
Cover with water and simmer until soft.
Add milk and chopped eggs, season and bring to a boil.
Serves 6.

ANNA HERSH, *Elizabethtown, Pa.*

## Celery Potato Soup

1 cup potatoes
1 cup celery
Salt and pepper

1 quart milk
2 tablespoons butter

Dice celery and potatoes and cook together until soft.
Add milk, butter and seasoning and bring to a boil.
Serves 6.

MRS. IRVIN BEACHY, *Salisbury, Pa.*

## Corn Chowder

4 slices bacon
1 tablespoon minced celery
1 tablespoon minced pepper
1 tablespoon minced onion
2 potatoes, diced

3 tomatoes
2 cups corn
2 pints milk
Salt and pepper

Chop bacon and place in pan to brown.
Add minced celery, pepper and onion.
Fry together until bacon is brown.
Add corn and sauté together for 3 minutes.
Add the chopped vegetables including potatoes and 1 cup of water.
Cover and cook slowly for 30 minutes.
Then add rich milk, and heat to boiling again.
Add chopped parsley.
Serves 4.

MRS. M. D. BURKHOLDER, *Harrisonburg, Va.*
MRS. CLAUDE M. SHISLER, *Souderton, Pa.*

## Corn Soup with Rivels

3 cups fresh or canned corn
2 quarts of water
1 cup rich milk
1 1/3 cups flour

1 egg
3 tablespoons butter
1½ teaspoons salt
Parsley

If fresh corn is used, cut kernels from the ear and cook for 10 minutes
in the water.

If canned corn is used, small, whole kernel corn is preferred. Bring to a
boil but do not cook.

Make a batter by mixing egg, flour and milk together.

Pour this batter through a colander, letting it drop into boiling corn.

Add butter and salt and cook slowly for 3 minutes in a covered pan.

Garnish with parsley.

Serves 6.

This soup should be eaten immediately, so that rivels retain their shape
rather than spread through soup.

MY GRANDMOTHER SHOWALTER

## French Onion Soup

2 medium-sized onions
2 ounces butter
1 quart of soup stock or milk

5 slices bread
¼ cup grated sharp cheese
Salt and pepper

Chop onions fine and fry in the butter until brown.

Add boiling soup stock or milk, and season.

When soup is ready to serve, add toasted bread cubes and grated
cheese.

Serves 4.

MRS. A. E. REESOR, *Markham, Ont., Can.*

## Potato Soup

2 cups diced potatoes
3 cups water
2 tablespoons butter

1 quart rich milk
1 onion
Salt and pepper

Cook potatoes in salt water until tender.

Drain, but save the water.

Run potatoes through a ricer, or mash them fine.

Add scalding hot milk, butter and potato water to the potatoes.

Grate the onion and put in soup tureen, pour the hot soup over it.

Serve with crackers or toasted bread.

Serves 8.

KATE B. HERSHBERGER, *Salisbury, Pa.*

## Potato Soup with Bacon and Browned Bread Cubes

| | |
|---|---|
| 3 large potatoes | 1½ cups bread cubes |
| 1 medium-sized onion | Salt and pepper |
| 1 quart water | ½ cup cream |
| 4 or 5 strips of bacon | |

Cook diced potatoes and onion in water until soft.

Cut bacon in small pieces and fry until brown.

Remove pieces of bacon from fat and toast small pieces of bread in meat fryings.

Add bacon and browned bread to soup, remove from heat and add cream.

Serves 4.

MRS. HARVEY FOGEL, *Grantsville, Md.*

## Potato Soup with Celery and Eggs

| | |
|---|---|
| 2 cups diced potatoes | 3 hard-cooked eggs, chopped |
| 1 medium-sized onion | 1 quart milk |
| ¼ cup celery | 1 tablespoon chopped parsley |
| 2 tablespoons butter | Salt and pepper |

Boil diced potatoes and onions together in 3 cups of water.

Add 1 teaspoon salt.

Add chopped celery when potatoes are partially cooked.

When potatoes are soft, pour in heated milk and add chopped eggs.

Add parsley and butter just before serving.

Serves 4.

MRS. J. IRVIN LEHMAN, *Chambersburg, Pa.*

## Old-fashioned Potato Soup

### With Dry Rivels

| | |
|---|---|
| 4 medium-sized potatoes | ½ cup flour |
| 1½ quarts water | 1 egg |
| 2 tablespoons butter | ¼ cup milk |
| Salt | ½ cup cream |

Cook diced potatoes in salt water until soft. Add butter.

To make rivels, rub egg and flour together, then add milk.

These are best made by cutting through mixture with two forks.

Drop rivels, which are no larger than a cherry stone, into boiling potatoes, stirring to prevent packing together.

Cook 5 minutes with kettle covered.

Add ½ cup cream.

Garnish with parsley or pieces of crisp bacon.
Serves 4.

Mrs. Andrew Beller, Castorland, N. Y.

## Salsify or Mock Oyster Soup

| | |
|---|---|
| 1½ cups diced salsify (oyster plant) | 1 quart milk |
| 1½ cups water | Salt and pepper |
| 1 tablespoon butter | |

Cook diced salsify in salt water until tender.
Add butter and rich milk and bring to a boil. Season to taste.
Serve with crackers.
Serves 6-8.

Annie Beachy, Salisbury, Pa.

## Split Pea Soup

| | |
|---|---|
| 1 ham hock | 1 large onion |
| 2½ quarts water | 3 medium-sized carrots |
| 2½ cups split peas | Salt and pepper |

Cook ham bone and peas together slowly for about 3 hours.
Dice onions and carrots and add 30 minutes before serving. Season.
Serves 8.

Mrs. M. W. Mishler, Sheridan, Ore.

## Turnip Soup

| | |
|---|---|
| 2 cups grated turnips | 1 tablespoon flour |
| 1 medium-sized onion | 1 teaspoon salt |
| 1 quart milk | 2 tablespoons chopped parsley |
| 2 tablespoons butter | |

Heat milk in double boiler with whole onion.
Rub flour and melted butter together into a paste and add to milk.
Add grated turnips and salt.
Cook until turnips are soft, approximately 10-12 minutes.
Remove the onion and sprinkle chopped parsley over the soup just
    before serving.
Serves 6.

Ruth Ann Sharp, Greenwood, Del.

## Vegetable Soup Without Meat

| | |
|---|---|
| 3 medium-sized potatoes | 3 medium-sized carrots |
| ½ cup rice | 1 onion |
| 4 tablespoons butter | ¼ teaspoon celery seed |
| 2 beef bouillon cubes | |

1 quart tomatoes
2 cups shredded cabbage

Salt and pepper
Water

Dice potatoes and cover with water.

When potatoes begin to cook, add rice, butter and salt.

Add diced carrots and onion, and shredded cabbage, and cook 10 minutes.

Then add tomatoes and water to make desired consistency.

Cook slowly together until all vegetables are soft.

Serves 8.

MRS. J. D. RAMER, *Elida, Ohio*

## Vegetable Soup with Meat

1 soup bone
¾ cup dried navy beans
1 onion
1 cup macaroni or noodles
3 medium-sized carrots, diced

1 quart tomatoes
½ cup diced celery
1½ cups shredded cabbage
Salt and pepper

Soak the beans overnight and drain.

Cook the soup bone in enough water to cover.

When tender, remove meat from broth and add beans.

When beans are almost soft, add diced vegetables and continue to cook for 20 minutes.

Season.

If hamburger is used, brown it in fat, add desired amount of water before adding vegetables.

Serves 8.

MRS. J. D. RAMER, *Elida, Ohio*

## Vegetable Soup to Can

1 peck tomatoes
10 onions
2 quarts corn
2 quarts Lima or soup beans
2 bunches celery
5 quarts water

1 large head cabbage, shredded
2 cups carrots, diced or ground
3 red peppers, chopped
2 green peppers, chopped
1 cup salt
1 teaspoon pepper

Cook beans separately, when almost soft, add carrots and celery.

Cook 10 minutes and add other vegetables and seasoning.

Cook slowly until all vegetables are tender.

Place in sterilized jars and seal.

Makes approximately 10 quarts.

ANNA GINGERICH, *Hartville, Ohio*

## MEAT, CHICKEN AND FISH SOUPS

### Beef Soup with Dumplings

| | |
|---|---|
| 1 soup bone with 2 pounds stewing beef | 1½ cups flour |
| 2 quarts water | 1 egg |
| Salt | ½ cup milk |

Cook meat until tender and remove from broth.

Add water until you have 2 quarts of broth.

Make dumplings by mixing beaten egg and milk into flour to form a batter the consistency of pancake batter.

Drop from a teaspoon into boiling broth.

Cook 8 minutes with cover on the kettle.

Serves 8.

MARY KEFFER, *Waterloo, Ont., Can.;* MRS. JOHN A. RHODES, *Dayton, Va.*

### Beef Noodle Soup

| | |
|---|---|
| 1 pound soup meat | 6 sprigs of parsley |
| 1 medium-sized onion | 1 tablespoon salt |
| 1 bay leaf | 1 package noodles (¼ pound) |
| 8 whole pepper kernels | |

Cook meat in 6 cups of water until almost tender. Add salt.

Put onion, pepper kernels and bay leaf in a spice holder or tie in a bag.

Add to meat and cook one-half hour longer, adding water as necessary.

Remove spices.

Cook noodles in salt water, drain and add to meat and broth.

Serves 4.

MRS. L. A. SCHROEDER, *Mountain Lake, Minn.*

### Chicken Soup

| | |
|---|---|
| 3 to 4 pound chicken (preferably a year-old hen) | 2½ teaspoons salt |
| 2½ quarts water | 2 cups cooked rice or noodles |

Cut chicken into serving pieces and bring to a boil.

Skim off top.

Allow to simmer 3 hours, adding more water as necessary.

Forty-five minutes before serving, skim off fat and add:

| | |
|---|---|
| 1 teaspoon pepper kernels | 1 bay leaf |
| 3 small pieces anise | 1½ inch stick cinnamon |
| 1 small onion | 2 tablespoons chopped parsley |

Just before serving add 2 tablespoons of butter.

Place cooked rice or noodles in soup bowl and pour soup over it.

Serves 6.

Mrs. John J. Becker, *Mountain Lake, Minn.*

## Chicken and Corn Soup

I chicken (preferably a 4-pound hen)
4 quarts of cold water
I onion, chopped
½ cup chopped celery and leaves
2½ cups fresh or frozen corn
2 cooked eggs (optional)
Salt and pepper

Cook chicken slowly until it is tender, adding salt 30 minutes before it is done.

Remove chicken and strain broth through a fine sieve.

Take meat from bones and cut in bite sized pieces. Set aside.

Add corn to broth and bring to boil.

Add chopped celery and seasoning and cook 5 minutes.

Five minutes before serving, add chicken, diced eggs, and rivels made from:

I cup flour
I egg
¼ cup milk

Rub this mixture together with 2 forks until the size of peas and drop into boiling soup.

Cover and cook gently for 5 minutes.

Serves 10. This is delicious!

Mrs. B. L. Bucher, *Dallastown, Pa.;* Ruth Slaymaker, *Leola, Pa.*

## Chicken Rice Soup

I chicken (preferably a one-year-old hen)
2 quarts water
½ cup chopped celery
I onion, chopped
Parsley
I cup rice
Salt and pepper

Cut up chicken in serving pieces.

Place in cooker, add water, celery, onion and parsley.

Cook slowly until chicken is tender.

Cook rice separately in salt water.

Drain and add to chicken just before serving.

Serves 6.

Mrs. Jacob Grove, *Hagerstown, Md.*

## Chili Soup

2 cups of pinto beans or one #2 can kidney beans
I pound hamburger
2 teaspoons salt

1 quart tomatoes
2 medium-sized onions

¼ teaspoon pepper
1 teaspoon chili powder

Cook beans until soft.

Put 2 tablespoons of fat in pan and brown the minced onion.

Add hamburger and fry until brown.

Add tomatoes to cooked beans and cook several minutes.

Then add beans to browned hamburger, add seasoning.

Simmer together 15 minutes.

Add water to obtain desired consistency.

Serves 6.

Mrs. Edward R. Kennel, *Strang, Neb.*
Mrs. Milton B. Hostetler, *Shanesville, Ohio*

## Delectable Lamb Soup

6 cups lamb broth
3 cups tomato juice
2 bay leaves

Salt and pepper
½ cup cream

Combine broth and tomato juice; then add seasonings and simmer until very hot.

Add ½ cup cream just before serving.

Serves 6.

Margaret Burton, *Highland Park, Mich.*

## Oyster Chowder

3 slices bacon or salt pork
2 cups raw diced potatoes
2 onions, diced
1 pint oysters
1½ teaspoons salt

¼ teaspoon pepper
1 quart hot milk
1 tablespoon butter
1 tablespoon flour

Fry bacon or pork until brown.

Add diced potatoes, onions, salt and pepper.

Cover with boiling water and simmer until tender.

Add hot milk and flour and butter paste.

Then add oysters, including liquor, and cook about 3 minutes or until edges begin to curl.

Serve with crackers.

Serves 6.

## Oyster Stew

1 quart milk
1 pint oysters
2 tablespoons butter
1 teaspoon salt

⅛ teaspoon pepper
1 tablespoon minced parsley or celery leaves

Bring milk to a boil in the top of a double boiler. Add salt.

Melt the butter in a saucepan.

Drain oysters and add one at a time to the butter.

When both the oysters in the butter and the milk are at the boiling point, pour oysters into milk.

Add minced parsley or celery leaves and serve at once.

Serves 6.

Mrs. W. K. Lederach, *Lederach, Pa.*

## Pork Soup

| | |
|---|---|
| 1 ham bone | 1 onion |
| 3 cups diced potatoes | 2 teaspoons salt |
| 2 cups macaroni | 1 cup sour cream |

Cook the ham bone until meat is almost tender.

Add diced potatoes, macaroni, minced onion and salt.

Cook until all is tender.

Just before serving, add sour cream.

Serves 6.

Mrs. William Yoder, *Hartville, Ohio*

## Salmon Soup

| | |
|---|---|
| 4 tablespoons of butter | 1 can salmon (2 cups) |
| 3 quarts of milk | Salt and pepper to taste |

Brown the butter in a kettle.

Add milk and seasoning.

When hot, add 1 can of salmon, flaked with a fork.

Let simmer 10 minutes.

Serve with crackers.

Serves 6-8.

Mrs. Wiltrude Miller, *Boswell, Pa.*; Catherine J. Miller, *Grantsville, Md.*

## Turkey Mushroom Soup

| | |
|---|---|
| Bones of 1 roast turkey | 1 onion |
| 2 quarts of cold water | 4 tablespoons uncooked rice |
| 1 carrot, chopped | 1 can condensed cream of |
| 1/3 cup chopped celery | mushroom soup |

Place turkey, vegetables and water in a kettle.

Cover and simmer for 2 hours. Strain.

This should make 1½ quarts of stock.

Add uncooked rice to stock and cook until soft.

Place mushroom soup in a pan, stir and slowly add turkey stock with
rice.

Bring to a boil and serve.

Serves 6. "A grand end to the noble bird!"

MRS. ENOS DELP, *Harleysville, Pa.*

# CREAM SOUPS

## Cream of Asparagus Soup

| | |
|---|---|
| 2 bunches of asparagus | 3 tablespoons flour |
| 1 small onion | 1 quart milk |
| 3 tablespoons butter | Salt and pepper |

Melt butter in saucepan, add flour and then milk to make a cream sauce.

Cook chopped asparagus for 20 minutes in salt water.

Sauté minced onion in 1 tablespoon of fat; when brown, add to
asparagus.

Then add asparagus to cream sauce.

Bring to a boil and serve.

Serves 6.

MRS. AMOS B. CHARLES, *Lancaster, Pa.*

## Cream of Potato and Onion Soup

| | |
|---|---|
| 2 frankfurters | 2 tablespoons butter |
| 1 onion | 1 tablespoon flour |
| 1 quart milk | 2 cups cooked riced potatoes |
| 1½ teaspoons salt | ¼ teaspoon pepper |

Wipe frankfurters with a damp cloth and slice in thin pieces.

Melt butter in a double boiler, add frankfurters and onions.

Cook 2 minutes.

Push frankfurters and onions to one side of pan and add flour.

When flour is well blended, add the milk gradually.

Then add potatoes and seasoning.

Cook until thickened and serve.

Serves 6.

MRS. WILLIAM SCHWEITZER, *Geneva, Neb.*

## Cream of Tomato Soup

| | |
|---|---|
| 3 tablespoons butter or fat | 1 tablespoon sugar |
| 2½ tablespoons flour | 2 teaspoons salt |
| 3 cups strained tomatoes or juice | 1 quart milk |
| 1 tablespoon minced onion | ⅛ teaspoon pepper |
| ¼ teaspoon celery salt | |

Melt butter in top of double boiler.

Add flour, salt, pepper and celery salt.

Add milk gradually and stir until thickened.

In a separate pan heat tomatoes and minced onion.

Cook until onion is soft and then strain.

Add tomatoes to milk slowly and stir.

If milk and tomatoes are both near boiling point and tomatoes are added slowly, this will not curd.

Should it curd, beat briskly with an egg beater.

Serves 6.

MRS. QUINTUS LEATHERMAN, *Souderton, Pa.;* ELIZABETH KAUFFMAN, *Nampa, Idaho*

## Tomato Soup to Can

| | |
|---|---|
| 3 gallons chopped tomatoes | 1¼ cups flour |
| 14 stems celery | 1½ cups sugar |
| 14 sprigs parsley | 1 teaspoon pepper |
| 12 bay leaves | 3 tablespoons salt |
| 8 medium-sized onions | ¼ pound butter |
| 20 whole cloves (optional) | |

Cook tomatoes, onions, celery and parsley together until soft. Strain.

Mix flour, sugar, salt and pepper with 2 cups water to form a paste.

Add flour paste to tomato mixture.

Bring to a boil, and add butter.

Pour into sterilized jars and seal.

Makes approximately 8 quarts.

MRS. OWEN F. SHOWALTER, *Broadway, Va.*

# MISCELLANEOUS SOUPS

## Grandma's Milk or Rivel Soup

| | |
|---|---|
| 2 quarts milk | 1½ teaspoons salt |
| 1 cup flour | 2 to 3 tablespoons cream |
| 1 large egg | |

Heat milk to boiling point in top of double boiler. Add salt.

To make rivels, see page 40.

When rivels are about the size of cherry stones, drop into hot milk.

Keep milk at boiling point for 3 to 5 minutes.

Serves 6 to 8.

MRS. CURTIS C. CRESSMAN, *New Hamburg, Ont., Can.*

# Egg Soup

1 quart milk                                2 cups toasted bread crumbs
3 eggs                                     1 teaspoon salt

Bring milk to boiling point.
Add the well-beaten eggs, stirring constantly.
Add toasted bread crumbs just before serving.
Season to taste.
Serves 4.                          Mrs. Milton B. Hostetler, *Shanesville, Ohio*

# Rice Pap Soup

1 cup rice                         1½ tablespoons flour
1½ quarts milk                 Brown or maple sugar
2 eggs

Boil rice in salt water until tender. Drain.
Bring milk to boiling point in top of double boiler.
Add rice and well-beaten eggs and cook one minute.
Add flour paste, made by mixing ¼ cup cold milk with flour, and cook
    several more minutes.
Pour into soup plates and sprinkle 1 tablespoon of brown or maple
    sugar over each plate.
Serve hot.
Serves 6.                            Mrs. C. L. Blough, *Grantsville, Md.*

# Toast Flour Soup

1½ quarts milk                 1 cup flour
2 tablespoons fat            Salt

Heat milk in top of double boiler.
Melt fat in skillet and add flour, stirring until it becomes a light brown.
Leave flour and fat in little lumps and drop into hot milk.
Keep at boiling point 5 minutes.
Season with salt.
Serves 6.                  Mrs. David A. Bontrager, *Haven, Kan.*

# COLD SOUPS

## Cold Soup or Farmer's Summer Supper Dish

2 quarts whole milk              ½ loaf white bread (approximately)
1 quart fresh or canned fruit, straw-    Sugar to taste, according to fruit used
    berries or peaches preferred

Add crushed fruit and sugar to cold milk.
Add enough broken bread to absorb milk. Serve.
A wide variety of fruits may be used.
Serves 6.

ERMA N. BENDER, *Grantsville, Md.*

## Pflaumenus
### *"Pluma Moos"*

| | |
|---|---|
| 1½ cup raisins | ½ cup flour |
| 1 cup dried prunes | ¼ cup sugar |
| ½ cup sugar | ½ teaspoon salt |
| 3 pints water | 3 cups milk |

Add water to dried fruits and cook until almost soft. Add ½ cup sugar
    during the last 5 minutes of the cooking period.
Make a paste of the milk, flour, salt and ¼ cup sugar.
Add thickening to fruit and stir until done.
If soup seems too thick, add more milk or a small amount of water.

KATIE WEDEL, *Newton, Kan.*

## Sour Cherry Soup

| | |
|---|---|
| 1 quart fresh sour cherries | 1 quart milk |
| 2 tablespoons butter | 4 slices toasted bread |
| 3 tablespoons flour | 1½ cups sugar |

Cook cherries until soft, add sugar.
Melt butter in skillet, add flour.
Stir until flour browns.
Mix with cherries and let get cold.
Add milk and toasted bread cubes just before serving.
Serve cold.
 Serves 6.

FANNIE M. WEBER, *Adamstown, Pa.*

# Meats
### and
# Meat Dishes
## Chapter III

SINCE MUCH OF THE MEAT THAT THE FARMER BUTCHERS TODAY FINDS its way to the freezing locker, there is little need of a special storehouse for meat, but go with me for a peep into Great-grandfather's old smokehouse.

It is late December, and butchering day has passed. In a large wooden barrel in one corner are many pieces of meat placed in criss-cross fashion, so that the air can circulate around them as the sugar cure is absorbed. Other pieces are suspended from the rafters by heavy twine, these having just been removed from the barrel. As we count the pieces of meat, we find there are 12 hams, 12 shoulders and 12 slabs of bacon, known as "middlings" by Grandmother. Thus we know that six hogs were butchered to meet the needs of a large family of growing children.

One smells the faint odor of wood chips. No doubt it was hickory that smoldered in a small iron pot in the corner so as to improve the flavor of the meat.

Along one side of the wall there are shelves filled with rows of gallon crocks. Each one of these is neatly covered across the top with brown paper and tied with a string. As you walk nearer you see written plainly on each one, "Sausage" or "Liver Pudding."

In addition to all this pork meat, Grandfather butchered a beef on shares with a neighbor sometime during the winter. It was necessary to have beef in order to make summer sausage (bologna) and jerks (home-cured dried beef). With such a bountiful supply of meat, it is no wonder that Grandmother's menu could include scrapple for breakfast, meat potpie for dinner, and fried ham for supper. The people who lived in houses that were inadequately heated, and who were up doing chores before the peep of dawn, required a heavier diet than we need today.

Most typical of our meat dishes today are the beef and chicken potpie, ponhaus and scrapple, pickled pigs' feet (souse) and roast pig stomach (Dutch goose). And one must not forget the *schnitz un knepp*. If it is prepared by cooking a ham bone and then adding the dried apple snitz, we may list it with the meat dishes. Family appetites differ, however, on how this old-fashioned favorite should be prepared. Many prefer only the flavor of the fruit and dumplings and do not use meat.

The smokehouse, like the old log house built over the spring, is numbered and found wanting among the buildings on the up-to-date farm today. "Time changes things," the poet says, and how true are his words!

## BEEF

### Barbecued Short Ribs

| | |
|---|---|
| 3 pounds short ribs of beef | 2 small onions, minced |
| 3 tablespoons fat | 1 cup catsup |
| 1 cup water | 2 teaspoons Worcestershire sauce |

Brown short ribs in the fat.

Make a sauce by simmering together for 20 minutes the onion, catsup, Worcestershire sauce and water.

Pour sauce over the browned ribs, cover and let simmer in a slow oven
at 325° for 2 hours.

Add water if needed.

Serves 6.

FANNIE G. GOOD, *Spring City, Pa.*

## Beef Birds

| | |
|---|---|
| 1 pound round steak | 1 teaspoon salt |
| 1 cup bread crumbs | ½ teaspoon sage or chopped parsley |
| 1 egg | 1 cup milk or broth |
| 1 small onion | |

Make a dressing by mixing together the bread crumbs, milk, egg and
seasoning.

Sprinkle salt over the meat and cut it in pieces 2 x 4 inches.

Spread each piece with dressing and roll.

Fasten with toothpicks or skewer.

Roll in flour and brown in hot fat.

Place in a pan or casserole, add hot water and cover.

Bake at 375° for 2 hours.

Remove toothpicks before serving.

Serves 4.

MRS. U. GRANT WEAVER, *Johnstown, Pa.*

## Beef and Biscuit

| | |
|---|---|
| 1 pound ground beef | ⅛ teaspoon pepper |
| ½ cup finely chopped onion | 2 tablespoons shortening |
| ½ cup chopped green pepper | 2 tablespoons flour |
| 1 teaspoon salt | 1 cup milk or water |

Brown meat, onion and pepper in hot fat.

Season with salt and pepper.

Add flour and blend, then add liquid and cook until thick.

For biscuit dough:

| | |
|---|---|
| 2 cups flour | 3 tablespoons shortening |
| 4 teaspoons baking powder | ¾ cup milk |
| 1 teaspoon salt | |

Roll biscuit dough ¼ inch thick, brush with melted butter and spread
with meat mixture.

Roll like a jelly roll and cut in 1¼ inch slices.

Place cut slices down in a greased baking pan.

Bake at 400° for 20 to 25 minutes.

Serves 6-8.

MRS. ISAAC GOOD, *East Earl, Pa.*

## Beef Croquettes

| | |
|---|---|
| 1 cup diced cold beef | Salt and pepper |
| 1 cup bread crumbs | 1 cup cracker crumbs |
| 1 egg, beaten | |

Chop cold roast beef and mix with bread crumbs. Season.

Beat the egg and work it in with the meat.

Shape mixture into patties or croquettes.

Roll in cracker crumbs or flour, or dip first in an egg beaten slightly and then roll in crumbs.

Fry in deep fat until a golden brown, approximately 4 minutes.

Makes 4-6 croquettes.

MRS. JACOB REIFF, *Hagerstown, Md.*

## Beef Roast

| | |
|---|---|
| 3 to 4 pounds, rib or sirloin | 1 small onion |
| 1 teaspoon salt per pound meat | 1 cup water |
| ½ cup flour | |

Wipe meat with a damp cloth.

Rub with salt, flour, pepper, and onion.

Place meat in roasting pan with fat side up.

Add 1 cup of water.

Do not cover unless a less tender cut is used.

If beef is fat, it will require no basting.

Time required for roasting depends on the shape of the cut.

For well-done roasts, the average cooking time is 30 minutes per pound of meat, for medium 25 minutes per pound, and 20 minutes for rare.

Roast at 325°.

MRS. CLARENCE YODER, *Midland, Mich.*

## Yorkshire Pudding

| | |
|---|---|
| ¾ cup milk | ½ teaspoon salt |
| ¾ cup flour | 1 teaspoon fat from roast to each |
| 1 egg | muffin pan |

Beat egg.

Add milk, flour and salt.

Continue to beat until well blended.

It is best to prepare this mixture 2 to 3 hours before baking.

Then add hot fat to muffin pans.

Have pans sizzling hot.

Fill muffin pans ¾ full.

Bake at 375° for 20 minutes.

This mixture may also be dropped from a spoon directly into roasting pan and baked.

Serves 6.

EDITH KEFFER, *Waterloo, Ont., Can.*

## Beef and Vegetable Stew

2 pounds beef, cubed
1 large onion
4 tablespoons fat or
   1½ inch cube suet
2 teaspoons salt
⅛ teaspoon pepper

1 cup diced carrots
4 large potatoes
½ pound green beans
1 cup tomatoes
½ cup water

Melt suet or fat in hot pan, add cubed beef and chopped onion and brown thoroughly.

Add green beans first, then diced carrots, potatoes, tomatoes and water.

Cook slowly for 3 to 3½ hours in a Dutch oven or 15 minutes in a pressure cooker.

Serves 8.

MRS. JOHN E. KAUFFMAN, *Bird-in-Hand, Pa.*

## Old-fashioned Beef Potpie

2 pounds stewing beef
6 cups water
1½ teaspoons salt
4 medium-sized potatoes
1½ cups flour

1 egg
3 tablespoons milk or water
1 teaspoon minced onion
1 teaspoon minced parsley

Cook meat in salt water until it is tender.

Remove meat from broth; add minced onion and parsley to broth.

Bring to boiling point and add alternate layers of cubed potatoes and squares of dough.

To make potpie dough, beat egg and add milk.

Add flour to make a stiff dough.

Roll out paper-thin and cut in inch squares.

Keep broth boiling while adding dough squares in order to keep them from packing together.

Cover and cook for 20 minutes, adding more water if needed.

Add meat and stir through potpie.

Serves 6 to 8.

GRANDMOTHER SHOWALTER

## Browned Stew with Dumplings

| | |
|---|---|
| 2 pounds cubed beef | 1½ teaspoons salt |
| 2 tablespoons flour | ⅛ teaspoon pepper |
| 3 tablespoons fat | 1 quart boiling water |
| 1 small onion | 1 teaspoon lemon juice |

Cut meat into small cubes.

Melt fat in hot skillet or Dutch oven.

Brown meat in fat, keep it sizzling hot until nicely browned.

Sprinkle flour, salt and pepper over meat.

Add the boiling water.

Cover the pan and lower heat so that meat simmers for 3 to 3½ hours.

One teaspoon lemon juice added at the same time the water is added
improves flavor and tenderizes meat.

To make dumplings take:

| | |
|---|---|
| 1 cup flour | 1 egg |
| 1½ teaspoons baking powder | 2 to 3 tablespoons milk |
| ½ teaspoon salt | 1 tablespoon shortening |

Stir quickly and drop from a spoon on simmering stew.

Cover and allow to cook 12 to 15 minutes. Delicious!

Serves 6-8.

ANN BECK, *Archbold, Ohio;* MRS. R. J. RICH, *Washington, Ill.*

## Breaded Oxtail

| | |
|---|---|
| 2 oxtails | ⅛ teaspoon pepper |
| 3 sprigs parsley | 1 egg, beaten |
| 1 bay leaf | 1 cup dry bread crumbs |
| 2 teaspoons salt | |

Wash oxtails and cut in 3 inch lengths; cover with boiling water.

Add parsley, bay leaf, salt and pepper.

Simmer until tails are tender, about 2½ hours.

Let cool in stock.

Drain meat and dip in beaten egg and then crumbs.

Fry in deep fat until brown.

The broth is delicious for soups.

GRACE E. ZOOK, *Belleville, Pa.*

## Casserole Meat Dish

| | |
|---|---|
| 2 cups cooked beef cubes | 1 teaspoon salt |
| 1 cup diced celery | ⅛ teaspoon pepper |
| 1 green pepper, chopped | ½ cup grated cheese |
| 1 can tomato soup | 3 cups cooked noodles |
| 1 can mushroom soup | 1 cup beef broth |

Arrange beef and vegetables in casserole in alternate layers with noodles and soups.

Top with noodles.

Bake in oven at 375° for 35 minutes. Add cheese last 5 minutes.

Serves 6.

DELLA STUTZMAN, *Milford, Neb.*

## Corned Beef Patties

| | |
|---|---|
| 2 cups flour | For Filling: |
| I teaspoon baking powder | 2 tablespoons butter |
| 1/2 teaspoon salt | 2 tablespoons minced onion |
| 6 tablespoons fat | 2 tablespoons flour |
| I egg, beaten | 1 1/4 cups cooked corned beef |
| 1/3 cup milk | 1 1/2 cups canned tomatoes |

Sift together flour, baking powder and salt.

Cut in shortening, add beaten egg and milk.

Roll out in 4½ inch squares ⅛ inch thick and fit into muffin tins.

Fill with corned beef mixture made as follows:

Melt butter, add chopped onions and cook until soft.

Blend in 2 tablespoons flour.

Add corned beef and tomatoes.

Simmer for 10 minutes.

When tarts are filled with corned beef mixture, fold edges of pastry to center and pinch together.

Bake at 425° for 20 minutes.

Serves 6-8.

STELLA HUBER STAUFFER, *Tofield, Alta., Can.*

## Dried Beef

### To Cure by Dry Salt Method

| | |
|---|---|
| 20 pounds of fresh beef (round steak) | I teaspoon saltpeter |
| 2 cups salt | 1/4 pound brown sugar |

Mix salt, sugar and saltpeter together, mashing out all lumps.

Divide this into 3 portions.

Cut pieces of meat lengthwise with grain so that slices will be crosswise.

These pieces are best if not more than 5 pounds.

Place meat in a large container and rub thoroughly with 1 portion of the salt-sugar mixture.

Follow the same procedure the second and third days.

Turn several times a day and let stand 7 more days.

Then hang in a warm place to drip.

When there is no more dripping, the pieces of meat can be smoked to improve flavor.

Wrap in clean muslin bags and hang in a cool place for six weeks before it is ready to eat.

MRS. OWEN F. SHOWALTER, *Broadway, Va.*

## "Grandmother's Jerks"

When serving "jerks" or smoked dried beef, try Grandmother's method of putting thin slices of beef into a vinegar-sugar-water solution (no salt) proportioned as for pickles (Chapter XIII).

Allow to stand 2 to 3 hours before serving.

CATHERINE J. MILLER, *Grantsville, Md.*

## Creamed Dried Beef

¼ pound dried beef
4 tablespoons butter
4 tablespoons flour

2½ cups water or milk
6 slices toast

Shred slices of dried beef into small pieces.

Melt butter in heavy pan and add dried beef.

Cook until the edges begin to curl and beef is slightly browned.

Sprinkle flour over beef and allow to brown slightly.

Slowly add liquid and cook over low heat, stirring constantly.

Cook until smooth and thickened.

Serve on hot toast.

Makes 6 servings.

MRS. JACOB A. SHENK, *Harrisonburg, Va.*

## Hamburgers

I pound ground beef
I cup bread or cracker crumbs
I onion, chopped
½ cup top milk

I egg
I teaspoon salt
⅛ teaspoon pepper

Soak bread crumbs in milk.

Mix all ingredients.

Shape in patties and fry in hot fat or on broiler pan until brown.

When meat is browned, gravy may be made by adding flour and water to the juice in the drip pan.

Serves 4-6.

MRS. A. L. TROYER, *Shickley, Neb.*

## Barbecued Hamburger

| | |
|---|---|
| 2 pounds hamburger | 2 tablespoons vinegar |
| I onion | 2 teaspoons prepared mustard |
| 1/2 cup catsup | I teaspoon Worcestershire sauce |
| 2 tablespoons brown sugar | I teaspoon salt |

Fry onion and hamburger in 4 tablespoons hot fat until it has lost its
raw, red color.

Stir until smooth and then add all the other ingredients.

Simmer about 20 minutes and serve with hamburger rolls.

Serves 8.

MRS. NORMAN LOUX, *Souderton, Pa.*

## Smothered Hamburger Patties

Make hamburger patties as in plain hamburger recipe (page 58).

Place in hot frying pan and brown well on both sides.

Add:

| | |
|---|---|
| 11 oz. tin of vegetable and beef stock | 1/2 teaspoon salt |
| 2 tablespoons minced onion | 1/3 cup water |

Cover tightly and simmer 30 minutes.

Serves 4-6.

MRS. MARK HARSHBARGER, *Dagmar, Mont.*

## Spanish Hamburger

| | |
|---|---|
| I pound hamburger | I cup chopped celery |
| 3 tablespoons fat | I green pepper, minced |
| I onion, minced | I can tomato soup |
| I teaspoon salt | 1/8 teaspoon pepper |

Fry onion and hamburger in hot fat until browned.

Add chopped celery, green pepper and seasoning.

Add tomato soup and simmer 30 minutes.

Serves 6.

MRS. LEILA STUTZMAN, *Albany, Ore.*

## Hamburger en Casserole

| | |
|---|---|
| I pound ground beef | 2 cups canned tomatoes |
| I onion, minced | 2 cups canned corn |
| 2 tablespoons fat | 4 tablespoons butter |
| I teaspoon salt | 5 tablespoons flour |
| 1/2 teaspoon sugar | I green or red pepper |

Fry onion in fat, add ground beef and brown well.

Add tomatoes and corn, sugar and salt.

Blend flour and butter together until smooth; then drop into mixture
   just prepared.
Stir and cook until thickened.
Pour into casserole and top with sweet pepper rings.
Bake at 375° for 45 minutes.
Serves 6.

MRS. PHEBE F. KRAUS, *Denbigh, Va.*

## Hamburger en Casserole

### *One-Dish Meal*

| | |
|---|---|
| 1 large onion, minced | 5 medium-sized potatoes, cooked |
| 2 tablespoons fat | ½ cup warm milk |
| 1 pound ground beef | 1 beaten egg |
| ½ pound cooked green beans | 1 teaspoon salt |
| 10 oz. can of tomato soup | ½ teaspoon pepper |

Brown onion and meat in hot fat.
Add beans and soup. Mix thoroughly.
Pour into greased baking dish.
Mash potatoes and add milk, egg and seasoning.
Put on top of meat mixture.
Bake in 350° oven for 30 minutes.
Serves 6.

MRS. ALICE BEILER, *Morgantown, Pa.*

## Old-fashioned Hash

| | |
|---|---|
| 3 cups leftover roast meat | 1½ teaspoons salt |
| 1 cup mashed potatoes | 1½ cups milk |
| 1 medium-sized onion | ½ cup bread crumbs |

Grind meat and onion in food chopper.
Add mashed potatoes, salt and milk. Mix well.
Place in a casserole and sprinkle crumbs over top.
Bake at 350° for 30 minutes.
Serves 6.

MRS. SARA NAFZIGER, *Harper, Kan.*

## Texas Hash

| | |
|---|---|
| 2 large onions | ½ cup uncooked rice |
| 3 tablespoons fat | 1 teaspoon chili powder |
| 2 green peppers, chopped | 1½ teaspoons salt |
| 1 pound hamburger | ¼ teaspoon pepper |
| 2 cups canned tomatoes | |

Fry minced onion and green peppers in fat until onions are brown.

Add hamburger and fry several minutes.

Then add tomatoes, rice and seasoning.

Pour into a large casserole, cover and bake at 375° for about 50 minutes.

Serves 8.

MRS. E. S. HALLMAN, *Tuleta, Tex.*

## Meat Balls in Tomato Juice

| | |
|---|---|
| I pound hamburger | 1/8 teaspoon pepper |
| I cup bread crumbs | 1/4 cup milk |
| I or 2 eggs | I quart tomato juice |
| I teaspoon salt | |

Mix ingredients well.

Shape into balls 1¼ inches in diameter.

Drop into boiling tomato juice.

Simmer for approximately 1½ hours.

Makes approximately 8 meat balls.

ETHEL LAHMAN, *Harrisonburg, Va.*

## Porcupine Balls

| | |
|---|---|
| I pound hamburger | 2 sticks celery, chopped |
| 4 slices bread | 1/4 cup uncooked rice |
| I egg, beaten | I teaspoon salt |
| I cup milk | 2 cups tomato juice |
| 2 medium-sized onions | |

Crumble bread and soak in milk.

Add beaten egg.

Mix with other ingredients (except tomato juice).

Shape into 8 balls and place in a greased casserole.

Pour tomato juice over the balls and bake 1½ hours in a 350° oven.

These balls may also be cooked in a pressure saucepan for 15 minutes.

MABEL LEHMAN, *Holsopple, Pa.;* MRS. REUBEN EBERLY, *Fayetteville, Pa.*

## Meat Loaf

| | |
|---|---|
| 1½ pounds hamburger | I or 2 eggs, beaten |
| I cup soft bread crumbs | I teaspoon salt |
| I cup milk or tomato juice | 1/8 teaspoon pepper |
| I medium-sized onion, minced | 6 strips bacon |

Soak crumbs in milk and add beaten egg.

Add meat, onion and seasoning.

Form into a loaf (do not pack) and place in baking dish; then put strips of bacon on top of loaf.

Bake at 375° for 1 hour.
Serves 6.

MRS. J. R. DILLER, *Hesston, Kan.*

This mixture may also be shaped in individual servings and placed in
greased muffin tins.
Spread top with a sauce made by combining the following:

3 tablespoons brown sugar          I teaspoon dry mustard
¼ cup catsup

MRS. RALPH MILLER, *Kalona, Iowa*

Another variation may be made by removing baked hamburger loaf
from pan and placing it in a broiler pan.
Spread with catsup and place under broiler for several minutes.

MRS. PEARL SCHMIDT, *Greensburg, Kan.*

*Horse-radish dressing* is good served with meat loaf.
Take:

¼ cup thick cream                  ¼ teaspoon salt
3 tablespoons grated horse-radish   I tablespoon vinegar

Mix vinegar and salt with grated horse-radish.
Whip the cream stiff and add gradually to horse-radish.

MRS. EZRA LONG, *Sterling, Ill.*

## Golden Meat Loaf

1½ pounds ground beef              2 teaspoons salt
I cup rolled oats                  ¼ teaspoon pepper
I cup raw grated carrots           1½ teaspoons Worcestershire sauce
½ minced onion                     3 hard-cooked eggs
2 eggs, beaten

Combine all ingredients, except hard-cooked eggs, and mix thoroughly.
Place half of mixture in a loaf pan 4 x 9 inches.
Cut eggs in half lengthwise and arrange in a row through the center of
the meat.
Place remainder of meat on top.
Bake at 350° for 1¼ hours.
Serves 6 to 8.

JENNIE A. L. GABLE, *York, Pa.*

## Meat Roll

1½ pounds hamburger
2 cups bread crumbs
1 onion
1 cup chopped celery

1½ teaspoons salt
⅛ teaspoon pepper
1 egg, beaten
2/3 cup milk

Mix hamburger with salt, pepper, beaten egg and ½ cup bread crumbs.
Add just enough milk to make it stick together.
Mix well, put on waxed paper and flatten out.
Spread on the meat a filling made of the remainder of the bread, chopped celery and onion.
Moisten with ½ cup milk or water.
Roll up like jelly roll.
Bake at 375° for 1 hour.
Serves 8.

ANNA HERSH, *Elizabethtown, Pa.*

## Meat Pie

1½ cups leftover meat
3 tablespoons flour
¼ cup broth or drippings
1 cup milk

½ teaspoon salt
⅛ teaspoon pepper
2 teaspoons grated onion
1/3 cup chopped pepper

Add flour to drippings and stir until blended.
Add milk and cook until thickened.
Add salt, minced onion and green peppers.
Stir meat into gravy and pour into pastry-lined dish.
Cover top with pastry (page 354).
Bake at 425° for 25 minutes.
Serves 6.

MRS. ELEANOR FREY, *Chambersburg, Pa*

## Meat with Sour Gravy

1 pound beef
½ cup chopped onions
2 tablespoons shortening
½ cup water

1 teaspoon salt
⅛ teaspoon pepper
1 cup bread crumbs
1½ tablespoons vinegar

Cut meat in serving pieces and pound it.
Melt fat in pan and add meat.
Season with salt, pepper and onions.
Add water, cover pan and let simmer 1 hour.
Add bread crumbs dampened with vinegar and simmer 5 more minutes.
Serves 6.

MRS. H. P. BALZER, *North Newton, Kan.*

## Meat Tarts (Piroshki)

Filling:

| | |
|---|---|
| 2 cups flour | 1/2 pound fresh or leftover meat, |
| 1/2 cup sour cream | chopped |
| 1 egg yolk | 1 onion, minced |
| 2 tablespoons butter | 1 tablespoon butter |
| | 1/2 teaspoon salt |

Sift flour and add melted butter. Stir until well blended.

Add sour cream and knead several minutes.

Roll out on floured board to 1/4 inch thickness.

Cut with a round biscuit cutter.

Place a spoonful of filling in center and close tightly by pinching into an oblong shape.

Brush with egg yolk and bake at 400° until crust is brown.

To make filling, brown the onion in butter and add the chopped meat and seasoning.

Stir until meat has lost its red color.

Makes 8 tarts.

MRS. HERBERT R. SCHMIDT, *Newton, Kan.*

## Mock Duck

| | |
|---|---|
| 1 thick round steak | 2 eggs |
| 2 cups bread crumbs | 1 teaspoon salt |
| 1/2 cup milk | 1/8 teaspoon pepper |

Make bread dressing as for stuffing for a fowl (pages 101 and 102).

Spread on meat and roll up carefully.

Fasten with skewers or tie with twine.

Place in a greased pan and bake at 375° for 1½ hours.

Serves 6.

MRS. SAM REDGER, *Greensburg, Kan.*

## Mock Turkey

| | |
|---|---|
| 1 loaf stale bread | 1 teaspoon salt |
| 1 quart milk | 1/8 teaspoon pepper |
| 1 carrot, grated | 1 pound ground sausage |
| 2 onions, minced | 1 teaspoon poultry seasoning |
| 2 stalks celery, chopped | 1 egg beaten |

Remove crust from loaf of bread; tear apart and moisten with warm milk. Crusts may also be used.

Add meat, chopped vegetables, seasoning and other ingredients.

Mix together well and place in a buttered baking dish.

Bake at 350° for 1½ hours.
This dish actually tastes like turkey. Try it!
Serves 6-8.

Mrs. David Burkholder, *Smithville, Ohio*

## Pigs in the Blanket

| | |
|---|---|
| 1 pound hamburger | 1 teaspoon salt |
| ¾ cup tomato juice | ¼ teaspoon pepper |
| 1 small onion, minced | ½ teaspoon Worcestershire sauce |

Make your favorite biscuit dough (pages 12 and 13).
Roll to ¼ inch thickness and cut into 4 inch squares.
Place one tablespoon meat mixture in center of each square.
Fold over dough so meat is covered.
Place in pan and bake at 425° for 40 minutes.
Makes 8 "pigs."

Mrs. Wade Good, *Harrisonburg, Va.*

## Pot Roast

| | |
|---|---|
| 3½ pounds rump or chuck | ⅛ teaspoon pepper |
| 1 onion | 2 tablespoons fat |
| 1½ teaspoons salt | ½ cup hot tomato juice or water |

Rub salt and pepper into meat and dip it in flour.
Brown meat and onion in 2 tablespoons fat until seared on all sides.
Place meat in casserole, Dutch oven, or electric skillet.
Add hot tomato juice or water.
Cover and bake at 350° for 3 hours.

Fannie G. Good, *Spring City, Pa.*

## Scalloped Beef

| | |
|---|---|
| 2 pounds stewing beef | Broth |
| ½ pound crackers | 1½ teaspoons salt |

Cook beef until tender.
Line baking dish with crushed crackers.
Add a layer of beef and then another of crackers.
Alternate until baking dish is ¾ full.
Cover with broth and then sprinkle 3 tablespoons very finely rolled
    crackers over the top.
Bake at 350° for 45 minutes.
Serves 6-8.

Mrs. Ella M. Herr, *Lancaster, Pa.*

## Shepherd's Pie

This is a good way to use leftovers from a holiday meal.

Line a greased casserole with mashed potatoes.
Fill with leftover vegetables and cubes of meat.
Add bread crumbs and gravy and seasoning.
Cover with mashed potatoes and bake at 350° for 40 minutes.
If you have no leftover gravy, beat an egg and add to it 1 cup milk.
Pour this over meat and vegetables before putting mashed potatoes
on top.

MRS. HENRY A. BISHOP, *Perkasie, Pa.*; MARIE BLOSSER, *Harrisonburg, Va.*

## Six-Layer Dinner

2 cups hamburger
2 cups sliced raw potatoes
2 cups chopped celery
1/2 cup diced onions

2 teaspoons salt
1/4 teaspoon pepper
1 cup diced green pepper
2 cups canned tomatoes

Place potatoes in bottom of greased casserole.
Add celery, then hamburger, onions and pepper.
Sprinkle salt and pepper on each layer.
Pour tomatoes over mixture in dish and garnish with green pepper rings.
Bake at 350° for 2 hours.
Serves 6-8.

MRS. VELMA MILLER, *Canton, Ohio*; MRS. ABNER MUSSELMAN, *Elmira, Ont., Can.*

## Steak and Onion Pie

1 cup onions, sliced
1/4 cup shortening
1 pound round steak, cubed
1/4 cup flour
2 teaspoons salt

1/2 teaspoon pepper
1/2 teaspoon paprika
2 cups raw potatoes, diced
2 1/2 cups boiling water
Pastry for 1 crust (page 354)

Cook onions slowly in melted fat. Remove onions.
Roll meat in mixture of flour and seasoning.
Brown meat in hot fat.
Add boiling water, cover and simmer 1 hour.
Add potatoes and cook 10 minutes longer.
Pour into greased casserole, lay cooked onions on top.
Cover with crust rolled ¼ inch thick.
Bake at 400° for 30-35 minutes.
Serves 6-8.

MRS. PHARES A. LANDIS, *Lancaster, Pa.*

## Swedish Meat Dish

| | |
|---|---|
| 8 tender cabbage leaves, whole | 1 teaspoon salt |
| 2½ cups ground steak | 1/8 teaspoon pepper |
| 1 onion, minced | ½ cup cooked rice |
| 1 green pepper, minced | 1½ cups sweetened tomato juice |

Parboil cabbage leaves for 3 minutes.

Mix meat, onion, pepper, rice and seasoning.

Put mixture into cabbage leaves, roll and fasten with skewers or tie with string.

Place in baking pan and pour over them the tomato juice sweetened with 1 tablespoon sugar.

Cover and bake at 375° for 35 minutes.

Serves 8.

MRS. A. E. REESOR, *Markham, Ont., Can.*

## Swiss Steak

| | |
|---|---|
| 2 pounds round steak 1 inch thick | 1/4 teaspoon pepper |
| 3 tablespoons melted fat | ½ cup flour |
| 1½ teaspoons salt | 3 cups tomatoes or tomato juice |
| 1 onion, minced | |

Rub salt and pepper into steak and dredge with flour.

Brown quickly on both sides in hot fat with the onions.

Add tomatoes, cover tightly and bake at 350° for 1½ hours.

This may also be prepared in an electric skillet at low temperature until tender.

JESSIE HAMILTON, *Sheridan, Ore.;* MRS. FOSTER THOMAS, *Holsopple, Pa.*

Instead of the tomatoes, a can of mushroom soup may be thinned with 1 cup milk and poured over browned steak.

Bake as in above recipe. This is delicious.

MRS. A. C. LOUX, *Souderton, Pa.*

## Three-Layer Dinner

| | |
|---|---|
| 1 pound hamburger | 1½ teaspoons salt |
| 1 small head cabbage | 1/8 teaspoon pepper |
| 3 cups diced raw potatoes | 1 cup milk |

Shred cabbage and put ½ of it in the bottom of a greased casserole.

Next add ½ of the diced potatoes and then ½ of the hamburger.

Sprinkle salt and pepper over each layer.

Add remainder in the same order, having hamburger on top.

Add milk and bake at 350° for 2 hours.

Serves 6-8.

MRS. WARD KREIDER, *Wadsworth, Ohio*

## Wigglers

| | |
|---|---|
| I pound hamburger | 1/3 cup chopped celery |
| 3 slices bacon | I small can mushrooms |
| I small onion, chopped | 1/2 lb. spaghetti, cooked |
| I cup cooked peas | 10 oz. grated cheese (mild or sharp) |
| 2 cups tomatoes | |

Fry bacon; when brown remove from pan.

Add onion and hamburger to bacon fryings and heat through.

Arrange meat, vegetables, and spaghetti in alternate layers in casserole.

Pour tomatoes over mixture; cover with grated cheese and bacon.

Bake at 350° for 1 hour.

Serves 6.

MRS. WILLIS BONTRAGER, *Shipshewana, Ind.*

# LAMB, PORK, AND VEAL

## LAMB

### Lamb Patties

| | |
|---|---|
| 3 cups cold roast lamb | I egg, beaten |
| I cup soft bread crumbs | 1/8 teaspoon pepper |
| I small onion | 3 tablespoons minced pickles |
| 1 1/2 teaspoons salt | 1/4 cup red currant jelly |

Grind roast lamb and onion through food chopper.

Mix with bread crumbs, beaten egg, minced pickle, salt and pepper.

A little broth or milk may be needed to moisten mixture.

Shape into 6 patties and brown on both sides in hot fat.

Set at low heat and add currant jelly.

Cover tightly and simmer for 15 minutes.

MRS. A. E. REESOR, *Markham, Ont., Can.*

### Roast Shoulder of Lamb

| | |
|---|---|
| 3 to 4 pounds shoulder of lamb | 1/8 teaspoon pepper |
| 1 1/2 teaspoons salt | Bread stuffing |

Have bone removed from shoulder.

Sew 2 sides of roast securely, leave other side open for stuffing.

Fill cavity with bread filling and sew together. (See following recipe.)

Rub salt and pepper on outside of roast.

Place on rack of roasting pan with fat side up and bake at 325° for approximately 2 hours.

Allow 35 minutes per pound.

ANNA MUSSER, *Adamstown, Pa.*

## Filling for Roast Shoulder of Lamb

| | |
|---|---|
| 1 onion | 1/4 teaspoon pepper |
| 3 tablespoons butter | 1 1/2 to 2 tablespoons milk or stock |
| 1 cup soft bread crumbs | 1/2 teaspoon parsley or sage |
| 1 teaspoon salt | |

Melt fat in pan, add minced onions and brown slightly.
Add the bread crumbs and seasoning.
Then add milk or stock.
Stuff into pocket of lamb shoulder.

ANNA MUSSER, *Adamstown, Pa.*

## Mint Sauce for Roast Lamb

| | |
|---|---|
| 4 tablespoons chopped mint | 4 tablespoons vinegar |
| 1/2 cup hot water | 1/2 teaspoon salt |
| 2 tablespoons sugar | |

Mix ingredients and bring to a boil.
Serve hot with roast lamb.

ANNA MUSSER, *Adamstown, Pa.*

# PORK

## Baked Ham

| | |
|---|---|
| 2 slices ham, 2/3 to 3/4 inch thick | 1 teaspoon dry mustard |
| 4 tablespoons brown sugar | Milk to cover |

Cut slices of meat through center of cured ham.
Place in a large flat roasting pan.
Rub with dry mustard and cover with brown sugar.
Add enough milk to barely cover ham.
Bake at 325° for 1 to 1¼ hours.
Milk should be absorbed.
This is delicious!
Serves 8 to 10.

## Baked Whole Ham

| | |
|---|---|
| 1 cured ham | 4 tablespoons brown sugar |
| Cloves | |

Let ham reach room temperature before placing it in the oven.
Place the ham, fat side up, in a roasting pan.
Add generous amount of water, then cover roasting pan.
Bake at 325°, allowing 16 minutes per pound for hams over 12 pounds.

When done, remove from oven and peel off the skin.

Cut shallow lines across the fat in form of squares or diamonds.

Stick with whole cloves and sprinkle with sugar.

Turn oven to 400°, put ham back in roaster and allow to brown slightly.

MRS. MENNO E. SCHMIDT, *Newton, Kan.*

A sauce made by mixing together the following and pouring it over
ham 45 minutes before ham is tender is also delicious.

| | |
|---|---|
| 1 cup vinegar | 1 teaspoon dry mustard |
| ½ cup brown sugar | 2 tablespoons flour |
| 2 cups boiling water | |

STELLA HUBER STAUFFER, *Tofield, Alta., Can.*

## Ham Loaf

| | |
|---|---|
| 1 pound fresh pork, ground | 1 teaspoon salt |
| 1 pound cured ham, ground | ⅛ teaspoon pepper |
| 1 cup bread crumbs | ¾ to 1 cup milk |
| 1 egg | |

Grind the meat and mix all the ingredients.

Shape in a loaf, dust with flour and place in a roasting pan.

Bake at 350° for 1½ to 2 hours.

At the end of 1 hour pour over the loaf either 1 cup of tomato juice or
a sauce made as follows:

| | |
|---|---|
| ¾ cup brown sugar | ½ cup water |
| 1 teaspoon dry mustard | ½ cup vinegar |

Mix and bring to a boil before pouring over ham loaf.

Serves 8.

MRS. ELMER J. HERR, *Hanover, Pa.;* MRS. D. C. HOSTETLER, *Orrville, Ohio*
MRS. MELVIN BIRKY, *Goshen, Ind.*

## Fried Ham with Cream Sauce

| | |
|---|---|
| 6 slices ham, 3x3½x¼ inches | 1 cup rich top milk |
| Flour | |

Cut slices of ham ¼ inch thick and large enough for a serving.

Roll in flour and fry until nicely browned on both sides.

Pour over the ham 1 cup of rich milk and then cover pan.

Simmer for 10 minutes.

This makes a delicious, unthickened gravy to serve over the fried ham.

Serves 6.

KATE BEACHY, *Grantsville, Md.*

## Fried Ham and Onion Gravy with Noodles

6 slices ham, 3x3½x¼ inches
3 onions

½ cup sour cream

Fry slices of ham until nicely browned.

Remove ham from pan and add the sliced onions to the ham drippings.

When onions are slightly browned, add sour cream.

Let come to a boil and pour over hot noodles.

To make noodles, or "keelka," take:

1 cup milk
1 teaspoon salt

2 eggs
Flour enough to make a stiff dough

Break eggs into a bowl and beat well.

Add the salt, milk and flour.

Roll the dough ¼ inch thick and cut into 1½ inch strips.

Dust dough with flour and lay 3 or 4 strips on top of each other.

Cut dough with a sharp knife into strips ⅛ inch wide to make noodles.

Drop noodles into boiling water and cook for 8 minutes.

Pour into a colander and rinse with warm water.

Serves 6.

MRS. JACOB M. FRANZ, *Mountain Lake, Minn.*

## Ham Puff

2 cups ground ham, cooked
1 cup ground cooked carrots
3 tablespoons melted butter
2 eggs, beaten
2 cups milk

2 cups flour
3 teaspoons baking powder
½ teaspoon salt
¼ teaspoon pepper

Sift together the dry ingredients.

Beat eggs and add milk; then add to flour mixture.

Then add ground carrots and ham and the melted butter.

Bake in greased casserole or muffin tins at 400° for 25-30 minutes.

Serves 6-8.

MYRTLE HUBER, *Bareville, Pa.*

## Ham Rolls with Cheese Sauce

2 cups flour
4 teaspoons baking powder
½ teaspoon salt
4 tablespoons fat

¾ cup milk
1 cup ground cooked ham
2 tablespoons soft butter
1½ tablespoons prepared mustard

Add butter and mustard to the ground ham.

Sift together flour, baking powder and salt and cut in fat.

Add milk to make a soft dough.

Roll out dough ¼ inch thick and spread with ham mixture.

Roll as a jelly roll and cut into slices 1½ inches thick.

Place cut side down in a greased pan and bake at 425° for 15 to 20 minutes.

When baked, serve with cheese sauce (page 133).

Serves 6.

ANNA LOIS UMBLE, *Atglen, Pa.*

## Ham Timbales

| | |
|---|---|
| 2 cups minced, cooked ham | ¾ teaspoon salt |
| 2 eggs, separated | ⅛ teaspoon pepper |
| 1½ cups bread crumbs | 1 teaspoon grated onion |
| 1½ cups milk | |

Combine the crumbs and milk and cook to a paste.

Add beaten egg yolks and seasoning to minced ham.

Then add crumb and milk mixture.

Fold in stiffly beaten egg whites.

Place in greased custard cups or timbale molds.

Set in a pan of hot water and bake at 350° for 30 to 35 minutes.

Serves 6-8.

LOUIDA BAUMAN, *Kitchener, Ont., Can.*

## Smothered Ham

| | |
|---|---|
| 1 slice ham 2 inches thick | ½ teaspoon salt |
| 1 cup bread crumbs | ¼ teaspoon pepper |
| 1 cup milk | 6 whole cloves |
| 1 tablespoon minced onion | ¼ cup brown sugar |

Use a slice of ham from the center of the ham.

Place in a roasting pan and pour over it 1 cup boiling water.

Stick cloves in the top of the slice.

Scald milk and add bread crumbs.

When soft, spread over ham and add seasoning.

Sprinkle brown sugar over top.

Bake at 350° for 2 hours.

Serves 6.

MRS. NELLIE HINES, *Birch Tree, Mo.*

## Stuffed Ham Steak with Sweet Potatoes

| | |
|---|---|
| 2 cups soft bread crumbs | 1 teaspoon dry mustard |
| 2 cups chopped seeded raisins | ¼ cup melted butter |
| ½ cup diced celery | 2 large slices of ham ½ inch thick |
| ¼ cup brown sugar | 3 large sweet potatoes |

Combine crumbs, raisins, celery, sugar, mustard and butter to form a stuffing.

Spread between slices of ham and tie securely with heavy cord.

Stick a few cloves in the fat.

Bake at 325° for 2 hours.

Forty-five minutes before serving, surround with halves of partly boiled sweet potatoes and continue to bake.

MRS. EARL HERTZLER, *Mechanicsburg, Pa.*

## Pork Chops, Breaded

| | |
|---|---|
| 6 pork chops | I egg, beaten |
| ¾ cup fine bread crumbs | ¼ cup milk |
| I teaspoon salt | ¼ cup boiling water |
| ⅛ teaspoon pepper | |

Add salt and pepper to bread crumbs.

Beat egg and add milk.

Dip chops in liquid and roll in crumbs.

Put 3 tablespoons fat in a skillet and brown chops.

Place chops in a baking pan or dish and add boiling water.

Cover and bake at 400° for about 50 minutes.

Serves 6.

## Pork Chops and Limas

| | |
|---|---|
| 1½ cups dried lima beans | 2 tablespoons sugar |
| 6 pork chops | ½ teaspoon dry mustard |
| ¼ cup chopped onion | I teaspoon salt |
| 1/3 cup catsup | ⅛ teaspoon pepper |

Soak Limas overnight.

Cook in salt water until almost soft.

Drain off the water and save it.

Brown the chops and remove from pan.

Mix catsup and seasoning with 1½ cups water in which beans were cooked.

Add Limas and chopped onion.

Place in a casserole or baking pan and lay browned chops on top.

Cover and bake at 350° for 1 hour.

Serves 6.

FLORENCE STRONG, *Mechanicsburg, Pa.*

## Pork Chops and Potatoes

6 pork chops
6 medium-sized potatoes
6 tablespoons flour

2½ cups milk
1½ teaspoons salt
⅛ teaspoon pepper

Brown the pork chops in fat.

Place a layer of raw sliced potatoes on top of chops.

Sprinkle with salt, pepper and flour.

Add another layer of potatoes, sprinkling flour and salt on each layer.

Pour the hot milk over the potatoes and add dots of butter.

Bake at 350° for 1 hour.

Serves 6.

Mrs. Dan Beachy, *Hartville, Ohio*

## Pork Chops and Rice

5 pork chops
½ cup uncooked rice
2 cups strained tomatoes

½ diced green pepper
1½ teaspoons salt
⅛ teaspoon pepper

Fry chops slightly in a hot pan.

Move chops to one side and add rice to the fat; allow it to brown.

Push rice to side of pan and brown the chops.

Add the diced pepper, tomatoes and seasoning.

Cover and cook slowly on top of stove for about 1 hour.

Serves 5.

Mrs. Nellie Hines, *Birch Tree, Mo.*

## Stuffed Pork or Lamb Chops

6 large pork or lamb chops
1½ cups bread crumbs
1 onion, minced
3 tablespoons melted butter

1 egg, beaten
1 teaspoon salt
⅛ teaspoon pepper
¼ cup hot water

Mix crumbs, melted butter, seasoning and beaten egg.

Add the hot water to make a bread filling.

Cut a pocket in each chop and fill with bread stuffing.

Sauté chops in a little fat until slightly brown.

Place in a roasting pan, add 1 cup hot water and the fat in which chops
were fried.

Cover and steam or bake slowly for 1 hour.

Serves 6.

Mrs. Walter Weaver, *Christiana, Pa.*

### Pickled Pigs' Feet or Souse

| | |
|---|---|
| 4 pigs' feet | 2 tablespoons salt |
| I cup chopped pickles | I tablespoon whole cloves |
| 2 cups vinegar | ½ teaspoon black pepper |
| 2 cups stock | I tablespoon broken cinnamon bark |

Scrape and clean feet well and put on to boil in enough salt water to cover.

Simmer for approximately 4 hours or until meat will separate from bones.

Mix stock in which meat was cooked with vinegar, salt, pepper and spices.

Bring to the boiling point and hold for 30 minutes.

Strain liquid to remove spices.

Place pieces of meat and chopped pickle in a flat dish or stone jar and pour the sour liquid over it.

Chill in refrigerator until perfectly cold.

Slice and serve.

The old recipe says, "This is very good for one who likes pigs' feet!"

KATE BEACHY, *Grantsville, Md.*

### Roasted Pig's Stomach

#### *Dutch Goose*

| | |
|---|---|
| I pig stomach | 2 cups shredded cabbage |
| 1½ pounds ground sausage | 2 tablespoons salt |
| I quart diced potatoes, raw | I teaspoon pepper |
| I onion, chopped fine | |

Remove the inner lining of the stomach and discard.

Wash stomach well and then soak in salt water several hours.

Drain and fill stomach with stuffing. Sew securely.

Use either of the following recipes for the filling.

#### I

Make a filling of raw diced potatoes, chopped onion and shredded cabbage.

Add seasoning and mix well.

#### II

Make a bread filling by browning diced onion and bread cubes in butter.

Mix with egg, parsley, and milk.

Stir in diced boiled potatoes and 1 pound sausage. Mix thoroughly.

Place stuffed stomach on a rack in a kettle, cover with water and cook
　　slowly until tender.

Then brown in a hot pan to which butter has been added.

Or

Place stuffed stomach in a roasting pan and bake at 350° for approxi-
　　mately 3 hours.

Serve with gravy made by adding flour and water to drippings in
　　roasting pan.

Serves 8 to 10.

　　Mrs. Barton Musser, *Adamstown, Pa.;* Mrs. Milton Huber, *Willow Street, Pa.*

## Pork Spareribs with Vegetables

| | |
|---|---|
| 4 pounds spareribs | 2 cups boiling water |
| 6 medium-sized potatoes, sliced | 2 teaspoons salt |
| 5 sliced carrots | 1/4 teaspoon pepper |
| 2 cups diced celery | 2 tablespoons flour |

Place spareribs in roasting pan, sprinkle with salt, pepper and flour.

Place potatoes, carrots and celery on top.

Add hot water.

Cover and bake at 350° for 1¼ hours.

Garnish with parsley.

Serves 8.

　　　　　　　　　　　　　　　Helen Weyant, *Grantsville, Md.*

## Pork and Vegetable Stew with Dumplings

| | |
|---|---|
| 1/2 pound pork, cubed | 3 medium-sized potatoes |
| 1 medium-sized onion | 3 carrots |
| 2 pints boiling water | 3 turnips |
| 2 teaspoons salt | 1/2 head cabbage |
| 1/4 teaspoon pepper | |

Fry pork cubes and minced onion together until slightly browned.

Add boiling water and season with salt and pepper.

Dice potatoes, carrots and turnips and add to meat.

Shred cabbage and add.

Fifteen minutes before serving, add dumplings to hot stew.

Use same recipe for dumplings as given with beef or chicken stew
　　(page 56 or 93).

Cover tightly and cook for 10 to 12 minutes.

Serves 6.

　　　　　　　　　　　　　　Mrs. Abner Musselman, *Elmira, Ont., Can.*

## Sausage and Bean Casserole

| | |
|---|---|
| 1 pound ground sausage | 1/4 teaspoon dry mustard |
| 3 1/2 cups cooked navy beans | 1 teaspoon salt |
| 1/4 cup chopped onion | 1/2 cup tomato juice |

Brown sausage and onion together.

Drain off excess fat.

Combine with beans and add seasoning.

Place in greased casserole and pour tomato juice over mixture.

Bake at 350° for 45 to 50 minutes.

Serves 6.

MRS. MARY HARTZLER, *Tiskilwa, Ill.*

## Baked Sausage Pie

| | |
|---|---|
| 1 pound fresh sausage | 1 1/2 teaspoons salt |
| 4 cups diced cooked potatoes | 1/8 teaspoon pepper |
| 2 onions, minced | Milk to cover mixture |
| 1/2 cup diced celery | Pastry for bottom and top crust |
| 1 tablespoon chopped parsley | (page 354) |

Line the bottom and sides of a flat baking dish with pastry.

Fill dish with alternate layers of fresh sausage and cooked, diced
potatoes.

Add onion, celery and seasoning.

Cover mixture with hot milk and add top crust.

Bake at 350° for 1 hour.

Serves 6-8.

MRS. ROY HUBER, *East Petersburg, Pa.*

## Sausage and Creamed Potatoes

| | |
|---|---|
| 1 pound sausage links | 1 1/2 teaspoons salt |
| 1 medium-sized onion | 1/4 teaspoon pepper |
| 6 to 8 potatoes | 1 cup milk |
| 2 tablespoons flour | |

Cut sausage in 1/2 inch lengths.

Chop the onion fine.

Mix meat and onion together and fry until slightly brown.

Add water to cover and cook 10 minutes.

Cut the potatoes in quarters, add to meat and season.

Cover and cook until vegetables are done.

Make a paste of the flour and milk.

Add to mixture and cook until thickened.

Serves 6-8.

MRS. HARVEY M. STOVER, *Souderton, Pa.*

## Sausage Casserole Dinner

¾ pound ground sausage
1 medium-sized onion
1 cup whole kernel corn
1 green pepper, diced
2 cups tomatoes

1½ cups cooked macaroni
1 teaspoon salt
¼ teaspoon pepper
½ cup buttered crumbs

Brown sausage and chopped onion in skillet.
Place in the bottom of a casserole.
Add alternate layers of macaroni, vegetables and seasoning.
Top with bread crumbs.
Bake at 350° for 1 hour.
Serves 6.

MRS. I. E. MILLER, *Fentress, Va.*

## Sausage Economy Loaf

1 pound sausage
2 cups mashed potatoes
1 onion, minced
1 egg

1 teaspoon salt
⅛ teaspoon pepper
½ teaspoon poultry seasoning

Mix all ingredients together and shape into a loaf.
Roll in oatmeal.
Bake at 350° for 1 hour.
Serves 6.

MRS. A. E. REESOR, *Markham, Ont., Can.*

## Sweet Potato Sausage Cakes

½ pound fresh sausage
1 teaspoon salt

2 cups raw sweet potatoes, shredded

Shred raw sweet potatoes and mix with sausage and salt.
Shape into 10 flat cakes.
Place in cold skillet and place over low heat.
Fry slowly until brown and crisp on both sides.
Serves 5 to 6.

MRS. S. J. BUCHER, *Harman, W. Va.*

## Scrapple

1½ cups liver pudding or sausage
3 quarts broth from cooked pudding
1 cup corn meal

3 cups whole wheat flour
1½ teaspoons salt
½ teaspoon pepper

Bring to a boil broth in which pudding meat was cooked.
Season with salt and pepper.
Stir into the boiling broth the corn meal and flour.

Add ground liver pudding.

This should be the consistency of corn meal mush.

Cook slowly in heavy pan or top of double boiler for approximately 30 minutes.

Pour in dishes to mold.

When cold, slice ¼ inch thick and fry in hot fat until brown and crusty on both sides.

Mrs. Frank Gehman, *Adamstown, Pa.;* Mrs. Henry Bechtel, *Spring City, Pa.*

## Snitz and Knepp

| | |
|---|---|
| 1½ pounds cured ham or 1 ham hock | 2 tablespoons brown sugar |
| 2 cups dried apples | |

Wash dried apples, cover with water and soak overnight.

In the morning, cover ham with cold water and cook slowly for 3 hours.

Add apples and water in which they soaked.

Add brown sugar and cook 1 hour longer.

For knepp or dumplings:

| | |
|---|---|
| 2 cups flour | 1 egg, beaten |
| 3½ teaspoons baking powder | 2 tablespoons butter |
| ½ teaspoon salt | 1/3 to ½ cup milk |

Sift together dry ingredients.

Stir in beaten egg and melted butter.

Add milk to make a batter stiff enough to drop from a spoon.

Drop batter by spoonfuls into boiling ham and apples.

Cover pan tightly and cook dumplings 10 to 12 minutes.

Do not lift cover until ready to serve.

Serves 8.

Mrs. Henry Delp, *Line Lexington, Pa.;* Mrs. N. H. Hess, *Lederach, Pa.*

## Snitz and Knepp

### Without Meat

Some people enjoy the flavor of this dish best when it is made without the ham.

Soak dried apple snitz according to preceding recipe and cook until soft.

Sweeten with brown sugar and add 3 tablespoons of butter or meat fryings.

Add dumplings as in preceding recipe.

Mrs. Roy E. Huber, *East Petersburg, Pa.*

## Sugar Cure for Pork

6 pounds salt
2 pounds brown sugar

1 ounce black pepper
1 ounce saltpeter

Mix and rub meat thoroughly with this mixture.

Repeat again in 2 days and a third time in 2 more days.

Lay pieces of meat on board and keep flat for 3 weeks.

By that time the sugar cure has been absorbed and the meat can be hung up and smoked.

This amount will cure approximately 350 pounds of pork.

MRS. FRANK VAN PELT, *Columbiana, Ohio*

# VEAL

## Veal Delicious

2 pounds veal steak, ¾ inch thick
3 tablespoons fat
1 onion
½ cup flour

1½ teaspoons salt
⅛ teaspoon pepper
2 cups sour cream

Cut veal in serving pieces.

Rub with salt and pepper and roll in flour.

Brown on both sides in hot fat.

Place in a roasting pan or casserole and cover with sour cream.

Slice onion in very thin pieces and lay on top.

Cover and bake at 350° for approximately 2 hours.

Serves 6-8.

MRS. SAMUEL NAFZIGER, *Kalona, Iowa*

## Veal Loaf

2 pounds ground veal shoulder
½ pound sausage or fresh pork
2 tablespoons catsup
2 tablespoons minced parsley
1 onion, minced

1 egg
½ cup dry bread crumbs
¼ cup hot milk
1½ teaspoons salt
¼ teaspoon pepper

Mix all the ingredients together and shape in a loaf.

Place in a loaf pan and bake at 350° for 1½ hours.

Brush occasionally with bacon fat.

Serves 6 to 8.

MRS. AMOS HORST, *Hagerstown, Md.*

## Veal Pie

| | |
|---|---|
| 4 cups cooked veal, cubed | 1/4 cup fat |
| 1 medium-sized onion, minced | 1 cup diced potatoes |
| 2 tablespoons diced bacon | 1/3 cup rice |
| 1 cup canned tomatoes | 2 tablespoons butter |
| 2 hard-cooked eggs, sliced | 1/4 teaspoon pepper |
| 1 teaspoon salt | 1 cup water |

Combine bacon, potatoes and onion and brown in hot fat.

Add the chopped veal and seasoning.

When slightly browned, add the water and cook several minutes.

Cook rice until soft, drain and add tomatoes. Season.

Pour the meat mixture in a greased baking dish.

Cover with rice and tomatoes and place sliced eggs on top.

Add small pieces of butter. Cover.

Bake at 375° for 30-35 minutes.

Serves 6 to 8.

MRS. DAN BEACHY, *Hartville, Ohio*

# RABBIT

## Fried Rabbit

| | |
|---|---|
| 1 rabbit, cut in serving pieces | 1 1/2 teaspoons salt |
| 1/4 cup fat | 1/8 teaspoon pepper |
| 1/2 cup flour | |

Dress the rabbit, cut in serving pieces; soak in salt water 6 to 8 hours.

Drain and roll in flour.

Place in a skillet containing the hot fat.

Fry pieces until a golden brown on both sides.

Season with salt and pepper.

Add 2 cups of water, cover and allow to steam until tender.

To make gravy, remove pieces of rabbit from the pan and add 2 tablespoons flour to the drippings.

Brown flour and then add water.

Stir until thickened.

Serves 6.

MRS. FRANK GEHMAN, *Adamstown, Pa.*

## Hasenpfeffer

| | |
|---|---|
| 8 or 10 pieces of dressed rabbit or pheasant | 1 teaspoon salt |
| | 1/4 teaspoon pepper |
| 1/4 cup fat | 1/2 teaspoon allspice or cloves |

1 medium-sized sliced onion     ½ cup vinegar
2 heads garlic                  1 can tomato purée
2 bay leaves

Roll pieces of meat in flour and sprinkle with salt and pepper.

Fry until a golden brown.

Place in a baking pan or casserole and add sliced onion, seasoning, vinegar and tomato purée.

Let simmer or bake at 350° for 1 to 1½ hours.

Serves 8 or 10.

MRS. FRANK HARDER, *Lima, Ohio*

## VARIETY MEATS

### Bologna Recipe

*Old Recipe*

75 pounds ground beef          3 ounces pepper
5 pounds brown sugar           2 ounces saltpeter
4 pounds salt

Mix as you would sausage and stuff tightly in muslin sacks 4 inches wide and 24 to 30 inches long.

Hang in cellar one week and then smoke to improve flavor.

Keep in a dry place 6 to 8 weeks before using.

A coat of paraffin applied to the bags with a brush will help to preserve bologna.

MRS. IRA NEWCOMER, *Seville, Ohio;* MRS. DAVID KORNHAUS, *Orrville, Ohio*

### Canadian Summer Sausage

66 pounds ground beef          5 pounds white sugar
33 pounds ground pork          1/3 pound pepper
4 pounds salt                  2 ounces saltpeter

Mix as you would sausage and stuff tightly in muslin sacks, 3½-4 inches wide and 2 feet long.

Hang in cellar for 1 to 2 weeks and then smoke.

Let dry for 6 to 8 weeks before using.

MRS. AMOS LEIS, *Wellesley, Ont., Can.*

### Frankfurters, Barbecued

¼ cup chopped onion            2 tablespoons vinegar
2 tablespoons brown sugar      3 teaspoons Worcestershire sauce
1 cup catsup                   ½ teaspoon prepared mustard
½ cup water                    ½ cup diced celery
2 tablespoons fat              12 frankfurters

Brown onions in hot fat.

Add remaining ingredients and cook together several minutes.

Split frankfurters and put into sauce.

Bake at 375° for 50 to 60 minutes.

MRS. JESSE HEISHMAN, *Harrisonburg, Va.*

## Frankfurter Casserole

| | |
|---|---|
| 1 pound dried Lima beans | 2 carrots, grated |
| 2¼ quarts water | 2 tablespoons butter |
| 3 teaspoons salt | 2 strips bacon |
| 9 frankfurters | |

Soak beans in 1½ quarts water for 2 to 3 hours.

Drain and add remaining water and simmer 45 minutes.

Split 4 frankfurters in half lengthwise and arrange in bottom of casserole.

Mix carrots, beans and salt together and pour into casserole.

Lay remaining frankfurters over top, leaving them whole.

Dot with butter and lay bacon over frankfurters.

Cover and bake at 350° for 30 minutes.

Uncover and bake 15-20 minutes longer or until bacon is crisp.

Yield, 6 servings.

MRS. ROBERT M. NACE, *Souderton, Pa.*

## Frankfurter Crown with Potato Dressing

| | |
|---|---|
| 1½ pounds frankfurters | Potato dressing |
| 3 slices bacon | |

Thread frankfurters through center on a string.

Tie ends of string and stand frankfurters in shape of a crown on a rack in a roasting pan.

Fill center with potato dressing made as follows:

| | |
|---|---|
| 4 slices bacon, diced | ⅛ teaspoon pepper |
| 1 tablespoon chopped onion | 1 quart bread cubes |
| 1 tablespoon chopped parsley | 1 egg |
| 1 teaspoon salt | 2 cups mashed potatoes |

Brown bacon, add onions and cook slowly.

Add seasoning and combine with bread, beaten egg and mashed potatoes.

Toss together and add water until mixture is desired consistency.

Lay 3 strips of bacon over the top of the dressing.

Bake at 375° until bacon browns, add ½ cup water, cover and cook 25 minutes.

Serves 8.

IVA TROYER, *Harper, Kan.*

## Frankfurter and Vegetable Casserole

| | |
|---|---|
| 5 cups sliced potatoes | 1½ teaspoons salt |
| 2 cups sliced carrots | ⅛ teaspoon pepper |
| 2 onions, sliced | 3 tablespoons flour |
| 1 pound frankfurters cut in | 2 cups milk |
| small pieces | 3 or 4 strips bacon |
| 1 tablespoon minced parsley | |

Arrange sliced vegetables and frankfurters in alternate layers, in a
greased 2 quart casserole.

Sprinkle each layer with salt, pepper and flour.

Pour scalded milk over ingredients.

Arrange bacon slices on top.

Cover and cook at 400° for 45 minutes.

Uncover last 10 minutes to crisp bacon.

Serves 8-10.

Mrs. Marlin Lauver, *Scottdale, Pa.*

## Frankfurter Quails

Make a lengthwise slit in the frankfurter.

Fill with a stick of sharp cheese ¼ inch thick.

Wrap each frankfurter in spiral fashion with a whole slice of bacon.

Fasten each with a toothpick.

Place split side up in a baking dish.

Bake at 425° for 20 minutes, turn if necessary to cook the bacon.

Edith Keffer, *Waterloo, Ont., Can.*

## Wieners Stuffed with Mashed Potatoes

Split wieners in half lengthwise.

Pile mashed potatoes on top.

Sprinkle grated cheese and paprika over potatoes.

Bake at 425° for 15-20 minutes.

Mrs. John Koppenhaver, *Perkasie, Pa.*

## Wieners in Tomatoes

Cut wieners in half lengthwise and simmer in hot fat until browned.

Add minced onion and brown.

Pour enough canned tomatoes or tomato juice over the wieners to
partially cover.

Continue to simmer for 20 minutes.

Mrs. Gilbert Lind, *Nampa, Idaho*

## Wiener Stew

| | |
|---|---|
| 1 pound wieners | 1/4 teaspoon pepper |
| 6 cups diced potatoes | 1 cup milk |
| 3 cups diced carrots | 3 pints water |
| 2 onions | 2 tablespoons flour |
| 2 cups diced celery | 2 tablespoons butter |
| 2 teaspoons salt | |

Cook potatoes, carrots, onions and celery in salt water until soft.

Add milk, sliced wieners and pepper and bring to a boil.

Thicken with flour and butter that have been rubbed together to form
a smooth paste.

Serve with a nippy salad.

Serves 8.

## Baked Liver

| | |
|---|---|
| 2 pounds beef or calves' liver | 1 teaspoon salt |
| 3 slices bacon | 1/8 teaspoon pepper |
| 2 onions | 2 tablespoons fat |

Melt fat in baking pan and add liver.

Place sliced onion and bacon over it and season with salt and pepper.

Bake at 350° for about 1¼ hours.

Serves 6.

STELLA HUBER STAUFFER, *Tofield, Alta., Can.*

## Liver and Vegetable Casserole

| | |
|---|---|
| 1 pound liver | 1 cup celery, diced |
| 1/4 cup flour | 2 cups carrots, diced |
| 4 tablespoons fat | 2 cups tomatoes |
| 2 onions, minced | 1 1/2 teaspoons salt |
| 1/8 teaspoon pepper | |

Roll liver in the flour.

Melt fat in hot pan and add liver, brown on both sides and add
seasoning.

Cut liver in 1½ to 2 inch cubes and arrange in a greased casserole.

Brown chopped onions, celery and carrots in fat and pour over the liver.

Sprinkle with salt and pepper and add tomatoes.

Bake at 350° for 1½ hours.

Serves 6.

MRS. FLORENCE YODER, *Columbiana, Ohio*

## Liver and Gravy

| | |
|---|---|
| 1 pound of liver, sliced thin | 2 tablespoons flour |
| 2 tablespoons fat | 1 teaspoon salt |
| 1 onion | 1/8 teaspoon pepper |
| Water | |

Melt fat and add minced onion and cook until light brown.
Add liver that has been sliced in thin pieces.
Stir frequently until liver is browned.
Then add 2 tablespoons flour and let it brown.
Add water until desired consistency is obtained. Season.
Cook until gravy is thickened.
Serves 6.

MRS. WILLIAM SCHWEITZER, *Geneva, Neb.*

## Liver Patties

| | |
|---|---|
| 1 pound liver | 1 teaspoon salt |
| 2 slices bacon | 1/8 teaspoon pepper |
| 1 small onion | 2 tablespoons flour |
| 1 green pepper | 1 egg |

Grind liver, bacon, onion and green pepper in meat grinder.
Add the beaten egg, salt, pepper and flour.
Mix well and drop from a spoon on a greased griddle.
Serves 6.

MRS. DANIEL LONGACRE, *Spring City, Pa.*

## Liver Loaf

| | |
|---|---|
| 1 1/2 to 2 pounds liver | 1 1/2 teaspoons salt |
| 1 1/2 cups mashed potatoes | 1/8 teaspoon pepper |
| 1 egg, beaten | 1/4 teaspoon dry mustard |
| 1 onion, minced | |

Fry liver until tender, but not crisp.
Chop into 1/2 inch cubes.
Add mashed potatoes, minced onion, beaten egg and seasoning.
Mix ingredients, shape in loaf, and bake at 350° for 1 hour.
Serve with the following sauce:

| | |
|---|---|
| 2 cups canned tomatoes | Salt and pepper |
| 1 tablespoon sugar | 2 cups crushed crackers |

Bring to a boil and pour over crushed cracker crumbs.

MRS. A. E. REESOR, *Markham, Ont., Can.*

## Liver Loaf with Carrots

| | |
|---|---|
| 1 pound liver | 1¾ cups bread crumbs |
| 2 eggs | 3 large carrots, cooked |
| 1 cup milk | 1 teaspoon salt |
| ½ cup ground salt pork | ⅛ teaspoon pepper |

Grind liver that has been previously cooked, using coarse knife of grinder.

Add eggs, crumbs, milk, ground salt pork and seasoning.

Slice cooked carrots in quarters lengthwise.

Place a layer of liver mixture in the bottom of a loaf pan.

Lay strips of cooked carrots on top.

Repeat with another layer of liver and carrots.

Bake at 375° for about 40 minutes.

Serves 6-8.

MRS. L. E. STUTZMAN, *Hickory, Va.*

## Liver and Bacon Loaf

### *Makes Excellent Sandwich Filling*

| | |
|---|---|
| 1½ pounds liver | ¾ cup corn meal |
| 4 slices bacon | 2 teaspoons salt |
| ¾ cup onion, minced | ½ teaspoon pepper |
| 2 shredded wheat biscuits, crumbled | 1 teaspoon powdered sage |
| 3 eggs, beaten | ½ cup catsup |
| 1 cup milk | 5 slices bacon |

Grind liver and 4 slices bacon through a food chopper, using medium blade.

Add remaining ingredients and mix thoroughly.

Place in a loaf pan lined with sliced bacon.

Place several slices of bacon on top.

Bake at 350° for 1 hour.

Serves 6-8.

R. GEISSINGER, *Old Zionville, Pa.*

## Liver Rice Cakes

| | |
|---|---|
| 1 pound pork liver | 1 teaspoon salt |
| 4 tablespoons fat | ¼ teaspoon pepper |
| ½ small onion | 1 egg |
| 1½ cups cooked rice | 1½ tablespoons milk |

Fry pieces of liver in hot fat until tender.

When cooled, grind liver and onions in food chopper.

Add rice, salt, pepper, egg and milk. Mix well.

Shape into cakes.

Melt fat in pan, add cakes and brown on both sides.
Serves 6.

Mrs. Grace E. Zook, *Belleville, Pa.*

## Tongue

| | |
|---|---|
| 1 beef tongue | 1 tablespoon sugar |
| 1 quart stock | 2 tablespoons vinegar |
| 1 pint catsup | 2 tablespoons flour |
| 1 onion | 2 tablespoons butter |
| 2 tablespoons minced parsley | 1/2 green pepper |
| 1/2 cup chopped celery | 2 teaspoons salt |
| 3 carrots | |

Wash and scrub the tongue well.

Cook in salt water for 2 hours.

Remove the skin.

Add chopped raw vegetables and seasoning to stock in which tongue
cooked and simmer together for 10 minutes.

Thicken with flour and butter paste.

Place tongue in a large baking pan and pour vegetable mixture over it.

Cover and bake at 350° for 2 hours.

Mrs. Bartram Leaman, *Denver, Pa.*

# Poultry and Fish

## Chapter IV

IN OUR GRANDMOTHER'S DAY IT WAS MORE ESSENTIAL THAT THE HOUSE and farm buildings be located near a spring than along a good road. For that reason, many of the older houses were approached by a long, narrow lane. When Grandmother chanced to look out her kitchen window around 9:30 in the morning to see a buggy coming up the lane, she made a hasty conclusion: company for dinner!

It seemed she was always prepared for such an occasion. In the chicken yard she kept several hens in a coop in order to fatten them for company dinners. As she hurried there, she repeated something she used to hear her mother say, "Roasted pigeons do not fly into one's mouth." By the time the guests had driven into the yard and hitched the horse, Grandmother was coming in with her decapitated hen. "I am so glad you folks came today," she called happily, "you see what we are having for dinner." Of course, there was always the smokehouse with its supply of cured pork to fall back on, but even ham was everyday fare in Grandmother's day. She seldom served it alone for company dinners without some apologies.

Besides roast chicken, Grandmother's specialties were chicken and dumplings, and chicken and oyster pie. There was pigeon potpie too, which Grandmother made when the boys of the family shot down a pigeon or two now and then. For variety, she had a brood of ducks or geese; these were more difficult to raise, so she aimed only to have enough for Thanksgiving and Christmas dinner.

A story handed down gives interesting information regarding the various names used for bread dressing used to stuff fowls. There was a large table of guests, and Uncle Dave, who was visiting from an adjoining state, was asked to pass the "dressing." Seeing only a look of dismay on his face, the host tried again, asking him to pass the "filling." Still not getting anywhere he suggested that he pass the "stuffing." "Oh," exclaimed Uncle Dave at last, "we call that ramming!"

The many types of canned fish that stand on our shelves today were unknown to Grandmother. Instead of the fish dishes we enjoy, she served mainly fried, fresh fish. The streams in her day had an abundant supply of fresh-water fish. To these streams Great-grandfather took his boys fishing at the close of harvest and haymaking. They had helped faithfully in the fields and this annual treat was one of their rewards. They usually went to a near-by river or creek in the evening, and there fished until they had caught enough to satisfy their appetites. Great-grandmother sat by the oil lamp quilting until they returned, so she could clean the fish. What a delicious breakfast the family enjoyed next morning! Fresh trout rolled in corn meal and fried in fat, along with plenty of fresh bread and butter!

## Procedure for Making White Sauce

A number of the recipes included in this chapter and elsewhere require a white sauce base. Directions are given here for making a white sauce. Where necessary, thick white sauces are described in individual recipes.

Melt fat in heavy saucepan or in top of double boiler.

Add flour and seasoning and stir until well blended.

Slowly add milk, stirring constantly until a smooth paste is formed. To shorten cooking time, milk may be heated separately.

## Thin White Sauce

| | |
|---|---|
| 3 tablespoons fat (butter preferred) | 1 teaspoon salt |
| 2 tablespoons flour | 2 cups milk |

## Medium White Sauce

| | |
|---|---|
| 4 tablespoons fat (butter preferred) | 1 teaspoon salt |
| 4 tablespoons flour | 2 cups milk |

# POULTRY

## Chicken a la King

| | |
|---|---|
| 2 tablespoons butter | 1/4 teaspoon pepper |
| 1 teaspoon minced onion | 3/4 cup milk |
| 1/2 cup flour | 1/3 cup chopped green pepper |
| 3 1/2 cups chicken stock | 1/3 cup red pimiento, chopped |
| 3 cups diced cooked chicken | 1 cup chopped mushrooms, cooked |
| 1 1/2 teaspoons salt | 2 egg yolks |

Sauté onion and green pepper in hot butter until slightly browned.
Remove from fat.
Add flour and blend into fat.
Add stock and cook until thickened.
Then add chopped chicken, cooked mushrooms and seasoning.
Heat together thoroughly.
Beat egg yolks and add milk.
Stir this into chicken and stir until blended. Add pimiento.
Remove from heat and serve.
Serves 8.

LOUISE REESOR, *Markham, Ontario, Can.;* MRS. L. M. CLEMMER, *Souderton, Pa.*

## Chicken Baked in Cream

| | |
|---|---|
| 1 young chicken cut in serving pieces | 1 1/2 teaspoons salt |
| 3 tablespoons butter | 1/8 teaspoon pepper |
| 1/2 cup flour | 1 1/2 cups sweet or sour cream |

Clean and cut chicken into serving pieces.
Sprinkle with salt and pepper and dredge in flour.
Melt butter in a skillet or roasting pan.
Fry chicken until a golden brown on both sides.
Place chicken in a casserole or roasting pan.
Pour the cream over the chicken.

Cover and bake at 350° for about 2 hours.
Serve with a gravy made from the fryings in the pan.
Serves 6.

Mrs. Clarence Swartzendruber, *Kalona, Iowa*
Mrs. B. L. Bucher, *Dallastown, Pa.*

## Chicken Casserole

| | |
|---|---|
| 2 cups diced cooked chicken | 1/4 teaspoon pepper |
| 2 cups soft bread cubes | 2 eggs, beaten |
| 2 tablespoons chopped parsley | 1 1/2 cups chicken broth |
| 1 teaspoon salt | 1 1/2 cups milk |

Place a layer of bread cubes in a greased casserole.
Then add a layer of chicken, parsley and seasoning.
Continue in alternate layers with bread cubes on top.
Beat eggs and add milk and broth.
Pour over mixture.
Bake at 350° for 45 minutes.
Serves 6.

Mrs. S. J. Bucher, *Harman, W. Va.*

## Creamed Chicken

| | |
|---|---|
| 2 cups cold diced chicken | 3 tablespoons butter |
| 2 cups milk | 1 egg |
| 1 teaspoon salt | 1/8 teaspoon pepper |
| 2 tablespoons flour | 1 tablespoon minced parsley |

Make a white sauce of the fat, flour, milk, and seasoning (page 90).
Add chopped chicken to white sauce and heat thoroughly.
Add beaten egg and parsley and blend together.
Remove from heat and serve.
This is good served on toast or in a noodle ring.
Serves 6.

Mrs. Jacob Reiff, *Hagerstown, Md.*

## Chicken Croquettes

| | |
|---|---|
| 2 tablespoons butter | 1/4 teaspoon onion juice |
| 2 1/2 tablespoons flour | 1/8 teaspoon pepper |
| 1 cup milk | 2 tablespoons minced parsley or celery |
| 2 cups minced cooked chicken | 2 eggs, beaten |
| 1 teaspoon salt | 1 cup dried bread crumbs |

Make a white sauce of the fat, flour and milk (page 90).
Add the finely chopped chicken and seasoning.

Cool thoroughly, then shape into croquettes.

Dip in crumbs, then beaten eggs and again into crumbs.

Fry in deep fat for 3-5 minutes.

Serves 6.

MRS. SIMON P. KRAYBILL, *Elizabethtown, Pa.*

## Chicken and Corn

| | |
|---|---|
| 2 tablespoons butter | 3 cups corn, fresh or canned |
| 2 tablespoons flour | 2 cups cooked diced chicken or |
| 1½ teaspoons salt | 1 chicken cut in pieces and fried |
| 1 cup milk | 1 green pepper |
| 1 cup light cream | ½ cup bread crumbs |
| 3 eggs, beaten | |

Make a white sauce with the fat, flour and milk (page 90).

Add the cream and beaten eggs to the thickened white sauce.

Remove from heat.

Arrange chicken and corn in alternate layers in greased casserole.

Pour egg and white sauce over the mixture.

Sprinkle lightly with crumbs and lay green pepper rings on top.

Bake at 350° for 1 hour.

Serves 6.

NAOMI GOOD, *Spring City, Pa.*; OLD PEOPLE'S HOME, *Maugansville, Md.*

## Chicken and Dumplings

| | |
|---|---|
| 1 chicken, a year-old hen preferred | For dumplings: |
| 1½ teaspoons salt | 1½ cups flour |
| Water to cover | ½ teaspoon salt |
| 3 medium-sized potatoes | 3 teaspoons baking powder |
| 1 small onion | 1 egg |
| 2 tablespoons chopped parsley | 2 to 3 tablespoons milk |

Cut chicken into serving pieces.

Cover with water and cook slowly until almost tender.

Add sliced potatoes and finely chopped onion, parsley and seasoning.

Cook 15 more minutes and then add the dumplings to the boiling broth and meat.

To make dumplings, sift dry ingredients together.

Add beaten egg and milk. Stir until well blended.

The dough should be stiff enough to drop from a spoon.

Drop dough from a teaspoon into boiling chicken.

Cover tightly and cook 10 more minutes.

Do not uncover until ready to serve.

Serves 6 to 8.

MRS. AMANDA TROYER, *Shickley, Neb.*; MRS. S. E. HOSTETTER, *Denbigh, Va.*

## Brown Fricassee Chicken with Dumplings

Dumplings:

| | |
|---|---|
| 1 chicken, cut in serving pieces | 2 cups flour |
| ½ cup flour | 4 teaspoons baking powder |
| 1 teaspoon salt | ½ teaspoon salt |
| 3 tablespoons butter | 2 teaspoons fat |
| 2 cups water | ½ cup rich milk |

Sprinkle pieces of chicken with salt and pepper and roll in flour.

Melt butter in a pan and fry chicken until a golden brown.

Add water and cover.

Cook slowly about 2 hours.

Make dough for dumplings and drop by spoonfuls into the hot chicken.

Cover and steam 10 minutes.

Thicken stock to make gravy after removing chicken and dumplings.

Serves 6.

MRS. D. D. DRIVER, *Hesston, Kan.*

## Fried Chicken

| | |
|---|---|
| 3½ pound fryer | 2 teaspoons salt |
| ½ cup flour | ⅛ teaspoon pepper |

Cut chicken into serving pieces.

Wash pieces of chicken, drain but do not wipe dry

Sprinkle well with salt and pepper mixture.

Place flour in paper bag and dredge pieces with flour by shaking them in bag until well covered.

Melt fat to a depth of ½ inch in a heavy skillet.

When fat is moderately hot, add pieces of chicken.

Do not crowd them in pan.

Turn the pieces to brown them on all sides.

If a crisp crust is desired, cover the pan for the first half hour of the cooking period, then uncover.

If a tender crust is desired, brown pieces with pan uncovered and then remove them to rack in roasting pan.

Cover and bake at 325° for 1 hour or in electric skillet for 30-40 minutes.

If desired, a pressure saucepan may be used for steaming after chicken has been fried a golden brown.

Serves 6.

MRS. EDGAR STRITE, *Hagerstown, Md.*

## Chicken Loaf

| | |
|---|---|
| 3 cups finely chopped cooked chicken | 2 tablespoons chopped parsley or celery |

2 cups fresh bread crumbs
2 cups cooked rice
1½ teaspoons salt
⅛ teaspoon pepper

2 tablespoons minced green pepper
1½ cups milk
1½ cups chicken broth
3 eggs, beaten

Mix ingredients in the order given, add beaten eggs, milk and broth last.
Shape in a loaf and bake at 350° for approximately 1 hour.
Serves 8.

Serve with the following sauce:

¼ cup fat
6 tablespoons flour
2 cups chicken broth
¼ cup cream

1 teaspoon salt
1 tablespoon minced parsley
½ teaspoon lemon juice
¼ pound fresh mushrooms (optional)

Brown chopped mushrooms in fat, add flour and broth.
Cook until thickened and then add seasoning and cream.
Serves 6-8.

MRS. R. J. RICH, *Washington, Ill.*

## Chicken Loaf with Peas

1 cup soft bread crumbs
2 cups milk
2 eggs, beaten
1 teaspoon salt

¼ teaspoon paprika
3 cups cooked diced chicken
½ cup cooked peas

Mix ingredients in the order given.
Pour into a greased loaf pan or ring mold.
Bake at 350° for 1 hour.
Let stand 10 minutes before turning out of mold.
May be served hot or cold.
Delicious when served with mushroom sauce.
Serves 8.

STELLA HUBER STAUFFER, *Tofield, Alta., Can.*

## Chicken and Noodles

1 stewing hen
½ pound package noodles
1½ teaspoons salt
4 tablespoons butter or fat

4 tablespoons flour
2 cups milk
3 cups chicken broth

Cook chicken until tender and remove meat from bones.
Cut chicken into ½ inch pieces.
Boil noodles in salt water for 20 minutes.
Then drain and rinse with warm water.
Make a thin white sauce with fat, flour and liquid. (Page 91.)
Add salt and pepper.

Add chopped chicken to white sauce.
Place a layer of chicken in greased casserole and then a layer of noodles.
Add another layer of chicken and noodles.
Crumble ½ cup corn flakes and put on top.
Bake at 350° for 1 hour.
Serves 8.

ANN BECK, *Archbold, Ohio*

## Chicken Oyster Pie

3 cups chopped cooked chicken
1 pint oysters
2 hard-cooked eggs
½ cup chopped celery

2 cups chicken broth
4 tablespoons flour
6 tablespoons water
1 recipe standard biscuit dough
(page 12)

Arrange chicken, oysters, celery and sliced eggs in alternate layers in a
greased casserole.
Heat chicken broth and thicken with the flour-water paste.
Pour sauce over contents of casserole.
Make biscuit dough, roll ¼ inch thick and cut into biscuits.
Place these on top of casserole.
Bake at 400° for 30 to 35 minutes.
Serves 8.

STELLA HUBER STAUFFER, *Tofield, Alta., Can.*

## Chicken and Oyster Casserole

1 chicken, cut in serving pieces
1 pint oysters
¼ cup melted butter or fat

1 cup cream or evaporated milk
1½ teaspoons salt
1 cup cracker crumbs

Season chicken with salt and pepper and roll in cracker crumbs.
Brown in fat and then place chicken in a greased casserole.
Roll oysters in cracker meal and salt, and place them between the pieces
of chicken in the casserole.
Pour cream over top.
Cover and bake at 350° for approximately 2 hours.
More cream may need to be added during the cooking period.
Serves 8.

MRS. C. R. EBY, *Hagerstown, Md.*

## Chicken Potpie (Slippery)

1 chicken, preferably a 4-pound hen
1 teaspoon salt

For potpie dough:
2 cups flour
½ teaspoon salt

Water to cover
4 medium-sized potatoes, sliced
2 tablespoons minced parsley

2 eggs
2-3 tablespoons water
1 tablespoon shortening

Cut chicken into serving pieces, cover with water and cook until tender. Season with salt.

When chicken is almost soft, add the sliced potatoes.

Add squares of potpie dough and cook 20 more minutes.

To make potpie dough, make a well in the flour and add the eggs and salt.

Work together into a stiff dough; if too dry add water or milk.

Roll out the dough as thin as possible (⅛ inch) and cut in 1 inch squares with a knife or pastry wheel.

Drop into the boiling broth, which should be sufficient to cover the chicken well. Cook 10-12 minutes.

Add the chopped parsley.

Serves 6 to 8.

MRS. HARVEY M. STOVER, *Souderton, Pa.;* MRS. J. C. CLEMENS, *Lansdale, Pa.*
MRS. AMOS KREIDER, *East Petersburg, Pa.*

Potpie may also be made by baking the squares of dough a golden brown before adding them to the chicken.

MRS. MAHLON BLOSSER, *Harrisonburg, Va.*

## Parsley Pinwheel Potpie

1 chicken or 2½-pound piece of beef
1 teaspoon salt
Water to cover
4 medium-sized potatoes
2 tablespoons chopped parsley

For potpie:
2 cups flour
1 teaspoon salt
3 teaspoons baking powder
4 tablespoons shortening
½ cup milk (approximate)

To make potpie, follow procedure for pastry (page 354).

Roll pastry dough in an oblong shape ⅛ inch thick.

Spread parsley over the dough and roll as a jelly roll.

Cut in 1½ to 2 inch lengths.

Place cooked pieces of chicken in a casserole, then add a layer of sliced raw potatoes.

Make a gravy of the chicken stock and pour it over the mixture in the casserole; have enough to cover.

Place pieces of dough on top of casserole with cut side down.

Bake at 425° for 25 minutes.

Serves 6-8.

MRS. ELMER MACK, *Souderton, Pa.*

## Baked Chicken Potpie

| | For potpie dough: |
|---|---|
| 1 chicken, preferably a 4-pound hen | 2 cups flour |
| 1 teaspoon salt | 1/2 teaspoon salt |
| Water to cover | 1/3 cup shortening |
| 4 medium-sized potatoes | 1 teaspoon baking powder |
| Parsley | 1/2 cup milk |

Cook the chicken in salt water and remove the meat from the bones.
Leave meat in as large pieces as possible.
Make pastry and line the bottom and sides of a baking dish.
Add pieces of chicken, then a layer of sliced potatoes.
Sprinkle with salt, pepper, parsley and minced onion.
Add another layer of chicken and potatoes.
Pour broth over mixture and place a pastry lid on top.
Cut holes in the lid to keep liquid from cooking out. Fasten edges
securely.
Bake at 350° for 1 hour.
This is delicious.
Serves 6-8.

Mrs. Aaron Groff, *Bareville, Pa.*

## Pressed Chicken

| | |
|---|---|
| 1 chicken | 1 tablespoon vinegar |
| 1½ teaspoons salt | 2½ pints chicken broth |
| Water to cover | 2 tablespoons gelatin |
| ⅛ teaspoon pepper | ½ cup chopped pickles (optional) |

Cook chicken in salt water until very soft.
Remove skin and bones.
Dice meat into small pieces and place in the dish it is to be molded in.
Dissolve gelatin in ½ cup cold water and add vinegar, broth, pepper, and
pickles.
Pour it over the meat and mix together well.
Place in refrigerator to mold.
Slice and serve, garnished with parsley.
Serves 8.

Mrs. David Swope, *Dayton, Va.*

## Roast Chicken

| | |
|---|---|
| 4½ pound hen | 1½ teaspoons ginger |
| 1 tablespoon salt | Bread dressing (see pages 101, 102) |

Rub inside of chicken with the mixture of salt and ginger (use 1¼
teaspoons salt for inside of fowl).

Stuff with favorite bread dressing recipe.

Lay a bread crust over dressing before trussing to keep it from coming out as the chicken roasts.

Rub outside of chicken with melted butter and sprinkle with remaining salt, to which 1 tablespoon of flour has been added, or cover fowl with a cloth dipped in melted fat.

Place in a roasting pan and add ½ cup water. Do not cover.

For first part of roasting period, place bird with the breast side down on a rack in a roasting pan.

In this position the thighs will cook more thoroughly without over-cooking the breast.

Roast at 350°, allowing 30 minutes per pound.

Turn the bird with the breast side up during the latter part of the roasting period.

If a soft rather than a crisp skin is preferred, cover the roasting pan for the last 30 minutes of roasting.

To test whether the bird is done, insert a sharp fork into the thickest part of the breast or thigh.

When done, the fork can be turned easily in the meat and the juice that runs out will show no trace of red.

If a cloth is not used to cover the fowl, it must be basted with hot drippings every 20 to 25 minutes.

Place bird on platter and remove strings and skewers used for trussing.

Makes 8-10 servings.

Serve with giblet gravy.

MRS. SAMUEL S. SHANK, *Broadway, Va.*

## Giblet Gravy

Simmer gizzard, heart and neck in 4 cups salted water, for 1 hour or until tender.

Add liver during last 10 minutes of cooking period.

Drain and reserve stock.

Chop the giblets in small pieces.

Remove 5 tablespoons of drippings from the roasting pan and add to giblets.

Add 5 tablespoons flour and stir until slightly browned.

Slowly add stock from giblets, stirring over low heat until gravy is smooth and thickened.

Cream or chicken stock may be added as desired.

MRS. SAMUEL S. SHANK, *Broadway, Va.*

## To Roast Turkey

Use same directions as for roasting chicken (page 98).

Weigh the stuffed bird and allow 18 to 20 minutes per pound for a medium-sized turkey (15 pounds). If bird is larger, allow 15-18 minutes per pound.

Remove roasted turkey to a large platter.

Use drippings for making cream or giblet gravy.

## Scalloped Chicken (I)

| | |
|---|---|
| I chicken hen, cooked | 6 cups chicken broth |
| 4 cups bread cubes | ½ cup fat |
| ½ cup chicken fat and butter | ¾ cup flour |
| I teaspoon sage | |

Remove the meat from the bones and dice it.

Melt the chicken fat and butter in a pan and add bread cubes, add chopped giblets and sage to make a bread filling.

Make a gravy by blending flour to melted fat and adding broth.

Add chopped chicken and parsley.

Put a layer of the bread dressing in the bottom of a casserole.

Add chicken and gravy and add a layer of dressing on top.

Bake at 350° for 35 to 40 minutes.

Serves 6-8.

MRS. FOREST KORNHAUS, *Orrville, Ohio;* MRS. SAMUEL TROYER, *Harper, Kan.*

## Scalloped Chicken with Mushroom Sauce (II)

| | |
|---|---|
| I chicken, cooked | 3 cups chicken broth |
| 2 cups cooked rice or bread cubes | I can mushroom soup |
| 3 eggs, beaten | |

Cook chicken until tender.

Remove meat from bones and cut into small pieces.

Beat eggs and add to rice, add chicken and broth.

Place mixture in a greased casserole and pour mushroom soup over it.

Sprinkle with bread crumbs and bake at 350° for 30 minutes.

Serves 6-8.

ANNA EIGSTI, *Buda, Ill.;* A SISTER, *South English, Iowa*

## Chicken Vegetable Treat

| | |
|---|---|
| 2½ to 3 pound chicken | 1/3 cup fat |
| ½ cup flour | 2 onions, chopped |
| I teaspoon salt | 8 carrots, chopped |
| ½ teaspoon paprika | 6 medium-sized potatoes, chopped |
| ¼ teaspoon pepper | |

Cut chicken into serving pieces, sprinkle with salt and pepper and roll
   in flour and paprika.

Brown chicken in hot fat.

Place in casserole or roasting pan, add 1 cup water, cover and bake for
   35 to 40 minutes at 350°.

Then place chopped onions, carrots and potatoes over chicken, add salt
   and more water if necessary.

Cover and continue baking 30 to 40 minutes.

Serves 6.

MRS. WILLIAM D. MOYER, *Souderton, Pa.*

## Wiggle Glacé

### An Old German Dish

| | |
|---|---|
| 1 chicken hen | For Noodles: |
| 1½ teaspoons salt | 2 cups flour |
| Water to cover | 2 eggs |
| 1 cup bread crumbs | ½ teaspoon salt |
| 3 tablespoons brown butter | 2 to 3 tablespoons water |
| 1 tablespoon minced parsley | |

Cook chicken until tender.

Remove meat from bones and cut it into small pieces. Add to broth.

Moisten bread crumbs with brown butter.

Make noodle dough by sifting flour and salt together. Make a well in
   flour and add eggs and water. Mix thoroughly.

Roll stiff dough out in oblong shape, moisten with chicken fat and
   spread with the buttered crumbs.

Roll as for a jelly roll and cut in 1 to 1½ inch pieces.

Bring chicken and broth to a boil and drop in pieces of dough.

Add minced parsley.

Cover and cook slowly for 20 minutes and serve.

Serves 6-8.

MRS. AARON STOLTZFUS, *Premont, Texas*

## Bread Dressing for Fowl (I)

| | |
|---|---|
| 1 quart soft bread cubes | 1 teaspoon minced onion |
| 3 eggs | 1 teaspoon salt |
| 2 cups milk | 1 teaspoon sage or poultry seasoning |
| 1 tablespoon chopped parsley | 2 tablespoons butter or chicken fat |

Beat eggs and add milk.

Pour liquid over bread crumbs.

Add melted fat, parsley, onion and seasoning and mix well.

Stuff fowl.

## Fried Bread Stuffing (II)

| | |
|---|---|
| 1 loaf bread | 1½ teaspoons salt |
| 2 cups mashed potatoes | ⅛ teaspoon saffron |
| 3 eggs | 1 minced onion or |
| 3 cups milk | ¼ cup celery if desired |
| 3 tablespoons chicken fat or butter | |

Beat eggs, add milk and pour over bread crumbs.

Add mashed potatoes and seasoning and mix together.

Melt 3 tablespoons of chicken fat or butter in a pan and add the mixture.

Let it simmer on top of the stove for 15 minutes.

Fill chicken while dressing is hot.

MRS. N. B. ZIMMERMAN, *Ephrata, Pa.;* MARY J. HOLSOPPLE, *Versailles, Mo.*

## Green Pepper Filling

| | |
|---|---|
| ½ cup diced green peppers | 2 cups milk |
| ½ cup diced, fried or cooked ham | 1 quart soft bread cubes |
| 2 eggs | 1 teaspoon salt |

Beat eggs.

Add salt and milk and mix thoroughly.

Pour mixture over bread cubes ½ inch square.

Add diced green peppers and ham.

Pour mixture into a flat, greased baking pan.

Bake at 350° for 25 to 30 minutes.

Serve with roast beef or chicken.

Makes 6-8 servings.

MRS. SAMUEL EBY, *Clearspring, Md.*

## Southern Corn Bread Dressing

| | |
|---|---|
| ½ cup chopped onion | For corn bread: |
| 1 cup chopped celery | 1 cup corn meal |
| ¼ cup chicken fat | ½ cup flour |
| 4 cups stale bread cubes | 1 cup sweet milk |
| 1 teaspoon salt | 3 teaspoons baking powder |
| ½ teaspoon poultry seasoning | 1 teaspoon salt |
| 1 egg | 1 egg |
| 1 cup chicken stock | 2 tablespoons shortening |

Mix corn bread according to recipe on page 14.

When baked, cool and crumble enough for 4 cups.

Cook minced onion and celery in fat until soft.

Add crumbed corn bread and white bread and fry until slightly brown.

Add salt, poultry seasoning and pepper.

Beat egg and add to chicken stock.

Pour liquid over the bread mixture and mix thoroughly.
This is enough stuffing for 2 roast chickens.

MRS. HARRY WOLGEMUTH, *Bareville, Pa.*

## Dressing Balls

| | |
|---|---|
| I loaf bread | 2½ cups chicken or beef stock |
| 2 eggs | 2 tablespoons minced parsley |
| ¼ cup chicken fat | ¼ teaspoon pepper |
| I. teaspoon salt | |

Break bread in small pieces. Remove crusts.
Add beaten eggs and melted chicken fat and mix well.
Add pepper and parsley and slowly add broth.
Moisten bread sufficiently to stick together when pressed into balls.
Melt 2 tablespoons of butter in a pan, place the balls in it and bake at
400° for 25 minutes.

MRS. H. D. H. SHOWALTER, *Broadway, Va.*

# FISH

## Deviled Clams

| | |
|---|---|
| I dozen clams | I teaspoon minced parsley |
| 2½ cups bread crumbs | I teaspoon salt |
| 3 eggs | ¼ teaspoon pepper |
| I tablespoon melted butter | Milk |
| I teaspoon minced onion | |

Cook clams in their own liquid in a double boiler for 1 hour.
Grind meat and add the bread crumbs browned in butter.
Cook 2 of the eggs and chop them.
Add chopped egg, parsley, onion, salt and pepper.
Add beaten raw egg and mix with above ingredients.
Use clam broth to moisten, if this is not sufficient liquid, add a little
milk.
Place filling in clam shells, dust with cracker crumbs and bake at 425°
for 15 to 20 minutes.

STELLA HUBER STAUFFER, *Tofield, Alta., Can.*

## Baked Fish

### *Fillet*

| | |
|---|---|
| 4 strips of bacon | I cup bread crumbs |
| 6 pieces of boned fish | I teaspoon salt |

Lay strips of bacon in the bottom of a flat baking dish.
Lay fish on bacon with skin side up and sprinkle with salt and pepper.

Sprinkle bread crumbs over top and bake at 400° for 45 minutes to
1 hour.
Serves 6.

MRS. S. J. BUCHER, *Harman, W. Va.*

## Baked Stuffed Fish (I)

3 to 4 pounds shad, rock
  or other large fish
2 teaspoons salt
2 onions

6 medium-sized potatoes
4 to 5 strips of bacon
I cup hot water

Clean fish and leave whole.
Rub salt on the inside and outside.
Place in a roasting pan.
Cut onion and potatoes into rather thick slices and lay these around the
  edge and inside of the fish.
Sprinkle vegetables with salt.
Lay strips of bacon on top of the fish.
Add hot water and bake at 375° for approximately 1¼ hours.
Serves 6 to 8.

MRS. PHEBE KRAUS, *Denbigh, Va.*

## Baked Stuffed Fish (II)

2 slices of halibut steak I inch thick
1½ teaspoons salt
Two 10½ ounce cans condensed
  vegetable soup
I tablespoon parsley
I lemon, sliced

For dressing:
I cup soft bread crumbs
I teaspoon salt
2 tablespoons scraped onion
Juice and rind of I lemon
¼ cup melted butter
I tablespoon minced parsley

Make stuffing and spread it between the two layers of halibut steak.
Sprinkle salt over fish and wrap securely with string to hold the two
  pieces together.
Cover with the condensed vegetable soup.
Bake at 375° for 45 to 60 minutes.
Garnish with parsley and lemon slices.
Serves 6-8.

MRS. R. E. GARBER, *Nampa, Idaho*

## Scalloped Fish

2 cups flaked cooked fish
2 hard-cooked eggs
2 cups medium white sauce
  (page 91)

I teaspoon salt
⅛ teaspoon pepper
I cup buttered bread crumbs

Chop cooked eggs and add to white sauce.
Arrange alternate layers of sauce and flaked fish in a greased casserole.
Cover with buttered crumbs.
Bake at 350° for 30 minutes.
Serves 6.

Mrs. S. J. Bucher, *Harman, W. Va.*

## Fried Oysters

| | |
|---|---|
| 1 pint oysters | ½ cup fat |
| 1 teaspoon salt | 1 cup cracker crumbs or corn meal |

Roll oysters in cracker crumbs or corn meal.
Melt fat in a skillet or heavy frying pan.
Add oysters and sprinkle with salt.
Fry on medium heat until a golden brown on both sides.

Mrs. H. D. H. Showalter, *Broadway, Va.*

## Oyster Fritters

| | |
|---|---|
| 1 dozen oysters, chopped | 2 eggs, beaten |
| 1 cup flour | ¼ cup milk |
| ½ teaspoon salt | ½ cup melted fat |

Chop raw oysters and add other ingredients.
Melt fat in a frying pan.
Drop oyster mixture by spoonfuls into the hot fat.
Fry until brown.
Makes 8 fritters.

Mrs. Norman Moyer, *Blooming Glen, Pa.*

## Oyster Pie

| | |
|---|---|
| 1 pint oysters | ¼ teaspoon pepper |
| 1 teaspoon salt | 1 tablespoon minced parsley |
| 4 medium-sized potatoes (or | 1½ cups milk |
| 2 cups crushed crackers) | Pastry for two crusts (page 354) |

Line flat baking dish with pastry.
Arrange alternate layers of oysters and sliced potatoes or crushed
crackers in a greased casserole.
Season with salt, pepper and parsley.
Add milk and oyster liquor.
Place a crust over top and bake at 375° for 45 minutes.
Serves 6.

Mrs. John Risser, *Hagerstown, Md.;* Myrtle Huber, *Bareville, Pa.*

## Scalloped Oysters

| | |
|---|---|
| 1 pint oysters | 1/4 teaspoon pepper |
| 4 cups crushed crackers or bread crumbs | 1/3 cup melted butter |
| 1 1/4 teaspoons salt | 2 cups oyster juice and milk |

Melt butter and add to crumbs.

Add alternate layers of crumbs and oysters in a greased casserole. Season.

Pour liquid over contents of dish and top with crumbs.

Bake at 375° for 30 minutes.

Serves 6.

Mrs. Jacob Grove, *Hagerstown, Md.*; Mrs. Abram Loux, *Souderton, Pa.*

## Salmon Puff or Soufflé

| | |
|---|---|
| 2 cups flaked salmon | 2 cups mashed potatoes |
| 2 tablespoons melted butter | 1 teaspoon minced onion |
| 2 tablespoons chopped celery | 1 teaspoon lemon juice |
| 2 tablespoons minced parsley | 2 eggs, separated |
| 1 teaspoon salt | |

Drain salmon and flake with fork.

Sauté chopped celery and parsley in the hot butter.

Combine with salmon and add mashed potatoes, salt, minced onion, lemon juice and egg yolks. Mix well.

Fold in stiffly beaten egg whites and pile lightly in a buttered baking dish.

Bake at 350° for 50 to 60 minutes.

Serves 6.

Mary C. Shenk, *Denbigh, Va.*; LaVerne Johnson, *Bluffton, Ohio*

## Salmon Loaf

| | |
|---|---|
| 2 cups canned salmon | 1 1/2 tablespoons minced parsley |
| 2 cups soft bread crumbs or cooked rice | 2 tablespoons melted butter |
| 1/2 cup milk | 1 teaspoon salt |
| 2 eggs, beaten | 1 teaspoon lemon juice (optional) |

Drain salmon, reserving the liquid.

Flake the fish and combine with all the other ingredients, including liquid from salmon.

Shape in a loaf and place in a greased baking pan.

Bake at 375° for 40 minutes.

Serves 6.

Serve with creamed peas or one of the following sauces:

1. White sauce to which catsup has been added just before serving.

2. Lemon sauce made by cooking together until thick:

| | |
|---|---|
| 1/2 cup butter | 1/2 teaspoon salt |
| 2 eggs | 1/8 teaspoon paprika |
| Juice of 1/2 lemon | 1/2 cup boiling water |

Mrs. Clarence E. Lutz, *Elizabethtown, Pa.*; Mrs. Howard Carter, *Sheldon, Wis.*
Mrs. Tobias Slabaugh, *Loogootee, Ind.*

## Creamed Salmon

| | |
|---|---|
| 2 cups flaked, canned salmon | 2 cups milk |
| 3 tablespoons flour | 1 1/2 teaspoons salt |
| 3 tablespoons fat | 1/2 teaspoon pepper |

Make a white sauce with the fat, flour and milk.

Add flaked salmon and seasoning.

Garnish with chopped parsley.

Serves 6.

## Salmon Croquettes

| | |
|---|---|
| 2 cups flaked salmon | 1 egg |
| 2 tablespoons fat | 3 tablespoons minced parsley |
| 4 tablespoons flour | 1 tablespoon lemon juice |
| 1 cup milk | 1 teaspoon Worcestershire sauce |
| 1 teaspoon salt | 1 cup bread crumbs |

Make a thick white sauce with the fat, flour and milk.

Add seasoning.

Mix together the drained salmon, parsley, lemon juice and Worcestershire sauce.

Add the beaten egg and then stir in the bread crumbs and white sauce.

Shape into croquettes and chill 2 to 3 hours.

Fry in deep fat.

Makes 8 croquettes.

Mrs. Ralph L. Vogt, *Hesston, Kan.*

## Salmon Pie

| | |
|---|---|
| 3 tablespoons fat | For topping: |
| 2 tablespoons flour | 1 cup flour |
| 1 cup milk | 1/2 teaspoon salt |
| 1 teaspoon salt | 1 1/2 teaspoons baking powder |
| 1 cup flaked salmon | 3 tablespoons butter |
| | 3/4 cup milk |

Make a white sauce with the fat, flour and milk.

Season with salt and pepper and add flaked salmon.

Put mixture in a greased shallow pan.

Mix the ingredients for topping and drop the soft dough by spoonfuls on top of the salmon mixture.

Bake at 400° for 30 minutes.

Serves 6.

MRS. DAVID PLANK, *Detroit, Mich.*

## Salmon Roll with Egg Sauce

| | |
|---|---|
| 2 cups canned salmon | 1½ teaspoons parsley, minced |
| 2 teaspoons minced onion | 1 recipe for biscuit dough (page 12) |

Flake salmon and add minced onion and parsley.

Mix biscuit dough and roll out in oblong shape to ¼ inch thickness.

Spread the salmon mixture on the dough and roll as a jelly roll.

Cut in slices 1¼ inches thick and bake at 400° for 25 minutes.

Serve with egg sauce made as follows:

    Melt and brown 2 tablespoons butter.

    Blend in 4 tablespoons flour and ¾ teaspoon salt.

    Stir in 2 cups milk and cook 2 minutes.

    Add 2 tablespoons of chopped parsley and 1 chopped hard-cooked egg.

Serves 6-8.

MRS. D. D. DRIVER, *Hesston, Kan.*

## Scalloped Salmon

| | |
|---|---|
| 2 cups salmon | 1 teaspoon salt |
| 2 cups milk | 2 cups cracker crumbs |
| 2 eggs | ¼ cup melted butter |

Flake the salmon.

Place alternate layers of salmon and crushed crackers in a greased casserole.

Beat eggs and slowly add hot milk, butter and salt.

Pour liquid over contents of casserole.

Bake at 375° for 40 minutes.

Serves 6.

MRS. E. S. HALLMAN, *Tuleta, Texas*

## Baked Tuna Loaf

| | |
|---|---|
| 2 cups flaked tuna | ½ cup celery, chopped |
| 3 cups bread crumbs | 1 small onion, chopped |
| 1 egg | One 10½ ounce can cream of chicken soup |
| 1 tablespoon minced parsley | |
| 1 teaspoon salt | ¼ teaspoon pepper |

Mix all the ingredients except the soup.

Shape in a loaf and place in a greased baking pan.

Pour chicken soup over top and bake at 375° for 30 minutes.

Serves 6.

Mrs. William A. Moyer, *Souderton, Pa.*

## Tuna Surprise

6 medium-sized potatoes, sliced
1 small can mushrooms
1/2 cup grated cheese
1 cup milk
1 1/2 cups flaked tuna
1/2 cup pimientos, chopped
1/2 cup buttered bread crumbs
1 teaspoon salt
1/4 teaspoon pepper

Arrange ingredients in alternate layers in a buttered casserole.

Pour milk over the contents and sprinkle with crumbs.

Bake at 375° for 1 hour.

Serves 6.

Alice Detwiler, *Birch Tree, Mo.*

# Cheese,
# Egg and Casserole Dishes

## Chapter V

Because of our swiss, german and dutch ancestry, it is easy to understand the reason for our fondness for many kinds of cheese. Some of the most typical of these recipes, no doubt brought from Europe, are cup cheese, egg cheese, soda cheese and stink cheese. Grandmother made each of them often enough to tell by the touch of her experienced fingers how much to scald the sour milk. She also knew when the curd had aged sufficiently to bring out the desired flavor of each type. That limb on the plum tree outside her kitchen window was a testimony to her many cheese makings. It was worn at the place where she always tied the bag of scalded curd to drain!

Grandmother traveled the path between her cook stove and egg basket rather frequently. Besides the numerous desserts which she prepared, all of those potpie, dumpling and noodle doughs called for eggs. It was no easy task to plan so that she would have enough eggs for cooking, and at the same time, have a basketful to exchange for groceries at the country store.

It was most interesting to see Grandmother making noodles. She did not even dream that the day would come when one could go to a store and buy noodles. She would never have been caught buying them, however, had it been possible—not Grandma! What machine could make as delicious noodles as she could! When she made noodles, she was never stingy with eggs, because she wanted them to be a deep yellow. Into a large bowl she would sift flour and salt. She would make a well in the flour and break eggs, one at a time, mixing with her fingers as she worked. When the dough was smooth and very stiff, she would divide it into equal parts and roll it into round balls the size of a large apple. These balls she would roll into a perfect round of dough 12 to 15 inches in diameter. They were as thin as she could possibly roll them.

Her next move was one of her own inventions. She had learned that these rounds of dough would dry quickly if she placed them in the sun. So she put one of her checkered tablecloths over the clothesline wire and hung the pieces of dough over the wire. She turned them numerous times during the drying process. Often there were 10 or 12 large pieces. When they had reached the stage of drying just before they would get hard enough to break, she removed them to the kitchen. There she rolled 3 or 4 pieces together as we roll a jelly roll. With a sharp knife she sliced across the roll, making fine strips. After they were all sliced, she let them dry until her meat was done and the broth was ready. She added some chopped parsley just before serving this favorite dish of the family.

Grandmother always had a half-dozen guineas around; these she kept for two reasons. They were her alarm clock in the morning as they called "pot rack, pot rack," and their eggs were considered far superior to chicken eggs as far as flavor was concerned. When she was to travel on the train, or ride a long distance by buggy, Grandmother never packed a lunch that did not contain hard-cooked guinea eggs. Because the shells were very hard, she cooked them about an hour before she was satisfied that they were done. At noon she took them from her bag and dipped the end in salt, which she had wrapped in a piece of brown paper. That egg eaten with buttered bread was as delicious to Grandmother as any fancy concoction we can spread in a sandwich today!

# CHEESE

## Cottage Cheese

1½ gallons sour milk  
1 teaspoon salt

½ cup cream

Heat milk slowly until it is too hot to hold your finger in it, approximately 115°.

Drain thoroughly in a cloth bag or strainer. Let stand in bag overnight to drain thoroughly.

When dry, crumble cheese curds fine and add the salt.

When serving, add the sweet cream and mix thoroughly.

Makes about 3½ cups.

MRS. SARAH WENGER, *Wayland, Iowa*

## Pennsylvania Cream Cheese

3 gallons thick sour milk  
1½ teaspoons soda  
½ cup butter

1½ cups sour cream  
¼ teaspoon butter coloring  
2 teaspoons salt

Heat the milk to 115° or until it is too hot to hold your finger in it.

Let stand at room temperature for 30 minutes.

Drain through a cloth; let stand overnight to drain thoroughly.

When dry, crumb the curds and mix with soda and butter.

Let stand for 2 hours.

Place in a double boiler, add 1 cup cream and allow curds to melt.

When cooked until smooth, stir in the remaining ½ cup cream to which butter coloring has been added.

Add salt and pour into a buttered dish to mold it.

MRS. G. P. SHOWALTER, *Broadway, Va.*  
MRS. ELIZABETH HARTZLER, *Marshallville, Ohio*

## Crock Cheese

1 gallon thick sour milk  
1½ tablespoons butter  
1½ teaspoons salt

2/3 cup cream  
½ teaspoon soda

Scald milk to 120° or until it is too hot to hold your finger in it.

Drain through a fine colander or cloth sack. Let stand overnight to drain thoroughly.

Place in a crock and crumble until fine. Add the salt and mix well.

Cover with a cloth and set to ripen at room temperature for 3 days.

Mix soda in the cheese and let stand 3 hours.

Melt butter in an aluminum pan or skillet and add the cheese.

Stir until dissolved and then add the cream.

Continue stirring until mixture comes to a boil.

Pour in flat dishes or bowls to mold.

Mrs. Ella Rohrer, *Wadsworth, Ohio*

## Old-fashioned Stink Cheese

To make this cheese, follow the preceding recipe, except to allow cheese
to ripen 5 days instead of 3 days.

It must be kept in a warm place while ripening.

Mrs. N. A. Lind, Sr., *Lebanon, Ore.*

## Cup Cheese

2½ gallons thick sour milk
1½ teaspoons soda

1½ teaspoons salt
½ cup water

Heat milk to 120° or until it is too hot to hold your finger in it.

Drain and allow to stand in bag until the next day.

Crumble curds or grind them fine in a food chopper.

Mix soda through cheese and place it in a crock.

Cover with a cloth and allow to stand 3 days at room temperature.

Stir each morning and evening.

At the end of the third day the cheese should appear yellow and
gummy, and have a sharp odor.

Set crock containing cheese in a boiler of hot water.

Add salt and water and stir until smooth.

Pour into custard cups. When cold it can be spread on bread.

Mrs. David Shirk, *Adamstown, Pa.*

## Egg Cheese

2 quarts sweet milk
I pint buttermilk or sour milk
I teaspoon salt

½ teaspoon sugar
4 eggs

Bring sweet milk to boiling point.

Beat eggs lightly, add sour milk, salt and sugar.

Beat slightly again.

Pour slowly into hot sweet milk.

Cover with a lid and let stand several minutes.

Stir slowly until it separates.

Remove cheese from whey by using a ladle with holes or a colander.

When set, serve with syrup.

Anna Farmer, *East Petersburg, Pa.;* Mrs. M. B. Horst, *St. Jacobs, Ont., Can.*

## Soda Cheese

| | |
|---|---|
| 1 gallon sour milk | 1 teaspoon salt |
| ½ teaspoon soda | 1 cup cream |
| 3 tablespoons butter | 1 egg |

Heat sour milk to 115°.

Cut through it both ways with a knife to aid in heating.

Pour into a cloth bag and let stand overnight to drain thoroughly.

When dry, crumble cheese and stir in soda and butter.

Let stand 5 hours.

Place in a double boiler and allow it to melt.

Add cream and stir until smooth.

Add salt and beaten egg and butter coloring.

Let come to a boil and then pour into a dish.

MRS. LEONARD JONES, MRS. M. J. BRUNK, *Harrisonburg, Va.*

## Caraway Cheese Balls

| | |
|---|---|
| 1 quart cheese curd made as for cottage cheese (page 112) | 1 teaspoon salt |
| 1 teaspoon caraway seed | Sour cream |

Use fresh cottage cheese curd from which all moisture has been removed.

Rub the curd fine between the fingers.

Place in a dish and cover with a cloth.

Allow to stand at room temperature for 3 to 5 days, stirring each morning and evening.

When cheese sticks together well, it is ready to mold.

Add the caraway seed, salt and enough cream to make the mixture stick together in balls the size of an egg.

Place cheese balls on a board in a dry place and allow to dry.

Turn each day for first few days in order to permit a crust to form on all sides.

After the crust is formed the cheese is ready to eat, but further aging improves flavor.

MRS. J. B. WARKENTIN, *Mountain Lake, Minn.*

## Cheese Fondue

| | |
|---|---|
| 6 slices of bread ½ inch thick | 2½ cups milk |
| 1 cup grated American cheese | ½ teaspoon salt |
| 3 eggs | |

Cut bread in cubes and place in the bottom of a greased, shallow baking dish.

Sprinkle with grated cheese.
Beat eggs, add milk and salt.
Pour liquid over bread and cheese.
Let stand 30 minutes.
Set in a pan of hot water and bake at 350° for 40 minutes.
This is delicious if sliced and served with creamed ham.
Serves 6-8.

RUTH SCHMIDT HERSHBERGER, *Harper, Kan*

## Cheese Rolls

### *An Old Favorite of Grandmother's Day*

| | |
|---|---|
| 2 cups flour | 1 teaspoon salt |
| 3 eggs | Milk to make a thin batter |

Beat eggs thoroughly and add salt.
Add flour and milk alternately to make a thin batter.
Put enough batter in a skillet to cover the bottom.
When brown underneath, place on waxed paper with brown side up.
Continue frying until all the batter is used.
Spread each cake with cottage cheese to which an egg has been added, and enough milk to spread.
Roll and place close together in a dripping pan and brown slightly in a moderate oven.
Makes about 8 rolls.

MRS. DEWEY WOLFER, *Sheridan, Ore.*

## Cheese and Noodle Ring

| | |
|---|---|
| 3 cups medium-wide noodles | 1 teaspoon salt |
| ½ pound processed cheese | ½ teaspoon paprika |
| 1 cup hot milk | 4 eggs, separated |
| 2 tablespoons butter | |

Cook the noodles in salt water until tender.
Drain and rinse with cold water.
Melt the cheese in the hot milk, add butter, salt and paprika.
Add to noodles and then fold in beaten egg yolks.
Beat egg whites until stiff and fold in gently.
Pour into a greased and chilled ring mold.
Place mold in a pan of hot water and bake at 350° for 45 minutes.
Serves 6-8.

STELLA HUBER STAUFFER, *Tofield, Alta., Can.*

## Cheese Soufflé

3 tablespoons butter
3 tablespoons flour
1 cup milk
½ teaspoon salt

3 eggs
1 cup grated American cheese
2 teaspoons grated onion (optional)
⅛ teaspoon paprika

Melt the butter, add flour and blend thoroughly.
Add milk to make a white sauce and cook until thickened.
Add cheese and stir until melted.
Then add the beaten yolks, salt, paprika and onion if desired.
Fold in the stiffly beaten egg whites.
Place in a greased casserole and set in a pan of warm water to bake.
Bake at 375° for about 40 minutes. Serve at once.
Serves 6.

MRS. MAHLON KING, *Parkesburg, Pa.;* MRS. EZRA LONG, *Sterling, Ill.*

## Cheese and Vegetable Casserole

1 cup processed cheese
¼ pound of spaghetti
2 cups cooked peas
1 chopped onion
1 green pepper, chopped

2 cups canned tomatoes
1 cup bread crumbs
1 teaspoon salt
¼ teaspoon pepper

Cook spaghetti in salt water until tender. Drain.
Place alternate layers of spaghetti and vegetables in a greased casserole.
Sprinkle with crumbs.
Bake at 375° for 35 minutes.
Then add the sliced cheese and return to oven until cheese is melted.
Serves 6-8.

MRS. MARY C. COULSON, *Hanover, Pa.*

## English Monkey
### *A Cheese Dish*

1 cup bread crumbs
1 cup milk
1 egg
1 tablespoon butter

¾ cup grated cheese
1 teaspoon salt
6 pieces hot buttered toast

Soak the bread crumbs for 15 minutes in the hot milk.
Melt the butter in the top of a double boiler and add the cheese.
When the cheese is melted, add the soaked crumbs and seasoning.
Then add the beaten egg and cook for 3 minutes.
Pour over the hot buttered toast and serve at once.
Serves 6.

MRS. MAURICE A. YODER, *Hesston, Kan.*

# EGGS AND EGG DISHES

## Eggs a la Golden Rod

6 hard-cooked eggs
2 cups thin white sauce (page 91)

8 slices toast
Salt and pepper

Chop egg whites and combine with white sauce.

Add salt and pepper.

Arrange slices of toast on a platter and pour the white sauce over them.

Mash the egg yolks through a sieve and sprinkle lightly over top.

Garnish with parsley.

Serves 8.

MRS. EMERY EIGSTI, *Wayland, Iowa;* MRS. JOHN A. LEHMAN, *Boswell, Pa.*

## Baked Egg with Cheese

6 hard-cooked eggs
1 cup grated cheese
2 cups bread crumbs

1/2 teaspoon salt
1/8 teaspoon pepper
1/2 cup cream

Slice eggs and arrange alternate layers of crumbs, egg and cheese in a
greased casserole.

Season with salt and pepper.

Pour cream over mixture and sprinkle with crumbs.

Bake at 350° for 30 minutes.

Serves 4-6.

MRS. SIMON HUBER, *Dayton, Va.*

## Egg Cutlets

4 tablespoons butter
6 tablespoons flour
1 1/2 cups milk
1 teaspoon salt
1 cup dry bread crumbs

1/4 teaspoon pepper
2 teaspoons minced parsley
1 teaspoon grated onion
10 hard-cooked eggs

Make a thick cream sauce with the fat, flour and milk. (See page 90.)

Add seasoning.

Chop hard-cooked eggs and add to cream sauce. Chill thoroughly in
refrigerator.

Shape into balls and roll in crumbs, then dip into beaten egg and in
crumbs again.

Brown in 1/2 cup hot fat.

Serve with favorite sauce.

Makes 8 cutlets.

NAOMI K. GROFF, *Lancaster, Pa.;* MRS. S. Z. RITTENHOUSE, *Souderton, Pa.*

## Eggs Lucian

| | |
|---|---|
| 2 cups medium white sauce (page 91) | 1 tablespoon grated onion |
| 2 cups cooked macaroni | 1/2 cup grated cheese |
| 1 teaspoon minced parsley | 6 hard-cooked eggs |
| 1 teaspoon salt | 1/4 teaspoon pepper |

Add minced onion and parsley to white sauce.

Then add cooked, drained macaroni and grated cheese.

Cut eggs in thick slices and add to mixture.

Place in a greased baking dish and cover with buttered crumbs.

Bake at 350° until crumbs are browned, approximately 30 minutes.

Serves 6.

MRS. LLOYD LEFEVER, *East Petersburg, Pa.*

## Plain Omelet

| | |
|---|---|
| 4 eggs | 1/2 teaspoon salt |
| 6 tablespoons milk or water | 1/8 teaspoon pepper |
| 2 tablespoons butter | |

Beat eggs enough to blend whites and yolks.

Add the liquid and seasoning.

Melt the butter in a heavy pan or skillet and add egg mixture.

Reduce the heat slightly. As omelet fries, lift it with a spatula to allow
uncooked part in center to run to edges and brown.

When omelet is brown underneath, mark lightly through the center
with the back of a knife. Fold in half and place on a hot platter.

Serves 4.

MRS. FANNY HERSHBERGER, *Grantsville, Md.*

## Bread Omelet

| | |
|---|---|
| 3 eggs | 1/8 teaspoon pepper |
| 1 1/2 cups milk | 1/2 teaspoon salt |
| 1 cup dry bread crumbs | 1/2 teaspoon baking powder |
| 2 tablespoons butter | 1 tablespoon cornstarch |

Soak the bread crumbs in the milk for 10 minutes.

Add beaten egg yolks, seasoning, baking powder and cornstarch.

Fold in the stiffly beaten egg whites.

Cook like plain omelet.

Serves 4-6.

MRS. LEVI H. MUSSER, *Mt. Joy, Pa.*

## Fluffy Omelet

| | |
|---|---|
| 4 eggs | 1/2 teaspoon salt |
| 4 tablespoons water or milk | 1/8 teaspoon pepper |
| 2 tablespoons butter | |

Beat egg yolks and add liquid and seasoning.
Fold in stiffly beaten egg whites.
Melt fat in a heavy pan and add egg mixture.
Cook omelet over low heat until it is a golden brown underneath.
Then place in the oven to dry omelet on top.
Bake at 375° for 10 to 15 minutes or until it no longer sticks to the finger
    when pressed lightly.
Cut lightly through the center and fold one-half over the other.
Place on a hot platter and serve at once.
Serves 4.

A SISTER

## Baked Omelet with White Sauce

| | |
|---|---|
| 3 tablespoons butter | I teaspoon salt |
| 3 tablespoons flour | 1/8 teaspoon pepper |
| I cup milk | 4 eggs, separated |

Cook fat, flour and milk together to make a white sauce.
Cool the white sauce and then add the beaten egg yolks and seasoning.
Add the stiffly beaten whites.
Pour in a greased baking pan or casserole and bake at 350° for 35
    minutes.
Serves 4.

MRS. CLARA HACKMAN, *Sterling, Ohio;* MRS. MARY WEAVER, *East Earl, Pa.*

## Scrambled Eggs

| | |
|---|---|
| 6 eggs | 3/4 teaspoon salt |
| 1/2 cup top milk | 1/4 teaspoon pepper |
| 2 tablespoons butter or fat | |

Stir eggs slightly with fork and add milk and seasoning.
Melt butter in a thick pan, skillet or double boiler.
Add egg mixture and cook slowly until creamy.
Stir constantly to avoid sticking.
Do not overcook.
Serve immediately.
Serves 5-6.

MRS. ANNIE HERSHBERGER, *Holsopple, Pa.*

## Spanish Eggs

| | |
|---|---|
| 6 hard-cooked eggs | I cup celery, chopped |
| 3 strips bacon | I teaspoon salt |

1 small onion, minced
2 cups canned tomatoes
1 green pepper, chopped

¼ teaspoon pepper
1 tablespoon flour

While eggs are cooking, cut bacon in small pieces and fry until crisp.
Remove bacon and cook onion in bacon fat.
Blend in the flour and add tomatoes, peppers and celery.
Simmer together 20 minutes and add bacon, salt and pepper.
Cut eggs in half lengthwise and arrange on a platter.
Pour hot sauce over eggs and serve at once.
Serves 6.

MRS. WILLIAM MARTIN, *Kitchener, Ont., Can.*

## Eggs Scalloped with Meat or Fish

6 hard-cooked eggs
¾ cup chopped meat or fish
¾ cup buttered bread or
  cracker crumbs

2 cups medium white sauce (page 91)
⅛ teaspoon pepper

Sprinkle the bottom of a greased casserole with buttered crumbs.
Add ½ of the chopped eggs.
Pour over the eggs ½ of the white sauce, then add a layer of chopped
  meat or fish.
Make a second layer, using the remaining ingredients.
Top with crumbs and bake at 375° for 20 minutes or until crumbs are
  brown.
Serves 6.

MRS. JACOB MARTIN, *Harrisonburg, Va.*

## Stuffed Eggs Supreme

6 hard-cooked eggs
6 tablespoons grated cheese, minced
  tongue or chopped celery
1 cup white sauce (page 91)

2 tablespoons cream
¾ teaspoon salt
¼ teaspoon pepper
6 slices buttered toast

Remove the yolks from the hard-cooked eggs and blend with grated
  cheese, tongue or celery.
Moisten with cream and add seasoning.
Refill centers of egg whites with the mixture.
Pour white sauce over buttered toast and arrange eggs on top.
Garnish with parsley.
Serve hot.
Serves 6.

ANNA MUSSER, *Adamstown, Pa.*

## Eggs in Bread Nests

4 slices bread, toasted          ½ teaspoon salt
4 eggs

Make toast and dip it in boiling water.
Butter slightly.
Beat egg whites until stiff and put on toast in the shape of a nest.
Drop yolk in the depression and sprinkle with salt and pepper.
Bake at 325° until delicately brown, about 25 minutes.
Serves 4.

LOUIDA BAUMAN, *Kitchener, Ont., Can.*

## Eggs in Ham Nests

1¾ cups cooked ground ham          1 teaspoon dry mustard
2 tablespoons ham fat              1 cup milk
2 tablespoons flour               6 eggs
¼ teaspoon salt

Melt fat, add flour and blend.
Add chopped ham and cook 2 minutes, stirring constantly.
Add salt, mustard and milk and cook slowly until thickened.
Pour into a greased shallow baking dish.
Make 6 hollows in the mixture and drop an egg into each.
Sprinkle with salt and pepper.
Bake at 325° for 25 minutes or until firm.
Serves 6.

MRS. WARD SHANK, *Broadway, Va.*

## Eggs in Noodle Nest

2 cups noodles ¼ inch wide          2 tablespoons butter
6 cups boiling water                ¼ teaspoon salt
1½ teaspoons salt                   ⅛ teaspoon pepper
½ cup milk                          6 eggs
1 cup grated cheese

Cook noodles in salt water until tender. Drain.
Add milk, cheese, butter, salt and pepper.
Mix well and turn into a greased casserole.
Make 6 depressions in the noodles with the back of a tablespoon.
Break an egg in each depression and sprinkle with salt and pepper.
Bake at 325° for about 25 minutes.
Serves 6.

MRS. CHESTER MARTIN, *Chambersburg, Pa.*

# MACARONI, NOODLES, RICE AND SPAGHETTI

## Chop Suey (American)

1 pound chopped beef or hamburger
2 onions
2 tablespoons fat
1 cup diced celery
4 cups of cooked rice, noodles or spaghetti

To make sauce:
1 tablespoon chow sauce
½ teaspoon salt
2 tablespoons cornstarch
1 tablespoon molasses
1 cup sliced mushrooms

Cut beef in small squares or grind it in a meat grinder.
Melt fat and add onions and meat.
Brown slightly and add celery, sauté 10 minutes.
Add 2 cups of hot water and bring to a boil.
Add thickened sauce made by combining the mushrooms, chow sauce, cornstarch, salt and molasses.
Simmer about 15 minutes.
Serve with plain boiled rice, chow noodles or spaghetti. Delicious!
Serves 6-8.

MRS. JOHN MILLER, Uniontown, Pa.

## Baked Macaroni and Cheese

2 cups macaroni
6 cups boiling water
1 teaspoon salt
2 tablespoons butter

1 tablespoon flour
1½ cups milk
1½ cups grated cheese
½ cup bread crumbs

Cook macaroni in salt water and drain.
Make a white sauce of fat, flour and milk (page 90).
Place a layer of macaroni in the bottom of a greased casserole.
Add grated cheese and white sauce.
Repeat until the casserole is filled.
Sprinkle crumbs over the top and bake at 375° for 30 minutes.
Serves 6.

MRS. ELIZABETH BRUBACHER, Waterloo, Ont., Can.
MRS. WILLIAM J. HUNSBERGER, Phoenixville, Pa.

## Macaroni with Hamburger

¼ pound macaroni
1½ quarts boiling water
2 teaspoons salt
¼ cup minced onion
1 green pepper, chopped

1 cup canned tomatoes
½ cup grated cheese
4 tablespoons butter or fat
½ pound hamburger
2 tablespoons flour

Cook macaroni in boiling salt water until tender. Drain.
Melt butter and add onion, green pepper and hamburger.

When brown, add flour and tomatoes and cook for 5 minutes.
Add macaroni and grated cheese. Season.
Place in a greased casserole and top with buttered bread crumbs.
Bake at 375° for 25 minutes.
Serves 6.

MRS. JESSE HARBALD, *Mechanicsburg, Pa.*

## Macaroni with Hamburger Balls

| | |
|---|---|
| 1 pound hamburger | 2 teaspoons salt |
| 2 medium-sized onions, minced | 1/4 teaspoon pepper |
| 1/4 pound macaroni | 1 cup canned peas |
| 1 1/2 quarts boiling water | 2 cups tomato juice |

Mix chopped onion, ½ teaspoon salt and pepper with hamburger.
Form into small balls and fry until brown.
Cook macaroni in salt water until tender. Drain.
Add peas, tomato juice and hamburger balls to the macaroni.
Simmer together for 10 minutes.
Serves 6-8.

MRS. FLORENCE C. FRIESEN, *Greensburg, Kan.*

## Macaroni Loaf

| | |
|---|---|
| 4 cups cooked macaroni | 1/2 cup bread crumbs |
| 2/3 cup grated cheese | 2 tablespoons onion |
| 2 cups canned tomatoes | 1 teaspoon salt |
| 2 tablespoons minced celery | 1/4 teaspoon pepper |
| 2 eggs | |

Mix all the ingredients together.
Place in a greased loaf pan.
Bake at 350° for 35 to 40 minutes.
Unmold and serve with either creamed dried beef or mushrooms,
cheese or tomato sauce. (Pages 133 and 134.)
Serves 6-8.

MRS. JACOB STOLTZFUS, *Belleville, Pa.*

## Baked Macaroni with Leftover Meat

| | |
|---|---|
| 2 cups cooked macaroni | 1/4 teaspoon pepper |
| 2 cups canned tomatoes | 1/4 cup minced onion |
| 1 cup leftover meat and gravy | 1 tablespoon butter |
| 1 teaspoon salt | 1 cup grated cheese |
| 1/2 cup boiling water | |

Melt fat in pan and add minced onion. Brown slightly.
Add meat and gravy.
Add tomatoes, salt, pepper and boiling water.

Cook slowly for 5 minutes and add grated cheese.

Put cooked macaroni in a greased casserole and pour meat mixture over it.

Bake at 375° for 25 minutes.

Serves 6.

MRS. STANFORD MUMAW, *Dalton, Ohio*

## Homemade Noodles

| | |
|---|---|
| 1½ cups flour | 3 tablespoons water |
| 1 teaspoon salt | 1 egg |
| 1 teaspoon fat | |

Make a well in the flour and add egg, salt and fat.

Rub together and add water to form a stiff dough. Knead.

Divide dough into three parts and roll each as thin as possible.

Spread rolled dough on a cloth and allow to dry partially.

Then cut dough into strips about 1½ inches wide and stack on top of each other. Then cut crosswise into fine shreds.

Or you may roll dough as a jelly roll and cut into fine shreds.

These are then ready to use like packaged noodles.

MRS. ELO SNYDER, *Breslau, Ont., Can.*

## Noodle Hamburger Casserole

| | |
|---|---|
| 1 pound hamburger | One 10½ oz. can tomato soup |
| 1 chopped onion | 1¼ cups water |
| ¼ pound noodles | ¼ pound grated cheese |
| 1 tablespoon fat | 1½ teaspoons salt |

Melt fat in pan and add onion and hamburger. Brown slightly.

Cook noodles in salt water until tender and drain.

Add browned meat to noodles.

Stir in tomato soup, water and grated cheese. Season.

Pour into a greased casserole and bake at 350° for 35 to 40 minutes.

Serves 6-8.

MRS. BERTHA LANDIS, *Sterling, Ill.;* MRS. GLEN BURKHOLDER, *Kalona, Iowa*

## Noodle and Beef Casserole

| | |
|---|---|
| ¼ pound noodles | ½ cup minced celery |
| 1 quart canned or cooked beef | 1 cup canned tomatoes |
| ½ teaspoon salt | ½ cup bread crumbs, buttered |
| ¼ cup minced onion | |

Cook noodles in boiling salt water until tender. Drain.

Put the canned meat and stock in a pan; add salt, onion, celery, tomatoes.

Cover and cook until the vegetables are tender.

Place the cooked noodles in a greased casserole and pour the meat mixture over them.

Sprinkle crumbs over top.

Bake at 350° for 30 minutes.

Serves 6.

EDNA MACK, *Souderton, Pa.*

## Noodle Ring

| | |
|---|---|
| 4 cups cooked noodles | 3 eggs, separated |
| ¼ cup melted butter | 1 teaspoon Worcestershire sauce |

Stir melted butter into cooked noodles.

Add well-beaten egg yolks and Worcestershire sauce.

Fold in stiffly beaten egg whites.

Place noodles in a greased ring mold.

Set mold in a pan of hot water and bake at 350° for 35 minutes.

Unmold carefully onto a large platter and fill the center with creamed peas or chicken.

Serves 8.

MRS. CLARENCE WHISSEN, *Broadway, Va.*

## Noodle-Salmon Casserole

| | |
|---|---|
| 4 cups cooked noodles | ¼ teaspoon pepper |
| 1 cup canned peas, drained | 1½ tablespoons flour |
| 2 cups flaked salmon, drained | 2 tablespoons butter |
| 1 cup milk | ¼ cup cracker crumbs |
| 1 teaspoon salt | |

Make a white sauce of the fat, flour, seasoning, milk and drained juices. (Page 90.)

Mix noodles, peas and salmon and turn into a greased baking dish.

Pour sauce over noodle mixture and top with cracker crumbs.

Bake at 350° for 25 minutes.

Serves 8-10.

MRS. STANFORD MUMAW, *Dalton, Ohio*

## Noodle Goulash

| | |
|---|---|
| ¼ pound noodles | 1 pound ground round steak |
| 1½ quarts water | 2 tablespoons flour |
| 1½ teaspoons salt | One 10½ oz. can vegetable soup |
| 1 large onion | 1¼ cups water |
| 2 tablespoons meat drippings | 1 cup canned tomatoes |
| ¼ teaspoon pepper | |

Cook noodles in salt water until tender. Drain.

Brown chopped onion lightly in the fat; add meat and cook slowly 10 minutes.

Add flour and blend into meat mixture.

Combine the noodles, soup, water and tomatoes. Season and add to meat.

Let simmer for 20 to 25 minutes on top of the stove or pour into a greased casserole and bake at 350° for 25 minutes.

Serves 6-8.

MRS. VELMA MILLER, *Canton, Ohio*

## Baked Noodles and Tuna with Mushrooms

| | |
|---|---|
| 1/3 pound noodles | I cup canned tuna |
| 1½ quarts boiling water | One 10½ oz. can mushroom soup |
| 1½ teaspoons salt | ¼ cup buttered crumbs |

Cook noodles in salt water until tender and drain.

Flake the tuna with a fork.

Mix with noodles and mushroom soup.

Turn into a greased baking dish.

Sprinkle with crumbs and bake at 350° for 40 minutes.

Serves 6.

MRS. DAVID GEHMAN, *Bally, Pa.*

## Filled Noodles

### Old

| | |
|---|---|
| 2 cups flour | 1½ cups mashed potatoes |
| I egg | 1½ quarts beef stock |
| ½ teaspoon salt | ¼ cup butter or meat fryings |
| 3 tablespoons water or milk | |

Make a stiff dough like noodle dough. (See page 124 for homemade noodles.)

Divide into 6 parts and roll each piece in a 4½ inch circle.

Spread each piece with 3 tablespoons mashed potatoes.

Turn over in a half-moon shape and pinch edges together securely.

Drop in boiling beef stock and cook for 10 minutes.

Do not cook more than 3 at one time.

Drain and fry in hot butter until brown on both sides.

Place in a dish and cover with hot beef stock.

Serves 6.

MRS. ELI H. GEHMAN, *Bally, Pa.*

## Potato Noodle Rolls
### *Very Old*

| | |
|---|---|
| 1 cup mashed potatoes | ½ teaspoon salt |
| 1 cup milk | Flour to make a stiff dough |
| 1 egg | (about 4 cups) |
| 1 tablespoon fat | 3½ teaspoons baking powder |

Add beaten egg, melted fat and salt to mashed potatoes.

Sift flour with baking powder and add alternately with milk.

Combine ingredients and knead dough a few minutes on floured board.

Pinch off pieces of dough the size of a small egg and roll each piece
with your hands until it is the thickness of your largest finger.

Fry in deep fat, as you do doughnuts.

Serves 6-8.

LIZZIE HERSHBERGER, *Johnstown, Pa.*

## Savory Noodles

| | |
|---|---|
| ¼ pound noodles | 2 cups chopped celery |
| 1½ quarts boiling water | 1 can tomato soup |
| 1½ teaspoons salt | 1/3 cup water |
| 1 tablespoon fat | ¾ cup grated cheese |
| ¾ pound fresh ground pork | ⅛ teaspoon pepper |
| 2 small onions, minced | |

Cook noodles in salt water until tender and then drain.

Brown meat and onion in fat and add remaining ingredients. Mix
together.

Pour into a greased casserole and bake at 350° for 45 minutes.

Serves 6-8.

MRS. ELMER J. HERR, *Hanover, Pa.*

## Wieners and Noodles

| | |
|---|---|
| ½ pound noodles | 2 tablespoons fat |
| 1½ quarts boiling water | 4 wieners |
| 1½ teaspoons salt | ¾ cup tomato juice |
| 1 onion, minced | |

Cook noodles in salt water until tender. Drain.

Melt fat and brown the onion.

Cut wieners in ¼ inch slices and add to onion.

When wieners are brown, add tomato juice.

Simmer 10 minutes.

Serve over noodles.

Serves 6-8.

MRS. S. J. BUCHER, *Harman, W. Va.*

## Noodles with Apples

2 cups boiled noodles
4 apples
4 tablespoons butter

¾ cup sugar
I teaspoon cinnamon

Wash, pare and cut apples in eighths.
Melt 2 tablespoons butter in a baking dish.
Place one-half of the noodles in the dish and then the apples.
Sprinkle with ½ the sugar and cinnamon mixture.
Cover with remainder of noodles.
Dot with butter.
Sprinkle remaining sugar and cinnamon on top.
Bake at 350° for 35 minutes.
Serves 4-6.

MRS. BETTY ROSENBURG, *Birch Tree, Mo.*

## Baked Rice and Cheese

I cup uncooked rice
I cup tomatoes
I medium-sized onion
I quart boiling water

5 tablespoons sugar
2 teaspoons salt
¾ pound cheese

Boil rice in water with tomatoes, onion, salt and sugar.
When rice is soft, place a layer of the mixture in a greased baking dish.
Then add a layer of diced cheese.
Add more of the rice mixture and top with cheese.
Bake at 350° for 35 to 40 minutes.
Serves 6.

MARY E. SUTER, *Harrisonburg, Va.*

## Rice and Curry

I pound hamburger
2 tablespoons fat
2 large onions, diced
1½ teaspoons curry powder
2 cups strained tomatoes

4 medium-sized potatoes, diced
1½ cups rice, uncooked
1½ quarts water
2 teaspoons salt

Brown hamburger and onions in the fat.
Add tomatoes, diced potatoes, curry and salt.
Add 1½ cups boiling water and cook slowly until potatoes are soft.
Cook rice in salt water and drain.
Serve curry mixture with the rice.
This is also good if chicken is used instead of beef.
Serves 6-8.

LOLA I. BRUNK, *Delphos, Ohio*

## Rice and Pork Casserole

6 pork chops
1 tablespoon fat
1 cup uncooked rice
1½ quarts water

2 teaspoons salt
2 red or green peppers
One 10½ oz. can tomato soup
¼ teaspoon pepper

Boil rice in salt water and drain.

Brown pork chops slightly in fat.

Place browned chops in the bottom of a casserole.

Add a layer of sliced pepper rings.

Add the rice and top with another layer of sliced peppers.

Pour the tomato soup, which has been diluted with ½ cup water, over the mixture.

Bake at 375° for 40 minutes.

Serves 6.

MARY C. BRENNEMAN, *La Junta, Colo.*

## Rice Vegetable Soufflé

1 cup cooked rice
¾ cup cooked green beans
¾ cup cooked carrots
2 tablespoons minced parsley
1 teaspoon grated onion

1 teaspoon salt
¼ teaspoon pepper
2 eggs, beaten
1 cup milk
3 tablespoons melted butter

Cook the rice in salt water and drain.

Chop all the cooked vegetables and mix with rice.

Season with salt, pepper, parsley and onion juice.

Beat eggs and add milk.

Mix with other ingredients.

Place in a greased baking dish and pour melted butter over the top.

Bake at 350° for 40 to 45 minutes.

Serves 6.

RUTH SCHMIDT HERSHBERGER, *Harper, Kan.*

## Spanish Rice

1 pound hamburger
4 cups cooked rice
2 small onions
2 cups tomatoes
1 green pepper

3 tablespoons fat
1½ teaspoons salt
¼ teaspoon pepper
1 teaspoon chili powder

Chop onions and pepper and cook in the fat until brown.

Add hamburger, salt, pepper and chili powder.

When meat is slightly brown, place alternate layers of cooked rice and meat mixture in a casserole.

Pour tomatoes over the contents of the dish and bake at 375° for approximately 35 minutes.
Serves 6-8.

Mrs. Roy Stutzman, *Haven, Kan.*; Mrs. Edna Selzer, *Canton, Kan.*
Mrs. Robert M. Nace, *Souderton, Pa.*

## Savory Rice

| | |
|---|---|
| ½ pound diced bacon | 3 tablespoons minced onion |
| ¼ cup bacon drippings | I teaspoon salt |
| 2/3 cup uncooked rice | ⅛ teaspoon pepper |
| 3 tablespoons chopped green pepper | 3¼ cups strained tomatoes or tomato juice |

Brown the diced bacon until nearly crisp.
Pour off fat in excess of ¼ cup and add uncooked rice, minced onion, pepper and seasoning.
Sauté until rice is light brown and then add tomatoes.
Cover and steam for 45 minutes on top of the stove.
Serves 6.

Mrs. W. M. Strong, *Mechanicsburg, Pa.*

## Sausage and Rice Casserole

| | |
|---|---|
| I pound ground sausage | One 10½ oz. can tomato soup |
| 2 cups cooked rice | I teaspoon salt |
| I medium-sized onion, chopped | ⅛ teaspoon pepper |
| 4 tablespoons grated cheese | |

Brown sausage in a pan.
Pour off excess drippings (about one-half).
Arrange alternate layers of rice and sausage in a greased casserole.
Sprinkle each layer with chopped onion and salt and pepper.
Pour tomato soup over the mixture and cover the top with grated cheese.
Bake at 375° for 35 to 40 minutes.
Serves 6.

Mrs. Allen Gingerich, *Lowville, N. Y.*

## Rice Ring

| | |
|---|---|
| I cup uncooked rice | 1½ teaspoons salt |
| 1½ quarts water | 3 tablespoons butter |

Cook rice in salt water until soft. Drain.
Add melted butter and mix thoroughly.

Press rice into a buttered ring mold and set in a pan of hot water for
    20 minutes or until rice has heated thoroughly.
Unmold on a platter and fill the center with creamed salmon or creamed
    chicken to which chopped olives have been added. (Pages 107
    and 92.)
Serves 6-8.

MRS. CLARENCE WHISSEN, *Broadway, Va.*

## Spaghetti Baked with Cheese

| | |
|---|---|
| ½ pound spaghetti | 1 teaspoon salt |
| 2 tablespoons fat | ⅛ teaspoon pepper |
| 1 tablespoon minced onion | 2 teaspoons sugar |
| 2 cups tomatoes | 1 cup grated cheese |

Cook spaghetti in salt water until tender. Drain.
Add minced onion to the fat and cook until soft.
Add tomatoes, salt, pepper and sugar to onion and cook for 10 minutes.
Mix sauce with spaghetti and add ½ cup grated cheese.
Put mixture in a greased baking dish and sprinkle with remaining
    cheese.
Bake at 375° for 25 minutes.
Serves 6-8.

MRS. EZRA LONG, *Sterling, Ill.*

## Spaghetti Dish

| | |
|---|---|
| 1 pound hamburger or sausage | 1½ teaspoons chili powder |
| 2 cups tomatoes | 1 teaspoon salt |
| ½ pound spaghetti | ½ cup grated cheese |
| 1 medium-sized onion, minced | |

Cook spaghetti in salt water until tender. Drain.
Brown hamburger or sausage and minced onion in a little fat.
Add tomatoes, spaghetti and seasoning.
Simmer 20 minutes on top of the stove.
Just before serving add ½ cup grated cheese.
Stir until cheese melts.
Serves 6-8.

MRS. FRANK SCHMIDT, *Greensburg, Kan.*; MRS. HERB FLICK, *Kitchener, Ont., Can.*

## Spatzlein (Little Sparrows)

| | |
|---|---|
| 1 egg | 2 quarts boiling water |
| 1 cup water | 1½ teaspoons salt |
| 2½ cups flour | |

Beat egg thoroughly.

Add water and beat until well blended with egg.

Add flour and beat until smooth.

Bring salt water to a boil and drop spatzlein into water.

To do this, tilt bowl containing batter in a position that it can be cut with the edge of a spoon as it pours over edge of bowl.

The spatzlein should be an inch long and ¼ inch in diameter.

Cook for 3 minutes after batter is all in the water.

Drain in colander and top with brown butter.

Makes 6 servings.

LENA MOSEMANN, *Lancaster, Pa.*

## Hungarian Goulash

| | |
|---|---|
| ½ pound spaghetti | 2 tablespoons fat |
| I pound hamburger | 1½ teaspoons salt |
| I green pepper, chopped | ½ pound cheese (Italian preferred) |
| I cup chopped onion | One 10½ oz. can tomato soup |

Brown onions, meat and green pepper in hot fat.

Cook spaghetti in salt water until tender, and drain.

Mix all the ingredients except cheese and cover with water (about 3 cups).

Simmer slowly for 30 minutes. Add cheese several minutes before serving.

Serves 6.

MRS. C. A. GRAYBILL, *Martinsburg, Pa.*

## Italian Spaghetti

| | |
|---|---|
| I pound hamburger | 1½ teaspoons salt |
| I medium-sized onion | I tablespoon fat |
| 2 green peppers | ½ pound spaghetti |

Mix the meat, chopped onion and green pepper. Add salt.

Shape meat into small balls and fry until brown.

Make a sauce with the following:

| | |
|---|---|
| ½ cup chopped onion | ¼ cup grated cheese |
| 2 green peppers | ½ cup catsup |
| I quart strained tomatoes | I tablespoon paprika |
| ¼ cup sugar | ½ teaspoon mustard |
| I teaspoon salt | ¼ cup chopped celery |

Mix together all the ingredients for the sauce and let simmer 1½ hours.

Add meat balls and simmer 1 hour longer.

Cook spaghetti in salt water until tender. Drain.

Pour meat and sauce over the spaghetti just before serving.
Sprinkle powdered cheese on top.
Serves 8.

MRS. HARRY A. DERSTINE, *Souderton, Pa.;* PAULA SEITZ, *Lancaster, Pa.*
MRS. EPENTUS FETTEROLF, *Lansdale, Pa.*

## Hot Tamale

| | |
|---|---|
| 3 cups diced onion | 3 cups milk |
| 3 tablespoons fat | 2 cups corn meal |
| 1½ pounds hamburger | 2 teaspoons salt |
| 1 quart tomatoes | 1½ teaspoons chili powder |
| 1½ cups corn, fresh or canned | 1 teaspoon Worcestershire sauce |
| 3 eggs | ¼ cup cracker crumbs |

Fry diced onions and hamburger in fat until slightly browned.
Add tomatoes, corn and seasoning and cook for 15 minutes.
Beat eggs and add milk and corn meal.
Arrange alternate layers of corn meal and meat mixtures in a baking
   dish.
Cover with cracker crumbs.
Bake at 350° for 35 minutes.
Serves 6-8.

MRS. C. F. DERSTINE, *Kitchener, Ont., Can.*

## Cheese Sauce

| | |
|---|---|
| 3 tablespoons shortening | 2 cups milk |
| (butter preferred) | ⅛ teaspoon pepper (optional) |
| 2 tablespoons flour | 1½ cups grated cheese |
| 1 teaspoon salt | |

Melt shortening over low heat. Add flour and seasoning.
Stir until well blended.
Gradually add milk, stirring constantly.
Cook until thick and smooth.
Add grated cheese and stir until it is melted.
Serve with meat, vegetables and casserole dishes.
Makes 2½ cups.

## Mushroom Sauce

| | |
|---|---|
| 1 cup thin white sauce (page 91) | 1 cup cream of mushroom soup, thinned with ¼ cup milk |

Add hot cream of mushroom soup to hot white sauce.
Serve with fish, meat or casserole dishes.
Makes 2 cups.

## Tomato Sauce

| | |
|---|---|
| 2 cups fresh or canned tomatoes | 1/2 teaspoon salt |
| 2 tablespoons onion, diced | 2 tablespoons butter |
| 4 whole cloves | 2 tablespoons flour |
| 2 teaspoons sugar | Chopped celery leaves (optional) |

Cook tomatoes, onion and seasoning together for 15 minutes.

Press through a sieve.

Melt fat over slow heat. Add flour and stir until well blended.

Slowly add hot strained tomatoes and cook until thick and smooth. Stir constantly.

Serve with fish, meat and casserole dishes.

Makes 1½ cups.

# Vegetables
## and
# Vegetable Dishes

## Chapter VI

WHEN IT CAME TO HAVING A BIG ENOUGH GARDEN, GRANDFATHER always had plenty of land. "Them that works hard, eats hearty," he used to say. If the vegetable garden near the house became too hemmed in by farm buildings that were enlarged as the needs of his growing family increased, he had a solution. It was easy enough to sacrifice an acre strip of ground from one of the fields nearest the house. When he had fenced in this land, he had a "vegetable patch."

Long rows of potatoes, corn, and green beans were planted in this so-called patch. There were also rows of pole butter beans. At each hill a tall pole was planted for the vines to trail on. Four of these poles were tied together near the top in wigwam fashion. There were also pumpkin vines, which wrapped themselves around the stalks of corn and produced big orange pumpkins in autumn. And there was always a cucumber bed to help meet the need for "the seven sours." When the soil was sandy enough, there were also beds of muskmelons and watermelons.

Onions, radishes, lettuce, peas and cabbage were planted in the garden, where it was handy for Grandmother to gather them in preparation for a meal. There were also tomatoes and parsnips and a bed of greens, mustard or turnip tops being the favorites.

The growing children of the family usually were assigned the task of keeping the patch clean. Nancy and Rebecca never minded this when it meant being relieved of washing the supper dishes in the cool of the day. But oh, how they hated that patch on a hot afternoon in mid-July! As they went down those long rows pulling weeds, or picking off potato bugs, one could have heard them frequently bemoaning the fact that they were farmer's daughters.

Grandmother had her own way of cooking vegetables. She scalded her cabbage and greens by pouring boiling water over them and allowing them to stand in it several minutes. Thus she removed some of the strong flavor and "got rid of impurities." The slightly colored water was then discarded and the vegetables were cooked from nine o'clock until noon! If beans were on the menu, the "speck," or salt pork, was put on to boil first thing after breakfast and the beans added shortly afterwards.

We know very little about Grandmother's special vegetable dishes, as she, like homemakers today, seldom cooked vegetables by a recipe. During those winters before much canning was done, the principal stand-bys were potatoes, dried vegetables and fermented foods like kraut. Among the dried foods, corn and green beans, known as "hay beans" to Grandmother, were most popular. After a preliminary cooking, they were spread on a cloth and dried in the sun on the porch roof. It was not unusual for Grandmother to have a hundred-pound sugar bag filled with dried hay beans, shelled beans or corn.

## Baked Acorn Squash

3 acorn squash
6 tablespoons honey or syrup
1 teaspoon salt

1 pound pork sausage
1 teaspoon sage

Wash each squash and cut in half.

Remove seeds and strings.

Put a tablespoon of honey or syrup in each half and sprinkle with salt and powdered sage.

Fill the cavity with pork sausage and top with bread crumbs.

Place halves in baking pan and add about 1 inch of water.

Cover and bake at 400° for 40 minutes.

Remove cover and allow to brown.

Serves 6.

MRS. SAMUEL NAFZIGER, *Kalona, Iowa*

## Baked Asparagus

| | |
|---|---|
| 1 No. 2 can asparagus tips or 15 to 20 tips of fresh asparagus | 5 hard-cooked eggs |
| 4 tablespoons butter | 1½ cups rich milk |
| 4 tablespoons flour | 1 teaspoon salt |
| 2 cups buttered bread crumbs | ⅛ teaspoon pepper |

Brown the bread crumbs in 2 tablespoons of butter.

Place half of the crumbs in the bottom of a baking dish.

Add cooked asparagus and chopped eggs in alternate layers.

Add seasoning.

Cover with remainder of crumbs.

Make a white sauce of 2 tablespoons butter, flour and milk.

Pour sauce over contents of the casserole and bake at 350° for 45 minutes. Grated cheese may be used instead of eggs.

Serves 6.

MRS. RALPH HEATWOLE, *Dayton, Va.*

## Green Beans with Bacon

| | |
|---|---|
| 1 quart green beans | 1 teaspoon salt |
| 4 slices bacon | 1½ cups hot water |

Wash the beans, string and snap in 1 inch lengths.

Dice bacon or salt pork and fry in the bottom of a saucepan or Dutch oven.

Add the beans and the water.

Cook until almost tender and add salt.

Serves 4 to 6.

CATHERINE J. MILLER, *Grantsville, Md.*

## Green Beans with Cream Sauce

### Old

| | |
|---|---|
| 1½ quarts green beans | 2 cups water |
| 3 tablespoons butter or meat drippings | 1½ teaspoons salt |
| 2 tablespoons flour | 1 cup sweet cream |

Wash the beans, string and snap in 1 inch lengths.

Melt butter in a saucepan and add flour.

When flour is slightly browned, add beans and water.

Stir occasionally during cooking.

Cook until almost tender and add salt.

Just before serving, add the cream.

There should be very little water on the beans at the end of the cooking
period.

Serves 6.

MRS. H. D. H. SHOWALTER, *Broadway, Va.*

## Baked Green Beans

| | |
|---|---|
| I quart cooked green beans | I teaspoon salt |
| One 10½ oz. can mushroom soup | ½ cup buttered bread crumbs |
| ½ cup water or milk | |

Place cooked beans in a baking dish.

Dilute soup with milk or water and pour over the beans. Season.

Cover with buttered bread crumbs.

Bake at 375° for 30 minutes.

Serves 6 to 8.

MRS. EDWARD GRABER, *Rittman, Ohio*

## Creole Green Beans

| | |
|---|---|
| I quart cooked green beans | 4 tablespoons butter |
| ¼ cup diced onion | ⅛ teaspoon pepper |
| ¼ cup diced green pepper | I teaspoon flour |
| I teaspoon salt | I cup canned tomatoes |

Sauté the onions, peppers and cooked green beans in the butter until
slightly brown.

Mix the flour, salt and pepper with the tomatoes.

Add tomato mixture to the beans and cook slowly together for 6 to 8
minutes.

Serves 5.

MRS. ALLEN BITIKOFER, *Canton, Kan.*

## Schnitzel Beans

| | |
|---|---|
| 4 slices of bacon or | 2 cups tomatoes |
| ¼ pound cubed ham | I teaspoon salt |
| 3 medium-sized onions, sliced | ¼ teaspoon pepper |
| I quart string beans | 1/3 cup boiling water |

Dice bacon or ham and fry until crisp.

Add sliced onions and fry until a light brown.

Then add string beans that have been cut into small pieces and brown
slightly.

Add tomatoes, seasoning and boiling water.
Cover and cook until beans are tender.
Serves 6.

MRS. HARRY GERBER, *Sugar Creek, Ohio*

## Sour String Beans

| | |
|---|---|
| 2 quarts cooked string beans | ¾ cup brown sugar |
| ¾ cup vinegar | 1 teaspoon salt |
| ¾ cup water | ¼ teaspoon pepper |

Cut the cooked beans in 1 inch lengths.
Make a syrup of the vinegar, water, sugar and salt.
Pour over the beans and bring to a boil. Serve.
This amount makes 2 quarts if canned.

MRS. HERBERT A. DERSTINE, *Souderton, Pa.*

## Baked Beans (I)

| | |
|---|---|
| 2 cups navy beans | 2 teaspoons salt |
| ¼ pound bacon or salt pork | 1½ cups tomato juice |
| 2 tablespoons molasses | 1 teaspoon dry mustard |

Soak beans overnight in cold water.
Drain in the morning and add 2 quarts fresh water.
Cook slowly until the skins burst.
Fry bacon or salt pork until crisp.
Add meat and drippings to beans.
Add other ingredients and place in a covered casserole.
Bake at 325° for 3 hours.
Keep beans covered with liquid while they cook.
Serves 6.

MRS. IDA MILLER, *Rittman, Ohio;* MRS. MARTIN S. GOOD, *Manheim, Pa.*

## Baked Beans (II)

| | |
|---|---|
| 4 cups navy beans | 2 teaspoons mustard |
| 3 teaspoons salt | ¼ teaspoon ginger |
| 1 onion, minced | ½ cup catsup |
| ½ cup molasses | ½ pound salt pork |

Soak beans overnight in cold water.
Drain and add 2½ quarts fresh water and minced onion.
Cook slowly until the skins burst.
Drain and save liquid.
Mix molasses, seasoning and catsup.
Add 2 cups of liquid from the beans.

Place a piece of pork in the bottom of the bean jar or baking dish.
Add the beans and place the remaining pork on top.
Pour molasses mixture over beans.
Add enough water to cover.
Bake with cover on for 5 hours at 300°.
Remove cover the last 30 minutes.
Add water as necessary during cooking process.
Serves 10.

MRS. SAM TROYER, *Harper, Kan.*

## Baked Beans (III)

2 cups navy beans
1 onion
¼ pound bacon
2 tablespoons butter

2 tablespoons cooking oil
2 tablespoons honey
2 apples, sliced in rings
1 teaspoon salt

Soak dried beans in water overnight. Drain.
Place whole onion, bacon slabs and butter in the bottom of a greased
    bean pot or baking dish.
Mix the oil and honey together and stir into the beans.
Pour beans into the pan and lay sliced apples over the top to keep them
    moist while baking.
Cover and bake at 300° for approximately 6 hours.
Do not stir. Add more liquid if necessary.
Serves 6.

MRS. A. E. REESOR, *Markham, Ont., Can.*

## Baked Limas

2 cups dried Lima beans
4 slices bacon or
    2 inch cube of salt pork
1 small onion
1 green pepper

1 cup canned tomatoes
2 teaspoons salt
1 teaspoon mustard
2 tablespoons brown sugar

Wash beans and soak overnight in cold water.
In the morning drain and add 2 quarts fresh water.
Cook until almost tender.
Pour beans in a buttered casserole.
Add minced pepper, onion, tomato and seasoning and mix together.
Place bacon or salt pork on top and bake with cover on casserole.
Add more liquid as necessary.
Bake 2 hours at 325°; leave uncovered the last 20 minutes.
Serves 6.

LOIS MININGER, *Hatfield, Pa.*; MRS. HETTIE GEHMAN, *Adamstown, Pa.*

## Creamed Limas

| | |
|---|---|
| 1 quart fresh Lima beans | 2 tablespoons butter |
| 2 teaspoons salt | 1/8 teaspoon pepper |
| 1½ teaspoons sugar | 1 cup whole milk |
| 1½ teaspoons flour | ¼ cup cream |

Cover beans with water and cook until tender and almost dry.

Add seasoning and milk.

When milk has come to a boil, add a paste made with the flour and cream.

Cook until thickened (2 minutes).

Serves 5.

MRS. MAUD DRIVER, *Waynesboro, Va.*

## Savory Limas

| | |
|---|---|
| ½ cup diced bacon | 3 cups fresh Lima beans |
| 2 tablespoons fat | 2 cups water |
| 1½ tablespoons flour | ½ cup top or evaporated milk |
| 1¼ teaspoons salt | ¼ teaspoon pepper |

Fry the bacon until crisp.

Blend flour in 2 tablespoons bacon fat.

Add salt and pepper and slowly stir in the water.

Add the fresh Lima beans and cook until tender.

Add milk and serve.

These may be cooked in a pressure saucepan.

Serves 5-6.

MRS. JACOB STOLTZFUS, *Belleville, Pa.*

## Kidney Bean Casserole

| | |
|---|---|
| 4 cups canned kidney beans | 2 tablespoons vinegar |
| 1 medium-sized onion, chopped | 3 tablespoons brown sugar |
| 2 teaspoons prepared mustard | 1 teaspoon salt |
| ½ cup catsup | 4 strips bacon |

Combine catsup, vinegar, mustard, salt and sugar.

Add to beans and minced onion.

Place in a baking dish and lay strips of bacon on top.

Bake at 375° for 45 minutes.

Serves 6 to 8.

MARGARET DERSTINE, *Souderton, Pa.*

## Soy Bean Casserole

| | |
|---|---|
| 2 cups dried soy beans | 2 cups diced celery |
| 2 quarts water | 2 tablespoons minced onion |

¼ cup diced salt pork
2 teaspoons salt
⅛ teaspoon pepper

2 tablespoons green pepper
6 tablespoons flour
2 cups milk

Soak beans overnight in sufficient water to cover.

Drain off water in the morning and add 2 quarts cold water.

Cook slowly until beans are soft.

Fry bacon cubes until light brown and add diced celery, onion and green pepper.

When vegetables are tender add flour, salt and pepper.

Gradually add the milk and stir until thickened.

Remove from heat and add soy beans.

Pour into a casserole and top with soft bread crumbs.

Bake at 350° for 35 minutes.

Serves 6.

STELLA HUBER STAUFFER, *Tofield, Alta., Can.*

## Bean Loaf

3 cups cooked navy, Lima or
   pinto beans
½ cup diced bacon or cheese
1 egg
1 teaspoon salt

⅛ teaspoon pepper
1 tablespoon minced parsley
2 tablespoons minced pepper
¼ cup milk

Mash the cooked beans through a coarse strainer.

Add the other ingredients and mix well.

Shape into a loaf and bake in a greased loaf pan.

Make a sauce by combining and cooking together the following:

1 tablespoon butter
2 tablespoons flour
3 tablespoons chopped onion

1 cup milk
1 cup cooked tomatoes

Pour sauce over the loaf while it is baking.

Bake at 350° for 40 minutes.

MRS. WILLIAM ROPP, *Detroit, Mich.;* MRS. PEARL AESCHLIMAN, *Fayette, Ohio*

## Mustard Beans

4 quarts beans
1 cup brown sugar
1 cup vinegar

1 cup water
3 tablespoons prepared mustard
3 teaspoons salt

Cook green or yellow wax beans in salt water until tender.

Water should be absorbed until cooking period is over.

Add sugar, mustard, vinegar and water. Bring to a boil.

These may be canned or served cold as a relish or pickle.

MRS. CALVIN STOVER, *Blooming Glen, Pa.*

## Lima-Corn Fritters

| | |
|---|---|
| 1 cup cooked Lima beans | 1 teaspoon salt |
| 2 cups canned or fresh corn | 1 teaspoon sugar |
| 4 tablespoons flour | 1/8 teaspoon pepper |
| 1 egg | 1/4 cup fat for frying |

Mash cooked beans through a coarse strainer.

Add corn, egg, flour and seasoning.

Drop mixture into hot fat and brown on each side.

Makes 8-10 fritters.

MRS. H. N. TROYER, *Hartville, Ohio*

## Grandmother's Dried Hay Beans

| | |
|---|---|
| 3 cups dried green string beans | 1 teaspoon salt |
| 1/4 pound bacon or salt pork | Water to cover |

Soak dried beans in warm water for 1 hour.

Cut bacon or salt pork into small cubes and fry in a Dutch oven or heavy saucepan until slightly browned.

Add beans and partially cover with water.

Cook until tender and most of the water is absorbed.

These beans, a favorite of Grandmother's day, are still enjoyed in many Mennonite families. They are dark in color and have a slight haylike flavor.

## Chili Con Carne

| | |
|---|---|
| 2 to 3 cups cooked kidney beans | 1 1/2 teaspoons chili powder |
| 1 pound ground or cubed beef | 2 cloves of garlic or 1 minced onion |
| 2 tablespoons chopped suet | 1 cup hot water |
| 1 1/2 teaspoons salt | 2 cups tomatoes |
| 1 tablespoon flour | |

Melt the suet and add garlic or onion.

When onion is slightly brown, add the ground or cubed meat.

Add flour, salt and chili powder to meat and blend together.

Then add canned tomatoes and hot water.

Cover and let simmer slowly for 1 hour, adding water if necessary.

Add kidney beans and bring to a boil.

Serves 6.

EDNA B. MILLER, *Nampa, Idaho*

## Harvard Beets

| | |
|---|---|
| 3 cups cooked diced beets | 1/4 cup vinegar |
| 1/2 cup sugar | 1/4 cup water |
| 1 tablespoon cornstarch | 2 tablespoons butter |
| 1 teaspoon salt | |

Mix the sugar, salt and cornstarch.

Add vinegar and water and stir until smooth. Cook for 5 minutes.

Add beets to the hot sauce and let stand for 30 minutes.

Just before serving, bring to a boil and add butter.

Serves 6.

MRS. ALVIN DETWEILER, *Souderton, Pa.;* MRS. LAURENCE SPEIGLE, *Boswell, Pa.*

## Beets with Savory Sauce

| | |
|---|---|
| 12 small beets | 1 cup milk |
| 4 tablespoons butter | 1 tablespoon lemon juice |
| 2 tablespoons flour | 1 teaspoon salt |
| 1 onion, minced | 1/8 teaspoon pepper |

Cook the beets until tender and slip off the skins.

To make the sauce, fry the onion in 2 tablespoons butter.

When slightly brown, add the flour and blend.

Then add the milk, gradually stirring until the sauce has thickened.

Add salt and pepper.

Work lemon juice into remaining butter and add to sauce.

Pour sauce over beets just before serving.

Serves 4.

MRS. A. E. REESOR, *Markham, Ont., Can.*

## Brussels Sprouts

| | |
|---|---|
| 1 quart Brussels sprouts | 2 cups medium white sauce |
| 1 teaspoon salt | (page 91) |
| 1/2 cup dry bread or cracker crumbs | 1/2 cup grated cheese |

Soak Brussels sprouts in salt water for 20 minutes. Drain.

Add water to partially cover. Cook until tender and then drain.

Place in a buttered baking dish and pour white sauce over the top.

Add crumbs.

Bake at 375° for 20 to 25 minutes. Add grated cheese during last 5 minutes of cooking period.

Serves 6.

MRS. A. E. REESOR, *Markham, Ont., Can.*

## Baked Cabbage

| | |
|---|---|
| 1 medium-sized head of cabbage | 1 1/2 cups hot milk |
| 1 teaspoon salt | 1 tablespoon flour |
| 1/8 teaspoon pepper | 2 tablespoons butter |
| 1/2 cup grated cheese | |

Cut cabbage in wedges ¾ inch thick.

Cook in salt water for 10 minutes.

Drain and place cabbage in a greased casserole.
Sprinkle with flour, salt, and pepper. Dot with butter.
Add hot milk and top with grated cheese.
Bake at 350° for 35 minutes.
Serves 6.

MRS. ELLA ROHRER, *Wadsworth, Ohio*

## Creamed Cabbage and Dried Beef

| | |
|---|---|
| ½ large head of cabbage | 1½ cups medium white sauce |
| ⅛ pound dried beef | (page 91) |
| | ½ cup buttered crumbs |

Cook coarsely chopped cabbage in salt water until tender. Drain.
Soak chopped dried beef in ½ cup warm water for 10 minutes.
Place cabbage and dried beef in alternate layers in a greased casserole.
Pour white sauce over mixture and top with buttered crumbs.
Bake at 350° for 25 minutes.
Serves 4.

MRS. ANDREW LEHMAN, *Marion, Pa.*

## Cabbage Bundles or Stuffed Cabbage Leaves
### *Golubtzi*

| | |
|---|---|
| 1 large head of cabbage | 2 tablespoons fat |
| ½ pound hamburger or chopped round steak | 1 teaspoon salt |
| | ¼ teaspoon pepper |
| 1 cup rice, cooked | One 10½ oz. can tomato soup |
| 1 onion, minced | ½ cup sour cream |

Remove outer leaves from the cabbage head and cook in salt water for about 5 minutes, or until leaves are flexible.
Drain and cool.
Add minced onion to 2 tablespoons of fat and brown slightly.
Add ground meat, cooked rice, and seasoning.
Drop a tablespoon of the mixture on the stem end of each cabbage leaf.
Start rolling from the rib end and tie securely with thread or fasten with toothpicks.
Place bundles in a baking pan and pour undiluted tomato soup over them.
Bake at 350° for 45 minutes or simmer slowly on top of the stove until tender.
Add sour cream 5 minutes before serving.
Serves 6.

MRS. HERMAN R. SCHMIDT, *Newton, Kan.;* MRS. N. A. LIND, SR., *Lebanon, Ore.*

## Stuffed Cabbage Head

| | |
|---|---|
| 1 large head of cabbage | 1 onion, minced |
| 1 pound ground beef | 3 strips of bacon |
| 1/2 cup soft bread crumbs | 1/2 cup milk |
| 1 egg, beaten | 1 teaspoon salt |
| 1 green pepper, minced | 1/4 teaspoon pepper |

Scoop out the center of a cabbage head enough to hold the stuffing.
Chop or grind beef and add diced bacon.
Add onion, green pepper and seasoning.
Beat egg, add the milk, melted butter and crumbs.
Mix all the ingredients together and stuff into the center of the cabbage
     head.
Tie in a cloth and steam or cook slowly for 1 to 1¼ hours.
Serves 6.

ELSIE MARTIN, *Kitchener, Ont., Can.*


## Fried Cabbage

| | |
|---|---|
| 6 cups finely shredded cabbage | 1/4 teaspoon dry mustard |
| 5 tablespoons fat | 1/2 teaspoon paprika |
| 1/2 teaspoon salt | 1/2 cup cream |
| 1 1/2 tablespoons sugar | 2 to 3 tablespoons vinegar |

Melt fat in a heavy saucepan and add cabbage.
Fry slowly for 15 minutes.
Stir every few minutes.
Mix other ingredients and add to the cabbage.
Heat to the boiling point and serve.
Serves 6.

MRS. AMOS BRENNEMAN, *Harrisonburg, Va.*


## Hot Slaw (I)

| | |
|---|---|
| 1 quart shredded cabbage | 1/2 cup water |
| 1 teaspoon salt | 2 tablespoons butter |
| 2 tablespoons sugar | 1/2 teaspoon mustard |
| 2 tablespoons vinegar | 1/2 cup sour cream |

Melt butter in a saucepan and add shredded cabbage.
Stir until butter is well mixed through the cabbage.
Add water and salt and cover tightly.
Cook for 10 minutes and then add the sugar, vinegar and mustard.
Simmer another minute and then add the sour cream.
Serves 4.

ANNA MILLER, *Denbigh, Va.*

## Hot Slaw (II)

Follow the preceding recipe, but omit the sour cream and add:

| | |
|---|---|
| 1 egg | 2 tablespoons of flour |
| 1½ cups milk | |

After cabbage has cooked 10 minutes it should be dry.
Add 1 cup of milk and the sugar and bring to the boiling point.
Beat egg, add flour and remaining ½ cup milk.
Add to cabbage mixture and stir until thickened.
Just before serving add vinegar and mustard.
Serves 4.

MRS. A. C. LOUX, *Souderton, Pa.*

## Dutch Cabbage

| | |
|---|---|
| 1 medium-sized head of cabbage | 1 teaspoon salt |
| 6 slices bacon | ¼ teaspoon pepper |
| 2 tablespoons flour | 6 medium-sized potatoes |
| 3 tablespoons fat | 2 cups cabbage broth or tomato juice |

Shred cabbage coarsely and cook in salt water until tender.
Cut bacon in small pieces and fry until crisp.
Blend flour with 3 tablespoons of bacon drippings and brown.
Add seasoning and liquid or tomato juice to make a gravy.
Add sauce to cabbage and place in a greased baking dish.
Cook potatoes in salt water until soft and then mash them.
Put mashed potatoes on top of the cabbage.
Bake at 375° for 25 minutes.
Serves 6.

MRS. AMIL ALLEN, *Birch Tree, Mo.;* MRS. S. HOWARD ATHINSON, *Perkasie, Pa.*

## Recipe for Making Sauerkraut (I)

Shred cabbage about ⅛ inch wide. Use a knife or cutter.
Add salt enough to taste good.
Mix salt through cabbage with your hands until it forms its own juice.
Pack tightly in quart jars.
Set jars in a large container.
Partly seal to let juice expand in fermenting.
After 3 days, seal tightly. Process in hot-water bath for 20 minutes.

MRS. LEWIS MARTIN, *Harrisonburg, Va.*

## Recipe for Making Sauerkraut (II)

Shred cabbage ⅛ inch wide.

Pack shredded cabbage in glass jars.

Do not pack tightly.

Add 1 teaspoon salt to each quart jar.

Fill jar with boiling water.

Seal tightly. Process in hot-water bath for 20 minutes.

Place jars in a pan while fermenting, as some of the juice will run out.

Mrs. Lewis Martin, *Harrisonburg, Va.*

## Sauerkraut with Spareribs

| | |
|---|---|
| I quart sauerkraut | 1½ pounds spareribs |

Cook spareribs until almost tender in sufficient water to cover (about 2 hours).

Add kraut and continue to cook for 40 minutes.

Serves 6.

Mrs. Lewis Martin, *Harrisonburg, Va.*

## Sauerkraut with Dumplings

| | |
|---|---|
| I quart sauerkraut | For dumplings: |
| ¼ pound salt pork | 1½ cups flour |
| 2 teaspoons sugar (optional) | ½ teaspoon salt |
| I cup soft bread crumbs, browned, or dumplings | 3 teaspoons baking powder |
| | I egg, beaten |
| | 5 tablespoons milk |
| | I tablespoon shortening |

Brown salt pork slightly, add water to cover and cook until almost soft.

Drain sauerkraut and rinse in cold water.

Add kraut and continue to cook for 40 minutes.

Add sugar.

Just before serving, add bread crumbs browned in butter or dumplings made by dropping dough from a spoon onto hot kraut.

Cook dumplings 12 minutes; keep pan tightly closed.

Serves 6.

Mrs. H. D. H. Showalter, *Broadway, Va.*

## Creamed Carrots

| | |
|---|---|
| 3 cups diced cooked carrots | I teaspoon salt |
| I small onion, minced | 1½ cups thin white sauce (page 91) |
| ½ cup chopped celery | |

Cook carrots and cut in cubes.

Cook diced celery and onion together; when soft, add to carrots.

Add white sauce and bring to a boil.
Serves 6.

MRS. FLORENCE C. FRIESEN, *Greensburg, Kan.*

## Delicious Creamed Carrots

| | |
|---|---|
| 4 cups sliced carrots | 1/8 teaspoon pepper |
| 3 tablespoons butter | 1/2 cup cream |
| 1/2 teaspoon salt | |

Cook carrots until tender and almost dry.
Brown the butter and add to carrots and simmer slowly for several minutes. Season.
Remove carrots from the heat and add the cream.
Serve immediately.
Serves 6.

MRS. J. D. RAMER, *Elida, Ohio*

## Carrot Loaf

| | |
|---|---|
| 3 cups cooked mashed carrots | 1 1/2 cups bread crumbs |
| 1 onion, minced | 1 cup milk |
| 1/2 cup minced celery | 2 eggs |
| 1 teaspoon salt | 2 tablespoons butter |

Fry onion in butter and add to mashed carrots.
Beat eggs, add milk and bread crumbs.
Mix together and add celery and seasoning.
Shape in a loaf and place in a greased loaf pan.
Bake at 350° for 40 minutes.
Serves 6.

MRS. NORMAN LANDIS, *Lansdale, Pa.*; LOUIDA STAUFFER, *Tofield, Alta., Can.*

## Carrots and Dumplings

| | |
|---|---|
| 3 cups carrots | Dumplings: |
| 1 teaspoon salt | 1 cup flour |
| Water | 2 teaspoons baking powder |
| | 1 teaspoon shortening |
| | 1/2 teaspoon salt |
| | 1/4 cup water or milk |

Cut carrots crosswise in 1 inch pieces.
Cook in salt water until tender.
To make dumplings, sift flour, salt and baking powder together.
Rub in shortening lightly with fingers.
Add water or milk to make a dough stiff enough to drop from a spoon.
Drop onto boiling carrots and cover tightly.

Cook for 10 to 12 minutes.
Do not remove cover until the end of the cooking period.
When serving, pour browned butter over the carrots and dumplings.
Serves 6.

MRS. ANNIE WEBER, Adamstown, Pa.

## Scalloped Cauliflower

| | |
|---|---|
| 1 large head of cauliflower | 1/2 teaspoon salt |
| 3 hard-cooked eggs | 1/4 teaspoon pepper |
| 2 cups medium white sauce | 1 cup buttered bread crumbs |
| (page 91) | 1/4 cup grated cheese |

Break the head of cauliflower into flowerets and cook in salt water until
tender. Drain.
Place alternate layers of cauliflower, diced egg and white sauce in a
greased casserole.
Put a layer of buttered crumbs and grated cheese over the top.
Bake at 375° for 25 minutes.
The cheese may be melted in the white sauce and only crumbs used on
the top if desired.
Serves 6.

MRS. FANNIE GABLE, York, Pa.

## Cooked Celery with Sweet-Sour Dressing

| | |
|---|---|
| 2 cups diced celery | 2 tablespoons flour |
| 1 teaspoon salt | 1 egg |
| 2 tablespoons sugar | 1 cup water |
| 1 1/2-2 tablespoons vinegar | 1/4 cup sour cream |

Cut celery in 1 inch pieces; the outside stems may be used.
Cook celery in salt water until tender and almost dry.
Make a dressing with the egg, flour, sugar, vinegar and water.
Bring dressing to a boil; when it thickens add the sour cream.
Pour dressing over the celery and serve at once.
Serves 5.

MRS. C. J. KURTZ, Elverson, Pa.

## Creamed Celery on Toast

| | |
|---|---|
| 2 cups diced celery | 1/2 cup top milk or thin white sauce |
| 1 teaspoon salt | (page 91) |
| 3 tablespoons butter | 6 slices toast |

Cut celery in 1/2 inch pieces and cook in salt water until tender.
By the end of the cooking period, the celery should be almost dry.
Add top milk or white sauce and bring to the boiling point.

Place on pieces of toast and garnish with browned butter.
Serve at once.
Serves 6.

ANNA HERSH, *Elizabethtown, Pa.*

## Baked Corn

2 cups corn, fresh, frozen, or canned
2 tablespoons fat
1½ tablespoons flour
1 cup milk
1 tablespoon sugar

1 teaspoon salt
⅛ teaspoon pepper
2 eggs
½ cup buttered crumbs

Melt the fat and add the flour.
Add milk gradually and bring to the boiling point, stirring constantly.
Add corn, sugar, salt and pepper and heat thoroughly.
Remove from heat and add beaten eggs.
Pour in a greased baking dish and sprinkle with buttered crumbs. Bake
at 350° for 35 minutes or until corn is firm.
Serves 4.

MRS. WILLIAM J. HUNSBERGER, *Phoenixville, Pa.*
MRS. EARL GROVE, *Dale Enterprise, Va.*

## Baked Corn and Tomatoes

4 cups cooked corn
6 medium-sized tomatoes, sliced
1 cup cooked Lima beans
1 teaspoon salt

⅛ teaspoon pepper
1 cup ground sausage, slightly
browned
1 cup cracker crumbs

Arrange ingredients in alternate layers in a greased baking dish. Season.
Top with crumbs and bake at 350° for 45 minutes.
Serves 6.

MRS. ELLA ROHRER, *Wadsworth, Ohio*

## Scalloped Corn

2 cups cooked or canned corn
1 cup milk
2/3 cup cracker or bread crumbs
3 tablespoons melted butter
½ teaspoon salt

⅛ teaspoon pepper
1 tablespoon sugar
2 eggs
1 teaspoon minced onion

Beat the eggs and add milk and crumbs.
Add the corn, onion, seasoning and melted butter.
Mix together well and pour in a greased casserole.
Bake at 350° for 40 minutes.
Serves 6.

MRS. WALTER WEAVER, *Christiana, Pa.*; MRS. HENRY HUBER, *Ronks, Pa.*

## Baconized Corn

4 cups fresh or canned corn
1 teaspoon salt
1/4 teaspoon pepper

1 1/2 teaspoons sugar
1 cup finely diced bacon

Place corn in a greased baking dish.
Season with salt, sugar and pepper.
Cover entire top of dish with finely diced bacon.
Bake at 350° for 35 minutes or until bacon is crisp.
Serves 6.

MRS. H. LANDIS, *Lancaster, Pa.*

## Fried Corn (I)

2 cups fresh corn pulp
2 tablespoons flour
3 eggs

3 tablespoons butter
1 teaspoon salt
1 cup rich milk

Split kernels and scrape from the cob.
Heat butter and add corn. Cook at moderate heat.
Keep turning corn with a spatula to prevent burning.
Combine beaten eggs, flour and milk. When corn is light brown, add
egg and milk mixture.
Let simmer slowly until thick.
Serves 6.

MRS. GLENN EBERSOLE, *Sterling, Ill.*

## Fried Corn (II)

3 cups fresh corn
2 green peppers, minced
2 eggs, beaten

1 teaspoon salt
3 tablespoons butter

Melt fat and add green pepper and corn.
Fry until a golden brown, stirring frequently.
Add salt and pepper.
When done, add 2 eggs and scramble them over the corn.
For variety, 1 cup of diced cooked potatoes or 1 cup of cream may be
added instead of the eggs.
Serves 6.

MRS. H. D. H. SHOWALTER, *Broadway, Va.*

## Corn Fritters

2 cups fresh corn, grated
2 eggs
1/4 cup flour
1 teaspoon salt

1/8 teaspoon pepper
1 teaspoon baking powder
2 tablespoons cream
4 tablespoons fat

Add beaten eggs, flour, baking powder, salt and pepper to the grated corn. Mix thoroughly.

Add the cream.

Melt the fat in a frying pan and drop corn mixture by spoonfuls into the hot fat.

Brown on both sides.

Makes 16-18 fritters.

MRS. ELIAS LINEDEMUTH, *Mt. Joy, Pa.;* MRS. DANIEL WITMER, *Markham, Ont., Can.*

## Corn Pudding

| | |
|---|---|
| 2 cups grated corn (fresh preferred) | 1 tablespoon sugar |
| 2 eggs | 2 tablespoons butter |
| 1 teaspoon salt | 1 tablespoon flour |
| 1/8 teaspoon pepper | 1 cup milk |

Grate corn and add salt, sugar, pepper, flour and melted butter.

Add beaten eggs and milk.

Pour into a greased baking dish and bake at 350° for 35 minutes.

Serves 6.

RUTH YOTHERS, *Souderton, Pa.;* MRS. LESTER CRIDER, *Chambersburg, Pa.*

## Corn Soufflé

| | |
|---|---|
| 1 1/2 tablespoons butter | 1 1/2 cups grated corn |
| 2 tablespoons flour | 1/2 teaspoon salt |
| 1 cup milk | 1/8 teaspoon pepper |
| | 2 eggs, separated |

Melt butter and add flour.

Add milk gradually and cook until thickened.

Add grated corn, beaten egg yolks and seasoning.

Fold in stiffly beaten egg whites.

Pour into a buttered baking dish.

Bake at 350° for 35 minutes.

Serves 4.

MRS. CHESTER HORST, *Orville, Ohio*

## Maryland Corn Pie

| | |
|---|---|
| 6 strips bacon | 3 cups fresh uncooked corn |
| 1 1/2 cups fine bread crumbs | 1 teaspoon salt |
| 1 green pepper, minced | 1/4 teaspoon pepper |
| 2 cups fresh tomatoes | 1 teaspoon sugar |
| 2 tablespoons butter | |

Place 3 strips of slightly cooked bacon in the bottom of a baking dish.

Place the other strips around the sides.

Add a layer of bread crumbs, and then a layer of peeled, sliced tomatoes and green pepper.

Sprinkle with salt, pepper and sugar.

Over this place a layer of corn and continue with alternate layers until the dish is filled.

Cover with bread crumbs and dot with butter.

Bake at 375° for 35 minutes.

Serves 6.

Mrs. M. D. Burkholder, *Harrisonburg, Va.*

## Dried Corn

| | |
|---|---|
| 2 cups dried corn | 2 teaspoons sugar |
| Water to partially cover | 1/2 cup cream |
| 1 teaspoon salt | |

Soak dried corn for 1 hour in warm water.

Cook corn until it is tender and most of the water is absorbed.

Add salt, sugar and cream and bring to a boil.

Serves 6 to 8.

Another Favorite of Grandmother's

## Baked Eggplant with Mushrooms

| | |
|---|---|
| 2 large eggplants | 1/2 teaspoon salt |
| 1 cup medium white sauce (page 91) | 1/2 cup bread crumbs |
| 1 small can mushrooms | 1/2 cup grated cheese |

Cook whole eggplant in salt water for about 12 minutes.

Cut in half lengthwise and scoop out inside. Do not break skin.

Cut the pulp into fine pieces.

Mix white sauce and chopped mushrooms with pulp.

Fill eggplant with mixture and top with crumbs and grated cheese.

Bake at 375° for 25 minutes.

Serves 8.

Grace E. Zook, *Belleville, Pa.*

## Baked Eggplant with Ham

| | |
|---|---|
| 1 large eggplant | 1/8 teaspoon pepper |
| 1/4 cup chopped onion | 1 egg, beaten |
| 2 tablespoons melted butter | 1/4 cup grated cheese |
| 1 cup cooked diced ham | 1/2 cup buttered bread crumbs |
| 1/2 teaspoon salt | |

Cook eggplant in salt water for 10-12 minutes.

Cut in half lengthwise and carefully scoop out center.

Cut the pulp into fine pieces.

Mix onion, ham, egg and seasoning with pulp of eggplant.

Refill hollowed-out center and top with buttered crumbs and grated cheese.

Bake at 375° for 20-25 minutes.

Serves 4.

MRS. HENRY HUBER, *Ronks, Pa.*

## Fried Eggplant

2 medium-sized eggplants
2 eggs
1 teaspoon salt

1 cup flour or cracker crumbs
½ cup fat

Pare eggplant and slice in rings ¼ inch thick.

Soak in salt water for 30 minutes.

Drain eggplant and dip into beaten egg.

Dredge with flour or roll in cracker crumbs.

Fry in hot fat until a golden brown on both sides.

Serve with tomato sauce (page 134).

Serves 6 to 8.

MRS. HUBERT PELLMAN, *Harrisonburg, Va.*

## Scalloped Eggplant

1 large eggplant
1 cup tomatoes
1 tablespoon minced green pepper
1 cup soft bread crumbs

½ teaspoon salt
2 tablespoons butter
3 strips bacon (optional)

Pare eggplant and cut into ¼ inch cubes.

Cook in salt water until tender and almost dry.

Add tomatoes, green pepper and seasoning.

Pour into a greased baking dish and top with buttered crumbs.

Strips of bacon may be placed over top.

Bake at 375° for 20 minutes.

Serves 5.

MRS. IRA S. MILLER, *Hanover, Pa.*

## Eggplant Soufflé

1 large eggplant
2 tablespoons butter
2 tablespoons flour
1 cup milk
1 cup grated cheese
¾ cup soft bread crumbs

2 teaspoons grated onion
1 teaspoon catsup
1 teaspoon salt
⅛ teaspoon pepper
2 eggs, separated

Pare eggplant and cut in ½ inch pieces.

Cook in salt water until tender and almost dry.

Make a white sauce with fat, flour and milk. (Page 90.)

When thickened, add mashed eggplant, seasonings, cheese, crumbs and beaten egg yolks.

Fold in stiffly beaten whites.

Pour into greased baking dish and bake at 350° for 40 minutes.

Serves 6.

MRS. VELMA MILLER, *Canton, Ohio;* MRS. MARLIN LAUVER, *Scottdale, Pa.*

## Creamed Mushrooms

| | |
|---|---|
| 2 pounds mushrooms | ⅛ teaspoon pepper |
| ½ cup butter | ½ cup flour |
| ½ cup water | 3 cups milk |
| ½ teaspoon salt | |

To clean mushrooms, pull caps from stems.

If young and tender, do not pare caps, brush them well.

Put the butter and water in a heavy saucepan or skillet.

Add cleaned mushroom caps and stems, salt and pepper.

Cover and steam slowly for 20 minutes or until dry.

Allow to brown slightly and then add flour.

Brown the flour, watching it carefully.

Add milk gradually and stir until thickened.

Serves 8.

MRS. WILLIS K. LEDERACH, *Lederach, Pa.*

## New Peas and Potatoes

| | |
|---|---|
| 3 cups fresh peas | 1½ cups top milk |
| 12 small new potatoes | 1½ teaspoons flour |
| 1½ teaspoons salt | 2 tablespoons butter |

Cook peas and potatoes separately in salt water until soft and almost dry.

Add peas to potatoes and pour the milk over them.

When milk is at the boiling point, add butter and flour that have been rubbed together.

Cook until slightly thickened and serve.

Serves 6.

This is a good way to stretch the first peas from the garden.

MRS. JAMES BAUMAN, *Oyster Point, Va.*

## Onion Pie

2 cups sliced onions
6 strips bacon

Salt and pepper
Pastry for one crust (page 354)

Line a pie pan with pastry.
Fill with thinly sliced onions.
Season with salt and pepper and add 2 tablespoons water.
Lay strips of bacon over the top.
Bake at 350° for 30 to 35 minutes.

MRS. MATTIE ZIGLER, *Denbigh, Va.*

## Caramel Cream Onions

12 small white onions
12 whole cloves
4 tablespoons brown sugar

4 tablespoons butter or margarine
½ cup cream or evaporated milk
1 teaspoon salt

Peel onions and cook in salt water until tender but not soft.
Place onions in a frying pan and sprinkle with sugar and butter and
cloves.
Cook over low heat, turning onions gently until they are caramelized.
Add cream or milk and cook until slightly thickened.
Serves 4.

PHOEBE KOLB, *Kitchener, Ont., Can.*

## Fried Onions and Apples

4 medium-sized onions, sliced
3 large tart apples, sliced
2 tablespoons butter

1 teaspoon salt
½ cup water

Heat butter in frying pan and add sliced onions.
Cook slowly until almost tender.
Pare and slice apples.
Then add sliced apples, water and salt.
Cover and cook until apples are soft.
Remove cover and fry until water is absorbed, and the apples and
onions are light brown.
Serves 4.

MRS. MELVIN WEAVER, *Ophir, Ky.*

## Parsnip Fritters

3 cups cooked parsnips
3 eggs
1 teaspoon salt
1 tablespoon flour

1 tablespoon sugar
3 tablespoons butter
1 cup milk

Mash cooked parsnips and add beaten eggs, flour, salt, sugar and milk.
Melt butter in a frying pan and drop mixture by spoonfuls into the
  hot fat.
Brown on both sides.
Serves 6.

MRS. A. E. REESOR, *Markham, Ont., Can.*

## Fried Parsnips

5 medium-sized parsnips
I teaspoon salt

2 tablespoons butter

Clean and scrape parsnips.
Cook whole in salt water until tender, but not soft.
Cut in quarters lengthwise and place in a greased baking dish.
Place dots of butter over parsnips and bake at 375° until slightly
  browned.
Serves 4.

MRS. WILLIAM JENNINGS, *Knoxville, Tenn.*

## Baked Stuffed Peppers (I)
### With Ham

8 medium-sized green peppers
I cup chopped ham
I onion, minced
½ cup cooked rice or
  cooked diced potatoes

½ teaspoon salt
⅛ teaspoon pepper
¼ cup buttered crumbs
¾ cup tomatoes
¼ cup grated cheese

Cut tops off peppers, remove seeds and veins.
Parboil in salt water for 5 minutes.
Mix ingredients, except crumbs and cheese, for the filling.
Stuff into pepper and top with buttered crumbs and grated cheese.
Arrange peppers in a greased baking dish.
Bake at 350° for 20 minutes and then turn to 400° for 5 minutes.
Serves 8.

MRS. MAUD DRIVER, *Waynesboro, Va.*; MRS. LIZZIE SNYDER, *Walnut Creek, Ohio*

## Baked Peppers (II)
### With Hamburger or Sausage

4 large green peppers
½ pound sausage or hamburger
I cup canned or fresh corn or
  Lima beans

½ cup crushed soda crackers
½ teaspoon salt
⅛ teaspoon pepper

Cut peppers in half lengthwise; remove seeds and veins.
Parboil for 5 minutes and allow to cool.

Brown meat slightly and mix meat, corn or Lima beans and seasoning.
Fill pepper halves and top with cracker crumbs.
Arrange in a greased baking dish.
Bake at 375° for 25 minutes.
Serves 6 to 8.

Mrs. D. M. Stoltzfus, *Talmadge, Pa.;* Ada E. Garber, *Elizabethtown, Pa.*
Mrs. Noble Blosser, *North Lima, Ohio*

## Potato Filling for Stuffed Peppers

| | |
|---|---|
| 1 cup hot mashed potatoes | ½ teaspoon poultry seasoning |
| 1 tablespoon minced parsley | 1 teaspoon salt |
| 1 egg, well beaten | 2 cups cubed stale bread |
| 2 tablespoons melted butter | ¼ cup diced celery |
| 1 small onion, minced | ⅛ teaspoon pepper |

Mix the mashed potatoes and beaten egg together.
Soak the bread in cold water and squeeze dry.
Add bread to potato mixture. Add other ingredients and mix well.
Stuff filling into green peppers that have been parboiled for 5 minutes.
This fills 6 to 8 peppers, according to the size.
Bake at 375° for 25 minutes.

Mrs. Ford R. Kreider, *Seville, Ohio*

## Potatoes Baked in Cheese Sauce

| | |
|---|---|
| 6 large potatoes, sliced | 1 teaspoon salt |
| 3 tablespoons butter | ¼ teaspoon paprika |
| 4 tablespoons grated cheese | ½ teaspoon catsup |
| 2 tablespoons flour | 1 green pepper, minced |
| 1½ cups milk | |

Melt butter in saucepan or top of double boiler.
Add the flour and stir until smooth.
Then add salt, paprika and catsup.
Pour in milk gradually and stir until thickened. Add grated cheese.
Cut raw or cooked potatoes in thin slices.
Place alternate layers of potatoes and peppers in a casserole.
Cover with sauce and repeat until all is used.
Bake at 350° for 35 minutes.
Serves 6.

Mrs. M. E. Weaver, *Annville, Pa.*

## Baked Potatoes and Tomatoes

| | |
|---|---|
| 4 cups raw, diced potatoes | 1 small onion, minced |
| ¼ cup tomato juice or pulp | 1 teaspoon salt |

½ cup water

¼ cup butter or meat fryings

⅛ teaspoon pepper

1 tablespoon minced parsley

Arrange alternate layers of potatoes, onion and seasoning in a greased casserole.

Mix water with tomato juice and pour over contents.

Bake at 350° for 45 to 50 minutes.

Serves 6.

MRS. ROLLIN HEATWOLE, *Harrisonburg, Va.*

## Creamed Potatoes with Parsley

3 cups raw diced potatoes

1 teaspoon salt

⅛ teaspoon pepper

¾ cup thin cream

2 tablespoons parsley

Cook potatoes in salt water until soft and almost dry.

Add cream, seasoning and chopped parsley and bring to a boil.

Serves 6.

SARA K. BEAN, *Creamery, Pa.*

## Potato Deutscher

7 medium-sized potatoes

6 slices stale bread

2 eggs

1 teaspoon salt

⅛ teaspoon pepper

2 cups milk

1 cup sour cream

Grate raw potatoes on a coarse grater.

Soak bread cubes in 1 cup milk.

Add beaten eggs to soaked bread and then add potatoes.

Add the remainder of the milk and seasoning.

Place in a greased baking dish and pour sour cream over the top.

Bake at 350° for 45 minutes.

Serves 6.

MRS. NOAH EBERSOLE, *Birch Tree, Mo.*

## Old-fashioned Fried Potatoes

5 cups sliced, cooked potatoes

3 tablespoons fat

1½ teaspoons salt

⅛ teaspoon pepper

1 cup cream, sweet or sour

Cook potatoes in jackets and allow to cool; peel and slice very thin.

Melt fat in frying pan; when hot, add potatoes, salt and pepper.

Fry until a golden brown; then add the cream.

Cover and allow to steam until the cream is absorbed.

Serves 6.

AUNT LINA RESSLER, *Scottdale, Pa.*; MRS. ERVIN J. YODER, *Myersdale, Pa.*

## French Fried Potatoes

4 cups raw potato strips          Salt
Fat for deep-fat frying

Pare medium-sized potatoes and cut lengthwise in strips ¼ inch wide.
Soak in ice water for 30 minutes.
Drain and dry between paper towels.
Drop a few at a time in hot fat and fry until nicely browned.
It is best to use a wire basket. Stir potatoes occasionally while they fry.
Drain on brown paper and sprinkle with salt.
Serves 6 to 8.

KATE BEACHY, *Grantsville, Md.*

## Potato Cakes

2 cups leftover mashed potatoes      2 tablespoons cream
1 large egg                            1 tablespoon minced onion, if desired
1 tablespoon flour                4 tablespoons fat

Mix ingredients and shape into flat cakes or drop from a spoon into
     hot fat.
Fry a golden brown on both sides.
Serves 6.

CATHERINE J. MILLER, *Grantsville, Md.*

## Potato Puffs

3 cups mashed potatoes        1 teaspoon salt
1 cup hot milk                  1½ tablespoons butter
2 eggs, separated            ¼ cup grated cheese
1 teaspoon parsley

Add beaten egg yolks to mashed potatoes.
Then add salt, parsley and milk and mix together.
Fold in stiffly beaten egg whites.
Drop by spoonfuls into a flat buttered baking dish, placing cakes an
     inch apart.
Greased muffin tins may also be used.
Sprinkle with grated cheese and bake at 400° for 20 minutes.
Serves 6.

MRS. EARL BUCKWALTER, *Hesston, Kan.*

## Volcano Potatoes

Use preceding recipe, but mold mixture into cones 3 inches high and
     place in a shallow baking dish.

Make a deep indentation in the top of each cone and fill with grated cheese sprinkled with paprika.

Bake at 425° for 12 to 15 minutes.

ANNA M. MILLER, *Denbigh, Va.*

## Mashed Potato Blend

| | |
|---|---|
| 4 cups mashed potatoes | ½ teaspoon salt |
| I cup mashed carrots | I tablespoon buttered parsley |
| I egg | ¼ cup cream |

Mix ingredients thoroughly.

Place in a greased baking dish and garnish with buttered parsley.

Bake at 375° for 25 minutes.

Serves 8.

NORA L. GROSS, *Doylestown, Pa.*

## Potato Balls

| | |
|---|---|
| 3 cups leftover mashed potatoes | ½ teaspoon salt |
| ¼ cup diced celery | ⅛ teaspoon pepper |
| 2 tablespoons butter | I cup fine cracker crumbs |

Melt butter in a saucepan and add minced celery.

Fry celery until soft; then add to mashed potatoes.

Add seasoning and shape into round balls.

Roll in cracker crumbs.

Fry in deep fat until a golden brown.

Makes 18 small balls.

MRS. JACOB M. KURTZ, *Fleetwood, Pa.*

## Potatoes with Ham

| | |
|---|---|
| ½ pound smoked ham | 1½ teaspoons flour |
| 6 large potatoes, sliced | ½ cup thin cream |
| I teaspoon salt | |

Cut ham into small cubes and cook until almost tender.

Then add sliced potatoes and salt.

When potatoes are soft and almost dry, add flour and cream that have been mixed together.

Bring to a boil and serve.

Serves 6.

KATE BEACHY, *Grantsville, Md.*

## Potatoes with Onions and Sour Dressing

| | |
|---|---|
| 4 cups diced raw potatoes | 2 tablespoons sugar |
| I cup sliced onions | 3 tablespoons vinegar |

2 tablespoons fat
2 teaspoons salt
I tablespoon flour

½ cup milk
½ cup cream

Cook potatoes in enough salt water to barely cover.

When they are nearly done, melt fat in a separate pan and fry the onions until light brown.

Blend sugar and flour with milk and cream to make a paste.

When potatoes are soft add the fried onions.

Then add the paste and vinegar and cook until it thickens.

There should not be more than ½ cup water on the potatoes when milk paste is added.

Serves 8.

CATHERINE J. MILLER, *Grantsville, Md.*

The sugar and vinegar may be omitted in the above recipe if desired. In that case the flour is added to the onions as they brown.

The milk and cream is poured in just before serving.

## Potatoes with Cabbage

½ pound salt pork or ham
½ large head cabbage, chopped
6 medium-sized potatoes

I teaspoon salt
I dried red pepper or a
little red cayenne pepper

Cook meat until almost tender.

Add chopped cabbage and cook 5 minutes.

Then add potatoes cut in 1 inch cubes.

Add salt and pepper and cook 20 minutes longer.

Serves 6.

CATHERINE J. MILLER, *Grantsville, Md.*

## Grandmother's Potato Pie

5 large potatoes, sliced
3 tablespoons butter
1½ teaspoons salt
⅛ teaspoon pepper

2 tablespoons minced parsley
I tablespoon flour
3 tablespoons water
Pastry for double crust pie
(page 354)

Line a flat baking dish with pastry.

Cut potatoes in thin slices and place in shell.

Sprinkle with salt, pepper, flour and parsley.

Add water and dot with butter.

Place crust on top and fasten securely. Cut a few small holes in it to keep it from running out.

Bake at 350° for 1 hour.

Serves 6.

MRS. IRVIN G. KOLB, *Spring City, Pa.*

## Scalloped Potatoes

| | |
|---|---|
| 6 cups raw potatoes, sliced thin | I onion |
| 4 tablespoons flour | 2½ cups hot milk |
| 2½ teaspoons salt | 2 tablespoons butter |
| ⅛ teaspoon pepper | |

Place a layer of potatoes in a buttered baking dish. Add minced onion.
Sprinkle with salt, pepper and flour, and dot with butter.
Repeat until all ingredients are used.
Pour hot milk over potatoes and bake at 350° for 1 to 1¼ hours.
Serves 6.

Mrs. Martin Good, *Manheim, Pa.*
Mrs. Wilmer Hochstetler, *Walnut Creek, Ohio*

Variations:

1. Make a white sauce with the milk, flour and butter (page 90).
   Melt ¼ cup grated cheese in the sauce.
   Pour over the potatoes.
2. Top with ⅔ cup soft bread crumbs and strips of bacon.
3. Add 1 cup grated cheese to the top of the potatoes 15 minutes before
   the cooking is completed.
4. Add 1 cup ground ham in alternate layers with the potatoes.

## Scalloped Potatoes with Endive

| | |
|---|---|
| 3 cups diced potatoes | ¼ teaspoon pepper |
| 1½ cups chopped endive | 4 slices bacon |
| I teaspoon salt | 2 cups milk |

Arrange raw, diced potatoes and chopped endive in alternate layers in
    a baking dish.
Sprinkle with salt and pepper.
Pour the milk over the mixture.
Top with strips of bacon and bake at 375° for 1 hour.
Serves 6.

Mrs. D. W. Lehman, *Harrisonburg, Va.*

## Potato Chips

| | |
|---|---|
| 12 large potatoes | Salt |
| Fat for deep-fat frying | |

Slice potatoes very thin on a vegetable slicer into a bowl of cold water.
Let stand 1 hour, adding ice cubes as necessary.
Drain and dry thoroughly between towels.
Drop in hot deep fat at 390° and fry until light brown.

Drain on brown paper and sprinkle with salt.
Do not use new potatoes.

ALICE SELZER, *Canton, Kan.*

## Candied Sweet Potatoes (I)

| | |
|---|---|
| 6 medium-sized sweet potatoes | ½ cup honey |
| 1 teaspoon salt | ½ cup orange juice |
| ¼ cup butter | |

Cook potatoes until soft, but not mushy.
Remove skins and cut in half lengthwise.
Arrange in a buttered baking dish and sprinkle with salt.
Heat together the butter, honey and orange juice.
Pour this mixture over the potatoes.
Bake at 400° for 25 minutes.
Serves 6.

MRS. VERNON MICHAEL, *Scottdale, Pa.*

## Candied Sweet Potatoes (II)

Follow Recipe I, but omit the orange juice and honey and add:

¾ cup water
1 cup of brown sugar

Melt the butter and sugar in a skillet and add the water.
Bring to a boil and then add sweet potatoes.
Cook slowly until liquid is thick and the potatoes are brown.
Serves 6.

MRS. JOHN A. LEHMAN, *Boswell, Pa.*

## Carameled Sweet Potatoes

| | |
|---|---|
| 5 medium-sized sweet potatoes | 3 tablespoons flour |
| 1 teaspoon salt | 8 marshmallows |
| 1 cup brown sugar | 1 cup thin cream |
| 2 tablespoons butter | ½ cup chopped nuts |

Cook potatoes until tender.
Drain and cool.
Cut in half lengthwise and arrange in greased baking dish.
Mix salt, sugar and flour and pour over potatoes.
Dot with butter.
Add marshmallows and nuts and pour cream over all.
Bake at 350° for 45-50 minutes.
Serves 5.

HILDA YODER, *Address Unknown*

## Sweet Potato Balls or Croquettes

| | |
|---|---|
| 2 cups mashed sweet potatoes | 6 marshmallows |
| 1 teaspoon salt | 1½ cups crushed corn flakes |
| 1½ tablespoons butter | 1 egg white |
| 1 tablespoon sugar | |

Cook sweet potatoes until soft; then mash very fine.

Season mashed sweet potatoes with salt, sugar and melted butter.

Shape potato mixture around a marshmallow.

Chill in refrigerator 30 minutes.

Dip balls into slightly beaten egg white and roll in corn flakes.

Place in a flat, greased baking dish and bake at 400° for 20 minutes or until golden brown.

Serves 6.

MRS. SAMUEL S. SHANK, *Broadway, Va.*

## Scalloped Sweet Potatoes and Apples

| | |
|---|---|
| 4 medium-sized sweet potatoes | ¼ cup butter |
| 3 large tart apples | ½ cup maple syrup or honey |
| 1 teaspoon salt | |

Cook the sweet potatoes and cut in slices ½ inch thick.

Slice apples in rings ½ inch thick. Do not pare.

Sauté apple rings in 2 tablespoons butter until light brown.

Arrange alternate layers of sweet potatoes and apples in a greased casserole.

Make a syrup of the remaining butter and maple syrup.

Pour over the ingredients and bake at 375° for 40 minutes.

Serves 6.

STELLA HUBER STAUFFER, *Tofield, Alta., Can.*

## Scalloped Sweet Potatoes and Pineapple

| | |
|---|---|
| 6 medium-sized sweet potatoes | ½ cup brown sugar |
| 6 slices of pineapple | ¼ cup butter |
| ¾ cup pineapple juice | 1 teaspoon salt |

Cook sweet potatoes in salt water until almost soft.

Slice cooked potatoes and arrange in alternate layers with chopped pineapple.

Blend brown sugar and butter together; then add pineapple juice.

Cook for 3 minutes and pour over sweet potatoes.

Bake at 375° for 30 minutes.

Serves 6 to 8.

MRS. E. M. GLICK, *Parkesburg, Pa.*

## Orange Sweet Potatoes

6 medium-sized sweet potatoes
1 cup orange juice
2 teaspoons grated orange rind
1 tablespoon cornstarch

3 tablespoons melted butter
1/3 cup white sugar
1/3 cup brown sugar
1 teaspoon salt

Cook potatoes in jackets until almost soft.

Remove skins and cut in quarters lengthwise.

Combine sugar, salt, butter, orange juice and rind and cook until thickened.

Arrange sweet potatoes in a greased baking dish and pour sauce over them.

Bake at 350° for 35 minutes.

Serves 6.

MRS. T. H. BERGEY, *Fentress, Va.*

## Mashed Sweet Potatoes

6 sweet potatoes
1 cup crushed pineapple
1/4 cup chopped walnuts

1 teaspoon salt
2 tablespoons butter
Juice of 1 orange

Bake the sweet potatoes whole until soft.

Cut a slice off, on side of each potato, and scoop out the center with a spoon.

Mash the potatoes and add other ingredients, mixing well.

Refill the shells with the mixture.

Serves 6.

FANNIE A. GABLE, *York, Pa.*

## Sweet Potato Pudding

2 cups mashed sweet potatoes
2 eggs
1 cup top milk
6 tablespoons sugar

1 teaspoon salt
2 tablespoons butter
8 marshmallows or
1/2 cup marshmallow whip

Cook sweet potatoes with skins on until soft.

Peel and mash and add sugar, salt, melted butter and rich milk.

Beat eggs well and add to mixture.

Pour in a buttered baking dish and top with marshmallows.

Bake at 350° for 45 minutes.

Serves 6.

MRS. WILLIAM JENNINGS, *Knoxville, Tenn.*
MRS. CHARLIE SHANK, *Chambersburg, Pa.*

## Baked Salsify

| | |
|---|---|
| 2 cups cooked salsify (oyster plant) | 1½ teaspoons salt |
| 2 eggs | ⅛ teaspoon pepper |
| 3 cups crushed soda crackers | 3 cups milk |
| 2 tablespoons butter | |

Clean salsify and cut in small pieces.

Cook in salt water until tender.

Break crackers in small pieces and place a layer in a greased baking dish.

Add a layer of salsify and sprinkle with salt and pepper.

Continue to add alternate layers until the contents are used.

Have cracker crumbs on top.

Beat eggs and add milk.

Pour this over ingredients.

Dot with butter.

Bake at 350° for 35 minutes.

Serves 6.

MRS. LIZZIE LE FEVRE, *Sterling, Ill.*

## Creamed Spinach on Toast

| | |
|---|---|
| 2 pounds spinach | 1 tablespoon butter |
| ½ cup thin cream | 1½ teaspoons flour |
| ½ teaspoon salt | 1 egg, beaten |

Cook spinach until tender.

Do not add water for cooking, as that which clings to the leaves when it is washed will be sufficient.

Chop and add ¼ cup cream, butter and salt.

Mix flour and beaten egg with remaining cream and cook until thickened.

Pour sauce over spinach.

Serves 6.

MRS. A. E. REESOR, *Markham, Ont., Can.*

## Scalloped Spinach

| | |
|---|---|
| 2 pounds spinach | 4 tablespoons melted butter |
| 2 eggs, beaten | ¾ teaspoon salt |
| 2 cups milk | ⅛ teaspoon pepper |
| 2 cups bread crumbs | ½ cup chopped bacon |

Cook and chop the spinach.

Add other ingredients, reserving bacon and ½ cup bread crumbs.

Mix thoroughly.

Sprinkle bread crumbs and chopped bacon on top.
Bake at 350° for 35-40 minutes.
Serves 6.

FANNIE A. GABLE, *York, Pa.*

## Succotash with Ham

| | |
|---|---|
| I ham butt | I teaspoon salt |
| 2½ cups fresh Limas | ¾ cup thin cream |
| 2½ cups fresh corn | |

Cook ham butt until tender and then remove from stock. Dice.
Add Lima beans to stock and cook until almost tender.
About 10 minutes before serving, add corn and diced ham.
Just before serving add hot cream.
Serves 8.

STELLA HUBER STAUFFER, *Tofield, Alta., Can.*

## Baked Tomatoes

| | |
|---|---|
| 3 cups canned or fresh tomatoes | 2 tablespoons butter |
| 2 tablespoons sugar | ¼ cup grated cheese |
| I teaspoon salt | I cup buttered bread crumbs |
| ⅛ teaspoon pepper | |

Place tomatoes in a greased baking dish.
Add sugar, salt and pepper.
Melt butter and rub into bread crumbs.
Sprinkle crumbs on top of tomatoes and then add grated cheese.
Bake at 350° for 35 minutes. Add grated cheese during last 10 minutes
of cooking.
Serves 6.

MRS. HENRY LAMBERTSON, *Pocomoke City, Md.*

## Fried Tomatoes

| | |
|---|---|
| 4 medium-sized tomatoes | ⅛ teaspoon pepper |
| ½ cup flour | 2 tablespoons brown sugar |
| ½ teaspoon salt | I cup cream |
| 3 tablespoons fat | |

Use ripe but firm tomatoes.
Do not remove skins.
Cut in slices ⅛ inch thick.
Roll in flour and fry in hot fat.
When browned on both sides, sprinkle with salt, pepper and brown
sugar.
Place tomatoes on a platter.

Add 1 tablespoon flour to fryings; when well blended add the cream.
Allow gravy to thicken and then pour it over the fried tomatoes.
Serves 5.

Mrs. Irvin G. Kolb, *Spring City, Pa.*; Mrs. Stanley Derstine, *Souderton, Pa.*

## Tomato Fritters

| | |
|---|---|
| 2 cups cooked tomatoes | 1/2 teaspoon salt |
| 2 eggs | 1/8 teaspoon pepper |
| 1 1/2 cups cracker crumbs | 1 1/2 teaspoons sugar |
| 1 small onion, minced | 3 tablespoons fat |

Beat eggs and add tomatoes, seasoning and cracker crumbs.
Stir until well blended.
Drop mixture from a spoon into hot fat.
Fry until brown on both sides.
Serves 6.

Elizabeth Gehman, *Mohnton, Pa.*

## Tomato Dumplings

| | For dumplings: |
|---|---|
| 3 cups tomato juice | 1 1/2 cups flour |
| 1/2 teaspoon salt | 1/2 teaspoon salt |
| 1 tablespoon sugar | 3 teaspoons baking powder |
| 1/8 teaspoon pepper | 1/2 cup milk |

Heat tomato juice, add salt, sugar and pepper.
Sift flour, ½ teaspoon salt, and baking powder together.
Add the milk and mix together into a stiff dough.
Drop dough from a teaspoon into hot juice to form dumplings.
Cover and cook for 12 minutes.
Do not remove cover until cooking period is over.
Serve at once.
Serves 6 to 8.

Mrs. Amanda Boley, *Hartville, Ohio*

## Tomato Soufflé

| | |
|---|---|
| 3 tablespoons butter | 1/4 pound cheese, diced |
| 4 tablespoons flour | 1/4 teaspoon paprika |
| 1/2 teaspoon salt | 1/2 teaspoon dry mustard |
| 1 cup condensed tomato soup | 3 eggs, separated |

Make a sauce of the butter, flour, salt and condensed tomato soup.
Place sauce over hot water and add diced cheese, paprika and mustard.
Stir until cheese is melted and sauce is smooth.

Remove from heat and add unbeaten egg yolks. Mix well.
Fold in stiffly beaten whites.
Pour in a greased baking dish and bake at 350° for 45 minutes.
Serve at once.
Serves 6.

STELLA HUBER STAUFFER, *Tofield, Alta., Can.*

## Baked Stuffed Turnips

| | |
|---|---|
| 4 medium-sized turnips | 1 teaspoon salt |
| 4 medium-sized tomatoes | 1/4 teaspoon pepper |
| 2 tablespoons uncooked rice | 1 tablespoon butter |
| 2 cups water | |

Chop the tomatoes and add rice, water and seasoning.
Cook until the rice is soft.
Scoop out the centers of the turnips, leaving a shell ½ inch thick.
Chop centers and add to tomato mixture.
Fill centers of turnips with stuffing.
Sprinkle with bread crumbs and place turnips in a greased baking dish.
Add ½ cup water, cover and bake at 350° for 1 hour.
Serves 4.

NORA L. GROSS, *Doylestown, Pa.*

## Turnips and Potatoes in Broth

| | |
|---|---|
| 3 medium-sized potatoes | Salt and pepper |
| 3 medium-sized turnips | 2½ cups beef broth |

Pare potatoes and turnips and slice in rings or cut in cubes.
Add broth and seasoning and cook until tender.
Just before serving, garnish with chopped parsley.

FROM GRANDMOTHER'S COOKBOOK

## Turnip Soufflé

| | |
|---|---|
| 1 cup cooked turnips | 1/8 teaspoon pepper |
| 2 tablespoons cream | 1 egg |
| 1 cup cracker or bread crumbs | 1 tablespoon sugar |
| 1 teaspoon salt | 1 cup milk |
| 1 tablespoon butter | |

Mash cooked turnips and add ½ cup crumbs, beaten egg, cream and
    seasoning.
Mix together and add milk gradually.
Place in a greased baking dish and cover with remaining crumbs and
    dots of butter.

Bake at 350° for 45 minutes.
Serve at once.
Serves 6.

Mrs. Arthur Ebersole, *Birch Tree, Mo.*

## Vegetable Croquettes

| | |
|---|---|
| 3 cups mashed potatoes | I teaspoon salt |
| I cup minced celery | ⅛ teaspoon pepper |
| 2 onions, grated | I egg |
| I cup grated carrots | Bread crumbs |

Do not add milk to mashed potatoes.
Mix ingredients together and shape into croquettes.
Dip into beaten egg and roll in dry bread crumbs. Chill.
Fry in deep fat until a golden brown.
Serves 6.

Mrs. Phares A. Landis, *Lancaster, Pa.*

## Vegetable Loaf

| | |
|---|---|
| I cup cooked peas | 2 cups milk or vegetable broth |
| I cup cooked carrots | 2 teaspoons salt |
| I cup cooked string beans | ½ teaspoon pepper |
| 2 cups mashed potatoes | ½ teaspoon celery salt |
| 3 tablespoons butter | I cup grated cheese |
| I onion, minced | ½ cup bread crumbs |
| 3 tablespoons flour | |

Arrange chopped cooked vegetables in layers or mix together in a
greased baking dish.
Melt fat in a saucepan, add onions and flour.
When slightly brown, gradually add the milk.
Add seasonings.
When sauce is smooth and thickened, add the grated cheese.
Stir until cheese is melted and remove from heat.
Cool slightly and then pour sauce over vegetables.
Sprinkle with crumbs.
Bake at 350° for 45 minutes.
Serves 8.

Mrs. H. Landis, *Lancaster, Pa.*

## Vegetable Pie

| | |
|---|---|
| I cup cooked meat, pork ribs preferred | For pastry: |
| 1½ cups potatoes, diced | I cup flour |
| | 2 teaspoons baking powder |

1 cup diced carrots
½ cup celery
1 teaspoon salt
¼ teaspoon pepper

2 tablespoons fat
½ teaspoon salt
¼ cup milk

Cook vegetables until almost soft.
Add to chopped meat and seasoning.
Place in greased baking dish.
Make pastry and pat dough to size of baking dish.
Lay on top of vegetables.
Bake at 350° for 45 minutes.
Serves 6.

Mrs. Eli Wenger, *Blue Ball, Pa.*

# Salads
## and
## Salad Dressings

### Chapter VII

SALADS ARE NOT LISTED AMONG THE RECIPES FOUND IN GRANDMOTHER'S old-fashioned cookbook. This fact is not too surprising, since the idea of having a salad with every dinner is a twentieth-century innovation.

It should be noted, however, that many of the foods we use in salads were a part of the diet of our great-grandparents. Those dishes of former days, although not called salads, consisted of lettuce, onions and radishes in late spring; cole slaw during the summer; endive, turnip slaw, and celery during crisp autumn days; and dandelion and water cress in early spring. In the absence of beautiful salad plates, these were served in fancy glass dishes, and were just another of the tasty foods arranged on Grandmother's table.

In winter the old wooden cabbage barrel, buried beneath the ground, provided slaw as long as the supply lasted. When it had been emptied, there was found a good substitute for salads in the row of pickles and relishes on the shelf in the cellar. Grandmother had made cucumber, beet, and green tomato pickle on those days before the first frost came to wilt her garden. These served to whet the appetites of her family members until spring came.

Most interesting is this bit of helpful advice found written among a list of home remedies in a quaint old recipe book: "At this season of the year [spring] too much cannot be said in favor of onions. Whether raw or cooked they are especially good, both medicinally and as a skin beautifier."

Salads have become so popular during the last few decades that we find almost every type of food being used in our newest recipes. We not only use vegetables and fruits, but we mix these together with a host of other foods in a way that would have horrified Grandmother!

One soon learns that she need not always follow a recipe in making a salad, but that she can be creative.

## MEAT, FISH AND EGG SALADS

### Chicken Salad

| | |
|---|---|
| 3 cups diced, cooked chicken | 1 teaspoon salt |
| 1½ cups diced celery | ⅛ teaspoon pepper |
| 3 hard-cooked eggs | 2/3 cup mayonnaise |
| 3 sweet pickles, chopped | 3 tablespoons cream |

Cut the cooked chicken in ½ inch pieces.

Chop celery and pickles and add to chicken.

Chop eggs, coarse, and add to mixture.

Add seasoning.

Add cream to mayonnaise; when smooth, mix with chicken.

Serve on lettuce.

Serves 8.

SADIE EASH, *Davidsville, Pa.;* MRS. P. R. KENNEL, *Sheckley, Neb.*

### Chicken Relish Mold

| | |
|---|---|
| 1 cup cooked chicken | 2 tablespoons minced onion |
| ¾ cup celery, sliced thin | ½ teaspoon salt |
| ¾ cup chopped carrots | 1 package lemon-flavored gelatin |
| ¼ cup diced sweet pickle | 2 cups hot water |

Dissolve gelatin in hot water.

Add salt and minced onion.

Chill; when slightly thickened, add chopped chicken and vegetables.
Pour into mold and chill until firm.
Unmold and garnish with mayonnaise and parsley.
Serves 6 to 8.

Mrs. Lillian Wought, *Cullom, Ill.*

## Crab Meat Salad

| | |
|---|---|
| 1 cup flaked crab meat | 1 teaspoon salt |
| 2/3 cup diced celery | Mayonnaise |
| 6 small tomatoes | |

Combine crab meat, diced celery and tomatoes that have been peeled,
    chilled and quartered.
Add mayonnaise enough to moisten well.
Serve on lettuce and garnish with hard-cooked eggs or parsley.
Serves 6.

Margaret Lambertson, *Pocomoke City, Md.*

## Salmon Salad

| | |
|---|---|
| 2 cups flaked salmon | 1/2 teaspoon salt |
| 1/2 cup minced celery | 1/8 teaspoon paprika |
| 1/2 cup shredded cabbage | Mayonnaise |

Flake salmon and add vegetables and seasoning.
Moisten with mayonnaise.
Serve on lettuce, garnish with hard-cooked eggs if desired.
Serves 6.

Edith Keffer, *Waterloo, Ont., Can.*

## Tuna Fish Salad

| | |
|---|---|
| 1 cup tuna fish | 1 minced green pepper |
| 1 cup shredded cabbage | 1 large carrot, diced |
| 1 cup cooked peas | 1 tablespoon minced onion |
| 1/2 cup diced celery | Mayonnaise |
| 1/2 teaspoon salt | |

Flake the tuna fish and add chopped vegetables and seasoning.
Toss together and mix with mayonnaise or salad dressing.
Serve on lettuce.
Serves 6.

Mrs. Rachel Powell, *South English, Iowa*

## Deviled Eggs

| | |
|---|---|
| 4 hard-cooked eggs | 2 teaspoons vinegar |
| 1/2 teaspoon salt | 1 tablespoon mayonnaise |

1/8 teaspoon pepper  
1/4 teaspoon mustard

1 tablespoon cream

Cut eggs in half lengthwise.

Remove yolks and mash until smooth.

Add other ingredients and mix well.

Refill the whites and garnish with paprika or parsley.

Serves 4.

MRS. SAMUEL RAMER, *Versailles, Mo.*

## Egg Pinwheel Salad

4 hard-cooked eggs  
4 small tomatoes  
1 cup salad dressing

Water cress, parsley or green pepper

Cut eggs in eighths lengthwise.

Peel tomatoes and chill.

Cut in eighths lengthwise.

Arrange egg and tomato slices alternately on a round platter to resemble a pinwheel.

Place salad dressing in center and garnish with greens.

Serves 4.

MRS. A. E. REESOR, *Markham, Ont., Can.*

# VEGETABLE SALADS

## Bean Salad

3 cups cooked navy or string beans  
4 hard-cooked eggs  
1 medium-sized onion  
1 large sour pickle, chopped

2 tablespoons vinegar  
1 1/2 teaspoons salt  
2/3 cup salad dressing

Chop eggs, onion and pickle.

If green string beans are used, cut in 1 inch lengths.

Add beans and seasoning.

Mix together and add salad dressing.

Serves 8.

MRS. L. P. SHOWALTER, *Broadway, Va.*

## Kidney Bean Salad

2 1/2 cups canned kidney beans, drained  
1/4 cup chopped celery  
2 hard-cooked eggs  
1 medium-sized onion, minced

1/2 teaspoon salt  
2 tablespoons sugar  
2 tablespoons vinegar  
1/4 cup salad dressing  
2 tablespoons cream

Chop eggs and combine with celery and onion.
Add beans that have been drained.
Mix ingredients together and chill.
Add cream to salad dressing and blend well through mixed vegetables.
Arrange on lettuce as desired.
Serves 6.

MRS. AARON GERIG, *Woodburn, Ind.*

## Beet Salad

6 small beets, cooked
1 medium-sized onion, diced
1½ cups shredded cabbage

Dressing:
1 egg, beaten
2 teaspoons sugar
1 teaspoon mustard
1 teaspoon salt
1 tablespoon flour
¼ cup vinegar
1 cup sour cream

Cook beets, peel and dice.
Mix with onion and cabbage.
Mix together the ingredients for the dressing. See directions for Cooked
    Salad Dressing (page 197).
Cook until thickened; then pour sauce over the vegetables.
Stir until well blended.
Serves 6.

MISS KIRCHHOFER, *Bluffton, Ohio*

## Beet and Apple Salad

2 cups cooked beets, diced
2 cups raw diced apple
2 hard-cooked eggs

½ cup salad dressing
¼ cup chopped nuts
Parsley

Mix together lightly the diced apples, beets and eggs.
Add salad dressing and garnish with chopped nuts and parsley.
Serves 6.

MRS. M. T. BRACKBILL, *Harrisonburg, Va.*

## Cabbage Salad (I)

1 small head of cabbage
1 cup drained pineapple cubes
1 dozen marshmallows

2 tablespoons sugar
½ teaspoon salt
4 tablespoons mayonnaise

Chop cabbage and add pineapple.
Cut marshmallows in small pieces and add to cabbage mixture.

Add sugar and salt to mayonnaise and mix with salad.
Serves 6.

THE MENNONITE HOME, *Maugansville, Md.*

## Cabbage Salad (II)

| | |
|---|---|
| 1 quart chopped cabbage | 2 tablespoons butter |
| 1 cup ground peanuts | 4 tablespoons sugar |
| ½ teaspoon salt | 4 tablespoons cream |
| 2 eggs | ½ cup vinegar |

Chop cabbage and add ground peanuts.
Make a cooked dressing with the remaining ingredients. See directions
for Cooked Salad Dressing (page 197).
When thickened, remove dressing from heat and cool.
Pour it over cabbage and peanut mixture.
Serves 6.

MRS. FLOYD NEWCOMER, *Seville, Ohio*

## Cole Slaw

| | |
|---|---|
| 4 cups finely shredded cabbage | 3 tablespoons sugar |
| ¼ cup sour cream | 1 teaspoon salt |
| ¼ cup vinegar | ⅛ teaspoon mustard |

Chop or shred the cabbage.
Mix together the sugar, salt, mustard, vinegar and sour cream.
Pour over cabbage and mix well.
Garnish with green pepper rings.
Serves 6.

STELLA HUBER STAUFFER, *Tofield, Alta., Can.*

## Carrot Salad

| | |
|---|---|
| 1 small head of lettuce | ¾ teaspoon salt |
| 4 medium-sized carrots | ½ cup vinegar |
| ½ cup raisins | ½ cup sugar |
| ¼ cup American cheese grated or chopped nuts | 1 cup sour cream |

Chop the lettuce into small pieces.
Grate carrots.
Mix together and add raisins.
Make a dressing with the sugar, salt, vinegar and sour cream.
Pour dressing over the salad mixture.
Serves 6.

JESSIE HAMILTON, *Sheridan, Ore.*

## Cucumber Salad

### Russian

1 quart thick sour milk or buttermilk
4 medium-sized cucumbers

1 tablespoon salt
2 tablespoons vinegar

Pare and slice cucumbers into thin rings.
Sprinkle with 1½ teaspoons salt and let stand 3 minutes.
Beat sour milk with an egg beater until smooth.
Add vinegar and remaining salt.
Drain cucumbers and add to milk.
This is rather thin and is eaten with a spoon.

MRS. JOHN A. WARKENTIN, *Mountain Lake, Minn.*

## Dandelion Salad

4 cups chopped dandelion
3 hard-cooked eggs
3 slices bacon

Dressing:
1½ tablespoons flour
1 teaspoon salt
1 egg
2 tablespoons sugar
¼ cup vinegar
2 cups milk or water

Wash and chop dandelion.
Cut bacon in pieces and fry until crisp.
Remove bacon from drippings.
To make dressing, mix together the dry ingredients, add egg, vinegar and water. Stir until well blended.
Cook in bacon drippings until thickened and cool slightly.
Pour dressing over dandelion and mix lightly. Garnish with sliced or chopped eggs and the crisp bacon.
Serves 6.

MRS. J. IRVIN LEHMAN, *Chambersburg, Pa.;* AUNT LINA RESSLER, *Scottdale, Pa.*

## Endive Salad

1 head of endive, well bleached
2 hard-cooked eggs
3 slices bacon
2 teaspoons sugar

1½ teaspoons flour
1 teaspoon salt
4 teaspoons vinegar
¾ cup cream

Wash and chop the endive.
Chop bacon and fry until crisp.
Remove from drippings.
Mix salt, sugar, and flour; add vinegar and cream. Stir until well blended.

Cook sauce in 2 tablespoons bacon drippings until thickened.
Pour hot mixture over endive and mix together lightly.
Garnish with eggs and bacon.
Serves 6.

EDITH KEFFER, *Waterloo, Ont., Can.*

## Fresh Garden or Spring Salad

| | |
|---|---|
| 1 medium-sized head of lettuce | 1 small onion, grated |
| 2 cups coarsely diced tomatoes | 1/4 cup sliced radishes |
| 1 cup sliced cucumbers | French dressing |

Chop vegetables and toss together lightly.
Chill and moisten with French dressing just before serving.
Serves 6.

MRS. CARL HARTMAN, *Waynesboro, Va.*

## Lettuce Salad

| | |
|---|---|
| 1 head of lettuce | 1/2 cup salad dressing |
| 1 onion, minced | 1 teaspoon mustard |
| 1/2 cup grated cheese | 2 tablespoons cream |
| 1 teaspoon salt | 2 tablespoons vinegar |
| 2 1/2 tablespoons sugar | |

Wash lettuce and chop coarsely.
Add minced onion and chopped or grated cheese.
Mix together salt, sugar, mustard, and cream. Add vinegar and salad
dressing and stir until smooth.
Pour over the lettuce and mix lightly.
Serves 6.

MRS. GEORGE BOLLINGER, *Marion, Pa.*

## Pea Salad

| | |
|---|---|
| 2 1/2 cups cooked peas | 1 small head of lettuce |
| 2 tablespoons chopped onion | 1/2 teaspoon salt |
| 4 tablespoons cream cheese | 1/2 cup salad dressing |
| 4 tablespoons chopped sweet pickles | 3 tablespoons cream |

Cut cheese and pickles in small pieces.
Add onion.
Mix with drained peas.
Add cream and salt to salad dressing.
Pour over vegetables and mix lightly.
Serve on lettuce leaves.
Serves 6.

MRS. AAL SCHLEGEL, *Shickley, Neb.*

## Potato Salad

8 medium-sized potatoes
4 hard-cooked eggs
1 medium-sized onion
2 small carrots, ground
1 cup celery, diced
1½ teaspoons salt

Dressing:

1 tablespoon flour
2 eggs
½ cup sugar
½ cup vinegar
1 teaspoon mustard
1½ cups water
2 tablespoons butter

Cook potatoes in jackets until soft.

Cool and peel.

Dice potatoes, eggs, onion and celery.

Grate carrots.

To make dressing, mix together the dry ingredients, add eggs, vinegar and water.

Melt butter in saucepan and add dressing.

Cook until thickened.

Cool and pour over potato mixture and mix lightly.

If desired, ½ cup of sandwich spread or mayonnaise may be added to dressing before it is poured over vegetables.

Serves 8 to 10.

MRS. RICHARD DANNER, *Hanover, Pa.;* MRS. G. P. SHOWALTER, *Broadway, Va.*

## German Potato Salad

6 frankfurters, cooked and chopped
4 cups hot diced potatoes
½ cup chopped celery
1 medium-sized onion, chopped
1 tablespoon chopped parsley
1½ teaspoons salt

1 tablespoon flour
2 tablespoons fat
1/3 cup sugar
1/3 cup vinegar
¼ teaspoon pepper
2/3 cup water

Fry chopped onion in hot fat until light brown.

Add flour and blend.

Then add sugar, salt, vinegar and water.

Bring to a boil, stirring constantly.

Pour dressing over the diced potatoes and chopped frankfurters.

Sprinkle with pepper and serve hot.

Serves 8.

MRS. E. KERMIT STYER, *Souderton, Pa.*

## Spinach Salad

4 cups chopped spinach
1 medium-sized onion

2/3 cup salad dressing
2 tablespoons cream

| 3 hard-cooked eggs | 2 tablespoons sugar |
| 1 teaspoon salt | 2 tablespoons vinegar |

Wash and chop spinach.

Dice onion and 1 hard-cooked egg and add to spinach.

Mix salt, sugar, cream and vinegar to the salad dressing.

Pour over the spinach.

Slice remaining 2 eggs and garnish salad.

Serves 6.

MRS. D. N. REESOR, *Markham, Ont., Can.*

## Sunshine Salad

| 1 cup shredded cabbage | 2 tablespoons lemon juice |
| 1 cup grated carrots | 3 tablespoons orange juice |
| 1 cup chopped apples | 2 teaspoons sugar |
| 1 teaspoon minced onion or green pepper | 1/2 teaspoon salt |

Mix together lightly the shredded cabbage, grated carrots, chopped
apples and minced onion or green pepper.

Place in a bowl and chill in refrigerator.

Mix together the salt, sugar and fruit juices.

Pour over the salad ingredients and serve.

Serves 6.

ETHEL CHARLES, *Lancaster, Pa.*

## Tomato Salad

| 6 medium-sized tomatoes | 2 tablespoons chopped parsley |
| 1 small onion | 1 teaspoon salt |
| 1 cup chopped celery | Mayonnaise |

Skin tomatoes and dice in a bowl.

Add minced onion and chopped celery.

Mix lightly and add mayonnaise and seasoning.

Garnish with chopped parsley.

Serves 6.

LENA KREIDER, *Palmyra, Mo.*

## Tomato, Celery and Cabbage Salad

| 1 cup diced tomatoes | 3 hard-cooked eggs |
| 1 cup chopped celery | Olives or small pickles |
| 1 cup chopped cabbage | French dressing or mayonnaise |

Mix together lightly the chopped vegetables.

Add mayonnaise or French dressing and serve on lettuce.

Garnish with olives or pickles, and hard-cooked eggs cut in lengthwise
pieces.

Serves 6.

MRS. D. B. BETZNER, *Kitchener, Ont., Can.*

## Turnip Slaw

6 medium-sized turnips
2/3 cup sour cream
2 tablespoons vinegar

2 tablespoons sugar
1 teaspoon salt
2 tablespoons minced parsley

Pare and grate raw turnips.

Pour over them a dressing made by combining the sugar, salt, vinegar
and cream.

Garnish with parsley.

Serves 6.

ANNA M. MILLER, *Denbigh, Va.*

# FRUIT SALADS

## Angel Salad

1 cup marshmallows, chopped
3 bananas or 1 pound white grapes
1 cup pineapple
1/2 cup crushed peanuts
1/2 cup whipping cream

2/3 cup pineapple juice
1 egg
2 tablespoons sugar
1 tablespoon cornstarch

Chop the marshmallows, bananas or grapes and pineapple.

Mix the marshmallows and fruit; then add the crushed nuts.

Make a cooked dressing of the egg, sugar, cornstarch and pineapple
juice.

Cool dressing and add the whipped cream.

Combine dressing with salad mixture and serve on lettuce.

Serves 6.

MARTHA MARTIN, *Salem, Ohio*

## Apple Salad

8 apples (Delicious preferred)
2 bananas
1/2 cup chopped celery
1/2 cup raisins

1/4 cup coconut
1/2 cup peanuts
1/2 cup walnuts
Juice of 1/2 lemon (optional)

Dice apples, do not pare them.

Place them in weak salt water while other ingredients are prepared or
add lemon juice and mix thoroughly. This keeps fruit from turning
dark.

Drain and add chopped celery, bananas, raisins, coconut and nuts.
Make one of the two following salad dressings and pour over the apple
 mixture.
Serves 6-8.

Dressing:

I. Make a cooked dressing of the following:

| | |
|---|---|
| I cup water | I tablespoon cornstarch |
| I teaspoon vinegar | ¼ cup cream |
| ¼ teaspoon salt | I teaspoon vanilla |
| I cup sugar | |

II. An uncooked dressing may be made as follows:

| | |
|---|---|
| ¼ cup peanut butter | ½ cup sugar |
| ¼ cup cream | ½ cup mayonnaise |

MRS. MAHLON BLOSSER, *Harrisonburg, Va.*

## Apple and Vegetable Salad

| | |
|---|---|
| 2 cups diced apples | Dressing: |
| ½ cup shredded carrots | 3 eggs |
| ½ cup diced celery | ½ cup sugar |
| ½ cup chopped peanuts | I tablespoon flour |
| | I tablespoon butter |
| | ¼ cup vinegar |
| | ½ cup cream |

Mix apples and chopped vegetables together.
Cook dressing until it thickens.
Add cream and allow to cool.
Pour dressing over salad mixture and serve.
Serves 6.

MRS. J. R. LANDIS, *Seville, Ohio*

## Avocado Pear Salad

| | |
|---|---|
| 2 avocado pears | I head lettuce |
| 3 hard-cooked eggs | I head garlic |
| 2 slices bread, toasted | French dressing |

Remove skin from the pears and chop in ½ inch pieces.
Chop eggs and lettuce, coarse.
Cut toasted bread into ½ inch cubes.
Rub the salad bowl with garlic.
Toss together lightly the lettuce, egg, bread and avocado pear.
Add French dressing.
Serves 6.

## Banana Salad

6 bananas
1/2 cup nut meats
1 cup chopped marshmallows

Dressing:
  2 cups water
  1 tablespoon cornstarch
  1 tablespoon vinegar
  1 cup sugar
  2 egg yolks
  1/8 teaspoon salt

Mix together the ingredients for the dressing and cook until thickened.
When cold, add the chopped bananas, nuts and marshmallows.
Mix together.
Serve on lettuce.
Serves 6.

MRS. RAYMOND BURKHOLDER, Orville, Ohio

## Candlestick Salad

4 slices pineapple
2 bananas

Maraschino cherries

Place a pineapple ring on lettuce.
Cut banana in half crosswise and stand one-half in an upright position
    in center of pineapple.
Make a cut in the tip of the banana and insert ½ of a cherry.
Serve with mayonnaise.
Serves 4.

MRS. HERSHEY WEAVER, Blue Ball, Pa.

## Christmas Salad

4 slices pineapple
1/2 cup Philadelphia cream cheese

Cranberry jelly
English walnuts

Place a pineapple ring on shredded lettuce.
On the pineapple put a heaping teaspoon of cream cheese.
Flatten out the cheese; on it place a star of cranberry jelly.
Place a small dot of cheese on top; in the center of it add half of an
    English walnut.
Serves 4.

MRS. JOHN KOPPENHAVER, Perkasie, Pa.

## Cranberry-Orange Relish

4 cups cranberries
2 oranges

3 apples
2 cups sugar

Wash berries and grind through food chopper.
Wash and core apples and chop very fine.

Peel oranges and remove seeds.

Grind rind and oranges through chopper.

Mix ingredients together and add sugar.

Let stand in refrigerator for 12 to 24 hours before serving.

Serves 8.

Mrs. Sam Redger, *Greensburg, Kan.*

Mrs. Henry Lambertson, *Pocomoke City, Md.*

## Foamy Salad

2 cups shredded cabbage
3 bananas, diced
1 cup crushed pineapple
1 cup sweet cherries

1 cup chopped nuts
1 cup marshmallows, chopped
1 cup mayonnaise
1 cup whipping cream

Combine cabbage, fruits, nuts and marshmallows.

Whip the cream and add to mayonnaise.

Pour dressing over salad mixture and blend.

Let stand in refrigerator 1 hour before serving.

Serves 6 to 8.

Mrs. Walter Shank, *North Lima, Ohio*

## Fruit Salad (I)

3 oranges
3 bananas
1 cup chopped pineapple

2 cups peaches or pears
(canned or fresh)
1 cup California grapes
1/4 cup chopped walnuts

Peel the oranges and separate into sections. Remove seeds and skin surrounding each section.

Cut grapes in half lengthwise and remove seeds.

Chop bananas and peaches or pears in ½ inch cubes.

Mix all ingredients and serve with favorite salad dressing or use as an appetizer or dessert.

Serves 6.

## Fruit Salad with Sweet Dressing (II)

3 oranges
3 apples
2 cups chopped pineapple
1 pound Malaga grapes

Dressing:
½ cup sugar
1 egg
1 tablespoon cornstarch
1½ tablespoons butter
1 cup milk
1 cup whipped cream

Peel and dice oranges and apples.

Cut grapes in half lengthwise and remove seeds.

Chop the pineapple and add to other fruits.
Combine and cook together the ingredients for the dressing.
Cool and add whipped cream.
Pour cold dressing over fruit.
Serves 6.

Mrs. Ralph Wingard, *Johnstown, Pa.*

## White Fruit Salad (III)

| | |
|---|---|
| 1 cup chopped pineapple | 1/2 cup chopped nuts |
| 1 cup white grapes | Juice of 1 lemon |
| 1 cup canned pears | 1 cup whipping cream |
| 12 marshmallows | 1/8 teaspoon salt |

Chop the pineapple, pears and marshmallows.
Split grapes in half lengthwise and remove seeds.
Mix fruit together and drain well.
Add nuts.
Add lemon juice and salt to whipped cream.
Mix together and chill for 6 to 8 hours before serving.
This salad is often used as a dessert.
Serves 6.

Mrs. Harvey Hershberger, *Sugar Creek, Ohio*

## Heavenly Salad

| | |
|---|---|
| 1 pound white grapes | Dressing: |
| One No. 2 can of pineapple | 3 egg yolks |
| (about 2¼ cups) | 1/2 teaspoon dry mustard |
| 1 pound marshmallows, chopped | 1/4 teaspoon salt |
| 1 cup chopped nuts | Juice of 2 lemons |
| 2 cups whipping cream | |

Split grapes in half lengthwise and remove seeds.
Add chopped pineapple and marshmallows.
Mix egg yolks, mustard, salt and lemon juice and cook until thickened. Cool.
Add whipped cream.
Pour dressing over fruit and mix lightly.
Let stand in the refrigerator overnight.
Add nuts just before serving.
Serve on lettuce or as a dessert.
Serves 8.

Mrs. Emanuel Lauver, *Mechanicsburg, Pa.;* Mrs. Ward Shank, *Sterling, Ill.*
Mrs. Leroy Hostetler, *Bellefontaine, Ohio*

## Pear and Pineapple Salad

3 cups canned pears
1 cup pineapple
1/2 cup raisins

1/2 head lettuce shredded
1/2 cup mayonnaise
1/2 cup cream

Chop the pears and pineapple.
Mix together and add raisins and shredded lettuce.
Mix mayonnaise and cream.
Pour dressing over salad mixture.
Serves 6.

MRS. AMANDA BOLEY, *Hartville, Ohio*

## Pineapple and Cheese Salad (I)

1 cup pineapple chunks
2 packages Philadelphia cream cheese
1/2 cup chopped nuts

Mayonnaise
3 tablespoons top milk

Drain pineapple.
Add chopped nuts.
Add top milk to cheese to soften it.
Add cheese and mix together.
Serve on lettuce.
Serves 4.

MRS. GRACE WINGARD, *Elverson, Pa.*

## Pineapple and Cheese Salad (II)

2 cups crushed pineapple
1 cup grated cheese
1 cup chopped nuts
Lettuce

Dressing:
1 cup pineapple juice
4 tablespoons sugar
1 tablespoon cornstarch
1/2 teaspoon salt
1 egg

Mix pineapple, grated cheese and nuts together.
Mix ingredients for dressing and cook until thickened.
Cool dressing and pour over salad mixture.
Serve on lettuce.
Serves 6.

MRS. DOUGLAS ALLEN, *Harrisonburg, Va.*

## Pineapple Salad

2 cups pineapple chunks
1 cup California grapes
1 cup chopped marshmallows
1 apple, diced

Dressing:
1/2 cup sugar
1 1/2 tablespoons cornstarch
2 eggs, separated

1 banana, diced
2 cups shredded cabbage

1 tablespoon vinegar
1 tablespoon butter
1 cup pineapple juice

Split grapes in half lengthwise and remove seeds.
Add chopped apple, banana, marshmallows and pineapple.
Mix together and add shredded cabbage.
Mix ingredients for dressing, reserving egg whites, and cook until thickened.
Chill and then add stiffly beaten egg whites.
Pour over salad mixture and blend together.
Serves 6 to 8.

MRS. JOHN R. VANPELT, *Columbiana, Ohio*

## Pineapple Salad

4 slices pineapple or
4 large peach halves, canned or fresh

1 cup whipped cream
Strawberries

Arrange lettuce on a large platter or individual plates if preferred.
Place pineapple rings or peach halves on lettuce.
Top with whipped cream and arrange strawberries around the salad.
Serves 4.

MRS. D. B. BETZNER, *Kitchener, Ont., Can.*

## Sunshine Salad

4 slices pineapple
4 apricot halves
4 teaspoons cream cheese
4 maraschino cherries

French dressing
Lettuce
Nuts (optional)

Place pineapple rings on lettuce.
Put apricot halves on top with the opening up.
Add a teaspoon of cream cheese to each.
Garnish with a cherry or chopped nuts.
Serve with French dressing.
Serves 4.

MRS. ROBERT NACE, *Souderton, Pa.*

# MOLDED SALADS

## Apricot, Pineapple Mold

2 packages orange gelatin
1 cup puréed apricots
1 cup crushed pineapple
2 cups hot water

For garnishing:
  4 pineapple rings
  8 apricot halves
  8 maraschino cherries

Dissolve gelatin in hot water.

Chill until it begins to congeal.

Add crushed pineapple and puréed apricots.

Do not drain fruits.

Pour into mold and allow to set.

Unmold on salad plate and garnish around edge of platter with pineapple rings, apricot halves and red cherries.

To do this, cut pineapple slices in half and arrange in scallops around edge of mold.

Turn apricot halves up, add a little mayonnaise and top each with a red cherry.

Place these between pineapple slices.

Very delicious and attractive.

Serves 6.

MRS. CARL G. SHOWALTER, *Broadway, Va.*

## Cardinal Salad

| | |
|---|---|
| 1 package lemon gelatin | 2 onions, grated |
| 1 cup boiling water | 1 tablespoon horse-radish |
| 3/4 cup beet juice | 3/4 cup diced celery |
| 3 tablespoons vinegar | 1 cup diced cooked beets |
| 1/2 teaspoon salt | |

Dissolve gelatin in beet juice and add boiling water. Cool.

Dice beets, add grated onion and chopped celery.

Season with salt, vinegar and horse-radish.

When gelatin begins to thicken, add vegetables and mix.

Unmold on lettuce.

Serves 6.

MRS. LEWIS H. REESOR, *St. Marys, Ont., Can.*

## Carrot and Pineapple Salad

| | |
|---|---|
| 1 package lemon gelatin | 1 cup crushed pineapple |
| 1 cup pineapple juice | 1 1/2 cups ground raw carrots |
| 1 cup boiling water | 1/2 cup chopped nuts |

Dissolve gelatin in hot water and add pineapple juice. Chill.

When this begins to thicken, add other ingredients.

Pour mixture into a mold and chill until set.

Unmold on lettuce.

Serve with mayonnaise.

Serves 6.

ANNA LEHMAN, *Boswell, Pa.*

## Cherry Salad

| | |
|---|---|
| 2 cups large Bing cherries | 2 tablespoons plain gelatin |
| 1 cup cherry juice | 1 cup orange juice |
| 1 cup sugar | 1 tablespoon lemon juice |
| English walnuts | |

Drain cherries.

Fill each cherry with a walnut half.

Place cherries in individual molds, filling each ½ full.

Dissolve sugar in cherry juice and bring to a boil. Remove from heat.

Soak gelatin in orange and lemon juice.

When dissolved, add to hot cherry juice.

When juice has cooled, pour over the cherries and allow to set.

Unmold on lettuce.

Serves 6.

MRS. HARRY FRANK, *East Petersburg, Pa.*

## Cottage Cheese and Pineapple Salad

| | |
|---|---|
| 1 package lemon or lime gelatin | ¼ teaspoon salt |
| 1 cup hot water | 1 cup cottage cheese |
| 1 cup pineapple juice | ½ cup chopped nuts |
| 1 cup crushed pineapple | Strips of green and red pepper |

Dissolve gelatin in hot water and add pineapple juice.

Chill until liquid begins to congeal.

Combine drained pineapple, cheese, nuts and salt and fold into gelatin mixture.

Pour into mold and chill until firm.

Unmold on lettuce and garnish with mayonnaise and strips of pepper.

Serves 6.

MRS. LYDIA BURTON, *Detroit, Mich.;* MRS. ARTHUR EBERSOLE, *Birch Tree, Mo.*

## Cranberry Salad

| | |
|---|---|
| ½ pound cranberries | ¼ cup chopped walnuts |
| 3 apples | 1 package cherry or strawberry gelatin |
| 1½ cups sugar | 1 cup hot water |
| 2 oranges or ½ cup crushed pineapple | 1 cup cold water |

Wash and grind cranberries through food chopper.

Pare and core apples and chop very fine.

Add chopped oranges, nuts and sugar.

Dissolve gelatin in hot water.

Add cold water.

When cool, add salad mixture.

Pour into mold and allow to congeal.

Unmold on lettuce.

Serves 6.

MABEL GEISER, *Seville, Ohio;* MARY E. SUTER, *Harrisonburg, Va.*
MRS. LEVI C. SCHROCK, *Kalona, Iowa*

## Crown Fruit Salad

| | |
|---|---|
| 1 tablespoon plain gelatin | 1 orange |
| 2 tablespoons cold water | 1/2 cup maraschino cherries |
| 1 cup fruit juice | 1/2 cup cream |
| 2 cups canned peaches or pears | 1/2 cup mayonnaise |

Soak gelatin in cold water.

Bring fruit juice to a boil and pour slowly over the gelatin. Cool.

Add cream to mayonnaise and stir until smooth.

Add mayonnaise to fruit juice and gelatin.

Blend well.

Cut peaches or pears into slices and maraschino cherries into halves.

When mixture begins to congeal, add fruit and cherries.

Pour into a mold and chill until firm.

Unmold on lettuce and garnish with clusters of grapes, bananas or
slices of canned fruit.

Serves 6.

MRS. BERTIE STALTER, *Elida, Ohio*

## Ginger Ale Salad

| | |
|---|---|
| 1 package lemon gelatin | 2 oranges |
| 1/3 cup hot water | 1 large grapefruit |
| 1 1/2 cups ginger ale | 1/2 cup diced celery |

Dissolve gelatin in hot water.

Add ginger ale and chill.

Peel oranges and grapefruit and remove sections with a sharp knife.

Add diced celery and fruit to gelatin when it begins to thicken.

Pour into mold and chill until firm.

Unmold on lettuce and serve with mayonnaise.

Serves 6.

NAOMI GROFF, *Lancaster, Pa.*

## Golden Glow Salad

| | |
|---|---|
| 1 package orange gelatin | 1 cup crushed pineapple |
| 1 cup boiling water | 1/4 teaspoon salt |
| 1 teaspoon lemon juice or vinegar | 1/4 cup maraschino cherries |
| 1 cup pineapple juice | Rind of 1 orange, ground |
| 1 cup grated carrots | |

Dissolve gelatin in boiling water.

Add pineapple and lemon juice and chill until slightly thickened.

Combine drained pineapple, grated carrots, cherries, orange rind and salt with gelatin.

Pour into mold and chill until firm.

Unmold on lettuce and serve with the following dressing:

| | |
|---|---|
| 1/4 cup pineapple juice | 1/4 cup sugar |
| 1/4 cup lemon juice | 1/2 cup whipped cream |
| 2 eggs | |

Combine eggs, juices and sugar and cook in top of double boiler until thick.

Add whipped cream just before serving.

Serves 6 to 8.

MRS. HOWARD STEVANUS, *Waterloo, Ont., Can.*

## New Manhattan Salad

| | |
|---|---|
| 1 package lemon gelatin | 1 cup tart apples, chopped |
| 1 cup boiling water | 1 cup English walnuts |
| 1 cup cold water | 1 cup chopped celery |
| 2 tablespoons vinegar | 1/4 teaspoon salt |

Dissolve gelatin in hot water.

Add cold water, salt and vinegar.

When slightly congealed, add the apples, nuts and celery.

Pour into mold and chill until firm.

Serve on lettuce.

Serves 6.

Dressing:

| | |
|---|---|
| 2/3 cup condensed milk | 1/2 teaspoon salt |
| 1/4 cup vinegar or lemon juice | 1 teaspoon dry mustard |
| 1 egg yolk | |

Combine ingredients and beat with a rotary beater until thick.

This makes 1¼ cups.

Use desired amount with salad.

MRS. LEIDY HUNSICKER, *Blooming Glen, Pa.*

## Perfection Salad

| | |
|---|---|
| 2 tablespoons plain gelatin | 1/2 cup sugar |
| 1/2 cup cold water | 1 teaspoon salt |
| 1/2 cup vinegar | 1 1/2 cups diced celery |
| Juice of 1 lemon | 1 1/2 cups shredded cabbage |
| 2 cups boiling water | 3 pimientos, chopped |

Soak gelatin in cold water.
Add hot water, vinegar, lemon juice, salt and sugar.
When jelly begins to thicken, add chopped vegetables.
Pour into mold and chill until firm.
Unmold on lettuce and garnish with mayonnaise.
Serves 6.

MRS. NOAH D. LEHMAN, *Orrville, Ohio*

## Pineapple-Cheese Salad

| | |
|---|---|
| 1 package lemon gelatin | 1 cup crushed pineapple |
| 1 cup hot water | 1/4 cup maraschino cherries |
| 1 cup pineapple juice | 1 package Philadelphia cream cheese |
| | (8 ounces) |

Dissolve gelatin in hot water.
Add pineapple juice and chill.
Mix to cheese 2 tablespoons cherry juice or cream.
When smooth, combine cheese with pineapple and chopped cherries.
When gelatin begins to thicken, add salad mixture.
Pour into mold and chill until firm.
Unmold on lettuce and garnish with mayonnaise and olives.
Serves 4 to 6.

MRS. DAVID MISHLER, *Johnstown, Pa.*

## Whipped Pineapple Salad

| | |
|---|---|
| 1 package lemon gelatin | 1 cup crushed pineapple |
| 1 cup hot water | 1 cup grated cheese |
| 1 cup cold water | 1 cup whipping cream |

Dissolve gelatin in hot water.
Add cold water and chill.
When jelly begins to thicken, whip it until light.
Add whipped cream, pineapple and cheese.
Pour into a mold and chill until firm.
Unmold and garnish as desired.
Serves 6.

MRS. CECIL SCHMIDT, *Greensburg, Kan.*

## Sweetheart Salad

| | |
|---|---|
| 2 cups crushed pineapple | 2 tablespoons lemon juice |
| 1/2 cup sugar | 2 tablespoons cherry juice |
| 1 1/2 tablespoons plain gelatin | 1 cup whipping cream |
| 1/4 cup cold water | 12 maraschino cherries |
| 6 ounces Philadelphia cream cheese | |

Dissolve gelatin in cold water.

Add pineapple to sugar. Bring to boiling point and add gelatin.

Stir until gelatin is dissolved.

Add lemon and cherry juice. Cool.

Mash cream cheese and add chopped cherries.

Combine with pineapple mixture, adding a small amount at a time.

Chill until slightly thickened.

Whip cream and blend with salad mixture.

Mold and chill.

Serves 8.

MRS. EPHRAIM LANDIS, *Blooming Glen, Pa.;* MRS. ROBERT NACE, *Souderton, Pa.*

## Jellied Tomato Salad

| | |
|---|---|
| 1 quart stewed tomatoes | 1 small onion |
| 2 tablespoons gelatin | 2 tablespoons sugar |
| ½ cup cold water | ½ teaspoon salt |
| 2 tablespoons celery leaves | ⅛ teaspoon pepper |

Cook tomatoes with seasoning. Strain.

Dissolve gelatin in cold water and add to hot tomato juice.

Pour into individual molds and chill until firm.

Unmold on lettuce and garnish with mayonnaise.

This salad may also be molded in a flat pan and cut in any desired shape.

Serves 8.

MRS. LEWIS H. REESOR, *Markham, Ont., Can.*

## Vegetable and Fruit Mold

| | |
|---|---|
| 1 package lemon gelatin | 1 cup diced celery |
| 1 cup boiling water | 1 cup grated cabbage |
| 1 cup cold water | 1 cup diced apples |
| 1 cup grated carrots | ½ cup chopped nuts |

Dissolve gelatin in hot water.

Add cold water and chill.

When gelatin begins to thicken, add grated carrots and cabbage, diced celery and apples.

Add chopped nuts and mix well.

Pour into mold and chill until firm.

Unmold on lettuce.

Serve with mayonnaise.

Serves 6.

MRS. JACOB F. KOLB, *Spring City, Pa.;* EDITH KEFFER, *Waterloo, Ont., Can.*

# MISCELLANEOUS SALADS
## Macaroni Salad

3 cups cooked macaroni
2 hard-cooked eggs
1 cup chopped celery
1 onion
1/2 head lettuce, shredded

Dressing:
1/2 cup sugar
1/2 cup vinegar
1/2 cup water
1 teaspoon salt
1/2 teaspoon dry mustard
1 tablespoon flour
2 eggs

Combine macaroni, chopped eggs and vegetables.

To make dressing, combine sugar, salt, mustard and flour. Add eggs and vinegar and mix well. Add water and stir until smooth. Cook until thickened.

Cool dressing slightly and pour over salad mixture.

Mix and serve.

Serves 8.

MRS. LABAN WADEL, *Shippensburg, Pa.*
MARY ELIZABETH LUTZ, *Elizabethtown, Pa.*

## Cracker Salad
### Old

18 soda crackers
1 1/2 cups tomato juice
1 cup chopped celery

1/4 cup chopped olives or sour pickles
1/2 cup mayonnaise

Crush crackers, breaking each into 4 or 5 pieces.

Add chopped celery and olives or pickles.

Season tomato juice with salt, sugar and pepper.

Pour juice over cracker mixture.

Add mayonnaise and mix slightly.

Serves 6.

MRS. AMOS K. MAST, *Cochranville, Pa.*; MARY SHANK, *Atglen, Pa.*

# SALAD DRESSINGS
## Cooked Salad Dressing (I)

1/2 cup sugar
1/2 cup vinegar
1/2 cup water
1 egg or 2 yolks

1 tablespoon cornstarch or flour
1 teaspoon dry mustard
1 teaspoon salt
1 tablespoon butter

Mix sugar, salt, cornstarch and mustard.

Add egg and beat well.

Add water and vinegar.

Cook in the top of a double boiler until thickened.
Add butter and serve on potato salad, lettuce or cabbage.
Makes 1½ cups.

MRS. SIMON P. KRAYBILL, *Elizabethtown, Pa.*; MRS. E. S. HALLMAN, *Tuleta, Texas*

## Cooked Dressing with Sour Cream (II)

| | |
|---|---|
| 1½ tablespoons flour | 3 tablespoons vinegar |
| 1 teaspoon salt | 2 tablespoons sugar |
| ½ teaspoon mustard | 1 cup sour cream |
| 1 egg | |

Mix sugar, flour, salt and mustard.
Add the egg and vinegar and mix well.
Add the sour cream and cook until dressing thickens.
Stir constantly.
Makes 1¼ cups.

MRS. EMILY KAUFFMAN, *Westover, Md.*; IDA MAE STECKLY, *Oakdale, Iowa*

## Cooked Salad Dressing with Evaporated Milk (III)

| | |
|---|---|
| 2 eggs, beaten | 2/3 cup vinegar |
| 1 teaspoon mustard | 1/3 cup water |
| 1 teaspoon salt | 1 cup evaporated milk |
| 1 cup sugar | |

Mix together the sugar, salt and mustard.
Add the beaten eggs and mix well.
Add vinegar and water and cook to a smooth paste.
Cool and add evaporated milk. Beat.
Makes 2 cups.

MRS. ANDREW K. STONER, *Bainbridge, Pa.*

## Cooked Mayonnaise

| | |
|---|---|
| 2 egg yolks | 1 teaspoon salt |
| 2 tablespoons vinegar | 1 cup salad oil |
| 2 tablespoons lemon juice | 1 tablespoon butter |
| ½ teaspoon mustard | 1/3 cup flour |
| ½ teaspoon sugar | 1½ cups water |

Put the first 7 ingredients together in a mixing bowl, but do not stir.
Make a white sauce of the butter, flour and water.
Pour hot sauce into first mixture and beat with a rotary egg beater
until thick and creamy.
This keeps in the refrigerator indefinitely.
Makes 2 cups.

ANNA HORST, *Blue Ball, Pa.*

## French Dressing

| | |
|---|---|
| 1 cup salad oil | 1 teaspoon grated onion |
| 1 cup vinegar | 1 tablespoon Worcestershire sauce |
| 2 tablespoons sugar | 1 cup catsup or |
| 1 teaspoon salt | condensed tomato soup |
| 1 teaspoon dry mustard | |

Mix sugar, salt, mustard and Worcestershire sauce together.

Add grated onion and catsup or tomato soup.

Add vinegar and pour on the oil slowly.

Place dressing in a bottle and keep in refrigerator.

Shake vigorously before using to blend ingredients.

Makes 1 pint dressing.

MRS. RUFUS BEACHY, *Mylo, N. D.;* ELVA GOOD, *Manheim, Pa.*

## Fruit Salad Dressing

| | |
|---|---|
| ½ cup lemon or orange juice | ½ cup sugar |
| ½ cup pineapple juice | 1 cup whipping cream |
| 2 eggs | ½ cup walnuts (optional) |
| 1½ tablespoons flour | |

Combine juices and stir slowly into sugar and flour mixture.

Cook in a double boiler until it thickens.

Add beaten eggs and cook 1 minute longer; remove from heat and cool.

Fold in whipped cream.

Makes 2½ cups dressing.

MRS. ELMER N. KAUFFMAN, *Manheim, Pa.*

## Mayonnaise

| | |
|---|---|
| 2 egg yolks | ½ teaspoon dry mustard |
| 1 teaspoon salt | 2 cups salad oil |
| ¼ teaspoon paprika | 4 tablespoons vinegar or |
| 2 teaspoons sugar | lemon juice |

Mix dry ingredients and moisten with vinegar or lemon juice.

Add mixture to beaten egg yolks.

Mix thoroughly and add the oil gradually, drop by drop at first.

Beat vigorously between additions of oil.

The mixture should become thick and smooth.

Makes approximately 3 cups dressing.

MRS. EDWARD YAUNCEY, *Lowville, N. Y.*

## Extender for Preceding Recipe

| | |
|---|---|
| 3 tablespoons cornstarch | 1 teaspoon salt |
| ¼ cup vinegar | 2 tablespoons sugar |
| 1 cup boiling water | |

Mix sugar and salt with the cornstarch.

Then add vinegar and boiling water.

Cook until thickened to a smooth paste.

Beat into the mayonnaise as soon as removed from the stove.

Mrs. Lou J. Miller, *Wellman, Iowa*

Variations may be made by adding tomato catsup, chopped pickles, sweet peppers or hard-cooked eggs to mayonnaise.

## Two-Minute Mayonnaise

| | |
|---|---|
| 1 egg, unbeaten | ¼ cup lemon juice or vinegar or a |
| 2 tablespoons sugar |    mixture of both |
| 1¼ teaspoons salt | 4 tablespoons cornstarch |
| ¼ teaspoon mustard | ¼ cup cold water |
| ¼ teaspoon paprika | 1 cup boiling water |
| ¾ cup salad oil | |

Place unbeaten egg in a bowl.

Add sugar, salt, mustard, paprika, oil and lemon juice or vinegar.

Do not beat.

Combine cornstarch and cold water and stir to a smooth paste.

Pour paste slowly into boiling water, stirring constantly, and cook until clear.

Add thickened mixture to ingredients in the bowl and beat with a rotary or electric beater until light.

For variation, add 1 cup of pineapple juice in place of the water in the cornstarch mixture.

One cup of whipped cream may also be blended into the mayonnaise with good results.

Mrs. Paul Bender, *Goshen, Ind.*

## Poppy Seed or Celery Seed Dressing

| | |
|---|---|
| 1 cup salad oil | 1 tablespoon grated onion |
| 1/3 cup vinegar | 1 teaspoon dry mustard |
| ½ cup sugar | 1 teaspoon salt |
| ½ teaspoon poppy seed or celery seed | |

Mix mustard, salt and sugar.

Add other ingredients and pour into a pint jar.

Keep in refrigerator and shake well before using.

Excellent served on grapefruit or orange slices.

Makes 1½ cups.

Zella Trimble, *Austin, Tex.*

# Cakes and Frostings

## Chapter VIII

DURING MY ROUNDS OF COLLECTING RECIPES I HAVE STUDIED A LARGE number of old handwritten notebooks that bear dates prior to the Civil War. As a result of this study, I have concluded that cake recipes held first place of importance to Grandmother. These cake recipes were not only the first ones recorded in her book but they occupied the greatest number of pages. This may be due to the fact that Grandmother recorded only those recipes which she did not use frequently enough to learn by memory.

Although there are numerous old cake recipes to be found, few of them are of any benefit to the ambitious young cake baker today. This is due to the fact that Grandmother took it for granted that anyone who could cook would know how to proceed without directions. She listed only the ingredients required without ever stating the procedure to follow. We can only guess if the recipe was meant for a loaf cake, a layer cake or a cookie.

Another characteristic regarding the earliest cake recipes is that many even failed to list flour among the essential ingredients. Again it must have been assumed that anyone would know to add enough flour to make a batter "just the right consistency."

When measurements for ingredients were given, they were usually of such nature that they are not meaningful today. One very old recipe calls for "two tins of flour and the third tin to the second ring." That may have meant a pint cup or a quart cup, or perhaps it referred to a special cup that is unknown to us at the present time. Another recipe called for a sixpenny crock of liquid and the third stated leavening in terms of five-cents worth of baking ammonia.

From a bride's book of 1844 comes a molasses cake recipe that calls for 10 "blubs" of molasses. This would indicate that the molasses was kept in a barrel and so much came out with each blub!

In Great-grandfather's day folks drove by horse and wagon 150 miles to Richmond, Virginia, once a year for sugar and other supplies. Thus we can understand why sugar was not plentiful enough to make fluffy frostings and decorate cakes as we do. Grandmother's two favorite "company cakes" were the rich pound cake that required no frosting, and the four-layered ribbon cake. Each of these layers was a different color: white, pink, yellow, and spice or chocolate. These layers were spread with bright currant jam and stacked one on top of another. From its lofty perch on the high cake stand this was a cake fit for a king!

The cake recipes in this chapter have been selected from approximately 600 recipes.

All have been tested in the laboratory and have been selected because they rated a high score.

## CAKES WITH SHORTENING

### Apple Butter Cake

| | |
|---|---|
| ½ cup shortening | 1 teaspoon cinnamon |
| 1 cup sugar | ½ teaspoon cloves |
| 4 eggs, beaten | ½ teaspoon nutmeg |
| 2½ cups all-purpose flour | 1 cup sour milk or buttermilk |
| 1½ teaspoons soda | 1 cup apple butter |
| ½ teaspoon salt | |

Cream the shortening.

Add sugar gradually and continue to cream until fluffy.

Add well-beaten eggs and mix thoroughly.

Sift flour; measure and sift again with salt, soda and spices.

Add dry ingredients alternately with sour milk.

Add apple butter and blend well into mixture.

Pour into a greased loaf pan 5 x 9 x 4 inches.

Bake at 350° for 45 to 50 minutes.

This cake has a delicious flavor and excellent keeping qualities.

Mrs. Ida Oswald, *Hudson, Ohio;* Mrs. Timothy Showalter, *Broadway, Va.*

## Applesauce Cake

| | |
|---|---|
| ½ cup shortening | 1 teaspoon soda dissolved in |
| 1½ cups sugar | 2 tablespoons hot water |
| 2 eggs, well beaten | 1 teaspoon cinnamon |
| 1½ cups applesauce, unsweetened | ½ teaspoon cloves |
| 2½ cups cake flour | 1 cup chopped seedless raisins |
| ½ teaspoon salt | ½ cup chopped nuts (optional) |

Cream shortening. Add sugar gradually and continue to beat until fluffy.

Add well-beaten eggs and combine thoroughly.

Sift flour; measure and sift again with salt and spices.

Add ⅓ of the applesauce to creamed mixture and blend.

Add dry ingredients alternately with remaining applesauce, beating thoroughly after each addition.

Dissolve soda in hot water and add to mixture. Mix thoroughly.

Chop raisins and nuts on a board and flour lightly.

Fold these into mixture.

Pour into a large, greased loaf pan 5 x 9 x 4 inches.

Bake at 350° for approximately 1 hour.

Excellent flavor and keeps well.

Mrs. Susan B. Lehman, *Chambersburg, Pa.*
Mrs. Quintus Leatherman, *Souderton, Pa.*

For variation, replace half of the applesauce with ¾ cup strained apricot pulp.

Mrs. C. R. Eby, *Hagerstown, Md.*

## Banana Cake

| | |
|---|---|
| ½ cup shortening | 2/3 teaspoon soda |
| 1 cup sugar | 5 tablespoons sour milk |
| 2 eggs | 1 cup banana pulp |
| 2 cups cake flour | 1 teaspoon vanilla |
| ½ teaspoon salt | |

Cream shortening.

Add sugar gradually and continue to beat until fluffy.

Add beaten eggs and vanilla and beat until light.

Sift flour; measure and sift again with dry ingredients.

Add dry ingredients alternately with milk.

Beat thoroughly after each addition.

Fold in banana pulp until well blended into mixture.

Pour into greased layer pans and bake at 350° for 30 minutes.

This makes 2 (9 inch) layers.

A very moist and tender cake.

RUTH KAUFFMAN, *Millersburg, Ohio*

## Boiled Raisin Cake

| | |
|---|---|
| 1 pound seedless raisins | 1½ teaspoons soda |
| 2 cups water | ¼ teaspoon nutmeg |
| 2/3 cup shortening | ½ teaspoon cloves |
| 1½ cups sugar (half brown and half white sugar) | 1 teaspoon cinnamon |
| | 1 cup sour milk or buttermilk |
| 3 cups all-purpose flour | 1 cup chopped nuts |
| 1 teaspoon salt | 1 teaspoon vanilla |

Chop raisins very fine and boil in the water until most of it is absorbed.

Add shortening to raisins and stir until it is melted.

Then add sugar and stir until it is entirely dissolved.

Sift flour; measure and sift again with salt, soda and spices.

Pour mixture into a bowl and add sifted dry ingredients alternately with milk.

Beat thoroughly after each addition.

Chop nuts and dust lightly with flour.

Add nuts to mixture and blend together.

Pour into a large, greased loaf pan 5 x 9 x 4 inches.

Bake at 325° for 1 hour and 15 minutes.

A splendid fruit type of cake with excellent keeping qualities.

MIRIAM SHAFFER, *Martinsburg, Pa.*

## Burnt Sugar Cake

| | |
|---|---|
| 1¾ cups sugar | ½ teaspoon salt |
| ¼ cup boiling water | 2½ teaspoons baking powder |
| ¾ cup shortening | 1 cup milk |
| 3 eggs, separated | 1 teaspoon vanilla |
| 2¾ cups cake flour | |

Melt ¼ cup sugar in a heavy pan.

Add boiling water and stir well. Set aside to cool.

Cream shortening and add remaining sugar gradually (1¼ cups).
Add beaten egg yolks and mix thoroughly.
Sift flour; measure and sift again with salt and baking powder.
Add sifted dry ingredients alternately with milk.
Beat thoroughly after each addition.
Add vanilla and burnt sugar mixture.
Blend well.
Fold in stiffly beaten egg whites.
Pour into greased layer pans.
Bake at 350° for 25 to 30 minutes.
Makes 2 (9 inch) layers.

Mrs. John Martin, *Hutchinson, Kan.;* Katie Rutt, *New Holland, Pa.*

## Busy Day Cake

| | |
|---|---|
| 1 2/3 cups all-purpose flour or | 1/3 cup shortening |
| 2 cups cake flour | 1 egg |
| 1 cup sugar | 2/3 cup milk |
| ½ teaspoon salt | 1 teaspoon vanilla |
| 2½ teaspoons baking powder | |

For ease in measuring: Pour milk into measuring cup up to ⅔ mark.
Add shortening, keeping it under the milk until it reaches the line
    indicating 1 cup.
Sift flour; measure and add sugar, salt, and baking powder. Sift again.
Add shortening, milk, unbeaten egg and vanilla all at once to sifted
    dry ingredients.
Beat well for 2½ minutes (electric mixer preferred).
If beating is done by hand, it is best to count the strokes. Try to average
    130 strokes per minute. This should be done rather rapidly.
Pour into a greased oblong pan 8 x 12 inches.
Bake at 350° for 35 to 40 minutes.
While cake is baking, mix together the following:

| | |
|---|---|
| 3 tablespoons melted butter | 2/3 cup brown sugar, packed |
| 4 tablespoons cream | ½ cup shredded coconut |

Spread mixture on cake while it is warm.
Do not remove cake from pan.
Put cake under the broiler until frosting begins to bubble.

Mrs. Tom Miller, *Walnut Creek, Ohio*

## Butter Cup Cake

| | |
|---|---|
| ½ cup shortening | ½ teaspoon soda |
| 1½ cups sugar | 1 cup buttermilk or sour milk |

2 eggs
1/2 teaspoon salt
2 1/3 cups cake flour
1 1/2 teaspoons baking powder

1 teaspoon vanilla or
1/2 teaspoon each of lemon, orange,
and almond extract

Cream shortening and add sugar gradually.

When mixture is fluffy, add well-beaten eggs and beat thoroughly.

Sift flour; measure and add salt, baking powder and soda. Sift again.

Add dry ingredients alternately with milk and flavoring.

Beat thoroughly after each addition.

Pour into greased layer pans.

Bake at 350° for 30 to 35 minutes.

Makes 2 (8 inch) layers.

A delicious cake with good flavor and texture.

MRS. DANIEL MARTIN, *Waynesboro, Va.*

## Chocolate Chip Cake

1/2 cup shortening
1 cup corn syrup (light or dark)
2 eggs
2 1/2 cups cake flour
1/2 teaspoon salt

2 1/2 teaspoons baking powder
1/2 cup milk
4 ounces chocolate chips
1 teaspoon vanilla
2 teaspoons grated orange rind

Cream shortening and add syrup.

Blend together and add beaten eggs. Beat again.

Sift flour; measure and add salt and baking powder. Sift again.

Add sifted dry ingredients alternately with milk and flavoring.

Beat thoroughly after each addition.

Fold in chocolate chips.

Pour mixture into greased layer pans.

Bake at 350° for 25 to 30 minutes.

Makes 2 (9 inch) layers.

Serve with sea foam or Seven-Minute Frosting (page 247).

MRS. TOM MILLER, *Walnut Creek, Ohio*

## Chocolate Cake

### *Modern Method*

Sift together:

1 3/4 cups cake flour
1 teaspoon baking powder
1 teaspoon soda
1 teaspoon salt

1 teaspoon cinnamon
1/2 cup cocoa
1 1/2 cups sugar

Add:

½ cup shortening and rub well into mixture
½ cup cooled strong coffee
1/3 cup buttermilk or sour milk

Beat 150 strokes.

Add:

Another 1/3 cup buttermilk or sour milk
2 eggs, unbeaten

Beat enough to blend ingredients thoroughly.

Pour into 2 greased layer pans.

Bake at 350° for 30 minutes.

Makes 2 (9 inch) layers.

This is a dark, rich chocolate cake.

MRS. JAMES CLYMER, *Lancaster, Pa.*

## Chocolate Nut Loaf

| | |
|---|---|
| I cup shortening | I teaspoon soda |
| 1¾ cups sugar | 3 (I oz.) squares chocolate |
| 4 eggs | I cup buttermilk or sour milk |
| 2½ cups cake flour | I cup chopped nuts |
| ½ teaspoon salt | I teaspoon vanilla |

Cream shortening and add sugar gradually.

Beat until fluffy.

Add well-beaten eggs and beat again.

Melt chocolate over water and allow to cool.

Sift flour; measure and add salt and soda. Sift again.

Add sifted dry ingredients alternately with milk and flavoring.

Beat thoroughly after each addition.

Add melted chocolate and chopped nuts.

Blend into mixture.

Pour into a large, greased loaf pan 5 x 9 x 4 inches.

Bake at 350° for 1 hour.

A very moist cake.

MRS. ABRAM SHANK, *Hagerstown, Md.*

## Red Chocolate Cake

First Part:

½ cup sugar
2/3 cup cocoa
½ cup water

Mix together and bring to boiling point. Cool.

Second Part:

| | |
|---|---|
| ½ cup shortening | I teaspoon soda |
| I cup sugar | ½ teaspoon salt |
| 2 eggs | ½ cup water |
| 2 cups cake flour | I teaspoon vanilla |

Cream shortening.

Add sugar gradually and beat until fluffy.

Add eggs and beat thoroughly.

Sift flour; measure and add salt and soda. Sift again.

Add sifted dry ingredients alternately with water and vanilla.

Combine with first mixture.

Pour into greased layer pans.

Bake at 350° for 30 minutes.

Makes 2 (8 inch) layers.

A delicious cake.

MRS. ALICE SCHROCK, *Tiskilwa, Ill.*

## Devil's Food Cake

| | |
|---|---|
| ½ cup shortening | ¼ teaspoon salt |
| 1¾ cups sugar | 1¼ teaspoons soda |
| 2 eggs | ½ cup sour milk or buttermilk |
| ½ cup cocoa | I cup boiling water |
| 2¼ cups cake flour | I teaspoon vanilla |

Cream shortening and add sugar gradually.

Beat until fluffy.

Add eggs and continue to beat. Add vanilla.

Sift flour; measure and sift again with cocoa and salt. Add alternately
with sour milk.

Add soda to boiling water, when dissolved add all at once to mixture.

Stir only enough to blend ingredients.

This makes a very thin batter.

Pour immediately into greased layer pans.

Bake at 350° for 25 to 30 minutes.

Makes 2 (8 inch) layers.

A very moist and fine-textured cake.

MRS. PERRY HOCHSTETLER, *Millersburg, Ohio*

## Prize Devil's Food Cake

### *With Sweet Milk*

| | |
|---|---|
| 2/3 cup shortening | 2¾ teaspoons baking powder |
| 1½ cups sugar | 3 one-ounce squares chocolate |

3 eggs, beaten
2 cups cake flour
½ teaspoon salt

¾ cup sweet milk
1 teaspoon vanilla

Melt chocolate in top of double boiler. Cool.
Cream shortening.
Add sugar gradually and beat until fluffy.
Add beaten eggs and continue to beat.
Add melted chocolate and blend into mixture.
Sift flour; measure and add salt and baking powder. Sift again.
Add sifted dry ingredients alternately with milk and flavoring.
Beat thoroughly after each addition.
Pour into greased layer pans.
Bake at 350° for 30 minutes.
Makes 2 (8 inch) layers.

Mrs. Jacob Neuenschwander, *Apple Creek, Ohio*

## Mahogany Cake

¾ cup shortening
2 cups brown sugar
3 eggs
3 cups cake flour
½ teaspoon salt

½ teaspoon soda
1 teaspoon baking powder
4 tablespoons cocoa
1½ cups thick sour milk
1 teaspoon vanilla

Cream shortening and add sugar gradually.
Beat until fluffy.
Add eggs and continue to beat.
Sift flour; measure and add salt, baking powder and soda. Sift again.
Add sifted dry ingredients alternately with sour milk and flavoring.
Beat thoroughly after each addition.
Pour into greased layer pans.
Bake at 350° for 25 to 30 minutes.
Makes 2 (8 inch) layers.
This cake is milder in flavor and lighter in color than the usual chocolate
cake.

Mrs. Edgar Strite, *Hagerstown, Md.*

## Saucepan Fudge Cake

Mix together:
4 tablespoons cocoa
½ cup boiling water
5 tablespoons shortening

Cook together for 2½ minutes.
Set aside to cool.

Then sift together:

| | |
|---|---|
| I cup flour | I teaspoon baking powder |
| ½ teaspoon soda | ¼ teaspoon salt |

Add to cooled mixture and mix thoroughly.

Add:

| | |
|---|---|
| I cup sugar | ¼ cup buttermilk or sour milk |
| I egg, well beaten | I teaspoon vanilla |

Beat until ingredients are well blended.

Pour into a greased loaf or layer pans.

If baked in a loaf, bake at 350° for 50 minutes.

If baked in layer pans, bake at 350° for 25 to 30 minutes.

Makes 1 loaf 3½ x 8 x 1½ inches or 1 (9 inch) layer.

Use a cream cheese frosting (page 246).

RUTH FRIEDT, *Medina, Ohio*

## Cinnamon Loaf Cake

| | |
|---|---|
| ¾ cup fat | ½ teaspoon salt |
| 1¾ cups sugar | 3½ teaspoons baking powder |
| 4 eggs | I cup milk |
| 3½ cups all-purpose flour or | I teaspoon vanilla |
| 4 cups cake flour | |

Cream shortening. Add sugar gradually and continue to beat until fluffy.

Add eggs, one at a time and beat until light.

Sift flour; measure and sift again with salt and baking powder. Add dry
ingredients alternately with milk and flavoring.

Beat thoroughly after each addition.

Pour into a large greased loaf pan.

One-half of recipe makes a loaf 3½ x 7 x 4 inches.

As soon as cake is removed from oven, spread with butter and sprinkle
with a cinnamon-sugar mixture.

This is not a rich cake, but is ideal served for lunch or toasted for
breakfast.

MRS. NOAH MARTIN, *Paramount, Md.*

## Coconut Cake

| | |
|---|---|
| I cup shortening | 2½ teaspoons baking powder |
| 1¾ cups sugar | I cup milk |
| 4 eggs, separated | I cup grated coconut |
| 3¼ cups cake flour | I teaspoon vanilla |
| ½ teaspoon salt | |

Cream shortening.

Add sugar gradually and beat until fluffy.

Add egg yolks and continue to beat.
Sift flour; measure and add salt and baking powder. Sift again.
Add dry ingredients alternately with milk and flavoring.
Beat thoroughly after each addition.
Fold in grated coconut and stiffly beaten egg whites.
Pour into greased layer pans.
Bake at 350° for 30 minutes.
Makes 3 (8 inch) layers.
This cake has an excellent flavor.

Mrs. Mary Burkholder, *Hagerstown, Md.*

## Cream Almond Cake

| | |
|---|---|
| 1 cup shortening | 2 teaspoons baking powder |
| 1½ cups sugar | 1 cup milk |
| 3 cups cake flour | 5 egg whites |
| ½ teaspoon salt | 1 teaspoon almond extract |

Cream shortening.
Add sugar gradually and beat until fluffy.
Sift flour; measure and add salt and baking powder. Sift again.
Add sifted dry ingredients alternately with milk and flavoring.
Beat thoroughly after each addition.
Fold in stiffly beaten egg whites.
Pour into greased layer pans.
Bake at 350° for 30 minutes.
Makes 3 (8 inch) layers.
An excellent white cake; light, moist and velvety.
A suggestion for topping is to sprinkle top of cake with shredded
coconut before putting into oven.
This will turn a golden brown while baking and can be used in place of
frosting.

Mrs. Jacob Grove, *Hagerstown, Md.*

## Date-Nut Loaf

| | |
|---|---|
| 1 pound walnut meats | 4 eggs, separated |
| 1 pound dates, chopped | ½ teaspoon salt |
| 1 cup all-purpose flour | 2 teaspoons baking powder |
| 1 cup sugar | 1 teaspoon vanilla |

Sift flour; measure and add salt and baking powder. Sift again.
Add to chopped dates and whole kernels of nuts.
Add sugar to mixture and stir until well blended.
Then add well-beaten egg yolks and beat.
Fold in stiffly beaten egg whites and vanilla.

Pour into a greased loaf pan 4½ x 9 x 4 inches.

Bake at 300° for 1½ hours.

A chewy cake that makes a good substitute for fruit cake at Christmas. Its flavor improves if allowed to stand for a time.

MRS. WARD SHANK, *Broadway, Va.;* MRS. NOAH ROTH, *Canby, Ore.*

## Dream Cake

Bottom part:

| | |
|---|---|
| ½ cup butter | 2 tablespoons sugar |
| 1 cup flour | |

Rub together like pastry and pat into a pan 8 x 12 inches.

Bake at 375° until light brown.

While this is baking, make top part as follows:

| | |
|---|---|
| 1½ cups brown sugar | 2 tablespoons flour |
| 2 eggs, well beaten | 1 teaspoon baking powder |
| 1 cup walnuts | ¼ teaspoon salt |
| ½ cup shredded coconut | 1 teaspoon vanilla |

Mix together as listed and pour mixture over bottom part.

Return to oven and bake at 350° for 35 minutes.

When slightly warm, cut in squares and roll in powdered sugar.

MARY KEFFER, *Waterloo, Ont., Can.;* MRS. ALVIN N. ROTH, *Wellesley, Ont., Can.*

## Dried Apple Cake

| | |
|---|---|
| 1 cup dried apples | 1¾ cups all-purpose flour |
| 1 cup dark syrup | 1 teaspoon baking soda |
| 1 egg | 1 teaspoon cinnamon |
| ¾ cup sour cream | ½ teaspoon cloves |
| 1 cup sugar | ½ teaspoon salt |

Soak dried apples overnight.

In the morning chop in small pieces and cook slowly in the syrup for 45 minutes.

While apples cool, pour sour cream into a bowl.

Add egg and beat thoroughly.

Add sugar and continue to beat.

Sift flour; measure and add salt, soda, and cloves. Sift again.

Add sifted dry ingredients to mixture.

Beat thoroughly and then add apples. Blend together.

Pour into a greased loaf pan 5 x 9 x 4 inches.

Bake at 325° for 1 hour.

This cake has an excellent flavor.

MRS. DAVID SWOPE, *Harrisonburg, Va.*

## Fruit Cake (Dark)

Sift together:

|  |  |
|---|---|
| 3 cups cake flour | 1/4 teaspoon nutmeg |
| 2 teaspoons baking powder | 1/4 teaspoon mace |
| 1 1/2 teaspoons cinnamon | 1/2 teaspoon salt |
| 1 teaspoon cloves |  |

Cream together:

|  |  |
|---|---|
| 1 cup shortening | 3 eggs, unbeaten |
| 1 1/2 cups brown sugar |  |

Cut with coarse blade of food grinder or chop very fine:

|  |  |
|---|---|
| 2 cups raisins | 1 cup figs |
| 2 cups dates |  |

Chop with a knife:

|  |  |
|---|---|
| 2 cups nuts | 2 tablespoons candied lemon peel |
| 1 cup candied cherries | 1/2 cup candied pineapple |
| 2 tablespoons candied orange peel | 1/4 cup candied citron |

Method of mixing:

To creamed shortening and sugar mixture add dry ingredients alternately with ½ cup peach or grape juice and 1 cup of jam (any kind).

To this mixture add lightly floured, chopped fruits and nuts.

Mix thoroughly.

Line a large tube or loaf pan with waxed paper.

Pour mixture into a greased pan.

Bake at 275° for 1 hour and then at 300° for approximately 2 more hours.

If top browns too soon, cover with brown paper.

This cake is best if made about Thanksgiving and kept in a tight container until Christmas.

MRS. JACOB SUDERMAN, *Goshen, Ind.;* MRS. GRACE WINGARD YODER, *Elverson, Pa.*

## Fruit Cake (White)

|  |  |
|---|---|
| 1/4 pound mixed lemon, orange and citron peel (candied) | 2 1/2 cups cake flour |
| 1 1/4 pounds (4 cups) crystallized fruit— cherries, apricots, pineapple and plums | 1 teaspoon baking powder |
|  | 1/2 teaspoon salt |
|  | 1 cup shortening |
| 1/2 cup preserved ginger | 1 cup sugar |
| 1/4 pound maraschino cherries | 1 tablespoon lemon juice |
| 1/4 pound blanched almonds | 8 egg whites |

Cut peel and crystallized fruit in thin slices.

Blanch almonds by allowing to stand in boiling water for 5 minutes.

Slip off skins and dry.

Sift flour; measure and add baking powder and salt. Sift again.

Add 1 cup of this mixture to sliced peel, fruit and nuts. Stir well.

Cream shortening until light.

Add ½ cup sugar and remaining flour gradually; beat until fluffy.

Add floured fruits and nuts.

Mix well.

Add lemon juice to egg whites and beat until stiff.

Fold into beaten whites the remaining ½ cup of sugar.

Fold egg whites into cake mixture.

Bake in large tube pan or 2 loaf pans 5 x 9 x 4 inches lined with waxed paper.

Bake at 250° for approximately 3 hours.

Makes a cake weighing 3½ to 4 pounds.

This cake is very attractive if whole almonds and pieces of colored fruit are arranged so as to make a design on top of the cake.

MRS. CARL G. SHOWALTER, *Broadway, Va.*

## Fruit Cake (Unbaked)

| | |
|---|---|
| 1 pound graham crackers | 1 cup nut meats |
| 1 pound seedless raisins | 1 pound marshmallows |
| 1 pound dried figs | 1 pint whipping cream |
| ½ cup maraschino cherries | |

Roll graham crackers very fine.

Chop cherries, figs, nuts and marshmallows.

Leave raisins whole unless very large.

Mix these ingredients together thoroughly.

Whip cream and fold into mixture.

Pour into an oblong loaf pan 5 x 9 x 4 inches. Pat mixture with bowl of spoon to make it smooth on top.

Place in refrigerator overnight.

When ready to serve, cut in slices and roll in powdered sugar.

This is delicious.

MRS. WALTER BURKHOLDER, *Harrisonburg, Va.*
MRS. OWEN F. SHOWALTER, *Broadway, Va.*

## Ice Water Cake

| | |
|---|---|
| ½ cup shortening | 1½ cups ice water |
| 2 cups sugar | 1 teaspoon vanilla |
| 3½ cups cake flour | ¼ teaspoon almond extract |
| ¾ teaspoon salt | 4 egg whites |
| 3 teaspoons baking powder | |

Cream shortening.

Add sugar gradually and beat until fluffy.

Sift flour; measure and add salt and baking powder. Sift again.
Add sifted dry ingredients alternately with ice water and flavoring.
Beat thoroughly after each addition.
Fold in stiffly beaten egg whites.
Pour into greased layer pans.
Bake at 350° for 30 minutes.
Makes 2 (8 inch) layers.
An excellent white cake.

MRS. S. J. BUCHER, *Harman, W. Va.*

## Lady Baltimore Cake

¾ cup shortening
1¾ cups sugar
3 eggs, separated
3 cups cake flour

½ teaspoon salt
3 teaspoons baking powder
1 cup milk
1 teaspoon vanilla or almond extract

Cream shortening.
Add sugar gradually and beat until fluffy.
Add egg yolks and beat thoroughly.
Sift flour; measure and add salt and baking powder. Sift again.
Add sifted dry ingredients alternately with milk and flavoring.
Beat thoroughly after each addition.
Fold in stiffly beaten egg whites.
Pour into greased layer pans.
Bake at 350° for 25 to 30 minutes.
Makes 3 (8 inch) layers.
An excellent plain or basic cake.

KATIE RUTT, *New Holland, Pa.*

## Maraschino Cherry Cake

Sift together:

2½ cups cake flour
1½ cups sugar

3 teaspoons baking powder
½ teaspoon salt

Add:

½ cup shortening
¼ cup maraschino cherry juice

½ cup milk
16 maraschino cherries, cut in eighths

Cut shortening into sifted dry ingredients. Add milk and cherry juice.
Beat vigorously with spoon or on medium speed of electric mixer for
2 minutes. Fold in cherries.

Add:

4 large unbeaten egg whites

Beat 2 more minutes.
Fold in ½ cup chopped nuts.
Pour in greased layer pans.
Bake at 350° for 30 minutes.
Makes 2 (9 inch) layers.

Rosa Wagler, *Loogootee, Ind.;* Esther King, *Parkesburg, Pa.*

## Marble Cake

White part:

| | |
|---|---|
| ½ cup shortening | ¼ teaspoon salt |
| 1 cup sugar | ½ cup sweet milk |
| 2½ cups cake flour | 4 egg whites |
| 2 teaspoons baking powder | 1 teaspoon vanilla |

Cream shortening.
Add sugar gradually and beat until fluffy.
Sift flour; measure and add salt and baking powder. Sift again.
Add sifted dry ingredients alternately with milk and flavoring.
Beat thoroughly after each addition.
Fold in stiffly beaten egg whites.

Dark part:

| | |
|---|---|
| ½ cup shortening | ¼ teaspoon salt |
| 1 cup brown sugar | 1 teaspoon each of cinnamon and |
| 4 egg yolks | cloves |
| ½ cup molasses | ½ teaspoon nutmeg |
| 2 cups cake flour | 1 cup sour milk |
| 1 teaspoon soda | |

Cream shortening.
Add sugar gradually and beat until fluffy.
Add molasses and egg yolks.
Beat until thoroughly blended.
Sift flour; measure and add soda, salt and spices. Sift again.
Add sifted dry ingredients alternately with sour milk.
Beat thoroughly after each addition.
Drop alternate spoonfuls of each batter into large, greased tube pan
    so as to make a marbled effect.
Bake at 350° for 1 hour.
Makes a very large cake.
This cake will not keep unless it is put under lock and key!

Mrs. John A. Rhodes, *Dayton, Va.*

When cold, cover with the following creamy cocoa frosting:

1/4 cup vegetable shortening
3 tablespoons cocoa
3 cups powdered sugar

1/4 teaspoon salt
I teaspoon vanilla
1/4 cup strong coffee

Blend shortening, salt and vanilla together.

Sift cocoa and powdered sugar and add to mixture alternately with coffee.

Stir until creamy and spread on cake.

SARAH M. GEHMAN, *Bally, Pa.*

## My Grandmother's Favorite Cake (Rochester Cake)

1/2 cup shortening
1 1/2 cups sugar
2 eggs
3 cups all-purpose flour
1/2 teaspoon salt

1 1/2 teaspoons soda
2 teaspoons cinnamon
I teaspoon cloves
I teaspoon nutmeg
1 1/2 cups sour milk

Cream shortening.

Add sugar gradually and beat until fluffy.

Add eggs and beat thoroughly.

Sift flour; measure and add salt, soda and spices. Sift again.

Add dry ingredients alternately with sour milk.

Beat thoroughly after each addition.

Pour into greased layer pans.

Bake at 350° for 30 minutes.

Makes 2 (9 inch) layers.

Filling:

3/4 cup sugar
2 tablespoons butter
I tablespoon cornstarch

3/4 cup raisins
I cup water

Combine cornstarch and sugar.

Add water and raisins.

Cook in a double boiler until thick and clear.

Add butter and remove from heat.

Spread between layers and on top of cake.

This is a very old recipe and makes a delicious cake.

MRS. EZRA SCHLABACH, *Goshen, Ind.*

## Nut Cake

1/2 cup shortening
1 1/2 cups sugar
3 eggs
2 1/2 cups cake flour
1/2 teaspoon salt

2 teaspoons baking powder
I cup milk
I cup chopped nuts
I teaspoon vanilla

Cream shortening.

Add sugar gradually and beat until fluffy.

Add egg yolks and beat until well blended.

Sift flour; measure and add salt and baking powder. Sift again.

Add dry ingredients alternately with milk and flavoring.

Beat thoroughly after each addition.

Fold in chopped nuts and stiffly beaten egg whites.

Pour into greased loaf or layer pans.

Bake at 350° for 30 minutes for layer cake and 1 hour for loaf cake.

Makes 2 (9 inch) layers or 1 loaf 4 x 8 x 3½ inches.

Mrs. N. G. Keyser, *Souderton, Pa.*

## Orange Layer Cake

| | |
|---|---|
| ¾ cup shortening | 1½ teaspoons grated orange rind |
| 2 cups sugar | ½ cup orange juice |
| 2 egg yolks | ¾ cup water |
| 3¼ cups cake flour | ½ cup moist shredded coconut |
| ½ teaspoon salt | 4 egg whites |
| 4 teaspoons baking powder | |

Cream shortening.

Add sugar gradually and beat until fluffy.

Add grated orange rind and beaten egg yolks. Beat again.

Sift flour; measure and add salt and baking powder. Sift again.

Add dry ingredients alternately with orange juice and water.

Beat just enough to blend ingredients.

Fold in shredded coconut and stiffly beaten egg whites.

Pour into greased layer pans.

Bake at 350° for 30 minutes.

Makes 3 (9 inch) layers.

Martha Witmer, *Columbiana, Ohio*

Filling:

| | |
|---|---|
| Juice and rind of 1 orange | 1 egg |
| 1 cup cold water | 1 tablespoon cornstarch |
| 1 cup sugar | |

Mix sugar and cornstarch together.

Add cold water to make a smooth paste.

Add orange juice and rind and beaten egg.

Beat until well blended.

Cook until thick and clear.

Spread between layers.

Phyanna Bauman, *St. Jacobs, Ont., Can.*

## Picnic Cake

| | |
|---|---|
| ½ cup shortening | ½ teaspoon salt |
| 1½ cups sugar | 3 teaspoons baking powder |
| 2 eggs | 1 cup milk |
| 2½ cups cake flour | 1 teaspoon vanilla |

Cream shortening.

Add sugar gradually and beat until fluffy.

Add eggs and beat until well blended.

Sift flour; measure and add salt and baking powder. Sift again.

Add dry ingredients alternately with milk and flavoring.

Beat thoroughly after each addition.

Pour into greased flat pan 7 x 10 x 1¼ inches.

Then make the following frosting:

| | |
|---|---|
| 12 marshmallows cut crosswise and placed on batter | ½ cup brown sugar |
| | ½ cup chopped nuts |

Mix sugar and nuts together and sprinkle over marshmallows.

Bake at 350° for 30 to 35 minutes.

MRS. MOSE HOFFMAN, *Goshen, Ind.*

## Pineapple Layer Cake

| | |
|---|---|
| ½ cup shortening | ¼ teaspoon soda |
| 1 cup sugar | 1½ teaspoons baking powder |
| 2 eggs | ¼ teaspoon each of almond, lemon |
| 1¾ cups cake flour | and vanilla extract |
| ¼ teaspoon salt | 2/3 cup crushed pineapple |

Cream shortening.

Add sugar gradually and beat until fluffy.

Add eggs and flavoring and beat until well blended.

Sift flour; measure and add salt, soda and baking powder. Sift again.

Add sifted dry ingredients alternately with crushed pineapple.

Mix together well.

Pour into greased layer pans.

Bake at 350° for 30 minutes.

Makes 2 (8 inch) layers.

MRS. RUFUS BEACHY, *Mylo, N. D.*

## Pork Cake

| | |
|---|---|
| 1 pound of ground pork | 5½ cups all-purpose flour |
| 2 cups boiling water | 1 tablespoon each of cloves and nutmeg |
| 2 cups sugar | |
| 1 cup molasses | 2 tablespoons cinnamon |
| 1 pound raisins | 1¼ teaspoons soda |

| ¼ pound citron | I cup chopped nuts |
| ½ teaspoon salt | I cup gum drops, chopped |

Pour boiling water over pork and allow to stand until almost cool.

Add soda to molasses and mix with sugar, combine with pork and blend together.

Sift flour; measure and add salt, soda and spices. Sift again.

Add dry ingredients. Mix together well.

Fold in chopped fruits, nuts and candy.

Pour into large, greased loaf pans.

Bake at 275° for 2½ to 3 hours.

One-half of recipe makes 1 large loaf 5 x 9 x 4 inches.

This is a good substitute for fruit cake and keeps for weeks.

MRS. MARK C. SHOWALTER, *Broadway, Va.*
ELIZABETH SHOWALTER, *Waynesboro, Va.*

## Potato Cake

| 2/3 cup shortening | 2 tablespoons cocoa |
| 2 cups sugar | I teaspoon cinnamon |
| 4 eggs | ½ teaspoon cloves |
| 2 cups cake flour | I cup chopped nuts |
| ½ teaspoon salt | I teaspoon vanilla |
| 2 teaspoons baking powder | I cup hot mashed potatoes |
| ½ cup milk | (not seasoned) |

Cream shortening.

Add sugar gradually and beat until fluffy.

Add eggs and beat until light.

Add hot mashed potatoes and blend together.

Sift flour; measure and add salt, baking powder, cocoa and spices. Sift again.

Add dry ingredients alternately with milk and vanilla.

Beat thoroughly after each addition.

Fold in slightly floured, chopped nuts.

Pour into greased loaf or layer pans.

Bake layers at 350° for 30 minutes and loaf for 1 hour.

Makes 2 (8 inch) layers or 1 loaf 4 x 8 x 3½ inches.

MRS. HERMAN RINKENBERGER, *Bradford, Ill.*

## Old-time Pound Cake

| 1½ cups butter | 8 eggs |
| 2 cups sugar | ½ teaspoon baking powder |
| 2¾ cups all-purpose flour or | ½ teaspoon salt |
| 3 cups cake flour | I teaspoon vanilla or lemon extract |

Cream butter.

Add sugar gradually and beat until fluffy.

Add eggs, 1 at a time, beating vigorously after each addition.

Sift flour; measure and sift again with salt and baking powder.

Add sifted dry ingredients alternately with eggs and flavoring.

Beat mixture until it is light enough to float when a little is dropped in water.

Pour into greased tube, loaf pan.

Bake at 350° for 1 hour.

This is a rich cake of golden-yellow color and a favorite of Grandmother's day.

MRS. RALPH HEATWOLE, *Dayton, Va.*

## Prune Cake

1/3 cup shortening
1 cup sugar
2 eggs
2½ cups cake flour
½ teaspoon salt

1 teaspoon soda
½ teaspoon cinnamon
1 cup sour milk
1 cup cooked prunes, chopped

Cream shortening.

Add sugar gradually and beat until fluffy.

Add eggs and beat again.

Sift flour; measure and add salt, soda and cinnamon. Sift again.

Add dry ingredients alternately with milk.

Beat thoroughly after each addition.

Add chopped prunes and blend into mixture.

Pour into greased loaf pan 4 x 8 x 4 inches.

Bake at 325° for 1 hour.

MRS. MOLLIE LEHMAN, *Croghan, N. Y.*

## Raisin Loaf Cake

¾ cup shortening
1½ cups brown sugar
2 eggs
3½ cups cake flour
½ teaspoon salt
½ teaspoon soda

3 teaspoons baking powder
½ teaspoon each of cloves, nutmeg, ginger
1 cup buttermilk or sour milk
1½ cup chopped raisins

Cream shortening.

Add sugar gradually and beat until fluffy.

Add eggs and beat until well blended.

Sift flour; measure and add salt, baking powder, soda and spices. Sift again.

Add sifted dry ingredients alternately with sour milk.
Beat thoroughly after each addition.
Chop raisins or grind through coarse blade of food grinder.
Dust raisins with flour and add to mixture.
Blend well.
Pour into greased loaf pan.
Bake at 325° for 1 hour.
Makes a large loaf 5 x 9 x 4 inches.

MRS. L. P. SHOWALTER, *Broadway, Va.*

## Raw Apple Cake

| | |
|---|---|
| ½ cup shortening | 1 teaspoon cinnamon |
| 1 cup sugar | 1½ cups finely chopped apples |
| 2 cups cake flour | (tart ones) |
| 2 eggs | 1 cup chopped raisins |
| ½ teaspoon salt | 1 cup chopped nuts |
| 1½ teaspoons soda | |

Sift flour; measure and add sugar, soda, salt and cinnamon. Sift again.
Work the shortening into this mixture as for pastry. Add beaten eggs.
Stir in chopped nuts and raisins that have been dusted with flour.
Add chopped apples and stir only enough to blend ingredients together.
Pour into a greased loaf pan.
Bake at 325° for 1 hour. Makes a loaf 4 x 8 x 3½ inches.
If apples are not tart, use only 1 teaspoon soda.

MRS. ALVA SWARTZENDRUBER, *Hydro, Okla.*

## Rotation Cake

*Grandma's Favorite*

| | |
|---|---|
| 1 cup butter | ½ teaspoon salt |
| 2 cups sugar | 3 teaspoons baking powder |
| 4 eggs | 1 cup sweet cream |
| 3 cups cake flour | 1 teaspoon vanilla |

Cream shortening.
Add sugar gradually and beat until fluffy.
Add eggs, 1 at a time and beat until light.
Sift flour; measure and add salt and baking powder. Sift again.
Add dry ingredients alternately with cream and flavoring.
Beat thoroughly after each addition.
Pour into large, greased loaf pan.
Bake at 350° for 1 hour.
Makes a large angel tube pan full (10 inch diameter).
A rich pound-type of cake with excellent flavor.

## Spice Cake

| | |
|---|---|
| ½ cup shortening | ½ teaspoon each of cloves and nutmeg |
| 2 cups brown sugar | ¾ cup of sweet milk and |
| 2 eggs | 3 teaspoons of baking powder |
| 2¼ cups cake flour | or |
| ½ teaspoon salt | 1 cup buttermilk or sour milk and |
| 1 teaspoon cinnamon | 1 teaspoon soda |

Cream shortening.

Add sugar gradually and beat until fluffy.

Add eggs and beat until light.

Sift flour; measure and add salt, spices and baking powder or soda. Sift again.

Add dry ingredients alternately with milk.

Beat thoroughly after each addition.

Pour into greased layer pans.

Bake at 350° for 25 to 30 minutes.

Makes 2 (9 inch) layers.

MRS. LLOYD EBERLY, *Salem, Ohio;* MRS. E. M. GLICK, *Parkesburg, Pa.*
ELIZABETH M. BATTERMAN, *Hanover, Pa.*

## Toasted Spice Cake

| | |
|---|---|
| ½ cup shortening | 1 teaspoon baking powder |
| 2 cups brown sugar | 1½ teaspoons cinnamon |
| 2 eggs, separated | 1 teaspoon cloves ˙ |
| 2½ cups cake flour | 1¼ cups sour milk |
| ½ teaspoon salt | 1 teaspoon vanilla |
| 1 teaspoon soda | |

Cream shortening.

Roll sugar until very fine and add gradually. Beat until fluffy.

Add egg yolks and beat again.

Sift flour; measure and add salt, soda, baking powder and spices. Sift again.

Add dry ingredients alternately with milk and flavoring.

Beat thoroughly after each addition.

Pour into a greased flat pan 8 x 12 x 1¼ inches.

Spread over mixture the following brown sugar meringue:

Beat the 2 egg whites until they are stiff enough to stand up in peaks.

Slowly add 1 cup light brown sugar to whites, beating until it is smooth.

Spread over cake batter and sprinkle with ½ cup finely chopped nuts or ½ cup shredded coconut.

Bake at 350° for 40 minutes.

MRS. FRANK RABER, *Detroit, Mich.;* MRS. MOSES STOLTZFUS, *Elverson, Pa.*

## Sour Cream Cake

| | |
|---|---|
| I cup sour cream (thick) | ½ teaspoon salt |
| I cup sugar | I teaspoon baking soda |
| 3 eggs | Grated rind of I lemon |
| 2 cups cake flour | I teaspoon lemon juice |

Combine sugar, egg yolks, lemon juice and rind, and sour cream.
Beat until well blended.
Sift flour; measure and add salt and soda. Sift again.
Add sifted dry ingredients gradually and beat thoroughly.
Fold in stiffly beaten egg whites.
Pour into greased loaf pan.
Bake at 350° for 45 to 50 minutes.
Makes a loaf 4 x 8 x 4 inches.
Cool and cover with orange frosting (page 247).

MRS. SAMUEL NAFZIGER, *Kalona, Iowa*

## Tiptop Cake

| | |
|---|---|
| ½ cup shortening | ½ teaspoon salt |
| 1½ cups sugar | 2 teaspoons baking powder |
| 2 eggs | I cup milk |
| 2¼ cups all-purpose flour | I teaspoon vanilla |

Cream shortening and add sugar gradually.
Add beaten eggs and beat until light and fluffy.
Sift flour; measure and add salt and baking powder. Sift again.
Add dry ingredients alternately with milk and flavoring.
Beat thoroughly after each addition.
Pour into greased loaf or layer pans.
Makes 2 (8 inch) layers or 1 loaf 3½ x 8 x 4 inches.
Bake at 350° for 30 minutes for layers and 45 minutes for loaf.
An inexpensive cake that even a child can make with success.

MRS. OTIS SUNDHEIMER, *Sugarcreek, Ohio*

## Tomato Lunch Cake

| | |
|---|---|
| 3 tablespoons shortening | ¼ teaspoon nutmeg |
| I cup brown sugar | I cup stewed tomatoes, strained |
| 2 cups cake flour | I cup chopped raisins or |
| ½ teaspoon salt | ½ cup raisins |
| I teaspoon soda | ½ cup chopped dried apricots |
| I teaspoon cinnamon | Orange peel, dates or citron (optional) |
| ¼ teaspoon cloves | |

Cream shortening and sugar together.
Sift flour; measure and add salt, soda and spices. Sift again.

Add dry ingredients alternately with strained tomatoes.

Chop dried fruits into small pieces and dust with flour.

Add fruits to mixture and blend together.

Pour into greased loaf pan.

Bake at 325° for 1 hour.

Makes a loaf 4½ x 8 x 4 inches.

A delicious flavor!

MRS. HERMAN RINKENBERGER, *Bradford, Ill.*

## Wedding Cake

| | |
|---|---|
| ¾ cup shortening | ¾ teaspoons salt |
| 1¾ cups sugar | 1¼ cups water or milk |
| 3½ cups cake flour | 6 egg whites |
| 3¾ teaspoons baking powder | 2 teaspoons vanilla |

Cream shortening and add sugar.

Beat until fluffy.

Sift flour; measure and add salt and baking powder. Sift again.

Add dry ingredients alternately with milk and flavoring.

Beat thoroughly after each addition.

Beat egg whites until stiff but not dry.

Fold into batter. Stir until well blended.

To make a large 3 tiered wedding cake make this recipe 3 times.

The first mixing will fill a 12 inch and an 8 inch cake pan.

The next mixing will make 2 layers (10 inches).

The third mixing will make a 12 inch and an 8 inch layer.

This will make 2 layers of each size.

Bake each layer at 350° for 30 to 35 minutes.

Frosting:

| | |
|---|---|
| 5 cups sugar | 24 marshmallows |
| 2 tablespoons vinegar | 1 teaspoon vanilla |
| ¾ cup cold water | 5 egg whites |

Combine sugar, vinegar and water and cook until it spins a thread.

Add marshmallows, cover and remove from heat.

Beat egg whites until stiff and then slowly pour boiled syrup into them.

Beat constantly with high speed on electric mixer or use rotary egg beater.

Hold back marshmallows until all the syrup has been poured into egg whites.

Then add marshmallows and beat until fluffy.

This is sufficient frosting to cover the large cake nicely and leave plenty to decorate with.

Add 4 tablespoons of powdered sugar with frosting used for decorating. Press through a decorator to make desired designs.

MRS. FRANK BEERY, *Dayton, Va.*

## Whipped Cream Cake

| | |
|---|---|
| 1 cup whipping cream | ½ teaspoon salt |
| 1 cup sugar | 2 teaspoons baking powder |
| 2 eggs | 1 teaspoon vanilla |
| 1½ cups cake flour | |

Whip cream until stiff.

Drop in eggs, 1 at a time and beat until light and fluffy.

Add sugar and vanilla and beat again.

Sift flour; measure and add salt and baking powder. Sift again.

Add dry ingredients gradually to mixture.

Beat well after each addition.

Pour into greased layer pan.

Bake at 350° for 35 minutes.

Makes 1 large layer (9 inch).

This cake is very fine grained and velvety in texture.

MRS. MARY A. STOLTZFUS, *Atglen, Pa.*

## White Mountain Cake

| | |
|---|---|
| ¾ cup shortening | 1 cup milk |
| 1¾ cups sugar | 5 egg whites |
| 3 cups cake flour | 1 teaspoon vanilla |
| ½ teaspoon salt | ½ teaspoon lemon or almond extract |
| 4 teaspoons baking powder | |

Cream shortening.

Add sugar gradually and cream until fluffy.

Sift flour; measure and add salt and baking powder. Sift again.

Add dry ingredients alternately with milk and flavoring.

Beat thoroughly after each addition.

Beat egg whites until stiff and fold into mixture.

Pour into greased layer pans.

Bake at 350° for 25 to 30 minutes.

Makes 3 (8 inch) layers.

Cover with Snow Cap Frosting (page 248).

MRS. LOREN WADE, *Sterling, Ill.*; MRS. DAVID EIMEN, *Iowa City, Iowa*

# CAKES WITHOUT SHORTENING
## Angel Food Cake

| | |
|---|---|
| 1 cup cake flour | 1 teaspoon cream of tartar |
| 1½ cups sugar, finely granulated | 1 teaspoon vanilla or |
| 1½ cups egg whites (11 to 12 eggs) | ½ teaspoon each of vanilla and |
| 2 tablespoons water | almond extract |
| ¼ teaspoon salt | |

Sift flour and measure.

Add ½ cup sugar and sift together 3 times.

Beat egg whites with rotary beater until frothy.

Add salt and cream of tartar.

Continue to beat until whites hold peaks.

Slowly add remaining sugar to beaten whites, folding it in with a wire whisk.

Add flavoring.

Then sift flour and sugar mixture, a tablespoon or two at a time, over beaten whites.

Fold in lightly with a down-up-over motion.

When well blended, pour into a large ungreased tube pan (10 inch diameter).

Cut through batter with a knife.

Bake at 350° for 1 hour.

Remove from oven and invert pan to cool.

MRS. HENRY EICHELBERGER, *Hydro, Okla.*; LOLA BRUNK, *Delphos, Ohio*
MRS. JOHN MARTIN, *Waynesboro, Va.*

## Cocoa Angel Food

Remove 3 tablespoons flour from cup and add 3 tablespoons cocoa.

Proceed as in preceding recipe.

MRS. MARY McNEIL TRISSEL, *Waynesboro, Va.*

## Yellow Angel Cake (Sponge)

| | |
|---|---|
| 5 egg yolks | 1½ cups sifted cake flour |
| 1 cup sugar, sifted | ½ teaspoon baking powder |
| 1 tablespoon cold water | 5 egg whites |
| ⅓ cup boiling water | ½ teaspoon salt |
| 1 teaspoon vanilla | ½ teaspoon cream of tartar |

Beat yolks until thick and lemon-colored.

Add cold water and vanilla.

Add sugar gradually and continue to beat.

Then add hot water gradually and beat 2 minutes.

Sift flour; measure and add baking powder. Sift again.
Sift 2 tablespoons at a time over egg yolk mixture and fold in gently.
Beat egg whites until frothy.
Add salt and cream of tartar.
Beat until whites hold peaks.
Carefully fold beaten whites into first mixture.
Pour into large, ungreased tube pan (10 inch diameter).
Bake at 350° for approximately 1 hour.
Invert pan to cool.
This is a large cake 10 inches in diameter and 5 inches high.

Mrs. Sadie Yoder, *Stuarts Draft, Va.;* Mrs. Howard Gnacey, *Kalona, Iowa*

## Sponge Cake

| | |
|---|---|
| 3 eggs | 1 teaspoon baking powder |
| 1 cup sugar, sifted | 3 tablespoons warm water |
| 1 cup cake flour | 1 teaspoon vinegar or lemon juice |
| ½ teaspoon salt | |

Beat whole eggs until thick and lemon-colored.
Add sifted sugar gradually and continue to beat.
Add water and flavoring and beat 2 minutes longer.
Sift flour; measure and add salt and baking powder. Sift again.
Add 2 tablespoons sifted dry ingredients at a time to egg-sugar mixture.
Fold in gently with a wire whisk.
When ingredients are well blended, pour into an ungreased tube pan.
Bake at 350° for 50 minutes.
Invert pan to cool.
A very good and economical cake.

Mrs. Jonas Freed, *Elroy, Pa.*

## Golden Sponge Cake

| | |
|---|---|
| 1 cup sugar, finely granulated | 2 teaspoons baking powder |
| 6 egg yolks | ½ cup boiling water |
| 1½ cups cake flour | Grated rind and juice of ½ lemon |
| ½ teaspoon salt | |

Beat yolks until thick and lemon-colored.
Add sifted sugar gradually and continue to beat.
Add lemon rind and juice.
Slowly add hot water and beat 2 minutes longer.
Sift flour; measure and add salt and baking powder. Sift again.
Add dry ingredients slowly to egg mixture.
Fold in gently

Pour into ungreased tube pan.

Bake at 350° for 45 to 50 minutes.

Invert pan to cool.

Makes a cake 8 inches in diameter and 5 inches high.

A good way to use yolks left from an angel cake.

MRS. QUINTUS LEATHERMAN, *Souderton, Pa.*

## Golden Sunshine Cake

| | |
|---|---|
| 5 egg yolks | 1/2 teaspoon salt |
| 1/3 cup cold water | 1 teaspoon cream of tartar |
| 1½ cups sugar, sifted | 5 egg whites |
| 1½ cups cake flour | 1 teaspoon vanilla or lemon extract |

Beat the egg yolks until thick and lemon-colored.

Add cold water gradually and continue to beat until light.

Add ¼ cup sifted sugar and beat thoroughly.

Add flavoring.

Sift flour; measure, and add remaining sugar and salt. Sift again and add slowly to yolk mixture.

Fold in gently.

Beat egg whites until frothy.

Add cream of tartar and continue to beat until whites hold peaks.

Fold whites gently into yolk-flour mixture.

Pour into ungreased tube pan.

Bake at 350° for 1 hour.

Invert pan to cool.

Makes a cake 10 inches in diameter and 5 inches high.

MRS. HENRY CLEMENS, *Telford, Pa.*

## Hot Milk Sponge

| | |
|---|---|
| 4 eggs | 2 teaspoons baking powder |
| 2 cups sugar | 1 cup hot milk |
| 2 cups cake flour | 1 teaspoon lemon juice or vanilla |
| 1/2 teaspoon salt | |

Beat whole eggs until thick and lemon-colored.

Slowly add sifted sugar and beat until well blended.

Add hot milk gradually, stirring vigorously.

Add flavoring.

Sift flour; measure and add salt and baking powder. Sift again.

Add 2 tablespoons at a time, sifting slowly over egg mixture.

Fold in flour with a wire whisk until ingredients are well blended.

Pour into ungreased tube pan.

Bake at 350° for 45 minutes.

Invert pan to cool.

Makes a cake 8 inches in diameter and 5 inches high.

Mrs. Henry Mininger, *Hatfield, Pa.*

## Jelly Roll

3 eggs
1 cup sugar
3 tablespoons water or milk
1 1/3 cups cake flour

1/2 teaspoon salt
1 1/2 teaspoons baking powder
Grated rind of 1 lemon

Beat eggs until thick and lemon-colored.

Add sifted sugar gradually and continue beating.

Add liquid and lemon rind and beat.

Sift flour; measure and add salt and baking powder. Sift again.

Sift slowly over egg mixture, folding in with a wire whisk.

Cover a shallow-sided, flat pan 12 x 16 x ⅛ inches with waxed paper.

Pour dough into pan. (It should not be over ¼ inch thick in pan.)

Bake at 400° for 12 to 14 minutes.

Turn out on damp cloth that has been sprinkled with powdered sugar.

Remove waxed paper and trim off hard crusts.

Spread with tart jelly and roll immediately.

Delicious.

Mrs. Omar A. Swartzendruber, *Parnell, Iowa*

## Pineapple Sponge Cake

6 eggs, separated
1½ cups sugar
1½ cups cake flour
½ teaspoon salt

1 teaspoon baking powder
½ cup of pineapple or orange juice
1 tablespoon lemon juice

Beat yolks until light and lemon-colored.

Add fruit juices.

Slowly add ¾ cup sugar and continue to beat.

Beat egg whites to a froth and add salt.

Continue to beat until whites hold peaks.

Gradually add remaining sugar to beaten whites.

Continue to beat until thoroughly blended.

Fold the yolk mixture into the whites and blend well.

Sift flour; measure and add salt and baking powder. Sift again.

Sift slowly over mixture and fold in gently.

Pour into ungreased tube pan.

Bake at 350° for 50 to 60 minutes.

Invert pan to cool.

Makes a large cake 10 inches in diameter and 5 inches high.

MRS. SARA HERR, *Martinsburg, Pa.*

## Russian Sponge Cake

4 egg yolks
2 cups sugar
1 cup boiling water
2¼ cups cake flour
½ teaspoon salt

1½ teaspoons baking powder
½ teaspoon cream of tartar
4 egg whites
1 tablespoon lemon juice

Beat egg yolks until thick and lemon-colored. Add lemon juice.

Add ½ cup sugar gradually.

Slowly add hot water and continue to beat.

Sift flour; measure and add baking powder, salt and 1 cup sugar. Sift again.

Add sifted dry ingredients, 2 tablespoons at a time, over yolk mixture.

Blend well.

Beat egg whites until foamy, add cream of tartar.

Add sugar gradually and continue to beat until whites hold peaks.

Fold egg whites into former mixture until well blended.

Pour into large, ungreased tube pan.

Bake at 350° for 1 hour.

Invert pan to cool.

Makes 1 large cake 10 inches in diameter and 5 inches high.

MRS. NOAH GEHMAN, *Bally, Pa.*

# CAKES FOR CHILDREN'S PARTIES
## Daffodil Cake

First part:

6 egg whites
¼ teaspoon salt
½ teaspoon cream of tartar

¾ cup sugar
½ cup cake flour
½ teaspoon vanilla

Beat egg whites until frothy.

Add salt and cream of tartar and continue beating until stiff but not dry

Gradually beat in sugar, adding 2 or 3 tablespoons at a time.

Gradually fold in flour, sifting it over mixture.

Add vanilla.

Pour mixture into ungreased tube pan 9 inches in diameter.

Second part:

6 egg yolks
1/2 cup sugar
2 tablespoons cold water
2/3 cup cake flour

3/4 teaspoon baking powder
1/2 teaspoon orange or lemon extract
1/2 teaspoon vanilla

Beat egg yolks until thick and lemon-colored.

Add water, flavoring and sugar and continue to beat.

Sift flour; measure and add baking powder. Sift again. Gradually add to egg foam.

Fold ingredients together until they are well blended.

Pour on top of the white batter and bake at 350° for 1 hour.

Invert pan to cool.

## Lily Cake

White part:

2/3 cup shortening
2 cups sugar
3 cups cake flour
1/2 teaspoon salt

2 1/2 teaspoons baking powder
2/3 cup milk
7 egg whites
1 teaspoon vanilla

Cream shortening.

Add sugar gradually and beat until fluffy.

Sift flour; measure and add salt and baking powder. Sift again.

Add dry ingredients alternately with milk and flavoring.

Beat thoroughly after each addition.

Beat egg whites until stiff but not dry; fold into mixture.

Pour into greased layer pans.

Bake at 350° for 30 minutes.

Makes 2 (9 inch) layers.

Yellow part:

1/2 cup shortening
1 cup sugar
7 egg yolks
1 2/3 cups cake flour
1/4 teaspoon salt

1 1/2 teaspoons baking powder
1/2 cup milk
1/2 teaspoon lemon extract
8 dried figs

Cream shortening.

Add sugar gradually and beat until fluffy.

Add beaten egg yolks and beat until light.

Sift flour; measure and add salt and baking powder. Sift again.

Add dry ingredients alternately with milk and flavoring.

Beat thoroughly after each addition.

Pour into greased layer pan.

Lay figs on top.

Bake at 350° for 30 minutes.

Makes 1 (9 inch) layer.

Use Seven-Minute Frosting (page 247) and top with coconut.

Place yellow layer in center, between 2 white layers.

MARY EARLY, *Dayton, Va.*

## Pansy Cake

First part:

| | |
|---|---|
| ½ cup shortening | ½ cup milk |
| 1 cup sugar | 3 egg whites |
| 2 cups cake flour | ½ teaspoon lemon extract |
| ¼ teaspoon salt | Few drops red coloring |
| 1½ teaspoons baking powder | |

Cream shortening.

Add sugar gradually and beat until fluffy.

Sift flour; measure and add salt and baking powder. Sift again.

Add dry ingredients alternately with milk and flavoring.

Add stiffly beaten egg whites and blend into mixture.

Divide batter into 2 equal parts.

Color half of batter pink.

Set this batter aside while second part is being made.

Second part:

| | |
|---|---|
| ½ cup shortening | 1½ teaspoons baking powder |
| 1 cup sugar | 3 tablespoons grated chocolate or |
| 3 egg yolks | cocoa |
| 2 cups cake flour | ½ cup milk |
| ¼ teaspoon salt | 1 teaspoon vanilla |

Mix as in first part except to add egg yolks to creamed sugar and shortening.

Remove ½ of batter and add to it the melted chocolate or cocoa.

Leave remaining half of batter yellow.

The total amount of batter will make 4 (8 inch) layers.

When pouring batter into pans make first layer white around edge then a ring of pink, yellow and brown in center.

Make second layer pink on outside edge then white, brown and yellow in center.

Make third layer yellow on edge then brown, white and pink in center.

Make fourth layer brown on edge then yellow, pink and white in center.

Bake at 350° for 25 to 30 minutes.

Cover with favorite frosting.

MRS. HENRY BROWN, *North Lima, Ohio*

## Watermelon Cake

White part:

| | |
|---|---|
| ½ cup shortening | 1½ teaspoons baking powder |
| 1 cup sugar | 1/3 cup milk |
| 1½ cups cake flour | 3 egg whites |
| ¼ teaspoon salt | 1 teaspoon vanilla |

Cream shortening.

Add sugar gradually and beat until fluffy.

Sift flour; measure and add salt and baking powder. Sift again.

Add dry ingredients alternately with milk and flavoring.

Beat thoroughly after each addition.

Fold in stiffly beaten egg whites.

Red part:

| | |
|---|---|
| ½ cup shortening | 2 teaspoons baking powder |
| 3 egg yolks | ½ cup sweet milk |
| 2 cups cake flour | 1½ cups seedless raisins |
| 1 cup sugar | ½ teaspoon red coloring |
| ¼ teaspoon salt | |

Cream shortening.

Add sugar gradually and beat until fluffy.

Add egg yolks and continue to beat.

Sift flour; measure and add salt and baking powder. Sift again.

Add dry ingredients alternately with milk.

Beat thoroughly after each addition.

Add slightly floured raisins and cake coloring and blend into mixture.

Pour batter into greased cake pan; a round tube pan is preferred.

Put white batter around outside edge of pan and a thin layer in bottom.

Pour red batter in center.

Add a thin layer of white batter on top.

Bake at 350° for 1 hour.

Cool and cover with Seven-Minute Frosting (page 247) to which green coloring has been added.

When cut, this will resemble a watermelon.

MRS. AMOS HORST, *Hagerstown, Md.*

# CUPCAKES

## Plain Cupcakes

| | |
|---|---|
| 2/3 cup shortening | ½ teaspoon salt |
| 1½ cups sugar | 2½ teaspoons baking powder |
| 2 eggs | 1 cup milk |
| 2½ cups cake flour | 1 teaspoon vanilla |

Cream shortening.

Add sugar gradually and continue to beat until fluffy.

Add eggs and beat until well blended.

Sift flour; measure and add salt and baking powder. Sift again.

Add dry ingredients alternately with milk and flavoring.

Beat thoroughly after each addition.

Fill greased cupcake or muffin pans ⅔ full.

Bake at 375° for 20 minutes.

Makes about 2 dozen cupcakes.

MRS. HENRY BECK, *Archbold, Ohio*

## Banana Cupcakes

½ cup shortening
1 cup sugar
2 eggs
1½ cups cake flour
½ teaspoon salt

½ teaspoon baking soda dissolved in
  1 tablespoon warm water
1 teaspoon baking powder
1 cup mashed bananas
1 teaspoon vanilla

Cream shortening.

Add sugar gradually and continue to beat until fluffy.

Add beaten eggs and vanilla and beat again.

Sift flour; measure and add salt and baking powder. Sift again.

Add dry ingredients alternately with water and soda and banana pulp.

Mix thoroughly and fill greased cupcake or muffin pans ⅔ full.

Bake at 375° for 20 minutes.

Makes 20 to 24 medium-sized cupcakes.

MRS. CLARENCE SWARTZENDRUBER, *Kalona, Iowa*

## Bit O' Chocolate Cupcakes

1/3 cup shortening
1 cup sugar
1 egg
2 cups cake flour
½ teaspoon salt

2½ teaspoons baking powder
¾ cup milk
1 package chocolate bits (6 ounces)
1 teaspoon vanilla

Cream shortening.

Add sugar gradually and beat until fluffy.

Add egg and beat again.

Sift flour; measure and add salt and baking powder. Sift again.

Add dry ingredients alternately with milk and flavoring.

Beat thoroughly after each addition.

Add chocolate bits and blend into batter.

Fill greased cupcake or muffin pans ⅔ full.
Bake at 375° for 20 minutes.
Makes 2 dozen cupcakes.

MRS. ROSCOE KRAMER, *Address Unknown.*

## Chocolate Surprise Cupcakes

| | |
|---|---|
| ½ cup shortening | I teaspoon baking powder |
| 2 cups brown sugar | (2 ounces) |
| 2 eggs | 2 squares unsweetened cholocate |
| 1¾ cups cake flour | ½ cup boiling water |
| ½ teaspoon salt | ½ cup sour milk |
| ½ teaspoon baking soda | I teaspoon vanilla |

Cream shortening.
Add sugar gradually and beat until fluffy.
Add eggs and beat again.
Grate chocolate and add boiling water.
Stir until dissolved.
Add to creamed mixture.
Sift flour; measure and add salt, soda and baking powder. Sift again.
Add sifted dry ingredients alternately with milk and flavoring.
Beat thoroughly after each addition.
Fill greased cupcake or muffin tins ⅔ full.
Bake at 375° for 20 minutes.
Makes 2 dozen cupcakes.
Cover with whipped cream or fudge frosting (page 245).

MRS. ALLEN SCHULTZ, *Milverton, Ont., Can.;* MRS. JACOB ALDERFER, *Souderton, Pa.*

## Cream Cupcakes

| | |
|---|---|
| 2 eggs | 2 cups cake flour |
| I cup cream | ½ teaspoon salt |
| I teaspoon vanilla | 2 teaspoons baking powder |
| I cup sugar | |

Beat eggs thoroughly and add cream, vanilla and sugar.
Beat again until well blended.
Sift flour; measure and add salt and baking powder. Sift again.
Add sifted dry ingredients gradually to mixture.
Beat thoroughly after each addition.
Fill greased cupcake or muffin pans ⅔ full.
Bake at 375° for 20 minutes.
Makes 2 dozen cupcakes.
If desired, shredded coconut may be sprinkled over cakes before baking.

MRS. NELSON HISTAND, *Culp, Ark.*

## Date and Nut Cupcakes

½ pound dates
½ cup shortening
1 cup brown sugar
1 egg
2 cups cake flour
½ teaspoon salt

½ teaspoon baking powder
1 teaspoon soda
1 cup boiling water
½ cup English walnuts
1 teaspoon vanilla

Cream shortening.

Add sugar gradually and beat until fluffy.

Add beaten egg and flavoring and blend thoroughly.

Pour boiling water over chopped dates and stir until a smooth paste. Cool.

Sift flour; measure and add salt, baking powder and soda. Sift again.

Add dry ingredients alternately with dates.

Blend together well and add slightly floured, chopped nuts.

Fill greased cupcake or muffin pans ⅔ full.

Bake at 375° for 25 minutes.

Makes 2 dozen cupcakes.

MRS. MENNO B. SOUDER, *Elroy, Pa.*

## Golden Orange Cupcakes

½ cup shortening
1 cup sugar
3 egg yolks
1¾ cups cake flour
½ teaspoon salt

3 teaspoons baking powder
1/3 cup orange juice
1/3 cup water
1 teaspoon vanilla

Cream shortening.

Add sugar gradually and beat until fluffy.

Add well-beaten egg yolks.

Sift flour; measure and add salt and baking powder. Sift again.

Add dry ingredients alternately with orange juice, water and flavoring.

Beat thoroughly after each addition.

Fill greased cupcake or muffin pans ⅔ full.

Bake at 375° for 20 minutes.

Makes approximately 20 cupcakes.

MRS. E. M. GLICK, *Parkesburg, Pa.*

## Peanut Butter Cupcakes

1/3 cup shortening
1½ cups brown sugar
½ cup peanut butter
2 eggs, beaten
2 cups cake flour

½ teaspoon salt
2½ teaspoons baking powder
¾ cup milk
1 teaspoon vanilla

Cream shortening.

Add sugar gradually and beat until fluffy.

Add peanut butter and blend into mixture.

Beat eggs and add. Beat again.

Sift flour; measure and add salt and baking powder. Sift again. Add dry ingredients alternately with milk and flavoring.

Beat thoroughly after each addition.

Fill greased cupcake or muffin pans ⅔ full.

Bake at 375° for 20 minutes.

Makes 2 dozen cupcakes.

MRS. I. K. METZLER, *Accident, Md.*

## Raisin Puffs

| | |
|---|---|
| ½ cup shortening | ¼ teaspoon salt |
| 3 tablespoons sugar | 2½ teaspoons baking powder |
| 2 eggs | ¾ cup milk |
| 2 cups cake flour | I cup seedless raisins |

Cream shortening.

Add sugar and beat until well blended.

Add beaten eggs and mix thoroughly.

Sift flour; measure and add salt and baking powder. Sift again. Add dry ingredients alternately with milk.

Beat thoroughly after each addition.

Add slightly floured raisins.

Blend into mixture.

Fill greased custard cups ⅔ full and set in boiling water.

Allow to steam for 30 minutes.

Serve with plain or fruit sauce, or cream and sugar.

Makes approximately 18 cupcakes.

LUELLA SHOUP, *Orrville, Ohio*

## Spice Cupcakes

| | |
|---|---|
| ½ cup shortening | ½ teaspoon soda |
| 2 cups brown sugar | I teaspoon baking powder |
| 2 eggs, separated | I teaspoon cinnamon |
| 2¼ cups cake flour | ½ teaspoon each of cloves and nutmeg |
| ½ teaspoon salt | I cup sour milk |

Cream shortening.

Add sugar gradually and beat until fluffy.

Add egg yolks and beat again.

Sift flour; measure and add salt, soda and baking powder. Sift again.

Add dry ingredients alternately with sour milk.

Beat thoroughly after each addition.

Beat egg whites until stiff and fold into batter.

Fill greased cupcake or muffin pans ⅔ full.

Bake at 375° for 20 minutes.

Makes 2 dozen cupcakes.

CAROL GLICK, *Sugarcreek, Ohio;* MRS. WILLIS MILLER, *Harrisonburg, Va.*

# MISCELLANEOUS CAKES

## Cinnamon Flop

2 cups cake flour
¾ cup sugar
2½ teaspoons baking powder
½ teaspoon salt

¼ cup shortening
1 egg
1 cup milk

Sift flour; measure and add baking powder, sugar and salt. Sift again.

Add shortening and rub together into fine crumbs.

Beat egg and add milk.

Add gradually to dry ingredients and beat until thoroughly mixed.

Put mixture into a greased pan 9 inches square.

Brush top with melted butter and sprinkle with ¾ cup of brown sugar
    and 1 teaspoon of cinnamon.

Bake at 375° for 25 to 30 minutes.

MRS. HARVEY STAHLY, *Nappannee, Ind.*

## Geburtstagkuchen and Kaffe

### *Birthday Cake and Coffee*

This is an original recipe from our Russian Mennonite refugees of
    World War II.

6 slices white bread (homemade)
6 slices rye bread (dark and heavy)
2 cups cottage cheese

2 cups skimmed milk
½ cup sugar
½ cup raw oatmeal

Spread slices of bread with cottage cheese and sprinkle with sugar.

Build up the slices of bread in alternate dark and light layers to form
    a loaf.

Pour as much skimmed milk over the loaf as it will absorb.

Cook oatmeal in 2 cups skimmed milk to form a medium-thick soup.

When it is cold, beat it with a rotary beater until it holds peaks.

Add sugar.

Spread this mixture over the cake.

Garnish with raw oatmeal flakes that have been toasted.

For the coffee:

Toast slices of rye bread until they are quite black.

Pulverize these slices of bread to form fine crumbs.

Use the crumbs to make coffee.

ELMA ESAU, *White Water, Kan.*

## Applesauce Gingerbread

| | |
|---|---|
| 1/3 cup butter | 1 teaspoon baking powder |
| ½ cup brown sugar | ½ teaspoon soda |
| ½ cup molasses | 1½ teaspoons ginger |
| 1 egg | 1 teaspoon cinnamon |
| 1¾ cup all-purpose flour or | 2 cups sliced apples |
|    2 cups cake flour | ¾ cup sour milk or buttermilk |
| ½ teaspoon salt | |

Cream butter and add sugar.

Beat until fluffy.

Add beaten egg and molasses and continue to beat until thoroughly blended.

Sift flour; measure and add salt, soda and baking powder. Sift again.

Add dry ingredients alternately with sour milk.

Beat thoroughly after each addition.

Cover bottom of greased pan with thin slices of apples.

Pour batter over apples and bake at 350° for about 45 minutes.

Makes a cake 8 x 10 x 1¼ inches.

MRS. LLOYD MILLER, *Pryor, Okla.*

Variation:

Use a deep loaf pan.

Melt 2 tablespoons butter in pan and add ¼ cup cane syrup.

Add 1 cup seedless raisins.

Cover with 1 cup thinly sliced apples.

Cook gently on top of stove or in oven for 15 minutes.

Add gingerbread batter and bake at 350° for 40 minutes.

MRS. MARY WEAVER, *East Earl, Pa.*

## Old-Fashioned or Soft Gingerbread

| | |
|---|---|
| ½ cup shortening | ½ teaspoon salt |
| ½ cup sugar | ½ teaspoon soda |
| 1 egg | 1 teaspoon baking powder |
| 1 cup dark molasses | 1½ teaspoons ginger |
| 2½ cups all-purpose flour or | 1 teaspoon cinnamon |
|    2¾ cups cake flour | 1 cup boiling water |

Cream shortening.

Add sugar gradually and beat until fluffy.

Add egg and beat well.

Add molasses and blend into mixture.

Sift flour; measure and add salt, soda, baking powder and spices. Sift again. Add dry ingredients gradually to mixture.

Add boiling water and stir until batter is smooth.

This is a thin batter.

Pour into waxed-paper-lined pan 8 x 10 x 2 inches.

Bake at 350° for 35 to 40 minutes.

Mrs. P. J. Blosser, *South English, Iowa;* Mrs. Amos C. Lehman, *Orrville, Ohio*
Mrs. M. G. Metzler, *Manheim, Pa.*

## Glorified Gingerbread

| | |
|---|---|
| ½ cup shortening | ½ teaspoon each of ginger and |
| 1 cup sugar | cinnamon |
| 2 cups all-purpose flour | |

Sift flour; measure and add spices. Sift again.

Rub fat into dry ingredients to make fine crumbs.

Take out ½ cup crumbs to sprinkle over top of mixture.

To the remaining crumbs add:

| | |
|---|---|
| 1 egg, beaten | 1 teaspoon soda |
| ½ cup molasses | ½ cup sour milk or buttermilk |
| ½ teaspoon salt | |

Beat until ingredients are well blended and batter is smooth.

Pour into greased, waxed-paper-lined pan.

Sprinkle with crumbs.

Bake at 350° for 45 minutes.

Makes a cake 8 x 8 x 1½ inches.

Esther Hershberger, *Kalona, Iowa;* Mrs. D. H. Bender, *Palmyra, Mo.*

## Chocolate Roll

Sift together:

| | |
|---|---|
| 6 tablespoons flour | ½ teaspoon baking powder |
| 6 tablespoons cocoa | ¼ teaspoon salt |

Then beat 4 egg whites until stiff and add:

| | |
|---|---|
| ¾ cup sifted sugar | 1 teaspoon vanilla |
| 4 beaten egg yolks | |

Sift dry ingredients slowly into egg-sugar mixture.

Blend thoroughly.

Line a shallow, waxed pan 9 x 12 inches with waxed paper.

Pour batter in pan to thickness of ¼ inch.

Bake at 400° for 15 minutes.

Remove from pan and turn out on a damp cloth sprinkled with powdered sugar.

Trim hard edges and spread with whipped cream or the following filling:

| | |
|---|---|
| 1 egg white | 3 tablespoons cold water |
| 1 cup sugar | 1 teaspoon cream of tartar |

Mix together and cook in double boiler over rapidly boiling water.

Beat mixture with rotary beater until it stands in peaks.

Remove from heat and add 1 cup shredded coconut.

Prepare this filling so it is ready to spread on cake as soon as it is removed from oven.

Roll as a jelly roll.

MARY E. SUTER, *Harrisonburg, Va.;* MRS. EARL DELP, *Line Lexington, Pa.*
MRS. AMOS MARTIN, *Chambersburg, Pa.*

# CAKE FROSTINGS

## Baked-on Frosting

| | |
|---|---|
| 1 egg white | ¾ cup brown sugar |
| ¼ teaspoon baking powder | ¼ cup chopped nuts |

Beat egg white until frothy.

Add baking powder and beat until stiff.

Gradually add brown sugar. Beat until creamy.

Spread on hot cake and sprinkle with chopped nuts.

Bake at 350° until bubbles form and it is a light brown.

MRS. EPHRAIM LANDIS, *Blooming Glen, Pa.*

## Banana Cake or Hurry Frosting (Toasted)

| | |
|---|---|
| 3 tablespoons butter, melted | 2 tablespoons sweet cream |
| 5 tablespoons brown sugar | 1 cup shredded coconut |

Combine ingredients and beat until well blended.

Spread on cake while it is hot.

Toast in the oven until lightly browned.

MRS. J. V. ALBRECHT, *Tiskilwa, Ill.;* MRS. S. S. EARLY, *Dayton, Va.*

## Banana Frosting

3 tablespoons mashed bananas          1½-2 cups confectioner's sugar
1 tablespoon lemon juice

Sift sugar, add crushed bananas and lemon juice.
Beat until smooth and creamy.
Spread on cake.

MRS. LEIDY HUNSICKER, *Blooming Glen, Pa.*

## Boiled Icing

2 cups sugar                          2 egg whites
½ cup corn syrup                      2 tablespoons sugar
½ cup water                          1 teaspoon vanilla

Cook 2 cups sugar, corn syrup and water to the soft ball stage (238°).
Do not stir after sugar is dissolved.
Beat egg whites until stiff, add 2 tablespoons sugar and beat thoroughly.
Slowly pour hot syrup into egg whites, beating constantly.
Beat until thick enough to spread. Add vanilla.
This will keep in a covered jar in the refrigerator for some time.
Add a few drops of water when ready to use.

MRS. MARY MILLER, *Westover, Md.*

## Brown Butter Icing

¼ cup butter, melted                  2 tablespoons hot water
2 cups confectioner's sugar          1½ teaspoons vanilla
2 tablespoons cream

Melt butter and keep it over a low flame until brown.
Remove from heat and add confectioner's sugar, cream, water and
vanilla.
Stir vigorously with electric or hand beater until smooth and creamy.
Spread on cake.

MRS. LAWRENCE SPEIGLE, *Boswell, Pa.*; CLARA HOSTETLER, *Pryor, Okla.*

## Brown Sugar Boiled Frosting

1½ cups brown sugar, firmly packed    2 egg whites
1/3 cup water                        1 teaspoon vanilla
1/8 teaspoon salt

Boil sugar and water together to 242° or to the firm ball stage (not
hard).
Beat egg whites until stiff and slowly add hot syrup.

Add salt and vanilla and beat until frosting will stand in peaks.
Spread on cake.

MRS. JACOB NEUENSCHWANDER, *Apple Creek, Ohio*

## Butter Frosting

3 tablespoons butter
1 tablespoon cream or strong coffee
1½ cups confectioner's sugar

½ teaspoon vanilla
½ teaspoon almond extract

Cream butter until soft.
Add sugar, cream or coffee and flavoring.
Beat with electric or hand beater until smooth and creamy.
Spread on cake.

MRS. JACOB NEUENSCHWANDER, *Apple Creek, Ohio*

## Butter Cream Frosting

½ cup butter
3½ cups confectioner's sugar
2 egg yolks

1 teaspoon grated lemon rind
2 tablespoons milk (approximately)

Cream the butter.
Add the salt and sifted sugar gradually.
Add egg yolks, lemon rind and milk.
Beat with electric or hand beater until smooth and creamy.
Spread on cake.

KATIE RUTT, *New Holland, Pa.*

## Caramel Frosting

3 cups brown sugar
1 cup top milk or thin cream

2 tablespoons butter
1 teaspoon vanilla

Mix ingredients together in a saucepan.
Stir until sugar is dissolved.
Cook syrup until it forms a soft ball when dropped in cold water (238°).
Cool until you can hold your hand on the bottom of the pan.
Beat until creamy and spread on cake.
Sprinkle with chopped nuts.

MRS. TOM MILLER, *Walnut Creek, Ohio;* MRS. IDA M. GABLE, *York, Pa.*

## Chocolate Icing

1 can condensed milk (15 ounce can)    2 squares chocolate (2 ounces)

Place ingredients in a double boiler and heat.
Cook until icing becomes thick and creamy.

Stir frequently.

Let cool and spread on cake.

This amount covers 2 flat layers or 1 layer cake.

MRS. ABRAM A. LANDIS, *Salford Heights, Pa.;* GRACE EASH, *Jerome, Pa.*

## Chocolate Icing Deluxe

| | |
|---|---|
| 1 large egg | 1/3 cup butter or margarine |
| 2 cups confectioner's sugar | 2 squares unsweetened chocolate |
| 1/4 teaspoon salt | 1 teaspoon vanilla |

Beat egg with electric or rotary beater until fluffy.

Sift the sugar and add gradually to the egg.

Add salt, soft shortening and melted chocolate.

Beat until smooth and creamy.

Add vanilla.

Spread on cake. CLARA HOSTETLER, *Pryor, Okla.*

## Chocolate Fluff Frosting

Blend together:

| | |
|---|---|
| 4 tablespoons butter | 1 teaspoon vanilla |
| 3/4 cup confectioner's sugar | |

Add:

| | |
|---|---|
| 3 squares chocolate, melted (3 ounces) | 1/4 teaspoon salt |

Beat 2 egg whites until stiff but not dry.

Add ¾ cup confectioner's sugar, 2 tablespoons at a time.

Combine the 2 mixtures and fold only until blended.

Spread on cake.

STELLA HUBER STAUFFER, *Tofield, Alta., Can.*

## Chocolate Fudge Frosting

| | |
|---|---|
| 2 cups granulated sugar | 1 tablespoon butter |
| 1 cup top milk | 1/8 teaspoon cream of tartar |
| 3 tablespoons cocoa | 1 teaspoon vanilla |

Mix ingredients together in top of double boiler and bring to a boil.

Stir only until sugar is dissolved.

Cook until syrup forms a soft ball in cold water (238°).

Remove from heat and add butter, vanilla and cream of tartar.

Cool until you can hold your hand on the bottom of the pan.

Beat until creamy.

Spread on cake.

MRS. JACOB NEUENSCHWANDER, *Apple Creek, Ohio*

## Cream Cheese Frosting

2 packages cream cheese (6 ounces)  
¾ cup confectioner's sugar  
I teaspoon lemon juice

Cream the cheese until soft.

Sift sugar and add it gradually.

Stir until smooth.

Add lemon juice and blend together.

Spread on cake.

This is especially good on spice cake.

MRS. C. R. EBY, *Hagerstown, Md.*

## Filling for Sponge Cake

½ box currants  
½ box seeded raisins  
½ pound seeded dates  
I coconut, grated  
I cup English walnuts  
I cup almonds  
2 cups sugar  
I cup water  
3 egg whites

Grind the dried fruits.

Grate coconut and chop the nuts.

Cook sugar and water until syrup reaches soft ball stage (238°).

Pour syrup over stiffly beaten egg whites.

Beat until stiff and then add fruit and nut mixture.

Spread on cake.

MRS. JESSE HEISHMAN, *Harrisonburg, Va.*

## Fresh Strawberry Frosting

3 tablespoons butter or  
vegetable shortening  
¼ teaspoon salt  
2½ cups confectioner's sugar  
¼ cup crushed strawberries  
I teaspoon vanilla

Blend together the salt and fat.

Add sifted sugar alternately with crushed berries.

Add vanilla and blend into mixture.

Spread on cake.

This frosting is especially good for angel and sponge cakes.

MRS. ABRAM HEEBNER, *Souderton, Pa.*

## Frosting for Gingerbread

I cup sugar  
¼ cup water  
2 egg whites  
¾ teaspoon lemon extract  
I cup shredded coconut

Boil sugar and water together until it spins a thread 5 to 7 inches long.
Beat egg whites until stiff then slowly add hot syrup.
Beat until thick and a good consistency to spread.
Add lemon extract.
Spread on gingerbread and sprinkle with coconut.

DELPHIA KURTZ, *Oley, Pa.*

## Orange Frosting

1 cup granulated sugar
1 tablespoon corn syrup
2 tablespoons cold water

1 egg white
2 tablespoons orange juice
1/2 teaspoon orange rind

Cook sugar, syrup and water together until it reaches the soft ball stage.
Pour syrup slowly over stiffly beaten egg whites.
Beat until thick and add orange juice and rind.
Spread on cake.

MRS. CLARENCE WHISSEN, *Broadway, Va.*

## Sauce for Plain Cake

1 cup whipping cream
1/2 cup sugar

4 tablespoons cocoa

Mix ingredients together well and let stand 2 hours before serving.
Then whip with electric or rotary beater until stiff.
Spread between layers and on top of plain cake.
Serve immediately.
This frosting cannot be kept long.

MRS. ROY SHANTZ, *Waterloo, Ont., Can.*

## Seven-Minute Frosting

2 egg whites, unbeaten
1 1/2 cups granulated sugar
5 tablespoons cold water

1 teaspoon corn syrup or
1/4 teaspoon cream of tartar
1 teaspoon vanilla

Combine egg whites, sugar, water and corn syrup in the top of the
    double boiler.
Mix thoroughly.
Place over rapidly boiling water and beat constantly with rotary beater
    until mixture will hold a peak.
This requires approximately 7 minutes.
Remove from heat.
Add vanilla and beat until thick enough to spread.
Spread on cake.

MRS. JENNIE A. L. GABLE, *York, Pa.;* MRS. LOUIS AMSTUTZ, *Apple Creek, Ohio*

## Snow Cap Frosting

1 cup sugar
1 egg white
3½ tablespoons cold water

½ teaspoon lemon extract
6 marshmallows

Combine sugar, water and egg white in top of double boiler.
Have water boiling rapidly in bottom of double boiler.
Beat with rotary egg beater until mixture begins to thicken.
Then add chopped marshmallows and beat until mixture holds peaks.
Add flavoring and blend into mixture.
Cover cake while frosting is hot.

MRS. LOREN WADE, *Sterling, Ill.*

## Two-Minute Frosting

5 tablespoons brown sugar
4 tablespoons evaporated milk
½ teaspoon vanilla

1 tablespoon butter
Confectioner's sugar

Combine sugar, milk and butter in a saucepan.
Bring to the boiling point and sift in enough confectioner's sugar to
make the right consistency to spread (approximately 1½-2 cups).
Add vanilla and beat until smooth and creamy.
Spread on cake.

MRS. M. D. BURKHOLDER, *Harrisonburg, Va.*

## Uncooked Honey Icing

6 tablespoons butter or margarine
3½ cups sifted confectioner's sugar
½ teaspoon salt

½ cup honey
4 tablespoons hot milk

Cream fat until soft, add sifted sugar and salt.
Add the honey very slowly.
Beat in the hot milk, a little at a time.
Stop adding milk when icing begins to look satiny.
Spread on cake.

STELLA HUBER STAUFFER, *Tofield, Alta., Can.*

## Walnut Icing

2½ cups confectioner's sugar
4 tablespoons hot rich milk

½ cup ground walnuts

Sift the sugar and slowly add hot milk to it.
When beaten until smooth and creamy, add ground nuts.
Spread on cake.

MRS. MABEL WINEY CLYMER, *Lancaster, Pa.*

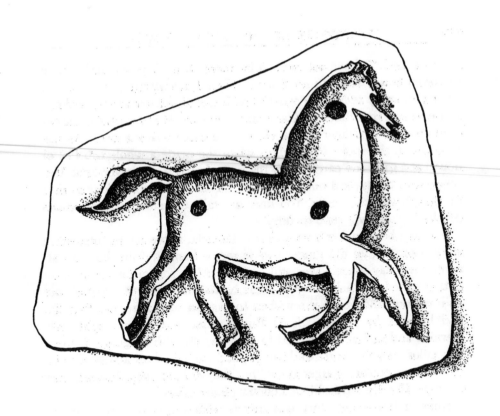

# Cookies

## Chapter IX

COOKIES WERE KNOWN TO GREAT-AUNT BARBARA ONLY AS "CAKES." Her two favorites were the old-fashioned ginger cookie, known also as leb kuchen, and the rich type of sugar cookie. The ginger cookie, still a favorite among our people, is a thick, chewy cookie always brushed with beaten egg to glaze it. The sugar cookie was usually made with sour cream and soda and then sprinkled with a mixture of sugar and cinnamon before it was baked.

Recently, during one of my rounds of collecting old recipes, I visited a dear 94-year-old granny. I had been told that she had made a name for herself during her younger days as the maker of the most delicious leb kuchen in her community. As I sat down and began to ask questions she only said, "I have not cooked for more than 15 years, and I have forgotten how I used to do things." Then I attempted once more to draw her out by telling her what I had heard about her ginger "cakes." Her eyes lost that faded look and with a gleam akin to youthful excitement she said, "Ginger cakes; oh, I have made many a one!" As she reminisced, she spoke of the days when she made a whole tub full of dough at a time and carried it to the springhouse to cool overnight. Her recipe was the typical one of her day, "Take just enough flour so that the dough will roll easily. You dare not take too much or the cookies will be dry and will stale readily."

A young homemaker from Ontario, Canada, wrote me an interesting story regarding an old ginger cookie recipe handed down by a great-aunt. "One day when I was still a small girl in school my Great-Aunt Esther called and asked me to come to visit her. She was getting old and had no children, so she wished to pass on several recipes that she had brought by memory from Europe. She had been taught only German and had never learned to write the English language. I drove five miles with the horse and buggy, and we baked all afternoon. She called these cookies 'ginger snaps,' but they did not snap. Instead, they are more like the old-fashioned chewy ginger cakes."

Another interesting story was sent in with a very old recipe called "ginger nuts." It is as follows: "These are small, round cookies which are so hard you have to suck them. My grandmother made them often and carried them to church hidden in a pocket in the folds of her skirt. She would use them, as needed, during church service to quiet and amuse her grandchildren."

There are other fascinating stories about cakes fried in deep fat and known in Grandmother's day as knee patches, plow lines and fasnachts. Peppernuts (pfeffernusse) and snicker doodles are two of the older recipes still popular enough to be worthy of a place in this book.

## DROPPED COOKIES
### Applesauce Cookies

| | |
|---|---|
| ½ cup shortening | ½ teaspoon salt |
| 1 cup sugar | ½ cup chopped raisins |
| 1 cup unsweetened applesauce | ½ cup chopped nuts |
| 1 teaspoon baking soda | 1 teaspoon cinnamon |
| 2 cups flour | ½ teaspoon cloves |

Cream shortening and sugar together.
Add applesauce and blend into mixture.
Sift flour.

Measure and add soda, salt and spices.

Sift again.

Add sifted dry ingredients and stir until smooth.

Add chopped raisins and nuts.

Drop from a teaspoon onto a greased baking sheet, spaced 2 to 3 inches
apart.

Bake at 375° for approximately 12 minutes.

Makes 4 dozen cookies.

MRS. EZRA LONG, *Sterling, Ill.*

## Brazil Nut Dainties

½ cup shortening
1 cup sugar
2 egg yolks
1 cup flour
¼ teaspoon salt

½ teaspoon grated lemon rind
3 tablespoons pineapple juice
6 tablespoons Brazil nuts, ground
½ cup Brazil nuts, sliced thin

Cream shortening and sugar together.

Add egg yolks and lemon rind and beat until fluffy.

Sift flour.

Measure and add salt.

Sift again.

Add sifted dry ingredients alternately with pineapple juice.

Stir until smooth.

Add coarsely ground nuts and blend into mixture.

Drop by teaspoonfuls onto a greased baking sheet, spaced 2 to 3 inches
apart.

Sprinkle with sliced Brazil nuts.

Bake at 375° for 10 to 12 minutes or until a golden brown.

Makes approximately 2 dozen cookies.

MRS. MARY GOOD, *Pottstown, Pa.*

## Carrot Cookies

½ cup shortening
1 cup brown sugar
½ cup granulated sugar
1 egg
1 cup cooked carrots, mashed

2 cups flour
½ teaspoon salt
1½ teaspoons baking powder
¾ cup raisins
1 teaspoon vanilla

Cream shortening and sugar together.

Add vanilla and eggs. Beat until fluffy.

Add cooked carrots that have been mashed and cooled.

Sift flour.

Measure and add salt and baking powder.

Sift again.

Add sifted dry ingredients and beat until smooth.

Add chopped raisins and blend into mixture.

Drop by teaspoonfuls onto a greased baking sheet, spaced 2 to 3 inches apart.

Bake at 375° for 10 to 12 minutes.

Makes about 3½ dozen cookies.

MRS. M. A. BENNER, *Mechanicsburg, Pa.*

Variation:

Spread orange frosting over carrot cookies while they are warm.

To make frosting, rub 1 teaspoon of soft butter into 1½ cups powdered sugar.

Add juice and grated rind of 1 orange.

Beat until smooth.

MRS. EVA COOPRIDER, *Hesston, Kan.*

## Chocolate Chip or Toll House Cookies

½ cup butter
½ cup brown sugar
½ cup granulated sugar
1 egg
1½ cups flour
½ teaspoon salt

½ teaspoon soda
1 package chocolate bits (7 oz.)
1 tablespoon hot water
1 teaspoon vanilla
½ cup chopped nuts (optional)

Cream shortening and sugar together.

Add egg, water and vanilla and beat until fluffy.

Sift flour.

Measure and add salt and soda. Sift again.

Add sifted dry ingredients and beat until smooth.

Add chocolate bits and nuts and blend into mixture.

Drop by teaspoonfuls onto a greased baking sheet, spaced 2 to 3 inches apart.

Bake at 375° for 10 minutes or until a light brown.

Makes about 4½ dozen cookies.

MRS. DAVE STEIDER, *Shickley, Neb.;* MRS. ALLEN YODER, *Grantsville, Md.*

## Chocolate Drop Cookies

½ cup shortening
1 cup brown sugar
2 eggs
1½ cups flour
½ teaspoon salt
1 teaspoon soda

½ cup cocoa or 2 ounce squares
of chocolate
½ cup milk
1 cup chopped nuts or
shredded coconut
1 teaspoon vanilla

Cream shortening and sugar together.

Add vanilla.

Add beaten eggs and continue to beat until fluffy.

Sift flour.

Measure and add cocoa, baking soda and salt.

Sift again.

Add sifted dry ingredients alternately with milk.

Beat until ingredients are well blended.

Add chopped nuts and blend into mixture.

Drop by teaspoonfuls onto a greased baking sheet, spaced 2 to 3 inches apart.

Bake at 375° for 10 to 12 minutes.

Makes 3½ dozen cookies.

Mrs. Joseph D. Backer, *Wolford, N. D.;* Mrs. David S. Mishler, *Johnstown, Pa.*

## Christmas Fruit Cookies

½ cup shortening
½ cup butter
2 cups sugar
3 eggs
3¼ cups flour
½ teaspoon salt
1 teaspoon cinnamon
½ teaspoon each of nutmeg and cloves
¼ cup milk
1 teaspoon lemon extract

1½ teaspoons vanilla
½ pound dates, chopped
½ pound raisins, chopped
¼ pound candied cherries
¼ pound candied pineapple
¼ pound citron
1 pound English or black walnuts, chopped
1 teaspoon baking soda

Cream shortening and sugar together.

Add eggs and flavoring.

Beat until fluffy.

Sift flour.

Measure and add salt and spices.

Sift again.

Add sifted dry ingredients alternately with milk.

Mix thoroughly after each addition.

Dissolve soda in 1 tablespoon water and blend well into mixture.

Add chopped fruits and nuts and blend well into mixture.

Drop by teaspoonfuls onto greased baking sheet, spaced 2 to 3 inches apart.

Bake at 350° for about 15 minutes or until lightly browned.

Makes approximately 12 dozen cookies.

Mrs. Willard Vogt, *Hesston, Kan.*

## Cinnamon Cookies

| | |
|---|---|
| 2 cups sugar | 1½ teaspoons cinnamon |
| 4 eggs | 1 teaspoon soda |
| 3 cups flour | ½ cup chopped nuts (optional) |
| ½ teaspoon salt | |

Combine sugar and cinnamon.

Beat eggs until light and add sugar and cinnamon mixture.

Sift flour.

Measure and add soda. Sift again.

Add sifted dry ingredients and stir until smooth.

Add chopped nuts and blend into dough.

Drop by teaspoonfuls onto greased baking sheet, spaced 2 to 3 inches apart.

Bake at 375° for 10 to 12 minutes or until lightly browned.

Makes 3 dozen cookies.

Let your children make these, as they are very easily made.

MRS. C. F. YAKE, *Scottdale, Pa.*

## Coconut Cookies

| | |
|---|---|
| 1 cup shortening (half butter) | 1 teaspoon soda |
| 2 cups light brown sugar | 1 teaspoon cream of tartar |
| 2 eggs | 2 tablespoons water |
| 3 cups flour | 2 cups grated coconut |
| ½ teaspoon salt | 1½ teaspoons vanilla |

Cream shortening and sugar together.

Add eggs, water and vanilla and beat until fluffy.

Sift flour.

Measure and add salt, soda and cream of tartar.

Sift again.

Add sifted dry ingredients and beat until smooth.

Add grated coconut and blend into mixture.

Drop by teaspoonfuls onto greased baking sheet, spaced 2 to 3 inches apart.

Bake at 350° for 10 to 12 minutes or until lightly browned.

Makes 3½ to 4 dozen cookies.

MRS. J. E. BRUBAKER, *Manheim, Pa.;* MRS. MAHLON KENNEL, *Shickley, Neb.*
RUTH STOLTZFUS, *Westover, Md.*

## Coconut Macaroons

| | |
|---|---|
| 1 can condensed milk (15 oz.) | 3 cups shredded coconut |

Combine milk and coconut.

Stir until all the coconut is well moistened.

Drop by teaspoonfuls onto greased baking sheet, spaced 2 to 3 inches apart.

Bake at 350° for 15 minutes or until lightly browned.

Remove from pan at once.

Makes 4 dozen cookies.

For variation, ½ cup chocolate chips or nuts may be added.

A SISTER, *Souderton, Pa.*

## Corn Flake Macaroons

| | |
|---|---|
| 2 egg whites | ½ teaspoon salt |
| ½ cup sugar | 1 cup grated coconut |
| ½ cup white syrup | 1 teaspoon vanilla |
| 2 cups corn flakes | |

Beat egg whites until frothy.

Add salt and continue to beat until very stiff but not dry.

Add 2 tablespoons sugar at a time and continue to beat.

Add syrup and vanilla and blend into mixture.

Lightly fold corn flakes and grated coconut into mixture.

Drop by teaspoonfuls onto greased baking sheet, spaced 2 to 3 inches apart.

Bake at 350° for 15 minutes or until lightly browned.

Makes about 3½ dozen cookies.

These are a chewy cookie. Delicious!

MRS. SAMUEL NAFZIGER. *Kalona, Iowa*

## Crunchy Crisps

| | |
|---|---|
| 1 cup shortening (half butter) | ¼ teaspoon salt |
| 1½ cups brown sugar | 2 teaspoons baking powder |
| 1 egg | 1 cup grated coconut |
| 1½ cups flour | 1 teaspoon vanilla |
| 1¼ cups rolled oats | |

Cream shortening and sugar together.

Add vanilla.

Add egg and beat until fluffy.

Sift flour.

Measure and add salt and baking powder.

Sift again.

Add dry ingredients and rolled oats to creamed mixture. Mix thoroughly.

Add grated coconut and blend well into dough.

Drop by teaspoonfuls onto greased baking sheet, spaced 2 to 3 inches apart or roll in small balls and press flat with a fork.

Bake at 375° approximately 12 minutes.

Makes about 3 dozen cookies.

MRS. ALVIN N. ROTH, *Wellesley, Ont., Can.*

## Grandmother's Ginger Balls or Ginger Nuts

| | |
|---|---|
| 1 cup shortening | 1½ teaspoons soda |
| 1 cup molasses | ½ teaspoon salt |
| 1 cup brown sugar | 1 teaspoon ginger |
| 3½ to 4 cups flour | ½ cup boiling water |

Cream shortening and sugar together.

Add molasses and continue to beat.

Sift flour.

Measure and add salt, soda and ginger.

Sift again.

Add sifted dry ingredients alternately with hot water.

Mix thoroughly.

Chill dough in refrigerator.

Roll into balls 1 inch in diameter and dip into granulated sugar.

Place balls on buttered baking sheets about 2 inches apart.

Bake at 350° for 12 to 15 minutes.

Makes approximately 6 dozen cookies.

MRS. E. SWARTZENTRUBER, *Breslau, Ont., Can.*
MRS. REUBEN B. EBERLY, *Fayettesville, Pa.*

## Gumdrop Cookies

| | |
|---|---|
| ½ cup shortening | ½ teaspoon soda |
| ½ cup brown sugar | ½ teaspoon baking powder |
| ½ cup granulated sugar | 1 cup gumdrops, chopped |
| 1 egg | 1 cup rolled oats |
| 1 cup flour | 1 cup corn flakes |
| ½ teaspoon salt | ½ cup grated coconut |

Cream shortening and sugar together.

Add egg and beat until fluffy.

Sift flour, measure and add salt, soda, and baking powder. Sift again.

Add sifted dry ingredients to creamed mixture and beat until well blended.

Then add chopped gumdrops, grated coconut, rolled oats and corn flakes.

Blend into dough.

Drop by teaspoonfuls onto greased baking sheet about 2 inches apart.
Bake at 350° for 15 minutes.

Makes about 4 dozen cookies.

EDITH KEFFER, *Waterloo, Ont., Can.*

## Hermits

| | |
|---|---|
| 1 cup shortening (half butter) | 1/2 teaspoon soda |
| 2 cups brown sugar | 1 1/2 teaspoons cinnamon |
| 2 eggs | 1/2 teaspoon each of cloves and nutmeg |
| 2 2/3 cups flour | 1/3 cup milk |
| 1/2 teaspoon salt | 2/3 cup chopped raisins |
| 2 teaspoons baking powder | 2/3 cup chopped nuts |

Cream shortening and sugar together.

Add eggs and beat until fluffy.

Sift flour.

Measure and add salt, soda, baking powder and spices. Sift again.

Add sifted dry ingredients alternately with milk.

Beat after each addition.

Add chopped nuts and raisins and blend into mixture.

Drop by teaspoonfuls onto greased baking sheet about 2 inches apart.
Bake at 350° for 12 to 15 minutes.

Makes about 5 dozen cookies.

FANNIE MARTIN, *Hinton, Va.;* MRS. MARTIN GERLACH, *Columbia, Pa.*

## Honey Drop Cookies

| | |
|---|---|
| 1/4 cup butter | 2 teaspoons baking powder |
| 3/4 cup honey | 2 tablespoons milk |
| 1 egg | 1 cup chopped nuts |
| 2 cups flour | 1 cup raisins, chopped |
| 1/2 teaspoon salt | |

Cream butter.

Add honey and beaten egg and beat until fluffy.

Sift flour, measure and add salt and baking powder.

Sift again.

Add chopped nuts and raisins to flour mixture.

Add dry ingredients alternately with milk to creamed mixture.

Mix thoroughly.

Drop by teaspoonfuls onto greased baking sheet, spaced 2 to 3 inches
apart.

Bake at 350° for 12 to 15 minutes.

Makes 4½ dozen cookies.

MRS. H. LANDIS, *Lancaster, Pa.*

## Jam Jams

| | |
|---|---|
| ¾ cup shortening | ½ teaspoon salt |
| 1 cup sugar | 2 teaspoons soda |
| 1 cup molasses | ½ teaspoon baking powder |
| 4 eggs | ½ cup sour cream |
| ¾ cup boiling water | 1 cup chopped raisins |
| 4 cups flour | |

Cream shortening and sugar together.

Add molasses and beat again.

Add eggs to creamed mixture and beat until fluffy.

Gradually add boiling water and stir until smooth.

Sift flour.

Measure and add salt, soda and spices.

Sift again.

Add sifted dry ingredients alternately with sour cream.

Mix thoroughly.

Add chopped raisins and blend into mixture.

Drop by teaspoonfuls onto greased baking sheet, spaced 2 to 3 inches apart.

Bake at 350° for 12 to 15 minutes.

Makes 6 to 7 dozen cookies.

MRS. OWEN F. SHOWALTER, *Broadway, Va.*

## Jumbies

| | |
|---|---|
| ½ cup shortening | 1 teaspoon soda |
| 1½ cups brown sugar | 2 tablespoons hot water |
| 3 eggs | 1 cup chopped nuts |
| 3 cups flour | 1 cup chopped dates |
| ½ teaspoon salt | 1 teaspoon vanilla |

Cream shortening and sugar together.

Add eggs and vanilla and beat until fluffy.

Sift flour.

Measure and add salt.

Sift again.

Add dry ingredients to mixture alternately with water in which soda has been dissolved.

Add chopped nuts and dates.

Drop by teaspoonfuls onto greased baking tin, about 2 inches apart.

Bake at 350° for approximately 15 minutes.

Makes 6 dozen cookies.

MRS. DAVID M. SNIDER, *Elmira, Ont., Can.*

## Lace Wafers

| | |
|---|---|
| I tablespoon butter | 1/2 teaspoon salt |
| I cup sugar | 2 teaspoons baking powder |
| 2 eggs | I teaspoon vanilla |
| 2 1/2 cups rolled oats | |

Cream shortening and sugar together.

Add vanilla.

Add eggs and beat until fluffy.

Combine rolled oats with salt and baking powder and add to creamed mixture.

Mix thoroughly.

Drop by teaspoonfuls onto greased baking sheet, spaced about 2 to 3 inches apart.

Bake at 375° for 12 minutes.

Makes 4 dozen cookies.

Mrs. L. Strong, *Waterloo, Ont., Can.*

## Lunch Box Cookies

| | |
|---|---|
| I cup shortening | 1/2 teaspoon salt |
| I cup brown sugar | 3 teaspoons baking powder |
| 3/4 cup granulated sugar | 1/2 cup milk |
| 2 eggs | 2 cups corn flakes |
| 2 cups flour | I teaspoon vanilla |

Cream shortening and sugar together.

Add vanilla and eggs. Beat until fluffy.

Sift flour.

Measure and add salt and baking powder.

Sift again.

Add corn flakes to dry ingredients.

Add dry ingredients to creamed mixture alternately with milk.

Mix thoroughly.

Drop by teaspoonfuls onto greased baking sheet, spaced about 2 to 3 inches apart.

Bake at 375° for 12 minutes.

Makes 5 dozen cookies.

Tillie Mae Hamilton, *Sheridan, Ore.*

## Mincemeat Cookies

| | |
|---|---|
| I cup shortening | I teaspoon soda |
| I cup brown sugar | I teaspoon cinnamon |
| I cup granulated sugar | 1/2 teaspoon each of cloves and nutmeg |

3 eggs
3 cups flour
1/2 teaspoon salt

I cup mincemeat
I cup chopped nuts

Cream shortening and sugar together.

Add eggs and beat until fluffy.

Sift flour.

Measure and add salt, soda and spices.

Sift again.

Add sifted dry ingredients to creamed mixture.

Mix thoroughly.

Add mincemeat and chopped nuts and blend into dough.

Drop by teaspoonfuls onto greased baking sheet, spaced 2 to 3 inches apart.

Bake at 350° for 12 to 15 minutes.

Makes 6 dozen cookies.

MRS. NATHAN G. KEYSER, *Souderton, Pa.*
MRS. J. MARK STAUFFER, *Harrisonburg, Va.*

## Molasses Crinkles

3/4 cup shortening
I cup brown sugar
I egg
4 tablespoons molasses
2 1/4 cups flour

1/2 teaspoon salt
2 teaspoons soda
I teaspoon cinnamon
I teaspoon ginger
1/2 teaspoon cloves

Cream shortening and sugar together.

Add egg and molasses and beat until well blended.

Sift flour.

Measure and add salt, soda and spices.

Sift again.

Add sifted dry ingredients to creamed mixture and mix thoroughly.

Chill dough in refrigerator.

Shape the chilled dough in balls 1 inch in diameter.

Roll balls in granulated sugar and place 2 inches apart on greased baking sheet.

Bake at 350° for 12 to 15 minutes.

Makes 4 dozen cookies.

MRS. J. IRVIN LEHMAN, *Chambersburg, Pa.*; MRS. SCHERTZ, *Falfurrias, Tex.*

## Nut and Fruit Cookies

I cup shortening (half butter)
1 1/2 cups sugar

1 1/2 tablespoons hot water
I teaspoon cinnamon

3 eggs
3½ cups flour
½ teaspoon salt
1 teaspoon soda

½ cup chopped raisins
½ cup currants
1 cup chopped nuts

Cream shortening and sugar together.

Add eggs and beat until fluffy.

Sift flour.

Measure and add salt and cinnamon.

Sift again.

Dissolve soda in hot water and add to creamed mixture.

Add half of sifted dry ingredients and mix thoroughly.

Fold in chopped fruits and nuts and remaining flour and stir until well blended.

Drop by teaspoonfuls onto a greased baking sheet, spaced 2 to 3 inches apart.

Bake at 350° for 15 minutes.

Makes 5 dozen cookies.

A SISTER, *Lancaster, Pa.*

## Orange Cookies

1 cup shortening
2 cups sugar
2 eggs
3½ to 4 cups flour
½ teaspoon salt

1 teaspoon soda
1 teaspoon baking powder
1 cup sour milk or buttermilk
Juice and grated rind of 1 orange

Cream shortening and sugar together.

Add eggs and beat until fluffy.

Add juice and grated rind of orange.

Sift flour.

Measure and add soda and baking powder.

Sift again.

Add sifted dry ingredients alternately with sour milk to creamed mixture.

Mix thoroughly.

Drop by teaspoonfuls onto greased baking sheet about 2 inches apart.

Bake at 375° for about 12 minutes.

Makes 6 dozen cookies.

Spread with orange frosting while cookies are warm (page 247).

MRS. DORA WYSE, *Scottdale, Pa.;* BETTY KAUFMAN, *Midland, Mich.*
LUCILLE VARNS, *Wooster, Ohio*

## Oatmeal Drop Cookies

| | |
|---|---|
| 1 cup shortening | 1 teaspoon soda |
| 1½ cups sugar | 2 cups rolled oats |
| 2 eggs | 1 teaspoon cinnamon |
| 1¾ cups flour | ½ cup sour milk |
| ½ teaspoon salt | 1 cup chopped raisins or dates |
| 1 teaspoon baking powder | ½ cup chopped nuts |

Cream shortening and sugar together.

Add eggs and beat until fluffy.

Sift flour.

Measure and add salt, soda, baking powder and cinnamon. Sift again.

Add rolled oats and mix thoroughly.

Add dry ingredients alternately with milk to creamed mixture.

Mix thoroughly.

Fold in chopped raisins or dates and nuts and stir until well blended.

Drop by teaspoonfuls onto greased baking sheet, spaced 2 to 3 inches apart.

Flatten with a fork.

Bake at 350° for 12 to 15 minutes.

Makes 6 dozen cookies.

    Mrs. Joe Shetler, *Midland, Mich.;* Mrs. Alva Swartzendruber, *Hydro, Okla.*

Variation:

One cup stewed, chopped prunes may be substituted for raisins or dates.

Follow directions in preceding recipe.

              Mrs. La Vern Miller, *Nampa, Idaho*

## Peanut Butter Cookies

| | |
|---|---|
| 1 cup shortening | 3 cups flour |
| 1 cup peanut butter | ½ teaspoon salt |
| 1 cup brown sugar | 2 teaspoons soda |
| 1 cup granulated sugar | 1 teaspoon baking powder |
| 2 eggs | 1 teaspoon vanilla |

Cream shortening and peanut butter together.

Add sugar and continue to beat.

Add eggs and vanilla and beat until fluffy.

Sift flour.

Measure and add salt, soda and baking powder.

Sift again.

Gradually add sifted dry ingredients to creamed mixture and mix thoroughly.

Chill dough in refrigerator for several hours.

Shape dough into balls 1 inch in diameter.
Place balls 2 to 3 inches apart on greased baking sheet.
Press flat with a fork.
Bake at 375° for 12 to 15 minutes.
Makes about 7 dozen cookies.

MARY BRUBAKER, *Harrisonburg, Va.;* SARAH M. GEHMAN, *Bally, Pa.*
MRS. JOSEPH D. HEATWOLE, *Bridgewater, Va.*

## Peanut Crunches

One cup finely crushed peanuts or peanut crunch may be substituted
for peanut butter.
Follow directions in preceding recipe.

MRS. MILTON ERNST, *Kitchener, Ont., Can.;* MRS. B. L. BUCHER, *Dallastown, Pa.*

## Pineapple Cookies

| | |
|---|---|
| 1/2 cup shortening | 1/2 teaspoon soda |
| 1/2 cup brown sugar | 1 teaspoon baking powder |
| 1/2 cup white sugar | 1/2 cup crushed pineapple, drained |
| egg | 1 teaspoon vanilla or lemon extract |
| 2 cups flour | 1/2 cup chopped nuts or shredded |
| 1/4 teaspoon salt | coconut (optional) |

Cream shortening and sugar together.
Add egg and flavoring and beat until fluffy.
Drain pineapple and add to creamed mixture.
Sift flour.
Measure and add salt, soda and baking powder.
Sift again.
Gradually add sifted dry ingredients and mix thoroughly.
Fold in chopped nuts or shredded coconut.
Drop by teaspoonfuls onto greased baking sheet, spaced 2 to 3 inches
apart.
Bake at 375° for 10 to 12 minutes.
Makes about 4 dozen cookies.

MRS. CLOYD KNAVEL, *Salix, Pa.;* MRS. WALTER WEAVER, *Christiana, Pa.*

## Popcorn Cookies

| | |
|---|---|
| 1 cup freshly popped corn | 1/8 teaspoon salt |
| 1 cup chopped nuts | 1/2 teaspoon baking powder |
| 1/2 cup sugar | 3 egg whites |

Put popcorn through food grinder and combine with nuts.
Beat egg whites until frothy; add salt and baking powder.

Continue to beat whites until stiff.

Add sugar gradually and beat until well blended.

Fold beaten whites into popcorn mixture.

Drop by teaspoonfuls onto greased baking sheet about 2 inches apart.

Bake at 350° for 12 to 15 minutes or until lightly browned.

Makes 2 dozen cookies.

## Raisin Cookies

| | |
|---|---|
| 2 cups raisins | 1 teaspoon baking powder |
| 1 cup boiling water | 1 teaspoon soda |
| 1 cup shortening | 1 teaspoon salt |
| 2 cups sugar | 1 teaspoon cinnamon |
| 3 eggs | 1/4 teaspoon each of cloves and nutmeg |
| 1 teaspoon vanilla | 1 cup chopped nuts |
| 4 cups flour | |

Add boiling water to raisins and cook for 5 minutes. Cool.

Cream shortening and sugar together.

Add eggs and vanilla and beat until fluffy.

Add cooled raisins to creamed mixture and mix thoroughly.

Sift flour.

Measure and add salt, soda, baking powder and spices. Sift again.

Add sifted dry ingredients and chopped nuts and blend well into mixture.

Drop by teaspoonfuls onto greased baking sheet, spaced 2 to 3 inches apart.

Bake at 350° for 12 to 15 minutes.

Makes 6 dozen cookies.

MRS. JACOB F. KOLB, *Spring City, Pa.*

## Ragged Robins

| | |
|---|---|
| 1/2 cup sugar | 1 cup chopped walnuts |
| 2 eggs | 1 cup chopped dates |
| 1 teaspoon vanilla | 2 cups corn flakes |

Beat eggs until lemon colored.

Gradually add sugar and vanilla and continue to beat until well blended.

Add chopped nuts and dates.

Fold corn flakes into mixture.

Shape into balls 1 inch in diameter and place 2 inches apart on greased baking sheet.

Bake at 350° for 12 to 15 minutes.

Makes 4 dozen cookies.

MRS. D. H. REIMER, *Altona, Man., Can.*

## Rock Cookies

| | |
|---|---|
| 1 cup shortening (half butter) | 1½ tablespoons hot water |
| 1½ cups brown sugar | 1 teaspoon cinnamon |
| 2 eggs | ½ teaspoon cloves |
| 2¾ cups flour | 1½ cups chopped dates or raisins |
| ½ teaspoon salt | 1 cup chopped walnuts |
| 1 teaspoon soda | |

Cream shortening and sugar together.

Add egg yolks and beat until fluffy.

Dissolve soda in hot water and add to creamed mixture.

Sift flour.

Measure and add salt and spices.

Sift again.

Add half of dry ingredients to mixture and mix thoroughly.

Combine remaining dry ingredients with chopped dates and nuts and add to dough.

Mix thoroughly.

Fold in stiffly beaten egg whites.

Drop by teaspoonfuls onto greased baking sheet, spaced 2 to 3 inches apart.

Bake at 350° for 12 to 15 minutes.

Makes 5 dozen cookies.

Mrs. Ephraim Delp, *Souderton, Pa.;* Mrs. Amos Leis, *Wellesley, Ont., Can.*

## Scottish Tea Cookies

| | |
|---|---|
| ¾ cup shortening (half butter) | ¼ teaspoon salt |
| ½ cup powdered sugar, sifted | 1 teaspoon vanilla |
| 2 eggs | ¼ cup chopped nuts (optional) |
| 1½ cups flour | |

Combine salt, sugar and shortening.

Work into flour as for pastry.

Beat eggs and add vanilla.

Add beaten eggs to flour mixture and stir until smooth.

Fold in chopped nuts.

Chill dough in refrigerator several hours.

Shape chilled dough into balls 1 inch in diameter and roll in powdered sugar.

Place balls on greased baking sheet 2 inches apart and flatten with spatula.

Bake at 350° for about 20 minutes.

After removing from oven, roll in powdered sugar or cool and spread with butter frosting (page 244).

Top with another cookie.

Makes 1½ dozen filled cookies.

Mrs. W. M. Strong, Mechanicsburg, Pa.

## Sour Cream Cookies

| | |
|---|---|
| ½ cup shortening | 1 teaspoon soda |
| 2 cups sugar | 1 cup sour cream |
| 2 eggs | 1 teaspoon vanilla |
| 4 cups flour | ¼ cup sugar-cinnamon mixture |
| ½ teaspoon salt | |

Cream shortening and sugar together.

Add vanilla.

Add eggs and beat until fluffy.

Sift flour.

Measure and add salt and soda.

Sift again.

Add sifted dry ingredients alternately with sour cream.

Mix thoroughly.

Drop by teaspoonfuls onto greased baking sheet, spaced 2 to 3 inches apart.

Sprinkle with sugar and cinnamon mixture.

Bake at 375° for about 12 minutes.

Makes 5 dozen cookies.

Mrs. O. O. Weaver, Canton, Kan.; Mrs. Mabel Lytle, Smithville, Ohio

## Spice Drop Cookies

| | |
|---|---|
| 1¼ cups shortening | 1 teaspoon soda |
| 1 cup brown sugar | 1 teaspoon baking powder |
| 1 cup granulated sugar | 1 teaspoon cinnamon |
| 3 eggs, separated | ½ teaspoon cloves |
| 3½ cups flour | 1 cup sour milk |
| 1 teaspoon salt | |

Cream shortening and sugar together.

Add egg yolks and one white and beat until fluffy.

Sift flour.

Measure and add salt, soda, baking powder and spices.

Sift again.

Add sifted dry ingredients alternately with sour milk to creamed mixture.

Mix thoroughly.

Drop by teaspoonfuls onto greased baking sheet, spaced 2 to 3 inches apart.

Beat remaining egg whites until stiff.

Add 3 tablespoons sugar and continue to beat until glossy.

Spread meringue on top of cookies and bake at 350° until a golden brown.

Makes 5 dozen cookies.

MARY BRUNK, *Washington, D. C.;* NANCY ZEHR, *Tavistock, Ont., Can.*

## Spritzes

| | |
|---|---|
| 1 cup butter | ½ teaspoon salt |
| 2/3 cup sugar | ¼ cup ground almonds |
| 3 egg yolks | 1 teaspoon vanilla |
| 2½ cups flour | |

Cream butter and sugar together.

Add vanilla.

Add unbeaten egg yolks and beat until fluffy.

Add ground almonds and blend into creamed mixture.

Sift flour.

Measure and add salt. Sift again.

Gradually add flour to creamed mixture and beat until smooth.

Chill dough in refrigerator for several hours.

Drop by teaspoonfuls onto ungreased baking sheet, spaced 2 to 3 inches apart.

Bake at 400° for 7 to 8 minutes.

Makes 4½ dozen cookies.

LA VERNE JOHNSON, *Bluffton, Ohio*

## Sweitzer Cookies

| | |
|---|---|
| 6 eggs | 4 cups flour |
| ½ teaspoon salt | 1 teaspoon vanilla |
| 2 cups sugar | |

Beat eggs and salt together for 10 minutes.

Add sugar gradually and continue to beat for 15 minutes.

Add flour and beat 20 minutes longer.

Drop by teaspoonfuls onto greased baking pans, spaced 2 to 3 inches apart.

Let stand in a cool place overnight.

In the morning bake at 375° for 10 to 12 minutes.

Makes 7 dozen small cookies.

MRS. ANNA AMSTUTZ, *Apple Creek, Ohio*

## Walnut Kisses

| | |
|---|---|
| 1 pound walnuts, finely chopped | 6 egg whites |
| 2 cups sugar | 1 teaspoon vanilla |
| 5 tablespoons flour | |

Beat egg whites until stiff but not dry.

Gradually add sugar and continue to beat until well blended.

Sift flour lightly over beaten whites and fold in with a wire whisk.

Add vanilla and nuts and blend into mixture.

Drop by teaspoonfuls onto greased baking sheets about 2 inches apart.

Bake at 325° for about 10 minutes.

Remove from pan at once.

Makes 6 dozen small cookies.

MRS. BENJAMIN BAER, *East Petersburg, Pa.;* MRS. AARON GROFF, *Bareville, Pa.*

# ROLLED COOKIES

## Butter Cookies

| | |
|---|---|
| 1½ cups shortening, butter preferred | 2 egg yolks |
| 1½ cups powdered sugar | 4 cups flour |

Cream shortening and sugar together until light and fluffy.

Add egg yolks and continue to beat.

Add sifted flour and stir until well blended into mixture.

Roll out on floured board to ⅛ inch thickness.

Cut with fancy shaped cutters and decorate with colored sugar or candies.

Bake at 375° until a golden brown (about 10 minutes).

Makes about 4 dozen cookies.

MRS. SIMON GINGERICH, *Goshen, Ind.*

## Date Filled Cookies

| | |
|---|---|
| 1 cup shortening | 2 teaspoons baking powder |
| 1½ cups brown sugar | ½ teaspoon salt |
| 2 eggs | 1 teaspoon soda |
| 4 cups flour | ¼ cup milk |
| 1 cup rolled oats | 2 teaspoons vanilla |

Cream shortening and sugar together.

Add vanilla.

Add eggs and beat until fluffy.

Sift flour.

Measure and add salt, soda and baking powder.

Sift again and add rolled oats.

Add dry ingredients alternately with milk.

Mix thoroughly.

Chill dough in refrigerator for several hours.

Roll out on lightly floured board to ¼ inch thickness.

Cut with a round cutter and spread with the following filling:

| | |
|---|---|
| 2 cups chopped dates | ¼ cup flour |
| 1 cup sugar | 1 cup water |

Combine sugar and flour and add to chopped dates.

Add water and stir until smooth.

Cook until thickened, stirring constantly.

Put a teaspoon of the filling on top of each cookie.

Cover with another piece of dough and fasten edges securely.

Place 1 inch apart on greased cookie sheet and bake at 375° until a golden brown.

Makes 2½ to 3 dozen cookies.

MRS. LIDA L. YODER, *Smithville, Ohio*

## Fig Filled Cookies

| | |
|---|---|
| ½ cup shortening (butter preferred) | 1 teaspoon soda |
| 1 cup sugar | ½ teaspoon salt |
| 2 eggs | ½ cup sour milk |
| 3½ cups flour | 1 teaspoon vanilla |

Cream sugar and shortening together. Add vanilla.

Add eggs and beat until fluffy.

Sift flour.

Measure and add salt and soda.

Sift again.

Add dry ingredients alternately with sour milk.

Beat after each addition.

Roll on floured board to ⅛ inch thickness.

Cut with cookie cutter and spread with fig jam or the following filling:

| | |
|---|---|
| 1½ cups chopped figs | 1 cup water |
| ½ cup sugar | ½ cup chopped nuts |
| 2 tablespoons flour | |

Combine sugar and flour.

Add chopped figs and nuts.

Add water and stir until smooth.

Cook until thickened, stirring constantly.

Put a teaspoon of filling on each cookie.

Cover with another cookie and fasten edges securely.

Place 1 inch apart on greased baking sheet.
Bake at 375° until a golden brown.
Makes 2½ to 3 dozen cookies.

Mrs. Ezra Yoder, *Tofield, Alta., Can.;* Mrs. Allen Gingerich, *Lowville, N. Y.*

## Old-Fashioned Ginger Cookies (Leb Kuchen)

| | |
|---|---|
| 2 cups shortening, melted | 2 tablespoons soda |
| 3 cups sorghum molasses | 1 tablespoon ginger |
| 1 cup sugar | 1 tablespoon cinnamon |
| 8 to 10 cups flour | 1½ cups buttermilk or sour milk |
| 1 teaspoon salt | |

Heat molasses and sugar together.
When sugar is dissolved, add shortening and stir until it is melted.
Remove from heat. Cool to lukewarm.
Sift flour, salt, soda and spices together.
Add sifted dry ingredients alternately with sour milk.
Stir until a medium-soft dough is formed.
Work dough with hands for 5 minutes.
Let chill in refrigerator for several hours.
Turn dough onto lightly floured board and roll ¼ inch thick.
Cut with large round cookie or a doughnut cutter with center removed.
Glaze with a beaten egg. (Dip a small piece of cheesecloth in beaten
   egg and rub lightly over cookie.)
Place 1 inch apart on greased cookie sheet.
Bake at 350° for 20 to 25 minutes.
This is the soft, chewy cookie that was a favorite of grandmother's day.
It is still very popular among many Mennonite families.
Makes 8 dozen large cookies.

Grandmother Keener, *Hagerstown, Md.;* Mrs. Aaron Lehman, *Castorland, N. Y.*
Ruth Slaymaker, *Leola, Pa.*

## Ginger Snaps

| | |
|---|---|
| 1 cup shortening | 7 cups flour, approximately |
| 2 cups dark molasses | 2 teaspoons ginger |
| ½ cup brown sugar | ½ teaspoon salt |
| ½ cup water | 2 teaspoons soda |

Combine molasses, sugar and water and cook together slowly for 15
   minutes.
Just before removing from heat, add shortening and ginger.
Stir until shortening is melted.
Cool mixture and add soda, salt and flour, which have been sifted
   together.

Mix ingredients thoroughly.

The dough should be very stiff.

Chill dough for several hours in refrigerator.

Turn out dough on a lightly floured board and roll as thin as possible.

Cut with round cookie cutter and place ½ inch apart on a greased cookie sheet.

Bake at 375° until crisp and golden brown.

Makes 8 dozen cookies.

These cookies improve if allowed to ripen in a stone jar for several weeks.

If desired, cookies may be spread with boiled frosting before being served.

MRS. JOSEPH E. BRUNK, *Goshen, Ind.*

## Graham Crackers

| | |
|---|---|
| 1 cup shortening | 1 teaspoon soda |
| 2 cups brown sugar | 2 teaspoons baking powder |
| 1 cup granulated sugar | ½ teaspoon salt |
| 2 cups white flour | 1 cup sweet or sour milk |
| 4 cups graham flour | 1 teaspoon vanilla |

Cream shortening and sugar together until fluffy. Add vanilla.

Sift flour.

Measure, and add salt, soda and baking powder.

Sift again.

Add sifted dry ingredients alternately with milk.

Mix thoroughly after each addition.

Chill dough in refrigerator overnight.

In the morning, turn out on floured board and roll as thin as possible.

Cut in squares or any shape desired.

Place 1 inch apart on a greased cookie sheet.

Bake at 350° until crisp and a golden brown.

Makes about 6 dozen cookies.

MRS. HENRY E. YODER, *Grantsville, Md.*

## Lemon Crackers

| | |
|---|---|
| 1 cup shortening | ½ teaspoon salt |
| 2¼ cups sugar | 2 cups milk |
| Approximately 7 cups flour | 1 ounce carbonate ammonia |
| 2 eggs | 1 teaspoon lemon extract |

Cream shortening and sugar together until fluffy. Add flavoring.

Add eggs and continue to beat.

Pulverize ammonia and dissolve in milk.

Sift flour and salt together and add alternately with milk.

Add only enough flour to make a medium-soft dough.

Chill in refrigerator for several hours.

Turn dough onto floured board and roll ⅛ inch thick.

Cut in squares or roll in one piece and mark in squares with back of knife.

Prick lightly with a fork before putting in the oven.

Place 1 inch apart on a greased baking sheet.

Bake at 375° until crisp and a golden brown.

Makes 6 to 7 dozen crackers.

MRS. EDGAR CLINE, *Broadway, Va.;* MRS. DAVID EIMEN, *Iowa City, Iowa*

## Maple Sugar Cookies

| | |
|---|---|
| ¼ cup butter | Approximately 3 cups flour |
| 2 cups maple sugar | ½ teaspoon salt |
| 1 cup thick sour cream | 1 teaspoon soda |
| 2 eggs | 1 teaspoon vanilla |

Cream butter and sugar together. Add vanilla.

Add eggs and beat until fluffy.

Add sour cream and blend into mixture.

Sift flour.

Measure and add salt and soda.

Sift again.

Add dry ingredients and work until dough is smooth.

Add more flour if necessary to make a medium-soft dough.

Chill in refrigerator for several hours.

Turn out on a lightly floured board and roll to ⅛ inch thickness.

Place 1 inch apart on a greased baking sheet.

Bake at 375° until a golden brown.

Makes about 4 dozen cookies.

MRS. SILAS BEACHY, *Accident, Md.*

## Old-Fashioned Molasses Cookies

| | |
|---|---|
| 1 cup shortening | 1 cup sugar |
| 4 cups flour | 1 egg |
| 1 teaspoon salt | ¼ cup hot water |
| 1 cup dark molasses | 1¼ teaspoons soda |

Sift flour and salt together and cut in shortening as for pastry.

In another bowl, combine molasses and sugar.

Add egg and beat well.

Dissolve soda in hot water and add to molasses mixture.

Combine crumb and molasses mixtures and stir until well blended.

Chill dough for several hours in refrigerator.

Turn out on a lightly floured board and roll to ¼ inch thickness.

Place 1 inch apart on a greased cookie sheet.

Bake at 375° until a deep rich brown.

After baking, these cookies will be cracked on top.

Makes 4 dozen cookies.

MRS. MARTHA KREIDER, *Wadsworth, Ohio*

## Raisin Bars

| | |
|---|---|
| 1 cup sour cream | 1 teaspoon baking powder |
| 1 cup sugar | ½ teaspoon salt |
| 2½ cups flour, approximately | 1 teaspoon vanilla |
| 1 teaspoon soda | |

Combine sugar and sour cream. Add vanilla.

Sift flour.

Measure and add soda, baking powder and salt.

Sift again.

Add sifted dry ingredients to cream and sugar mixture.

Add more flour if necessary to make a dough that can be rolled.

Roll very thin and spread with the following filling:

| | |
|---|---|
| ¾ cup sugar | 1½ cups chopped raisins |
| ¾ cup water | 1½ tablespoons flour |

Combine sugar and flour.

Add water and raisins.

Cook until mixture thickens, stirring constantly.

Cut dough in strips 1½ x 3 inches.

Spread with filling and cover with another strip.

Press edges tightly together.

Place 1 inch apart on a greased cookie sheet.

Bake at 375° for 20 to 25 minutes.

MRS. ERNEST YODER, *Salisbury, Pa.*; MRS. PAUL A. MAUST, *Grantsville, Md.*

## Raisin Filled Cookies

| | |
|---|---|
| 1 cup shortening | 4 teaspoons baking powder |
| 2 cups sugar | 1 teaspoon soda |
| 2 eggs | 1 cup milk |
| Approximately 5½ cups flour | 2 teaspoons vanilla |
| 1 teaspoon salt | |

Cream shortening and sugar together. Add vanilla.

Add eggs and beat until fluffy.

Sift flour.

Measure and add salt, soda and baking powder.

Sift again.

Add sifted dry ingredients alternately with milk.

Stir until smooth.

Add more flour if necessary.

Chill dough for several hours in refrigerator.

Turn out on lightly floured board and roll to ⅛ inch thickness.

Cut with round cutter and place 1 inch apart on a greased cookie sheet.

Spread with the following filling:

| | |
|---|---|
| 2 cups ground raisins | 2 tablespoons flour |
| 1 cup sugar | ½ cup chopped nuts |
| 1 cup water | |

Combine ingredients and cook until thick, stirring constantly.

Cool before spreading on cookie.

Put a teaspoon of filling in center of each and cover with another round of dough.

Press edges together.

Bake at 400° for 10 to 12 minutes.

Makes 4 dozen cookies.

MRS. M. T. BRACKBILL, *Harrisonburg, Va.;* NETTIE WITMER, *Columbiana, Ohio*
MRS. LEIDY HUNSICKER, *Blooming Glen, Pa.;* MRS. JOHN H. LANDES, *Lititz, Pa.*

Variation:

## Monkey Faces

Use preceding recipe.

Before putting top round of dough on cookie, use a thimble to cut eyes and mouth.

Do not cut through dough but press deep enough so that shape will remain in baked cookie.

This was Grandmother's way of decorating cookies.

ELIZABETH KREIDER, *Lancaster, Pa.*

## Sand Tarts or Saint Hearts

| | |
|---|---|
| 1 cup shortening | 1 teaspoon salt |
| 2 cups granulated sugar | 2 teaspoons baking powder |
| 3 eggs | 1 teaspoon vanilla or |
| 3½ to 4 cups flour | lemon extract |

Cream shortening and sugar together.

Add eggs and flavoring and beat until fluffy.

Sift flour.

Measure and add salt and baking powder.

Sift again.

Add sifted dry ingredients.

Stir until a medium-soft dough is formed.

Chill several hours in refrigerator.

Roll very thin and cut in fancy shapes.

Brush tops with rich milk and sprinkle with sugar and cinnamon.

Decorate with pecan halves.

Place 1 inch apart on a greased cookie sheet.

Bake at 350° for 8 to 10 minutes.

Makes 4 to 5 dozen cookies.

The oldest recipe books call these cookies Saint Hearts.

> Mrs. Samuel Martin, *Hagerstown, Md.;* Mrs. Richard Danner, *Hanover, Pa.*

## Sugar Cookies

| | |
|---|---|
| 1 cup shortening | 1 teaspoon salt |
| 2 cups sugar, granulated or light brown | 1½ teaspoons baking powder |
| | 1 teaspoon soda |
| 2 eggs | ¼ cup milk |
| Approximately 5 cups flour | 1 teaspoon vanilla |

Cream shortening and sugar together. Add flavoring.

Use half butter for good flavor.

Add eggs and beat until fluffy.

Sift flour.

Measure and add salt, soda and baking powder.

Sift again.

Add sifted dry ingredients alternately with milk.

Stir until dough is smooth.

Chill in refrigerator for several hours.

Roll out to ¼ inch thickness and cut in fancy shapes.

Place 1 inch apart on greased cookie sheet and bake at 400° for 8 to 10 minutes.

Makes about 6 dozen cookies.

> Mrs. Caroline Stutzman, *Sweet Home, Ore.;* Edith Mast, *Boyertown, Pa.*

## Old-Fashioned Sugar Cookies

Follow preceding recipe, but replace milk and shortening with 1 cup sour cream.

Omit baking powder and use 2 teaspoons soda.

Add more flour if necessary.
Dough should be soft, but not sticky.
Delicious!

Mrs. Perry Shank, *Broadway, Va.;* Mrs. D. B. Betzner, *Kitchener, Ont., Can.*

## Trilbys

| | |
|---|---|
| 2 cups shortening, half butter | I teaspoon salt |
| 3 cups brown sugar | 2 teaspoons soda |
| 6 cups flour | I cup buttermilk |
| 4 cups rolled oats | I teaspoon vanilla |

Cream shortening and sugar together.
Add vanilla.
Sift flour.
Measure and add salt, soda and rolled oats.
Add dry ingredients alternately with buttermilk.
Mix thoroughly.
Chill in refrigerator for several hours.
Turn out on lightly floured board and roll to ⅛ inch thickness.
Cut with round cookie cutter and place 1 inch apart on greased baking
     sheet.
Bake at 375° until a golden brown.
Makes 8 dozen cookies.
When cookies are cold, spread with the following filling:

| | |
|---|---|
| 2 cups finely chopped dates | I cup water |
| I cup sugar | 2 tablespoons flour |

Combine ingredients and cook until thick.
Let cool before spreading on cookie.
Top with another cookie.
Delicious!

Mrs. S. P. Zook, *Sterling, Ohio*

## REFRIGERATOR COOKIES

### Butterscotch or Refrigerator Cookies

| | |
|---|---|
| I cup shortening | I teaspoon salt |
| 4 cups brown sugar | 1½ teaspoons baking powder |
| 4 eggs | 2 teaspoons soda |
| 7 to 8 cups flour | 2 teaspoons vanilla |

Cream shortening and sugar together.
Add vanilla.
Add eggs and beat until fluffy.

Sift flour.

Measure and add salt, soda and baking powder.

Sift again.

Add sifted dry ingredients and mix to a smooth, stiff dough.

Shape into long rolls 2½ to 3 inches in diameter and chill in refrigerator overnight.

When ready to bake, cut roll in thin crosswise slices with a sharp knife.

Place slices 1 inch apart on an ungreased baking sheet.

Bake at 400° for about 8 minutes.

Makes about 10 dozen cookies.

ELIZABETH KREIDER, *Wadsworth, Ohio;* MRS. IRA S. JOHNS, *Goshen, Ind.*

## Crispy Caramel Cookies

| | |
|---|---|
| 1 cup shortening | 1 teaspoon soda |
| 2 cups brown sugar | 1 teaspoon cream of tartar |
| 2 eggs | ½ teaspoon salt |
| 3 cups flour | 1 teaspoon vanilla |

Cream shortening and sugar together.

Add vanilla.

Add eggs and beat until fluffy.

Sift flour.

Measure and add salt, soda and cream of tartar. Sift again.

Add sifted dry ingredients and work until a smooth, stiff dough is formed.

Chill for 15 minutes and then shape into rolls 2½ inches in diameter.

Let rolls stand in refrigerator overnight, then slice ⅛ inch thick and place 1 inch apart on ungreased baking sheet.

Bake at 400° for about 8 minutes.

Makes about 5 dozen cookies.

MRS. ALLEN GINGERICH, *Lowville, N. Y.*

## Date Pinwheel Cookies

| | |
|---|---|
| 1 cup shortening | 4 to 4½ cups flour |
| 2 cups brown sugar | 1 teaspoon salt |
| ½ cup granulated sugar | 1 teaspoon soda |
| 3 eggs | 1 teaspoon cinnamon |

Cream shortening and sugar together.

Add eggs and beat until fluffy.

Sift flour.

Measure and add salt, soda and spices.

Sift again.

Add sifted dry ingredients to creamed mixture, and beat until smooth.

Chill dough in refrigerator for several hours.

Divide chilled dough in 2 parts.

Roll to ¼ inch thickness and spread with the following filling:

| | |
|---|---|
| 1½ cups ground dates or raisins | 1 cup water |
| 1 cup sugar | ½ cup nuts |

Combine dates, sugar and water and cook until thick, stirring constantly.

Remove from heat and add nuts.

Cool and spread on rolled pieces of dough.

Roll as a jelly roll and chill thoroughly in refrigerator.

Slice in rings ⅛ inch thick and place 1 inch apart on greased cookie sheet.

Bake at 375° until a golden brown.

Makes 3½ dozen cookies.

MRS. MARY LAUBER, *Sheridan, Ore.;* MRS. M. A. BENNER, *Mechanicsburg, Pa.*
MRS. MILTON ROHRER, *Orrville, Ohio*

Variation:

Instead of fruit filling, spread rolled dough with melted chocolate and sprinkle with grated coconut and chopped nuts.

Follow directions given above.

MRS. DAVID S. MISHLER, *Johnstown, Pa.*

## German Christmas Cookies

| | |
|---|---|
| 1 cup shortening, half butter | 4 cups flour |
| ½ cup sugar | ½ teaspoon salt |
| 3 eggs | 1 teaspoon grated lemon rind |

Blend shortening and sugar together.

Add grated rind.

Add eggs, reserving 1 white and beat mixture until light.

Sift flour.

Measure and add salt. Sift again.

Slowly add sifted dry ingredients and work to a smooth, stiff dough.

Shape into rolls 2 inches in diameter and chill for several hours in refrigerator.

Slice ⅛ inch thick and roll on a board with flat part of the hand into fingerlike sticks. Shape like an S.

Chill again.

Dip in slightly beaten egg white and then into granulated sugar.

Bake at 325° until a golden brown.

Makes 6 dozen cookies.

MRS. CHRISTINE HORSCH, *Scottdale, Pa.*

## Oatmeal Refrigerator Cookies

| | |
|---|---|
| 1/2 cup shortening | 1 1/4 cups flour |
| 1 cup brown sugar | 1 cup rolled oats |
| 1 egg | 1/2 teaspoon salt |
| 2 tablespoons water | 1/2 teaspoon soda |
| 1/2 teaspoon vanilla | 1/2 cup chopped raisins |
| 1/4 teaspoon almond extract | 1/4 cup chopped nuts |

Cream shortening and sugar together.

Add egg, water and flavoring.

Beat until fluffy.

Sift flour.

Measure and add salt and soda.

Sift again.

Add oats to dry ingredients.

Add dry ingredients to creamed mixture and stir until well blended.

Add finely chopped nuts and raisins.

Shape into rolls 2¼ inches in diameter and chill overnight in refrigerator.

Slice ⅛ inch thick and place 1 inch apart on greased baking sheet.

Bake at 375° for 8 to 10 minutes.

Makes 3 dozen cookies.

MRS. FRED OURS, *Harrisonburg, Va.;* MRS. DAN CRESSMAN, *St. Jacobs, Ont., Can.*
MRS. DUANE R. YODER, *Kalona, Iowa*

## Peppernuts (Pfeffernusse) (I)

| | |
|---|---|
| 1/3 cup shortening | 1/2 teaspoon salt |
| 1 cup sugar | 1 cup sweet cream |
| Approximately 6 cups flour | 1 cup milk |
| 3 teaspoons baking powder | 1 teaspoon peppermint extract |

Cream shortening and sugar together.

Add flavoring.

Add sweet cream and beat until fluffy.

Sift flour.

Measure and add baking powder and salt.

Sift again.

Add sifted dry ingredients alternately with milk.

Beat until a medium-soft, smooth dough is formed.

Chill dough in refrigerator for several hours.

When thoroughly chilled, divide dough into 5 or 6 parts.

Remove one portion from refrigerator at a time and turn out on lightly floured board.

Cut off small portions and form into fingerlike sticks, rolling with the flat part of hand.

Lay sticks in parallel rows and cut across, making pieces the size of a small marble.

Place pieces close together on a greased baking sheet.

Bake at 425° until they begin to turn a light, golden brown.

These cookies are especially popular at Christmas time in many Mennonite homes.

ELIZABETH WARKENTIN, *Mountain Lake, Minn.*

## Pfeffernusse (II)

4 eggs
1 pound powdered sugar
About 4 cups flour
1 teaspoon cinnamon
½ teaspoon cloves

½ teaspoon nutmeg
1 teaspoon soda
½ teaspoon salt
Grated rind and juice of 1 lemon

Beat eggs until frothy.

Gradually add powdered sugar and lemon juice and rind.

Sift flour.

Measure and add salt, soda and spices.

Sift again.

Add sifted dry ingredients to egg and sugar mixture.

Beat until a medium-soft, smooth dough is formed.

Chill dough in refrigerator and carry out directions given in preceding recipe.

MRS. JULIA C. AUGSPURGER, *Hamilton, Ohio*

## Springerle Cookies

1 pound sugar (2 cups)
4 eggs
4 cups flour

10 drops anise oil
2 tablespoons anise seed

Add sugar gradually to well beaten eggs and continue to beat for 15 minutes with electric mixer, or 30 minutes with rotary beater.

Add anise oil and blend into mixture.

Gradually add sifted flour and stir until a smooth, stiff dough is formed.

Chill dough in refrigerator.

Roll out on lightly floured board to ¼ inch thickness.

Then roll with a springerle roller or on a springerle board to make designs.

Press firmly and cut on line of imprint.

Place cookies 1 inch apart on ungreased baking sheet.

Sprinkle with anise seed and let stand in a cool place overnight to dry.

Bake at 375° for 3 minutes and then reduce heat to 325° for about 12 minutes longer.

When baked, these cookies should be light in color and appear frosted. Keep cookies in a tight can for 2 or 3 weeks before using. To soften, put an apple in container a day or so before they are served. Makes about 4 dozen cookies.

MRS. BERNICE HOBBS, *Iowa City, Iowa;* MRS. J. D. WARKENTIN, *Beulah, N. D.*

## SPREAD COOKIES
### Apple Oatmeal Bars

| | |
|---|---|
| 1 cup flour | 1/2 cup shortening |
| 1/2 teaspoon salt | 2 1/2 cups sliced apples |
| 1/2 teaspoon soda | 2 tablespoons butter |
| 1/2 cup brown sugar | 1/2 cup granulated sugar |
| 1 cup rolled oats | |

Sift flour.
Measure and add salt, soda, and brown sugar.
Sift again.
Add oatmeal flakes.
Cut shortening into mixture until it is crumbly.
Spread ½ of mixture in a greased baking pan 7 x 10 inches.
Arrange sliced apples over crumb mixture.
Dot with butter and sprinkle with granulated sugar.
Cover with remaining crumbs.
Bake at 350° for 40 minutes.
Cut in squares or bars while still warm.
Makes 18 to 20 squares.

MRS. JACOB HULBERT, *North Lima, Ohio*

### Brownies

| | |
|---|---|
| 2 squares unsweetened chocolate (2 ounces) | 1/2 cup flour |
| 1/3 cup shortening | 1/2 teaspoon baking powder |
| 1 cup sugar | 1/2 teaspoon salt |
| 2 eggs, beaten | 1 cup chopped nuts |
| | 1 teaspoon vanilla |

Melt chocolate and shortening together.
Beat eggs thoroughly and add sugar.
Combine egg and chocolate mixtures and blend together.
Sift flour.
Measure and add baking powder and salt.
Sift again.
Add dry ingredients and blend into mixture.

Add chopped nuts and vanilla.

Spread dough in a greased pan 8 x 10 x 1½ inches.

Bake at 350° for 30 minutes.

Cool slightly and cut in squares or bars.

These cookies keep well.

Makes 2 dozen squares.

MRS. EMERY EIGSTI, *Wayland, Iowa;* LAVERN JOHNSON, *Bluffton, Ohio*
MRS. WARD SHANK, *Broadway, Va.*

## Butterscotch Squares

| | |
|---|---|
| ¼ cup butter | 1 teaspoon baking powder |
| 1 cup brown sugar | ¼ teaspoon salt |
| 1 egg | ½ cup chopped nuts |
| 1 cup flour | 1 teaspoon vanilla |

Melt butter and blend with sugar.

Add egg and beat vigorously.

Sift flour.

Measure and add baking powder and salt.

Sift again.

Add dry ingredients to egg and sugar mixture and mix together well.

Add chopped nuts and vanilla.

Spread dough in a greased pan 8 x 8 inches.

Bake at 350° for 30 minutes.

Cut in squares or bars while warm.

Makes 18 to 20 squares.

MRS. BARBARA STUTZMAN, *Kalona, Iowa*

## Coconut Squares (I)

| | |
|---|---|
| ½ cup butter | ¼ teaspoon salt |
| 1½ cups brown sugar | 2 tablespoons flour |
| 1 cup flour | ½ teaspoon baking powder |
| 2 eggs, beaten | 1½ cups grated coconut |
| 1 teaspoon vanilla | 1 cup chopped nuts |

Combine butter and ½ cup brown sugar.

Add 1 cup flour and work with fingers to make crumbs.

Press mixture into a greased baking pan 8 x 10 inches.

Bake at 250° for 10 minutes.

While dough is baking, prepare the following mixture:

Beat eggs and add remaining brown sugar and vanilla.

Sift remaining flour with salt and baking powder.

Add dry ingredients to egg and sugar mixture.

Fold in grated coconut and chopped nuts.

Pour mixture over top of dough in the oven and continue to bake for 25 minutes.

Cut in squares while warm.

Makes 2 dozen squares.

MRS. ALLAN BACHMAN, *Putman, Ill.*

## Coconut Squares (II)

| | |
|---|---|
| 1/3 cup shortening | Topping: |
| 1/2 cup sugar | 1 egg white |
| 2 eggs, separated | 1 cup brown sugar |
| 1 1/2 cups flour | 1 cup grated coconut |
| 1/4 teaspoon salt | 1/2 cup chopped nuts (optional) |
| 1 teaspoon baking powder | 1/2 teaspoon vanilla |
| 2 tablespoons milk | |
| 1 teaspoon vanilla | |

Cream shortening and sugar together.

Add egg yolks and one white, beat thoroughly.

Sift flour.

Measure and add salt and baking powder.

Sift again.

Add milk and vanilla alternately with dry ingredients.

Pour dough into a greased baking pan 8 x 10 inches.

Cover with topping made as follows:

Beat remaining egg white until stiff.

Add brown sugar gradually and blend well into white.

Add vanilla, grated coconut and chopped nuts. Fold into mixture.

Spread topping on dough.

Bake at 325° for 30 minutes.

Cut in squares while warm.

Makes 2 dozen squares.

MRS. SAMUEL CHRISTENEN, *Nampa, Idaho*

## Date Bars

| | |
|---|---|
| 2/3 cup shortening | 1 teaspoon baking powder |
| 1 cup brown sugar | 1/2 teaspoon salt |
| 2 eggs | 1 cup chopped dates |
| 1 cup flour | 1 cup chopped nuts |

Cream shortening and sugar together.

Add eggs to creamed mixture, and beat until light and fluffy.

Sift flour.

Measure and add baking powder and salt.

Sift again.

Add sifted dry ingredients to mixture.

Fold in chopped dates and nuts.

Turn into a greased baking pan 8 x 10 inches.

Bake at 350° for about 25 minutes.

Cut in bars while still warm and roll in powdered sugar.

Makes 2 dozen bars.

MARIAN ZOOK, *Christiana, Pa.*

## Frosted Creams

| | |
|---|---|
| 1 cup shortening | ½ teaspoon salt |
| 1 cup sugar | 1½ teaspoons soda |
| 1 cup dark molasses | 1 cup sour milk or buttermilk |
| 2 eggs | 1 teaspoon cinnamon |
| Approximately 4 cups flour | ½ teaspoon ginger |

Cream shortening and sugar together.

Add eggs and beat until light.

Add molasses and beat again.

Sift flour.

Measure and add salt and soda.

Sift again.

Add sifted dry ingredients alternately with sour milk. Mix thoroughly.

Spread dough in a thin layer on greased cookie sheets.

Bake at 350° for 20 to 25 minutes.

When cold, spread with boiled sugar frosting and cut in squares.

For frosting take:

| | |
|---|---|
| 1¼ cups sugar | 2 egg whites |
| 4 tablespoons water | ½ teaspoon vanilla |

Cook sugar and water together until it spins a thread 5 to 7 inches long.

Pour over stiffly beaten egg whites, stirring constantly.

Beat until smooth.

Add flavoring.

Makes 4 dozen squares.

This is an old favorite.

MRS. J. J. HOSTETLER, *Canton, Ohio;* MRS. EMERY M. YODER, *Kalona, Iowa*

## Fruit Cookies

| | |
|---|---|
| ½ cup shortening | 1 teaspoon cinnamon |
| 1 cup sugar | ¼ teaspoon ground cloves |
| ½ cup molasses | ½ cup sour milk |
| 2 eggs | 1 cup seedless raisins |

2½ cups flour
½ teaspoon salt
1 teaspoon soda

¼ cup each of candied orange and
lemond rind
½ cup chopped nuts

Cream shortening and sugar together.

Add eggs and beat thoroughly.

Add molasses and blend well into mixture.

Sift flour.

Measure and add salt, soda and spices.

Sift again.

Add sifted dry ingredients alternately with sour milk.

Mix thoroughly after each addition.

Add chopped fruits and nuts, then fold into mixture.

Spread in a greased, shallow baking pan, 10 x 12 inches.

Bake at 375° for 25 minutes.

Cut in squares or bars while still warm.

Spread with favorite frosting.

Makes 2½ dozen squares.

Excellent at Christmas time!

Mrs. O. O. HERSHBERGER, *Hesston, Kan.;* Mrs. ABRAM BERGEY, *Bothwell, Ont., Can.*
Mrs. H. C. LAUVER, *Archbold, Ohio*

## Ginger Creams

2/3 cup shortening
1¼ cups brown sugar
1 cup molasses
5½ cups flour
1 teaspoon soda
½ teaspoon salt

1 teaspoon ginger
1 teaspoon cinnamon
½ teaspoon cloves
1 cup hot water or coffee
1 cup raisins, chopped

Cream shortening and sugar together.

Add molasses and beat thoroughly.

Sift flour.

Measure and add salt, soda and spices.

Sift again.

Add sifted dry ingredients alternately with hot water.

Beat only until ingredients are blended together.

Fold in chopped raisins.

Spread dough on greased cookie sheet.

Bake at 375° for about 20 minutes.

Cut in squares when cooled and spread with favorite frosting.

Makes 3½ dozen squares.

Mrs. ILA WEAVER, *Millersburg, Ohio*

## Golden Bars

| | |
|---|---|
| 2/3 cup shortening | 1/2 teaspoon salt |
| 2 cups brown sugar | 2 teaspoons baking powder |
| 2 eggs | 3/4 cup chopped nuts |
| 1 1/2 cups flour | 1 teaspoon vanilla |

Cream shortening and sugar together.

Add eggs and beat until fluffy.

Sift flour.

Measure and add salt and baking powder. Sift again.

Add sifted dry ingredients and blend well into mixture.

Fold in chopped nuts and vanilla.

Spread in a greased shallow pan, 8 x 12 inches.

Bake at 350° for 25 to 30 minutes.

Makes 2½ dozen bars.

Roll in powdered sugar if desired.

Mrs. Ruth Eby, *Westover, Md.*

## Pecan Squares

| | |
|---|---|
| 2/3 cup shortening | Topping: |
| 1 cup brown sugar | 1 egg |
| 1 egg | 1/2 cup brown sugar |
| 2 cups flour | 1 cup chopped pecans |

Cream shortening and sugar together.

Add egg and beat until fluffy.

Add flour and work well into mixture.

Spread on a greased sheet, 11 x 16 inches.

Beat remaining egg and spread over top of mixture.

Sprinkle with brown sugar and top with chopped nuts.

Bake at 350° for 20 to 25 minutes.

Makes 3½ dozen squares.

Mrs. Adolf Johnson, *Sweet Home, Ore.*

# Desserts

## Chapter X

I SOMETIMES BELIEVE THAT GREAT-GRANDMA ROCKED HER BABIES TO SLEEP with tunes other than the well-known lullaby, "Rockabye Baby." One of these must have been "seven sweets and seven sours," for every young lady grew up believing that no dinner was complete without its seven sweets and seven sours.

Several years ago I visited a friend who lived in the heart of that region where Pennsylvania Dutch cookery is well known. There was only one thing she did not know about cooking: that was when she had enough! Her guests had eaten heartily of the main dinner, and then began the merry-go-round of desserts. Hesitating as I tried to select one of the four or five desserts passed, I said, "My dear, you expect too much of your guests." She looked surprised for a moment, as if she did not understand, and then in self-defense said, "Ach, well, peaches aren't a dessert; they are just fruit. And rice pudding I will not call a dessert either. It is just another dish, and certainly any good cook would have pie and cake with company dinner."

Besides the cakes and pies, the popular desserts of yesteryears consisted of baked puddings and old-fashioned custards. Not uncommon were steamed suet puddings, bread pudding, cherry dumplings, apple roll, short cakes and fruit custards.

The fondness of our ancestors for the heavier type of foods induced them to serve dumplings as a dessert as well as a main dish. There are still to be found numerous kinds and sizes of dumplings made according to family tastes. The old-time dampf knepp, made by dropping big balls of yeast dough onto hot fruit to steam is most delicious. There are the smaller dumplings such as cherry dumplings, which are made by dropping a baking powder leavened dough from a spoon. In mentioning these rich fruit desserts one must not forget "Pluma Moos," the favorite of many Mennonites of Russian background. This is made by cooking together a number of dried fruits, and thickening them with a flour paste to which a cup of sweet cream is added.

Although Grandma did not grace her table with lighted candles and bouquets of flowers, she nevertheless laid a beautiful table. There was always quite a display of color in the large variety of desserts. There were decorative notes, too, in the cut glass, or beautifully painted cream pitcher and sugar bowl, which accompanied even the richest of desserts. Near the center of the table stood the tall glass cake stand, which was polished until it sparkled before Grandma placed on it the golden pound cake.

What could make a prettier picture than a dish of spiced crab apples? Those dainty butter molds added touches of color too. It seemed each granny tried to outdo her neighbor by displaying the most unusual one. My own grandmother's favorite was a work of art and patience. She curled the edges of a round ball of butter with a screw, pushing outward and down, to form a perfectly shaped pineapple.

# CUSTARDS AND SOFT PUDDINGS

## Baked Cup Custards

| | |
|---|---|
| 4 eggs | 4 cups milk |
| 1/2 cup sugar | 1/2 teaspoon vanilla |
| 1/2 teaspoon salt | Nutmeg (optional) |

Beat eggs slightly.

Add sugar, salt and vanilla.

Scald milk and pour it slowly over egg mixture.

Stir until thoroughly mixed.

Pour into custard cups, filling them two-thirds full.

Sprinkle with nutmeg if desired.

Set cups in a pan and pour hot water around them until it comes to the level of the custard.

Bake at 325° approximately 40 minutes, or until a silver knife comes out clean when inserted in the center of the custard.

Do not let water in pan boil.

Custard may also be baked in a casserole.

To unmold custards, they must be thoroughly chilled.

Serve with whipped cream if desired.

Makes 8 custards.

MABEL YODER, *Grantsville, Md.*; MRS. I. B. LAPP, *Oley, Pa.*

## Banana Pudding

| | |
|---|---|
| 2 boxes vanilla pudding | 1 teaspoon vanilla |
| 4 cups milk | 14 graham crackers |
| 1 cup whipping cream | 4 bananas |
| 1 tablespoon sugar | |

Combine pudding and milk and stir until smooth.

Cook until thickened, stirring constantly.

Remove from heat and cool.

Whip the cream and add sugar and vanilla.

To the cold custard add ⅔ of the whipped cream, 3 diced bananas and 10 graham crackers rolled very fine.

Combine ingredients well and pour into serving dish.

Spread the remaining cream on top of mixture.

Garnish with remaining crumbs and sliced bananas.

Makes 6-8 servings.

MRS. CLAYTON SHANK, *Harrisonburg, Va.*

## Butterscotch Pudding

| | |
|---|---|
| 1 cup brown sugar | 3 cups milk |
| 2 eggs, beaten | 2 tablespoons butter |
| 3 tablespoons flour | 1 teaspoon vanilla |
| ¼ teaspoon salt | |

Melt butter in a skillet.

Add sugar and salt and mix well.

Slowly add 2 cups milk.

Heat to boiling point.

Make a paste by adding remaining milk to the flour.

Add to mixture, stirring constantly until it is thickened.

Beat eggs. Add ½ cup hot mixture to eggs and then add eggs to pudding.

Cook for 2 minutes and remove from heat.

Add flavoring.

Chill and garnish with ground peanuts, whipped cream or crushed bananas as desired.

Makes 6-8 servings.

IRMA ALDERFER, *Souderton, Pa.;* LIZZIE HORST, *Wadsworth, Ohio*

## Chocolate Vanilla Pudding

| | |
|---|---|
| 3 cups milk | ¼ teaspoon salt |
| I cup sugar | I tablespoon butter |
| 3 eggs, separated | I teaspoon vanilla |
| 2½ tablespoons cornstarch | |

Scald 2½ cups milk in top part of double boiler.

Combine sugar, salt and cornstarch.

Add remaining milk to make a smooth paste.

Add some of the hot milk to the paste and mix thoroughly.

Then add paste to hot milk and cook until thickened, stirring constantly.

Beat egg yolks and add some of the hot pudding.

Then add egg yolks to mixture and cook for 2 minutes.

Remove from heat and add butter and vanilla.

Chill thoroughly and then top with the following meringue:

Beat egg whites until stiff.

Add 5 tablespoons sugar and 1 ounce of unsweetened chocolate, melted.

Continue to beat until meringue has a sheen.

Spread chocolate meringue on pudding.

Serves 8.

MRS. SAMUEL SHREINER, *East Earl, Pa.;* MRS. ELLA MARTIN, *Adamstown, Pa.*

## Coconut Custard

| | |
|---|---|
| 3 cups milk | ¼ teaspoon salt |
| I cup sugar | ½ teaspoon vanilla |
| 3 eggs, beaten | I coconut, grated |
| 2 tablespoons cornstarch | |

Scald 2½ cups milk in top of a double boiler.

Mix sugar, salt and cornstarch and add remaining milk to make a smooth paste.

Add some of the hot milk slowly to the paste and then add all to the
    scalded milk.

Stir until thickened.

Beat eggs and add slowly to custard, stirring constantly.

Cook for 2 minutes.

Remove from heat.

Add ⅔ of the grated coconut and the vanilla.

Garnish the chilled custard with whipped cream and the remaining
    coconut.

Makes 6-8 servings.

MRS. ELMER J. HERR, *Hanover, Pa.*

## Baked Coconut Custard

| | |
|---|---|
| 2 cups soft bread crumbs | 3 eggs, beaten |
| 4 cups milk | 2 tablespoons butter |
| ¾ cup sugar | I teaspoon orange extract |
| ¼ teaspoon salt | I cup grated coconut |

Soak bread crumbs in milk for 15 minutes.

Add sugar, salt and beaten eggs. Blend together.

Add melted butter, flavoring and coconut and stir until thoroughly
    mixed.

Pour into a casserole dish and bake at 350° for approximately 40
    minutes or until a silver knife comes out clean when inserted in the
    custard.

Makes 8 servings.

LEVINA STEINER, *Dalton, Ohio*

## Coconut Cream Tapioca

| | |
|---|---|
| I quart milk (4 cups) | 3 tablespoons minute tapioca |
| I cup sugar | ¼ teaspoon salt |
| 4 eggs, separated | ½ cup shredded coconut |

Scald milk in top of double boiler.

Add salt and minute tapioca and cook 15 minutes or until clear.

Stir frequently.

Combine egg yolks, sugar and coconut.

Add some of the hot mixture and stir until a smooth paste is formed.

Add paste to hot tapioca and continue to cook for 2 minutes, stirring
    constantly.

Pour into a greased baking dish.

Cover with a meringue made by adding 4 tablespoons sugar to stiffly
    beaten egg whites.

Sprinkle with coconut.

Bake at 300° for 15 minutes or until a golden brown.

Makes 6-8 servings.

Mrs. B. L. Bucher, *Dallastown, Pa.*

## Grape Juice Tapioca

2½ cups water
¾ cup sugar
1 cup grape juice

2/3 cup minute tapioca
Juice of 1 lemon

Combine sugar and water and boil together until sugar is dissolved.

Add tapioca and cook until clear.

Add lemon juice and grape juice and continue to cook for 3 minutes.

Serves 6.

Mrs. Melvin Weaver, *Ophir, Kan.*

## Rhubarb Tapioca

2 cups chopped rhubarb
24 stewed prunes
¼ cup prune juice

½ cup sugar
½ cup minute tapioca
¾ cup cold water

Soak tapioca in cold water for 30 minutes.

To the chopped rhubarb add stewed prunes, prune juice and sugar.

Cook together for 5 minutes.

Add tapioca and cook until mixture is transparent.

Serve hot or cold.

Top with whipped cream if desired.

Makes 6-8 servings.

Mrs. Eli Amstutz, *Apple Creek, Ohio*

## Red Blushing Apple Tapioca

4 or 5 tart apples
½ cup sugar
2 tablespoons minute tapioca

2 tablespoons red cinnamon candy
1½ cups hot water
1 tablespoon lemon juice

Pare and core apples.

Cut in eighths lengthwise.

Combine sugar, water and cinnamon candy.

Cook until dissolved, stirring constantly.

Add apples and cook until tender.

If syrup has boiled down, add enough water to make 1 cup.

Put syrup in top part of double boiler.

Add tapioca and cook 15 minutes. Stir frequently.

Remove from heat and add lemon juice. Pour thickened syrup over apples.

Makes 6 servings.

For variation, strawberries or pineapple may be added.

MRS. JENNIE SAYLOR, *Boswell, Pa.*

## Cornstarch Pudding or Soft Custard

| | |
|---|---|
| 1 quart milk (4 cups) | 2 tablespoons cornstarch |
| 4 tablespoons sugar | 1/4 teaspoon salt |
| 3 eggs, separated | 1 teaspoon vanilla |

Scald 3½ cups milk in top of a double boiler.

Combine sugar, salt and cornstarch.

Add remaining milk to make a smooth paste.

Add some of the hot milk to the paste and then stir paste into scalded milk.

Cook until thickened.

Beat egg yolks and add some of the hot custard.

Slowly add beaten yolks to mixture and cook for 2 minutes.

Remove from heat and add vanilla.

Beat egg whites until stiff, add 1 tablespoon powdered sugar.

Fold beaten whites into custard.

This may be served in sherbet glasses topped with whipped cream or poured over fresh fruit or sponge cake.

Makes 6-8 servings.

NAOMI S. DERSTINE, *Souderton, Pa.;* MRS. P. R. KENNEL, *Shickley, Neb.*

## Date Butterscotch Pudding

| | |
|---|---|
| 1 cup brown sugar | 1 cup boiling water |
| 2 tablespoons cornstarch | 1 egg |
| 1/4 teaspoon salt | 3 tablespoons butter |
| 1/2 cup cold water | 1/2 cup chopped dates |

Combine sugar, salt and cornstarch.

Add cold water to make a smooth paste.

Add boiling water and cook until thickened, stirring constantly.

Beat egg and add a little of the hot mixture.

Then add egg to pudding and cook one minute longer.

Remove from heat and add butter and chopped dates.

Chill and serve plain or with whipped cream if desired.

Makes 6 servings.

MRS. AARON STEINER, *Dalton, Ohio*

## Floating Island Custard

| | |
|---|---|
| I quart milk (4 cups) | 2 tablespoons cornstarch |
| 2 eggs, separated | ¼ teaspoon salt |
| ½ cup sugar | I teaspoon vanilla |

Scald 3½ cups milk in top of double boiler.

Combine sugar, salt and cornstarch.

Add remaining milk to make a smooth paste.

Slowly add paste to hot milk and cook until thickened.

Stir constantly.

Beat egg yolks, add some of the hot custard.

Then add egg yolks to custard and cook 2 minutes longer.

Remove custard from heat and add vanilla. Chill.

Beat egg whites until stiff, add 4 tablespoons of sugar and ½ teaspoon vanilla.

Drop meringue by spoonfuls onto chilled custard.

Top with red jelly.

Meringue may also be dropped by spoonfuls into a shallow baking pan with bottom covered with hot water.

Bake at 325° until a golden brown and then place on top of custard.

Makes 6-8 servings.

MARTHA LEHMAN, *Apple Creek, Ohio*

## Graham Cracker Pudding

| First Part: | Second Part: |
|---|---|
| 2 cups milk | 1/3 cup whipping cream |
| 1/3 cup sugar | 1/3 cup sugar |
| 3 tablespoons flour | ⅛ teaspoon salt |
| I egg | I teaspoon vanilla |
| ½ teaspoon salt | |
| I teaspoon vanilla | |
| 2 cups graham cracker crumbs | |
| 2 cups sliced bananas | |

Scald 1½ cups milk in top of double boiler.

Combine flour, sugar and salt.

Add ½ cup milk and stir to a smooth paste.

Add paste slowly to hot milk and cook until thickened.

Stir constantly.

Beat egg and add some of the hot mixture.

Add egg to custard and cook 1 minute longer.

Remove from heat and add vanilla. Chill.

Add sliced bananas and blend into pudding.

To make second part:

Whip cream and add sugar, salt and vanilla.

Mix together well and fold into pudding, reserving some for topping.

Add cracker crumbs and blend into mixture.

Garnish with some of the whipped cream topping.

Makes 6 to 8 servings.

Bananas may be omitted.

Mrs. Ervin J. Yoder, *Meyersdale, Pa.*

## Grape Nut Pudding

½ cup grape nuts
½ cup brown sugar
I egg, beaten
I tablespoon cornstarch
⅛ teaspoon salt

2 cups milk
½ cup raisins
½ cup chopped nuts
I teaspoon vanilla

Combine brown sugar, salt and cornstarch.

Add beaten egg and blend into mixture.

Add grape nuts and milk and beat thoroughly.

Dust raisins and chopped nuts with flour and fold into mixture.

Add vanilla.

Pour into greased baking dish and bake at 350° until firm (approximately 45 minutes).

Makes 6 servings.

Mrs. Eli Amstutz, *Apple Creek, Ohio*

## Lemon Custard

3 eggs, separated
I cup sugar
¼ cup butter
2½ tablespoons cornstarch

¼ teaspoon salt
2 cups water
I large lemon

Slice the lemon and add water.

Bring to a boil and cook until strength is extracted. Drain.

Combine sugar and butter and cream together.

Add egg yolks and beat thoroughly.

Add hot lemon juice to creamed mixture and bring to a boil.

Add ¼ cup cold water to cornstarch and stir until it is a smooth paste.

Add cornstarch paste to hot mixture and cook until thickened and clear.

Remove custard from heat.

Add stiffly beaten egg whites and blend lightly into mixture.

If desired, this may be poured into a casserole and baked at 325° until slightly browned.

Makes 6 servings.

Mrs. Carrie Bell, *Oley, Pa.*

## Lemon Chiffon Pudding

| | |
|---|---|
| 1 cup sugar | 1/4 cup lemon juice |
| 3 tablespoons butter | Grated rind of 1/2 lemon |
| 4 tablespoons flour | 1 cup milk |
| 1/4 teaspoon salt | 3 eggs, separated |

Combine sugar, flour, salt and butter.

Add lemon juice and rind and beaten egg yolks.

Beat until ingredients are thoroughly blended.

Add milk and blend into mixture.

Fold in stiffly beaten egg whites.

Pour into a greased baking dish and set in a pan of hot water.

Bake at 350° for 45 minutes.

Serve warm.

Makes 6 servings.

Mrs. C. D. Kauffman, *Hesston, Kan.*

## Lemon Sponge Custard

| | |
|---|---|
| 3 tablespoons butter | 1/8 teaspoon salt |
| 3/4 cup sugar | 1 cup milk |
| 2 eggs, separated | Juice and grated rind of 1 lemon |
| 2 tablespoons flour | |

Combine sugar, flour and salt.

Add butter and rub into mixture.

Add beaten egg yolks and lemon juice and rind and beat well.

Add milk and beat until smooth.

Fold in stiffly beaten egg whites.

Pour mixture in a greased casserole or custard cups and set in a pan of hot water.

Bake at 350° for 45 minutes.

Serve warm.

Makes 6 servings.

Mary E. Landis, *La Junta, Colo.;* Mrs. Mahlon King, *Parkesburg, Pa.*

## Orange Pudding

| | |
|---|---|
| 5 oranges | 2 tablespoons cornstarch |
| 1 cup sugar | 1/4 teaspoon salt |
| 1 quart milk | 2 eggs |

Slice oranges in thin slices and spread in bottom of serving dish.

Sprinkle orange slices with ½ cup sugar.

Scald 3½ cups milk.

Combine remaining sugar, salt and cornstarch.

Add ¼ cup milk and stir to a smooth paste.
Add paste to scalded milk and cook until thickened.
Beat egg yolks and add slowly to hot mixture.
Continue to cook for 2 minutes.
Beat egg whites until stiff, spread on top of orange slices.
Pour hot custard over the top of beaten whites.
Serves 8.

MRS. LIZZIE C. ALDERFER, *Souderton, Pa.*

## Pineapple Meringue Pudding

2 cups crushed pineapple
1 tablespoon cornstarch
¼ cup sugar
¼ teaspoon salt
1 tablespoon lemon juice

2 eggs, separated
6 lady fingers or small pieces of
   sponge cake
2 tablespoons sugar
½ teaspoon vanilla

Combine ¼ cup sugar, salt and cornstarch together in a saucepan.
Add crushed pineapple and juice and stir until smooth.
Cook until slightly thickened (about 5 minutes).
Separate eggs and add ¼ cup hot sauce to beaten yolks.
Mix well and stir into remaining pudding.
Break lady fingers or sponge cake into small pieces and place in greased
   custard cups.
Add hot pudding and top with meringue made by beating 2 tablespoons
   sugar in stiffly beaten egg whites.
Add vanilla to whites.
Bake at 325° for 12 to 15 minutes or until meringue is a golden brown.
Serve hot or cold.
Makes 6 servings.

MRS. NORMAN LANDIS, *Lansdale, Pa.*

## Pumpkin Custard

2 cups sieved pumpkin
1 cup soft bread crumbs
2 eggs, separated
1½ cups milk
1 cup sugar

½ cup shredded coconut
3 tablespoons melted butter
¼ teaspoon salt
1 teaspoon orange flavoring

Combine ingredients in order listed, reserving the egg whites.
Mix together well.
Pour into a baking dish.
Bake at 325° until mixture thickens and is slightly browned.
Beat egg whites until stiff and add 2 tablespoons sugar.

Spread whites on top of custard and brown slightly.

This is delicious served hot or cold.

Makes 6-8 servings.

MRS. BERTHA BEERY, *Dayton, Va.*

## Creamy Rice Pudding

| | |
|---|---|
| ¼ cup uncooked rice | 6 tablespoons sugar |
| 2 cups milk | ¼ teaspoon salt |
| 2 eggs, separated | 1 teaspoon vanilla |

Wash rice, drain and add to milk.

Cook covered in top of double boiler until rice is tender (about 45 minutes).

Beat egg yolks thoroughly. Add 4 tablespoons sugar and salt.

Stir some of the rice mixture into beaten yolks.

Then add yolks to hot mixture and cook 2 minutes.

Stir constantly.

Remove from heat and add vanilla.

Beat egg whites until stiff, add 2 tablespoons sugar.

Fold beaten whites into custard.

Chill and serve.

Beaten whites may be spread on top of custard and browned delicately in the oven.

One cup of raisins may be cooked in custard if desired.

Makes 6 servings.

MRS. PHOEBE KOLB, *Kitchener, Ont., Can.*

## Glorified Rice

| | |
|---|---|
| 2 cups cooked rice | 24 marshmallows, quartered |
| 1 cup pineapple (cubed) | ½ cup sugar |
| 1 cup whipping cream | 1 cup chopped apples |

Combine cooked rice, pineapple chunks, marshmallows, sugar and chopped apples.

Let stand for 1 hour.

Whip cream and fold into mixture just before serving.

Garnish with maraschino cherries, red raspberries or strawberries.

Fresh peaches may be added in place of pineapple.

Makes 6 servings.

Delicious!

MRS. NELSON THOMAS, *Clarksville. Mich.*

## Rice Mold with Lemon Sauce

| | |
|---|---|
| 1 cup cooked rice | ¼ cup cold water |
| 4 tablespoons lemon juice | 1 cup boiling water |
| 1 teaspoon grated rind | 1 egg |
| 1 cup sugar | 2 tablespoons cornstarch |
| ⅛ teaspoon salt | 1 tablespoon butter |

Cook rice and drain.

Press rice into a buttered mold.

Place in refrigerator to chill.

Turn out on serving plate and pour the following sauce over it:

Combine cornstarch with cold water and stir to a smooth paste.

Add boiling water and bring to a boil.

Beat egg. Add sugar, salt, fruit juices and rind.

Add a little of the hot mixture to egg and then add egg to hot mixture.

Cook about 2 minutes longer, stirring constantly.

Remove from heat and add butter.

Pour hot sauce over rice ring and serve.

Makes 6 servings.

Mrs. H. F. Reist, *Premont, Texas*

# STEAMED AND BAKED PUDDINGS

## Bread Pudding

| | |
|---|---|
| 2 cups bread cubes | 3 tablespoons butter |
| 2 cups milk | 1 teaspoon vanilla |
| ¼ cup sugar | ½ teaspoon cinnamon (optional) |
| 2 eggs | ¼ teaspoon nutmeg (optional) |
| ½ teaspoon salt | |

Use bread a day old. Cut into cubes ¼ inch square.

Place cubes of bread in a buttered baking dish.

Scald milk and add butter and sugar.

Beat eggs slightly and add salt and vanilla.

Pour scalded milk over beaten eggs and mix thoroughly.

Then pour mixture over bread cubes and blend together.

Set baking dish in a pan of hot water.

Bake at 350° for about 1 hour or until a knife comes out clean when inserted in center.

Makes 6 servings.

Serve hot or cold with cream or favorite sauce.

Mrs. Kenneth Seitz, *Camp Hill, Pa.*

Variations:

Add ½ cup raisins and ¼ cup nuts to mixture just before serving.

MRS. A. D. AMSTUTZ, *Apple Creek, Ohio*

When pudding is done, spread with tart jelly (currant).

Beat 2 egg whites until stiff, add 6 tablespoons sugar gradually.

Add ½ teaspoon vanilla.

Continue to beat until stiff, then pile meringue lightly on pudding and
return to the oven to brown.

RUTH SLAYMAKER, *Leola, Pa*

## Brown Sugar Pudding

| | |
|---|---|
| 1 cup sugar | Syrup: |
| 2 cups flour | 1½ cups brown sugar |
| 2 teaspoons baking powder | 1 1/3 cups water |
| ¼ teaspoon salt | 2 tablespoons butter |
| 1 cup milk | |
| 1 teaspoon vanilla | |

Combine brown sugar, water and butter and cook together 5 minutes
to make syrup.

While syrup cooks, sift sugar, flour, baking powder and salt together.

Add vanilla to milk and pour all at once into dry ingredients.

Beat until thoroughly mixed.

Pour syrup in a buttered baking dish.

Drop dough by spoonfuls on top of hot syrup.

Bake at 350° for 45 minutes.

Makes 6 servings.

MRS. ANDREW TROYER, *Hartville, Ohio*

## Baked Chocolate Pudding

| | |
|---|---|
| 1 cup flour | ½ cup milk |
| ¼ teaspoon salt | 2 tablespoons melted butter |
| 2 teaspoons baking powder | ½ cup chopped nuts |
| 1½ tablespoons cocoa | 1 teaspoon vanilla |
| ¾ cup sugar | |

Sift first five ingredients together.

Add milk and vanilla and stir to a smooth batter.

Add melted butter and chopped nuts and blend well into mixture.

Pour into a greased baking dish and bake at 350° for about 45 minutes.

Serve hot with cambridge or chocolate sauce (page 349).

Makes 6-8 servings.

MRS. ARTHUR EBERSOLE, *Birch Tree, Mo.;* MRS. ALLEN GINGERICH, *Lowville, N. Y.*

## Carrot Pudding

| | |
|---|---|
| 1 cup grated raw carrots | 1 teaspoon soda |
| 1 cup grated raw potatoes | 1/3 cup hot water |
| 1 cup sugar | 1 cup raisins |
| 1/3 cup shortening | 1/2 cup chopped figs |
| 1 cup flour | 1/2 cup chopped dates |
| 1/2 teaspoon salt | 1/2 cup chopped nuts |
| 1 teaspoon cinnamon | |

Cream shortening and sugar together.

Add grated carrots, potatoes and chopped dried fruit.

Sift flour; measure and add salt, soda and spices. Sift again.

Add sifted dry ingredients alternately with hot water.

Add chopped nuts and blend into mixture.

Turn into a well-greased pan or mold with cover and steam for 3 hours.
Serve with favorite sauce.

Makes 8 servings.

MRS. AMOS BRUBAKER, SR., *Lebanon, Ore.;* MRS. HENRY SALA, *Holsopple, Pa.*

## Christmas Pudding

| | |
|---|---|
| 1½ cups light cream | ¾ pound dried figs |
| 1½ pounds brown sugar | 1 cup shredded coconut |
| 1 tablespoon butter | 1 cup almonds, chopped |
| ¾ pound chopped dates | 1 teaspoon vanilla |

Combine sugar, cream and butter in a saucepan.

Cook until the soft-ball stage has been reached (238°).

Remove from heat and beat until creamy.

Add chopped fruits and nuts.

Roll with hands into rolls of desired size.

Wrap in waxed paper and store in a cool place for 2 weeks.

Cut in slices when ready to serve and roll in powdered sugar.

MRS. AMOS LEIS, *Wellesley, Ont., Can.*

## Cottage Pudding

| | |
|---|---|
| 1/3 cup shortening | 1/2 teaspoon salt |
| 1 cup sugar | 2 teaspoons baking powder |
| 2 eggs | 1/2 cup milk |
| 1½ cups flour | 2/3 teaspoon vanilla |

Cream shortening and sugar together.

Add unbeaten eggs and beat thoroughly.

Sift flour and measure.

Sift dry ingredients together and add alternately with milk and vanilla.

Stir only enough to blend ingredients together.

Pour into greased pan 8 x 8 inches.

Bake at 375° for about 25 minutes.

Serve with butterscotch, chocolate or orange sauce (pages 349 and 351).

Crushed fresh berries or fruits are also delicious with this cake.

Makes 8 servings.

MRS. ABE MILLER, *Elida, Ohio*

## Cracker Pudding

| | |
|---|---|
| 4 cups milk | 2 cups coarse cracker crumbs |
| 2 eggs, separated | I cup shredded coconut |
| ½ cup sugar | I teaspoon vanilla |

Scald milk in top of double boiler.

Beat egg yolks and add sugar.

Add this mixture gradually to scalded milk. Stir constantly.

Allow to cook for one minute and then add cracker crumbs and coconut.

Stir until cracker crumbs are soft and mixture is thick.

Remove from heat and add vanilla.

Pour into a buttered baking dish.

Spread with meringue made by beating 3 tablespoons sugar into stiffly
    beaten egg whites.

Bake at 350° until meringue is a golden brown.

Makes 6-8 servings.

MRS. LAMON SAYLOR, *Holsopple, Pa.*; MRS. ELLEN LIVINGSTON, *Davidsville, Pa.*

## Date Pudding (I)

| | |
|---|---|
| I pound dried dates, chopped | ½ teaspoon salt |
| I teaspoon soda | 2 cups flour |
| I cup boiling water | I teaspoon baking powder |
| 2 eggs | I cup chopped nuts |
| I cup sugar | I cup sugar |
| 2 tablespoons shortening | 2/3 cup boiling water |

Add soda to ½ pound dates; pour boiling water over mixture.

Beat eggs, add 1 cup sugar and melted shortening.

Combine this mixture with hot dates.

Add flour, salt and baking powder that have been sifted together.

Fold chopped nuts into mixture.

Pour in a greased baking dish and bake 40-45 minutes at 325°.

To make dressing:

Add 1 cup sugar and boiling water to remaining ½ pound dates.

Cook until sauce is thickened like syrup.

Pour over pudding while hot, just before serving.

Serves 6-8.

MRS. BERTIE STALTER, *Elida, Ohio*

## Date Pudding (II)

Syrup:
- 1 cup brown sugar
- 1 cup water
- 1 tablespoon butter

Batter:
- 1/2 cup brown sugar
- 1/2 cup milk
- 1 cup flour
- 1 cup dates, chopped
- 1/2 cup chopped nuts
- 2 teaspoons baking powder
- 1/4 teaspoon salt

Combine 1 cup brown sugar and water; cook together 3 minutes to make syrup.

Remove from heat and add butter.

To make batter:

Sift sugar, flour, baking powder and salt together.

Add milk and stir until smooth.

Fold in chopped dates and nuts, blending well into mixture.

Pour syrup in a greased baking dish.

Pour batter on top of hot syrup and bake at 350° for 35 to 40 minutes.

Serve plain or with whipped cream.

Makes 6 servings.

ELSIE MAY MUMAW, *Dalton, Ohio*

## Fig Pudding (Steamed)

- 2 1/2 cups dried figs
- 1 cup sour milk
- 1 1/4 cups ground suet
- 1 tablespoon cornstarch
- 1 1/2 cups fresh bread crumbs
- 2 eggs
- 1 1/2 cups flour
- 1 1/4 teaspoons soda
- 3 tablespoons grated orange rind
- 1/2 cup orange juice
- 1 cup corn syrup
- 1/2 teaspoon nutmeg
- 3/4 teaspoon salt

Chop dried figs and add sour milk.

Cook together in the top of a double boiler until figs are soft.

Add syrup and ground suet and blend into mixture.

Add beaten eggs and mix thoroughly.

Sift flour and measure.

Sift flour, cornstarch, salt, soda and nutmeg together.

Add dry ingredients and bread crumbs to mixture alternately with orange juice and rind.

Pour mixture into a greased pan or mold and steam for 3 hours.

This pudding should be prepared 3 to 4 weeks before serving.

Serve as fruit cake.

Makes 10-12 servings.

MARY KEFFER, *Waterloo, Ont., Can.*

# Hasty Pudding

Batter:
- 2 tablespoons butter
- 1/3 cup brown sugar
- 1 cup flour
- 1½ teaspoons baking powder
- ¼ teaspoon salt
- ½ cup milk
- 1 cup raisins

Syrup:
- 1 cup brown sugar
- 2 cups boiling water
- 1 tablespoon flour
- 1 tablespoon butter
- 1 teaspoon vanilla

Cream butter and sugar together.

Sift flour and measure.

Sift flour, salt and baking powder together.

Add dry ingredients alternately with milk to creamed mixture.

Beat thoroughly after each addition.

Dust raisins with flour and add to batter.

Pour mixture into a greased 8 inch baking pan.

Cover with syrup.

To make syrup, combine sugar and flour.

Add boiling water and stir until smooth.

Cook until slightly thickened and then remove from heat and add butter and vanilla.

Pour syrup over batter and bake at 350° for about 45 minutes.

Makes 6-8 servings.

Mrs. Floyd Wideman, Tofield, Alta., Can.; Mrs. Sam Leis, Wellesley, Ont., Can.

# Plum Pudding (Steamed)

- 2 2/3 cups dry bread crumbs
- 1¼ cups flour
- 4 cups raisins (seedless)
- 1 package dried figs, chopped (6 ounces)
- 2 cups ground suet
- 1¼ cups sugar
- 1 cup molasses
- 1 teaspoon nutmeg
- 1 teaspoon allspice
- 4 eggs
- 2 teaspoons salt
- 1 cup applesauce or chopped raw apples
- ¼ cup candied orange or lemon peel (optional)

Combine ingredients in the order given.

Mix thoroughly.

Pour into small greased loaf pans or molds.

Steam for 5 hours over boiling water or for 1 hour in a pressure cooker at 15 pounds pressure.

Serve with favorite fruit sauce.

This amount will fill 2 molds of 2 quart capacity.

Mrs. Preston A. Marshall, Pocomoke City, Md.

## Baked Rice Pudding

| | |
|---|---|
| 1/4 cup rice | 1/2 teaspoon salt |
| 1 quart milk, scalded | 1 tablespoon butter |
| 1/3 cup sugar | 1/8 teaspoon nutmeg (optional) |

Clean rice and wash thoroughly.

Add other ingredients and pour into a greased baking dish.

Bake at 325° for approximately 2 hours or until rice is tender.

Stir occasionally, folding in brown layer which forms on top.

Serve while warm.

Makes 6 servings.

ADA E. GARBER, *Elizabethtown, Pa.*; R. GEISSINGER, *Old Zionsville, Pa.*

## Suet Pudding

| | |
|---|---|
| 1 cup ground suet | Sauce: |
| 1 cup molasses | 1 1/2 cups brown sugar |
| 1 cup boiling water | 2 tablespoons butter |
| 3 1/2 cups flour | 3 tablespoons vinegar |
| 1 teaspoon soda | 3 cups water |
| 1 teaspoon cinnamon | 1/2 teaspoon vanilla |
| 1/2 teaspoon cloves | |
| 1/2 cup raisins | |

Combine ground suet, boiling water and molasses.

Sift flour and measure.

Sift flour, soda and spices together and add to mixture.

Beat until thoroughly mixed.

Dust raisins with flour and blend into mixture.

Pour into a greased pan or mold with cover and steam 2 hours.

Serve pudding while warm with hot sauce.

To make sauce, combine sugar, water and vinegar.

Bring to a boil and cook for 3 minutes.

Remove from heat and add butter and flavoring.

Makes 6-8 servings.

MRS. NORMAN M. YODER, *Stuarts Draft, Va.*; ALICE S. SCHMIDT, *Harper, Kan.*

## Walnut and Apricot Pudding (Steamed)

| | |
|---|---|
| 1 cup white flour | 1 egg, beaten |
| 3/4 cup graham flour | 1/2 cup orange juice |
| 1 teaspoon baking powder | 1/2 teaspoon grated orange rind |
| 1/2 teaspoon soda | 1 cup chopped, dried apricots or |
| 1/4 teaspoon salt | prunes |
| 1/4 cup butter | 1/2 cup English walnuts |
| 1/2 cup honey | |

Sift flour; measure and add baking powder, soda and salt.
Sift again.

Add graham flour.

Melt butter in a saucepan and remove from heat.

Add honey and well-beaten egg.

Blend thoroughly.

Then add orange juice and grated rind, chopped fruits and nuts.

Combine this mixture with sifted dry ingredients and mix until thoroughly blended.

Pour into 1 large greased mold or into 10 small individual molds.

Steam for 2 hours if a large mold is used and 1 hour for individual molds.

Serve with favorite sauce.

Makes 10 servings.

STELLA HUBER STAUFFER, *Tofield, Alta., Can.*

## Walnut Date Surprise Pudding

| | |
|---|---|
| 1/3 cup butter | 1/4 teaspoon cloves |
| 1 cup brown sugar | 1/4 teaspoon nutmeg |
| 1/2 cup flour | 2/3 cup milk |
| 1 teaspoon soda | 1/2 cup chopped dates |
| 1/4 teaspoon salt | 1 cup chopped walnuts |
| 1/2 teaspoon cinnamon | 1 1/4 cups dry bread crumbs |

Cream butter and sugar together well.

Sift flour, salt, soda and spices together and add to creamed mixture alternately with milk.

Mix thoroughly.

Dust chopped nuts and dates with flour and blend into mixture along with bread crumbs.

Steam in a greased mold or top of double boiler for 1¼ hours.

Serve hot or cold with cream or fruit sauce (page 350).

Makes 6-8 servings.

MRS. ESTHER ZEHR, *Castorland, N. Y.*

# FRUIT DESSERTS

## Baked Apples

| | |
|---|---|
| 6 large red baking apples | 1 teaspoon cinnamon |
| 1 tablespoon butter | 1/2 cup water |
| 6 tablespoons sugar | 1/2 cup corn syrup |

Wash and pare apples ⅓ of the way down from stem end.

Remove cores, leaving apples whole.

Place apples in a flat baking dish.

Place pared end up.

In the center of each apple put ½ teaspoon butter and 1 tablespoon of sugar and cinnamon mixture.

Combine water and syrup and pour over apples.

Bake at 350° for approximately 45 minutes.

Baste occasionally to keep juicy and to glaze.

For variation, use peppermint candies, honey, chopped dates, seedless raisins or English walnuts as fillings for apples.

MRS. B. L. BUCHER, *Dallastown, Pa.*

Another variation:

Mix together and pour over apples before baking:

| | |
|---|---|
| 1 cup raw oatmeal flakes | 1 cup brown sugar |
| ½ cup butter | 1 cup hot water |

MRS. S. H. ESH, *Belleville, Pa.*

## Apple Brown Betty

| | |
|---|---|
| 3 cups tart apples, diced | ¼ teaspoon salt |
| 1½ cups soft bread crumbs | 1 teaspoon cinnamon |
| 2/3 cup brown sugar | 2 tablespoons lemon juice |
| ¼ cup butter, melted | 1/3 cup water |

Add melted butter to bread crumbs.

Combine apples, sugar, salt and cinnamon.

Place a layer of buttered bread crumbs in bottom of a greased casserole.

Add a layer of diced apples and another of crumbs.

Continue with alternate layers, having bread crumbs on top.

Combine lemon juice and water and pour over mixture.

Bake at 350° for 1 hour.

Makes 6 servings.

ANNA HACKMAN, *South English, Iowa*

## Caramel Apples

| | |
|---|---|
| 6 red baking apples | ⅛ teaspoon salt |
| 1 cup brown sugar | 1 tablespoon butter |
| ½ cup water | 1 cup milk |
| 1 tablespoon cornstarch | ½ teaspoon vanilla |

Wash and pare apples ⅓ of the way down from stem end. Leave whole.

Remove cores and cook in syrup made of sugar and water.

When apples are tender, remove to serving dish.

Combine cornstarch and milk to make a smooth paste.

Bring cornstarch to boiling point and then add syrup in which apples were cooked.

Cook for 10 minutes or until cornstarch is thoroughly cooked.
Remove from heat and add butter, salt and vanilla.
Pour over apples and serve.
Serves 6.

FANNIE M. WEBER, *Adamstown, Pa.*

## Cinnamon Apples

| | |
|---|---|
| 4 tart apples, sliced | ½ cup water |
| 1 cup sugar | ½ pound red cinnamon candy |

Pare and slice apples into eighths.
Combine sugar, water and candy to make syrup.
Bring to a boil and when sugar and candy are dissolved, add sliced
  apples.
Cook until apples are soft.
Makes 4 servings.

MRS. MARTIN GERLACH, *Columbia, Pa.*

## Apple Crisp

| | |
|---|---|
| 8 baking apples | ¾ cup flour |
| 1 cup brown sugar | ½ cup butter |
| 1 teaspoon cinnamon | ½ cup water |

Wash, pare, quarter and core apples.
Cut each quarter lengthwise into 3 or 4 slices.
Put sliced apples in bottom of a buttered baking dish.
Add water.
Combine sugar, cinnamon and flour and rub butter into mixture to
  make crumbs.
Spread crumbs over top of apples, patting them down evenly.
Bake at 375° for approximately 40 minutes. Leave uncovered.
Serve with cream.
Makes 6-8 servings.

MRS. RAYMOND NACE, *Souderton, Pa.;* MRS. PAUL YODER, *Goshen, Ind.*

## Apple Crunch or Delight

| | |
|---|---|
| 1 quart sliced apples | For topping: |
| 1 cup sugar | ¾ cup oatmeal flakes |
| 1 tablespoon flour | ¾ cup brown sugar |
| 1 teaspoon cinnamon | ¼ cup melted butter |
| ⅛ teaspoon salt | ¼ teaspoon soda |

Pare and slice apples.
Combine sugar, salt, cinnamon and flour and sprinkle over apples.

Put apples in bottom of greased baking dish.

Combine oatmeal, brown sugar and soda.

Add melted butter and rub into oatmeal mixture to make crumbs.

Place crumbs on top of apples, patting them down evenly.

Bake at 375° for approximately 40 minutes.

Makes 6-8 servings.

Serve with rich milk or whipped cream as desired.

> Mrs. Will Schlegel, *Milford, Neb.;* Mrs. John Weaver, *Columbiana, Ohio*
> Edna Sommerfeld, *Canton, Kan.*

## Maple Apples

6 tart apples       1½ cups water
1 cup maple syrup

Wash, pare and core apples. Leave whole.

Combine water and syrup and bring to a boil.

Add apples and simmer until tender.

Turn frequently to insure even cooking.

When apples are done, remove from pan and continue to cook syrup until thickened.

Pour syrup over apples.

Serve warm or cold with cream.

> Mrs. Irene Moshier, *Lowville, N. Y.*

## Old-fashioned Apple Dumplings

| | |
|---|---|
| 6 medium-sized baking apples | Sauce: |
| 2 cups flour | 2 cups brown sugar |
| 2½ teaspoons baking powder | 2 cups water |
| ½ teaspoon salt | ¼ cup butter |
| 2/3 cup shortening | ¼ teaspoon cinnamon or nutmeg |
| ½ cup milk | (optional) |

Pare and core apples. Leave whole.

To make pastry, sift flour, baking powder and salt together.

Cut in shortening until particles are about the size of small peas.

Sprinkle milk over mixture and press together lightly, working dough only enough to hold together.

Roll dough as for pastry and cut into 6 squares and place an apple on each.

Fill cavity in apple with sugar and cinnamon.

Pat dough around apple to cover it completely.

Fasten edges securely on top of apple.

Place dumplings 1 inch apart in a greased baking pan.

Pour over them the sauce made as follows:

Combine brown sugar, water and spices.

Cook for 5 minutes, remove from heat and add butter.

Bake at 375° for 35 to 40 minutes.

Baste occasionally during baking.

Serve hot with rich milk or cream.

MRS. FORREST OGBURN, *Dallastown, Pa.;* MRS. U. GRANT WEAVER, *Johnstown, Pa.*
MRS. JAMES BAUMAN, *Oyster Point, Va.*

## Apple Roll-ups

Follow directions in preceding recipe, but chop the apples.

Roll pastry in one large piece ¼ inch thick.

Spread with melted butter and ½ cup brown sugar to which ½ teaspoon
cinnamon has been added.

Add chopped apples and roll as a jelly roll.

Cut in slices 1¼ inches thick.

Place slices in greased baking pan 1 inch apart.

Cover with syrup (see preceding recipe).

Bake at 375° for 35 to 40 minutes.

Delicious served hot with rich milk.

MRS. BERTHA LANDIS, *Sterling, Ill.;* ANNA LOIS UMBLE, *Atglen, Pa.*
MRS. M. D. STUTZMAN, *Kingman, Alta., Can.*

## Apple Fritters

| | |
|---|---|
| 1 cup flour | |
| 1½ teaspoons baking powder | 1 egg, beaten |
| ½ teaspoon salt | ½ cup milk plus 1 tablespoon |
| 2 tablespoons sugar | 1½ cups apples, chopped |

Sift dry ingredients together.

Beat egg and add milk.

Pour into dry ingredients.

Stir until the batter is smooth.

Pare apples and dice or slice very thin.

Add apples to batter and blend together.

Drop by spoonfuls into deep hot fat 370° to 375°.

Fry until a golden brown on all sides.

Makes 12 to 15 fritters.

MRS. IDA HERSHBERGER, *Parnell, Iowa;* MRS. AARON STOLTZFUS, *Premont, Texas*
MRS. MATILDA YODER, *Iowa City, Iowa*

## Swiss Apple Rings

Pare and core apples. Leave whole.

Slice in crosswise rings ¼ inch thick.

Dip apple rings in fritter batter of preceding recipe and fry according
to directions.

Sprinkle with sugar and serve hot.

MRS. H. E. BRENNER, *Creston, Ohio*

## Apple Goodie

For topping:

¾ cup sugar
1 tablespoon flour
⅛ teaspoon salt
½ teaspoon cinnamon
2 cups sliced apples

½ cup oatmeal
½ cup brown sugar
½ cup flour
¼ cup butter
⅛ teaspoon soda
⅛ teaspoon baking powder

Sift sugar, flour, salt, cinnamon together and combine with sliced
apples.

Mix together well and place in the bottom of a greased casserole.

To make topping, combine dry ingredients and rub in butter to make
crumbs.

Put crumbs on top of apple mixture.

Bake at 375° for 35 to 40 minutes.

Serve hot or cold with rich milk.

Makes 6 servings.

MARY HOSTETLER, *Iowa City, Iowa*

## Apple Grunt

½ cup sugar
2 tablespoons shortening
1 egg
1 cup flour
½ teaspoon salt

1 teaspoon baking powder
½ teaspoon soda
½ cup sour milk or buttermilk
1½ cups sliced apples
½ teaspoon vanilla

Cream sugar and shortening together.

Add egg and beat.

Add soda to sour milk and stir into mixture.

Sift dry ingredients together and add, beating thoroughly.

Add sliced apples and blend into mixture.

Pour into greased shallow baking dish.

Rub together the following for crumbs:

6 tablespoons brown sugar
1½ teaspoons flour

½ teaspoon cinnamon
1½ tablespoons butter

Sprinkle crumbs over top of mixture.

Bake at 375° for 35 to 40 minutes.

Serve hot with rich milk.

Makes 4-6 servings.

MRS. LOUELLA PLETCHER, *Middleberry, Ind.*

## Apple Pandowdy

| | |
|---|---|
| 1 quart sliced apples | Topping: |
| 1 cup brown sugar | 1 cup flour |
| 1/4 cup flour | 1/2 teaspoon salt |
| 1/2 teaspoon salt | 2 teaspoons baking powder |
| 1 tablespoon vinegar | 2 1/2 tablespoons shortening |
| 1 tablespoon butter | 1/2 cup milk |
| 3/4 cup water | |
| 1 teaspoon vanilla | |

Pare and slice apples.

Place in the bottom of a large flat baking dish.

To make syrup, combine sugar, flour, salt, vinegar and water.

Bring to a boil and cook for 2 minutes.

Remove from heat and add butter and vanilla. Cool.

Pour cooled syrup over apples.

Make topping by cutting shortening into sifted dry ingredients.

Add milk and stir only until mixture is wet.

Drop topping by spoonfuls over apple mixture.

Bake at 400° for 35 minutes.

Serve with rich milk or cream.

Makes 6-8 servings.

MRS. ELEANOR FREY, *Chambersburg, Pa.*

## Apple Sponge Pudding
### *Very Old*

| | |
|---|---|
| 6 medium-sized apples | 1 teaspoon baking powder |
| 2 eggs, separated | 1/2 cup water |
| 1 cup sugar | 1 teaspoon vanilla or lemon extract |
| 1 cup flour | 2 tablespoons butter |
| 1/2 teaspoon salt | 2 cups brown sugar |

Wash, pare and slice apples.

To make batter, beat egg yolks and add sugar.

Sift dry ingredients together and add alternately with water and flavoring.

Fold in stiffly beaten egg whites.

Melt butter and brown sugar in bottom of large, flat baking dish.

Add sliced apples.

Pour batter over top of apples.

Bake at 350° for 45 minutes.

Turn upside down to serve.

Serve with cream.

Makes 8 servings.

MRS. RAYMOND DOERR, SR., *Millersville, Pa.*

## Stewed Sweet Apples

3 cups sweet apples
2/3 cup brown sugar
1/4 teaspoon salt

1 1/2 tablespoons flour
2 cups water
1/4 cup rich milk

Wash, pare and core apples.
Cut in thin slices lengthwise.
Add water and cook until apples are soft but not mushy.
Five minutes before apples are done, add sugar and salt.
Add milk to flour and stir to a smooth paste.
Add paste to apples and cook until slightly thickened, stirring constantly.
Remove from heat, pour into serving dish and sprinkle with cinnamon.
Serve warm.
A favorite dish of Grandmother's day.
Makes 6 servings.

MRS. EARL EASH, *Elverson, Pa.*

## Apricot Sauce

1 pound dried apricots
2 1/2 cups water
1 tablespoon cornstarch

2 cups boiling water
1/2 cup sugar
1/2 cup crushed pineapple

Soak dried apricots in 2½ cups water for 1 hour.
Cook until tender and rub them through a fine sieve.
Add sugar and 2 cups boiling water to pulp and bring to a boil.
Mix cornstarch with ¼ cup water to make a smooth paste.
Add paste to apricot pulp and cook until thickened, stirring constantly.
Remove from heat and add crushed pineapple.
Makes 6 servings.

## Apricot Upside Down Cake

18 apricot halves
1/2 cup shortening
1 cup brown sugar
3 eggs, separated
1 cup granulated sugar

5 tablespoons apricot juice
1 cup cake flour
1 teaspoon baking powder
1/4 teaspoon salt

Melt butter in large frying pan.
Add brown sugar.
Arrange apricot halves on top of sugar-butter mixture.
Beat egg yolks until light.
Add granulated sugar and apricot juice.
Sift flour and measure.
Sift flour, salt and baking powder together.

Add to mixture.
Fold in stiffly beaten egg whites.
Pour mixture over apricots and bake at 375° for 35 to 40 minutes.
Serve upside down.
Garnish with whipped cream.
Makes 6-8 servings.

MRS. TITUS MILLER, *Falfurrio, Texas*

## Berry Sturm

| | |
|---|---|
| 1 quart berries (raspberry, blackberry or blueberry) | 12 slices bread (a day old) |
| ¾ cup sugar | 1 pint rich milk |

Mash fruit and add sugar.
Cut bread into small cubes and add to berries.
Let stand 10 minutes and then add cold milk.
This dish is of Swiss origin.
Makes 6 servings.

MRS. GROVER SOLDNER, *Bluffton, Ohio*

## Blackberry Cobbler

| | |
|---|---|
| 3 tablespoons butter | 2 tablespoons vinegar |
| 1 cup sugar | ½ teaspoon each of cinnamon and cloves |
| 1 egg | |
| 1½ cups flour | ¼ cup blackberry juice or milk |
| ½ teaspoon salt | 2/3 cup blackberries |
| 1 teaspoon soda | |

Cream butter and sugar together.
Add egg and beat until fluffy.
Sift flour and measure.
Sift dry ingredients together and add alternately with juice and vinegar.
Beat thoroughly after each addition.
Add berries and stir just enough to blend into dough.
Pour into a greased baking pan 8 inches square.
Bake at 350° for approximately 40 minutes.
Makes 6 servings.

MRS. ESTHER MOSHIER, *Castorland, N. Y.*

## Steamed Blueberry Mush

### *An Old Favorite*

| | |
|---|---|
| 4 cups blueberries | 2/3 teaspoon salt |
| 2 cups sugar | 3½ teaspoons baking powder |
| 1 tablespoon butter | ¾ cup milk |
| 2 cups flour | 1 teaspoon lemon juice |

Sift flour and measure.

Sift flour, baking powder and salt together.

Add butter and work it into dry ingredients.

Add milk and beat until thoroughly mixed.

Add sugar and lemon juice to berries.

Fold into batter, stirring just enough to blend together.

Pour into a buttered mold, cover tightly and steam for 45 minutes.

Serve warm with rich milk or cream.

Makes 6 servings.

## Cherry Cobbler

| | |
|---|---|
| 1/4 cup shortening | 1 tablespoon tapioca |
| 1 cup sugar | 1 tablespoon lemon juice |
| 1 egg | 2 tablespoons butter |
| 1 1/2 cups flour | 1/3 cup milk |
| 1/2 teaspoon salt | 2 cups cherries, seeded |
| 2 teaspoons baking powder | |

Sift flour and measure.

Sift flour, baking powder, salt and sugar together.

Cut shortening into dry ingredients.

Beat egg and add milk.

Combine with flour mixture.

Stir until flour is damp.

Pour cherries into a greased, shallow baking dish.

Sprinkle with tapioca, add lemon juice and butter.

Drop batter in 6 mounds on top of cherries.

Bake at 400° for 30 minutes.

Serve warm with milk or cream.

Makes 6 servings.

Mrs. Charles Vanpelt, *Columbiana, Ohio*; Mrs. Edgar Thomas, *Holsopple, Pa.*

Variation:

Replace 1 cup of cherries with 1 cup pineapple chunks and follow directions as given.

Mrs. Clayton Rohrer, *Wadsworth, Ohio*

## Cherry Dumplings

| | Dumplings: |
|---|---|
| 4 cups cherries | 1 1/2 cups flour |
| 1 cup sugar | 2 teaspoons baking powder |
| 3 cups water | 1/4 cup sugar |
| | 1 egg |
| | 1/4 cup milk |
| | 1/2 teaspoon salt |

Wash and seed cherries.
Add water and sugar and cook until soft.
Drain cherries from juice.
Bring juice to boiling point and add dumplings.
To make dumplings:
Sift flour, salt, sugar and baking powder together.
Beat egg slightly and add milk.
Combine with flour mixture, and beat until a smooth, stiff dough.
Drop by spoonfuls into boiling cherry juice.
Cover and cook 12 minutes.
Add cherries and serve hot.
Makes 6-8 servings.
Delicious!

MRS. H. E. BRENNER, *Creston, Ohio*

## Grandma's Cherry Pancakes or Fritters

| | |
|---|---|
| 1¼ cups flour | 1 cup milk |
| ½ teaspoon salt | 2 cups fresh or canned cherries (sour |
| 2 eggs | or sweet cherries may be used) |
| 3 tablespoons sugar | |

Sift flour and measure.
Sift flour, sugar and salt together.
Beat eggs and add milk.
Combine with flour mixture.
Beat until a smooth batter.
Add drained pitted cherries and blend into mixture.
Drop by spoonfuls onto a well greased, hot skillet.
Fry until the edges curl and cakes are brown on both sides.
Sprinkle each cake generously with sugar and stack in layers on a plate.
Makes 12-16 pancakes.
A very old recipe.

MRS. C. F. YAKE, *Scottdale, Pa.*

## Cherry Knepplies

| | |
|---|---|
| 1 quart canned sour cherries | 2 cups flour |
| 1 cup water | 2 eggs |
| 3 tablespoons cornstarch | ¾ cup milk |
| Add sugar to suit taste | 2/3 teaspoon salt |

Bring cherries to the boiling point.
Combine cornstarch and water to make a paste.

Add paste to cherries and cook until thickened, stirring constantly.

Remove from heat but keep warm.

To make knepplies, sift flour and salt together.

Make a well in the flour and add eggs.

Stir with a fork and add milk to mixture.

Stir until a smooth, thick batter is formed.

Drop batter into 1½ quarts of boiling salt water.

To drop it, tilt bowl containing batter at an angle so that batter comes just to edge of bowl.

As it is about to drop off into salt water, cut it with the side of a spoon so that about ½ teaspoon of batter drops at once. Every fourth or fifth time dip spoon in boiling water to keep batter from sticking to spoon.

Let boil one minute after all the batter is in the kettle.

Remove from heat and drain through a colander.

Melt ¼ cup of butter and let it brown.

Pour browned butter over knepplies.

To serve, pour thickened cherries over little balls of dough.

Makes 6 servings.

In former times this dish was used as a main course, and in a few communities it is still served that way.

The old folks used to say that "as long as it gives knepplies and cabbage the Dutchman will not die!"

To the younger generation this dish is delicious as a dessert.

MRS. SARAH STEINER, *Orrville, Ohio*

## Cherry Moos

| | |
|---|---|
| 1 quart sour cherries, seeded | 5 tablespoons flour |
| 2 quarts water | 1 cup sweet cream |
| 2/3 cup sugar | |

Add water to cherries and cook until soft.

Add half of sugar to cherries.

Combine remaining sugar with flour and add cream to make a smooth paste.

Add paste to cherries and cook until thickened, stirring constantly.

Serve warm or cold as desired.

Makes 6-8 servings.

MRS. H. B. FAST, *Mountain Lake, Minn.*

## Cherry Rolls

| | |
|---|---|
| I egg | ¾ teaspoon salt |
| ¾ cup sour cream | 2 tablespoons sugar |
| 2 cups flour | 2 cups drained cherries |
| ¼ teaspoon soda | 2 tablespoons butter |
| 2½ teaspoons baking powder | I teaspoon cinnamon |

Beat egg and add sour cream.

Sift flour; measure and add salt, soda and baking powder. Sift again.

Add sifted dry ingredients and stir until well mixed.

Toss onto a slightly floured board and roll in an oblong piece ¼ inch thick.

Spread lightly with soft butter and cover with cherries.

Sprinkle cherries with cinnamon and sugar.

Roll up like a jelly roll and cut in crosswise slices 1¼ inches thick.

Place slices close together, cut side turned up in a greased baking pan.

Pour over them the following sauce:

| | |
|---|---|
| 1/3 cup brown sugar | 1½ cups cherry juice |
| 1/3 cup white sugar | Few drops red coloring |
| 1½ tablespoons cornstarch | ½ teaspoon almond extract |
| 1½ tablespoons butter | |

Combine dry ingredients, add liquid, coloring and flavoring.

Bring to a boil. When slightly thickened, add butter and pour over rolls.

Bake at 375° for 25 minutes.

Makes 12 rolls.

LEVINA STEINER, *Dalton, Ohio;* MRS. ADA MILLER, *Elida, Ohio*

## Dampf Knepp or Caramel Dumplings

| | |
|---|---|
| I cup warm water | Syrup: |
| I egg | 3 cups water |
| I teaspoon salt | 2 cups brown sugar |
| 3 tablespoons sugar | I tablespoon butter |
| I tablespoon shortening, melted | |
| I yeast cake (small) | |
| Flour (approximately 2½ to 3 cups) | |

Dissolve yeast in warm water.

Beat egg and add sugar and salt.

Combine yeast and egg mixture.

Add flour and melted fat and work to a smooth soft dough.

Turn out on a floured board and knead for several minutes.

Place dough in a greased bowl and brush surface with melted shortening.

Cover and let rise in a warm place until double in bulk.

Divide dough into 6 parts, work into smooth round balls and let rise until light.

Place on top of boiling syrup. To make syrup, combine water, brown sugar and butter and cook together for 5 minutes.

Cover and cook slowly for 25 to 30 minutes.

Do not remove lid.

Serves 6.

An old favorite of Grandmother's day.

Raisins may be added to syrup if desired.

MRS. EDGAR STRITE, *Hagerstown, Md.*; MRS. BETTY BECK, *Archbold, Ohio*

## Blueberry Roly-Poly

| | |
|---|---|
| 1/2 cup shortening | 1/2 teaspoon soda |
| 1/2 cup brown sugar | 1/2 cup boiling water |
| 1/2 cup molasses | 1 teaspoon cinnamon |
| 1 egg | 1/2 teaspoon nutmeg |
| 2 1/4 cups flour | 1 1/2 cups fresh berries |
| 1/2 teaspoon salt | |

Cream shortening and sugar together.

Add egg and molasses and beat until light.

Sift flour; measure and add salt and spices. Sift again.

Dissolve soda in boiling water.

Add dry ingredients alternately with hot water.

Mix well. Then fold in floured berries.

Pour into a greased baking pan and bake at 350° for 35 minutes.

Serve with the following sauce:

| | |
|---|---|
| 1 cup sugar | 1 egg, beaten |
| 1 tablespoon flour | 1 tablespoon butter |
| 1/2 cup boiling water | 1/4 cup sweet cream |
| 1/4 teaspoon salt | 1 teaspoon vanilla |

Combine sugar, flour, and salt.

Slowly add boiling water and stir to a smooth paste.

Cook sauce for 3 minutes, stirring constantly.

Add beaten egg and cook 1 minute longer.

Remove from heat and add butter, sweet cream and vanilla.

Stir until well blended.

Makes 6-8 servings.

MARY E. SUTER, *Harrisonburg, Va.*; MRS. ADA SHANK, *Clearspring, Md.*

## Peach Fritters

| | |
|---|---|
| 1 cup flour | 1 egg |
| 1½ teaspoons baking powder | 1/3 cup milk |
| ¼ teaspoon salt | 1 tablespoon shortening |
| 2 tablespoons sugar | 8 halves canned peaches |

Sift flour; measure and add baking powder, salt and sugar.
Beat egg and add milk.
Add to dry ingredients and beat well.
Add melted fat and mix thoroughly.
Dip peach halves into batter and brown in shallow fat in a frying pan.
Sprinkle with sugar and serve warm.
Makes 8 fritters.

MRS. AARON H. MARTIN, *Adamstown, Pa.*

## Peach Skillet Pie

| | |
|---|---|
| 2 cups flour | 1/3 cup shortening |
| 1 teaspoon salt | 1/3 to ½ cup milk |
| 4 teaspoons baking powder | 8 fresh peaches |

Sift flour; measure and add salt and baking powder. Sift again.
Cut in shortening as for pastry.
Add milk all at once, just enough to make a soft dough.
Turn out on floured board and roll a round piece ¼ inch thick and
several inches larger in diameter than the skillet used.
Place dough in bottom of skillet, let edges hang over the outside.
Then fill with sliced peaches and sprinkle with ¼ cup sugar, to which
has been added ½ teaspoon cinnamon.
Dot with butter.
Fold edges back toward center to partially cover.
Leave center of pie uncovered.
Bake at 400° for 25 to 30 minutes.
Serve warm with rich milk.
Makes 6-8 servings.

MRS. JACOB F. KOLB, *Spring City, Pa.*

## Pear Betty

| | |
|---|---|
| 1 quart canned pears | Juice of 1 lemon |
| ½ cup sugar | 2 cups soft bread crumbs |
| ½ teaspoon cinnamon | 2 tablespoons melted butter |
| ¼ teaspoon each of nutmeg and ginger | |

Drain juice from pears and slice them in lengthwise pieces.
Sift together sugar and spices.
Add sugar mixture and lemon juice to pears.

Add melted butter to bread crumbs and blend together.

Place a layer of buttered crumbs in the bottom of a greased baking dish.

Add a layer of the pear mixture.

Repeat alternate layers, having crumbs on top.

Bake at 350° for 25 to 30 minutes.

Serve with whipped cream or rich milk.

Makes 6 servings.

HANNAH MACK, *Souderton, Pa.*

## Pineapple Upside Down Cake

| | |
|---|---|
| 1 can pineapple slices (8 to 10 slices) | 1/2 teaspoon salt |
| 3 tablespoons shortening | 1 1/2 teaspoons baking powder |
| 1 cup sugar | 1/2 cup milk |
| 3 eggs | 1 cup brown sugar |
| 1 1/2 cups flour | 3 tablespoons butter |

Melt butter in a skillet or heavy baking pan.

Add brown sugar and stir until well blended.

Arrange pineapple slices in an attractive pattern.

To make batter:

Cream shortening and sugar together.

Add eggs and beat until light.

Sift flour and measure.

Sift flour, salt and baking powder together and add alternately with milk.

Beat thoroughly after each addition.

Pour batter over fruit and bake at 350° for 45 to 50 minutes.

Invert pan on a rack or plate.

Serve with whipped cream.

English walnuts or pecans may be added to brown sugar and butter before adding batter.

Makes 6-8 servings.

MRS. NORMAN KRAYBILL, *Elizabethtown, Pa.*
MRS. OLIVER HAMILTON, *Tuleta, Texas*
MRS. CORA WEAVER, *Johnstown, Pa.*

## Pluma Moos

| | |
|---|---|
| 2 quarts water | 1/2 cup sugar |
| 1 cup seedless raisins | 6 tablespoons flour |
| 1 cup dried prunes | 1/2 teaspoon salt |
| 1/4 cup dried peaches | 1 teaspoon cinnamon |
| 1/4 cup dried apricots | 1 cup sweet or sour cream |

Wash fruit and add warm water.

Cook until almost tender and then add sugar.

While fruit is cooking, prepare flour paste by combining flour, salt, cinnamon and cream.

When fruit is done, slowly add flour paste, stirring constantly.

Cook until slightly thickened.

Serve warm.

This dish is served traditionally as a dessert or side dish in some Mennonite communities for Easter, Pentecost or Christmas dinners.

Makes 8 servings.

MRS. JACOB M. FRANZ, *Mountain Lake, Minn.*

## Prune Whip

2 cups prune pulp
3 egg whites
½ cup sugar

¼ teaspoon salt
2 tablespoons lemon juice

Beat egg whites with salt until stiff but not dry.

Add sugar gradually, beating into whites.

Add lemon juice to prune pulp and gradually beat into egg whites.

Continue to beat until mixture is fluffy.

Pile lightly into individual serving dishes and chill.

Or pour into a greased baking dish, set in a pan of water and bake at 300° for 25 minutes.

Serve with whipped cream or a custard sauce (page 350).

Makes 6 servings.

Variations:

Other fruits such as apricots, bananas, fresh peaches or strawberries may be used.

MRS. J. H. FLISHER, *Nampa, Idaho*

## Raisin Pudding

1 cup flour
1 cup sugar
2 teaspoons baking powder
¼ teaspoon salt
½ cup milk

1 cup seedless raisins
2 cups boiling water
1 cup brown sugar
1 tablespoon butter

Sift flour and measure.

Sift flour, granulated sugar, baking powder and salt together.

Add raisins and milk and mix thoroughly.

Pour into a greased baking pan.

Make sauce by combining brown sugar, butter and boiling water.
Pour hot sauce over dough and bake at 350° for 35 to 40 minutes.
Serve warm with rich milk.
Makes 6 servings.

MRS. EDWARD SELZER, *Canton, Kan.;* MRS. JESSE SPICHER, *Belleville, Pa.*

## Raisin Shortcake with Orange Sauce

2 cups flour
2½ teaspoons baking powder
½ teaspoon salt
4 tablespoons shortening
1 egg
½ cup milk or water

For raisin filling:
1½ cups water
2/3 cup raisins
2 teaspoons cornstarch
¼ cup sugar

Sift flour; measure and add baking powder and salt. Sift again.
Cut in shortening as for pastry.
Add beaten egg and beat again.
Add liquid slowly and beat until a smooth dough.
Turn out on floured board and roll ½ inch thick.
Cut with biscuit cutter and place on greased baking sheet.
Bake at 400° for 12 to 15 minutes.
When baked, split cakes and spread with raisin filling.
To make filling, cook raisins in water, when almost done add sugar.
Dissolve cornstarch in ¼ cup cold water and add to raisins.
Cook until slightly thickened, stirring constantly.
Serve with orange sauce (page 351).
Makes 6-8 servings.

MRS. ABNER MUSSELMAN, *Elmira, Ont., Can.*

## Rhubarb Crunch

Mix until crumbly:
1 cup flour, sifted
¾ cup uncooked oatmeal
1 cup brown sugar, packed
½ cup melted butter
1 teaspoon cinnamon
Prepare 4 cups diced rhubarb

Combine the following:
1 cup sugar
2 tablespoons cornstarch
1 cup water
1 teaspoon vanilla

Press half of crumbs in a greased 9 inch baking pan.
Add diced rhubarb.
Combine second mixture and cook until thick and clear.
Pour over rhubarb.
Top with remaining crumbs.
Bake at 350° 35 to 40 minutes.

Cut in squares and serve while warm.
This is delicious served plain or with cream.
Makes 8 servings.

MRS. LEWIS STRITE, *Harrisonburg, Va.*

## Rhubarb Pudding (I)

| | |
|---|---|
| 1½ cups flour | 1/3 cup butter or margarine |
| ½ teaspoon salt | 4 cups diced rhubarb |
| ¼ teaspoon cinnamon | 1 cup brown sugar |
| ½ cup sugar | 1 tablespoon lemon juice |

Sift flour; measure and add salt, sugar and cinnamon. Sift again.
Cut in shortening as for pastry.
Mixture will be crumbly.
Place ½ of crumb mixture in the bottom of a greased 8 inch cake pan.
Press down rather firmly.
Combine rhubarb, brown sugar and lemon juice.
Spread over top of crumb mixture.
Add remaining crumbs and press down with a spoon.
Bake at 375° for 40 to 45 minutes.
Serve warm with rich milk or cream.
Makes 6 servings.

FRANCES AMSTUTZ, *Dalton, Ohio*

## Rhubarb Pudding (II)

| | |
|---|---|
| 3 slices white bread | For custard: |
| 1 cup diced rhubarb | 1 egg |
| 1/3 cup brown sugar | ¼ cup sugar |
| ⅛ teaspoon nutmeg | 1 cup milk |
| 1 tablespoon butter | |

Cut bread in small cubes.
Place half of bread cubes in a greased baking dish.
Then add rhubarb and sprinkle with sugar and nutmeg.
Top with remaining bread cubes and dot with butter.
Beat egg, add sugar and milk.
Pour mixture over contents of baking dish.
Bake at 350° for approximately 40 minutes or until a silver knife comes
 out clean when inserted in pudding.
Serve warm or cold with rich milk or cream.
Makes 6 servings.

MRS. LESTER D. AMSTUTZ, *Apple Creek, Ohio*

## Rhubarb Upside Down Cake

| | |
|---|---|
| ¼ cup shortening | ½ teaspoon salt |
| 1 cup sugar | 1 cup milk |
| 1 egg | 2 cups diced rhubarb |
| 2 cups flour | 1 cup brown sugar |
| 2½ teaspoons baking powder | 2 tablespoons butter |

Melt butter in a skillet or heavy baking pan.

Add brown sugar and diced rhubarb.

To make batter:

Cream shortening and sugar together.

Add egg and beat.

Sift flour; measure and add baking powder and salt. Sift again.

Sift dry ingredients together and add alternately with milk.

Pour batter over rhubarb and bake at 375° for 40 to 45 minutes.

Turn upside down on plate to serve.

Serve with rich milk or cream.

Makes 6 servings.

MRS. GALEN MILLER, *Canton, Ohio*

## Strawberry Shortcake

| | |
|---|---|
| 2½ cups flour | 1 cup sugar |
| 2 teaspoons baking powder | 1 cup milk |
| ½ teaspoon salt | 2 tablespoons butter |
| 2 eggs | 1 teaspoon vanilla |

Sift flour; measure and add baking powder and salt. Sift again.

Sift dry ingredients together.

Beat eggs and add sugar, milk and flavoring.

Combine egg mixture with dry ingredients.

Add melted butter and beat until thoroughly blended.

Pour into 2 greased 8 inch cake pans.

Bake at 375° for 25 to 30 minutes.

Spread strawberry whip between layers and on top.

To make whip:

Boil 1 cup sugar and ½ cup water together until syrup spins a thread when dropped from a fork.

Pour syrup over 2 stiffly beaten egg whites.

Add 2 cups crushed strawberries.

After spreading whip between layers and on top of cake, garnish with whole berries.

Makes 6-8 servings.

MRS. ED UMBLE, *Gap, Pa.*

# FROZEN DESSERTS
## ICE CREAMS, ICES AND SHERBETS

### Freezer Ice Cream (Vanilla Custard)

For 1 gallon freezer:
- 1 quart milk
- 2 cups sugar
- 4 tablespoons flour
- 1/2 teaspoon salt
- 6 egg yolks or 4 whole eggs
- 2 quarts light cream
- 1 tablespoon vanilla

Scald milk in top of double boiler.

Combine flour, salt and sugar.

Add ½ cup cold milk to make a smooth paste.

Add paste slowly to hot milk, stirring constantly.

When custard thickens, add beaten eggs and cook 2 minutes longer.

Remove from heat and add vanilla. Cool.

When cool, add cream and stir until well blended.

Scald can and dasher of the freezer and add custard.

Do not fill can more than 3 inches from top to allow for expansion.

Assemble freezer and crush ice.

Measure ice and salt, using 5 parts ice to 1 part salt.

Pack ice solidly around can, completely covering the top of can.

Turn the crank slowly the first 5 minutes.

Then turn rapidly until cranking becomes difficult.

Remove lid of can and take out dasher.

Push ice cream down from the sides of can.

Use layers of waxed paper over top cream before returning lid, or plug hole in lid with a cork.

Cover with more ice and salt mixture.

Lay newspaper over top.

Keep packed in a cool place to allow cream to ripen for several hours.

Mrs. James Horst, *Columbiana, Ohio*

### Quick Freezer Ice Cream

For 1 gallon freezer:
- 1½ quarts light cream
- 1 quart milk
- 2 cups sugar
- 1/2 teaspoon salt
- 4 eggs
- 1 tablespoon vanilla

Combine milk and cream.

Add sugar, salt and vanilla and stir until well blended.

Beat eggs and add to mixture.

Pour into scalded freezer can and adjust lid and crank of freezer.

Add finely chopped ice, 5 parts ice to 1 part salt.

Turn crank slowly for first 6 minutes, then turn rapidly.

Add more ice and salt as needed.

When frozen, pack in salt brine and allow to ripen for several hours.

Makes 3 quarts.

## REFRIGERATOR ICE CREAM

### Vanilla Ice Cream (Uncooked Base)

2 cups milk
1 tablespoon plain gelatin
½ cup cold water
1 cup sugar

¼ teaspoon salt
1 cup whipping cream
2 teaspoons vanilla

Scald milk in top of double boiler.

Add sugar and salt and stir until dissolved.

Soak gelatin in cold water.

Add gelatin to milk and blend together. Cool.

Add vanilla and pour into freezing tray.

Freeze until firm throughout.

Remove from tray, put in a bowl and break up with a wooden spoon.

Beat with electric mixer or rotary beater until free from hard lumps.

Fold in whipped cream and return to freezing tray.

Set control on refrigerator between normal and fast freezing to hold
  until ready to serve.

Makes 6 servings.

Mrs. Henry A. Bishop, *Perkasie, Pa.*

Variation:

Add 1 cup evaporated milk to mixture just before pouring it into
  freezing tray.

When cream is removed from tray to beat, add ½ cup sour cream in
  place of the cup of whipping cream.

Stir until sour cream is well blended into mixture.

Return to tray and follow previous directions.

Florence C. Friesen, *Greensburg, Kan.*

### Caramel Refrigerator Ice Cream

½ cup sugar
1½ cups milk, scalded
⅛ teaspoon salt
2 egg yolks

1 cup cream
1 teaspoon vanilla
½ cup nut meats

Heat ¼ cup sugar slowly in heavy skillet until melted and slightly
  browned.

Add scalded milk to melted sugar and stir until sugar is completely
   dissolved.
Add remaining sugar and salt to beaten egg yolks.
Add yolks gradually to milk and sugar mixture.
Cool and pour into freezing tray.
Chill until mushy and then remove from tray and beat.
Add whipped cream and vanilla.
Line tray with broken nuts, add cream and freeze until firm.
Makes 6 servings.

MRS. LUELLA LAYMAN, *Harrisonburg, Va.*

## Chocolate Refrigerator Ice Cream

1½ squares unsweetened chocolate     ¼ teaspoon salt
    (1½ ounces)     2 eggs
2 cups milk     1 cup cream
2/3 cup sugar     2 teaspoons vanilla
1 tablespoon flour

Chop chocolate and melt it in top of double boiler.
Add 1½ cups milk and heat to boiling point.
Combine sugar, salt and flour with remaining milk and stir until a
   smooth paste.
Add to hot milk and cook until thickened, stirring constantly.
Add beaten eggs and cook 2 minutes longer.
Remove from heat and cool.
When cool, add vanilla and whipped cream.
Pour into freezing trays and stir 3 or 4 times during freezing.
Makes 6-8 servings.

MRS. LEVI SHRAG, *Lowville, N. Y.*

Variation (Uncooked Base):
Add 1 tablespoon gelatin to hot milk in place of flour paste.
Dissolve gelatin in ½ cup cold milk before adding it to hot milk.

MRS. MAHLON KING, *Parkesburg, Pa.*

## Frozen Peach Custard

2½ cups milk     ¼ teaspoon salt
¾ cup sugar     1 teaspoon vanilla
3 eggs     1½ cups sliced peaches
1 tablespoon flour

Scald 2 cups milk in top of double boiler.
Combine sugar, salt and flour and add remaining milk to make a
   smooth paste.

Add flour paste to hot milk and cook until thickened, stirring constantly.
Add beaten eggs and cook 2 minutes longer.
Chill and add vanilla and sliced peaches.
Pour into freezing tray and freeze.
Stir several times during freezing.
Makes 6 servings.

MRS. FOREST KORNHAUS, *Orrville, Ohio*

## Honey Refrigerator Ice Cream

| | |
|---|---|
| ¾ cup honey | 2 cups whipping cream |
| 3 eggs | 1 teaspoon vanilla |
| ¼ teaspoon salt | |

Heat honey to boiling point and slowly add to well-beaten eggs.
Add salt.
Beat with rotary beater or electric mixer until thick.
Cool and add whipped cream and vanilla.
Pour into 2 freezing trays and freeze.
Stir once during freezing.
Makes 8 servings.

MRS. JOHN P. DUERKSEN, *Hesston, Kan.*

## Mocha Ice Cream

| | |
|---|---|
| 1 tablespoon gelatin | 1 cup brown sugar |
| ½ cup cold coffee | 1 teaspoon vanilla |
| 1 small can evaporated milk | 1 cup whipping cream |
| 2 cups milk | ½ cup nuts or shredded coconut |

Dissolve gelatin in cold coffee.
Let stand 5 minutes and then melt over hot water until clear.
Combine evaporated milk, brown sugar, vanilla and milk.
Add dissolved gelatin and stir until thoroughly mixed.
Add whipped cream and pour into mold and allow to set in refrigerator.
Garnish with nuts, coconut or maraschino cherries.
Makes 6-8 servings.

MRS. WILLIAM G. DETWEILER, *Orrville, Ohio*

## Quick Refrigerator Ice Cream

| | |
|---|---|
| 1 can condensed milk | ¼ teaspoon salt |
| 1 cup cold water | 1 teaspoon vanilla or banana extract |
| 2 cups whipping cream | |

Dilute milk with water.
Add flavor and salt.

Fold mixture into whipped cream and pour into tray.
Freeze for 1 hour, remove from tray and beat until smooth.
Return to tray and freeze until firm.
Makes 6-8 servings.

MRS. CLIFFORD CRESSMAN, *E. Kitchener, Ont., Can.*

## Quick Peppermint Ice Cream

20 marshmallows
I cup hot milk
I cup crushed or ground
peppermint candy

¼ teaspoon salt
I cup whipping cream
I teaspoon vanilla

Cut marshmallows into small pieces and add to hot milk.
Stir until dissolved, add salt and remove from heat.
Cool and chill.
Fold marshmallow mixture into whipped cream and beat until smooth.
Fold in crushed candy and vanilla.
Pour into freezing tray and freeze until firm.
Stir 2 or 3 times during freezing.
Makes 8 servings.
Candy may also be dissolved in hot milk if desired.

MRS. FRANK G. GOOD, *Spring City, Pa.*

## Pineapple-Orange Ice Cream

I cup crushed pineapple
Juice of 2 oranges
I tablespoon lemon juice

I cup sugar
4 cups milk
I cup thin cream

Combine crushed pineapple, orange and lemon juice with sugar.
Let stand 30 minutes to blend the flavors.
Add milk and cream and freeze in hand freezer or tray of electric
refrigerator.
If frozen in tray, stir every 20 minutes during first hour of freezing.
Makes 8 servings.

MRS. SIMON GINGERICH, *Goshen, Ind.*

## Apricot Ice

I cup sugar
½ cup corn syrup
2 cups boiling water

1 1/3 tablespoons lemon juice
2 cups apricot pulp and juice

Combine sugar, syrup and 1 cup water.
Cook to the soft ball stage.
Remove from heat and add remaining water and juice.
Add apricot pulp that has been rubbed through a sieve.

Cool and pour into freezing tray.

Set control for fast freezing.

Freeze until firm throughout.

Remove from tray and break up with a wooden spoon.

Beat with rotary or electric beater until smooth.

Return to refrigerator to complete freezing.

Makes 6-8 servings.

MRS. CARL G. SHOWALTER, *Broadway, Va.*

## Orange Ice

| | |
|---|---|
| I cup orange juice | 1/2 cup corn syrup |
| 1 1/2 cups water | I teaspoon grated orange rind |
| 3/4 cup sugar | I tablespoon lemon juice |

Combine syrup, sugar, water and grated orange rind.

Place over low heat and stir until sugar is dissolved.

Bring to a boil and cook for 5 minutes without stirring. Cool.

Add orange and lemon juice. Mix well.

Freeze in a hand freezer or electric refrigerator.

If a freezer is used, use same directions as for ice cream (page 326).

If frozen in a refrigerator, set control for fast freezing and freeze until firm.

Remove from tray and break up with a wooden spoon.

Beat with an electric or rotary beater until a thick mush free from hard lumps.

Return to refrigerator to complete freezing.

Makes 6-8 servings.

ANNA HERSH, *Elizabethtown, Pa.*

Variation:

If lemon ice is desired, replace orange juice and rind with ⅜ cup lemon juice and 1 tablespoon lemon rind.

## Maple Mousse

| | |
|---|---|
| 1 1/2 teaspoons plain gelatin | I cup whipping cream |
| 1/4 cup cold water | 1/2 teaspoon vanilla |
| 1/2 cup boiling maple syrup | 1/8 teaspoon salt |

Dissolve gelatin in cold water and let stand 5 minutes.

Slowly add hot maple syrup to gelatin. Stir until smooth.

Cool and add whipped cream, salt and vanilla.

Pour into freezing tray and set the control for fast freezing.

Do not stir during freezing.

Makes 6 servings.

MRS. JOHN DANFORD, *Dayton, Ohio*

# SHERBETS

## Buttermilk Pineapple Sherbet

| | |
|---|---|
| 1 cup crushed pineapple | 2 cups buttermilk |
| ¾ cup sugar | 1 egg white |
| Juice of 1 lemon | |

Combine sugar and crushed pineapple.

Add lemon juice and buttermilk.

Freeze until firm and then remove from tray and break up with a wooden spoon.

Beat with electric mixer or rotary beater until smooth.

Add stiffly beaten egg white and blend into mixture.

Return to refrigerator to finish freezing.

Makes 6-8 servings.

MRS. ARTHUR EBERSOLE, *Birch Tree, Mo.*

## Lemon Milk Sherbet

| | |
|---|---|
| 1 cup sugar | 1/3 cup lemon juice |
| 2½ cups milk | |

Add the sugar to the lemon juice and stir until dissolved.

Add milk slowly to lemon juice; stir constantly to keep from curdling.

Pour in freezing tray and follow directions given in preceding recipe or freeze in hand freezer, following directions for ice cream (page 326).

Makes 6-8 servings.

MRS. NAOMI BOSHART, *Lowville, N. Y.*

## Lime Sherbet

| | |
|---|---|
| 1 package lime gelatin | ¼ cup lemon juice |
| 1 cup sugar | 2½ cups milk |
| 1 cup water | |

Combine sugar and water and cook together for 2 minutes.

Pour hot syrup over gelatin.

Stir until gelatin is dissolved.

Add lemon juice and cool.

Add milk and blend together well.

Pour into freezing trays and freeze until firm.

Remove to bowl and break into chunks with a wooden spoon.

Beat with electric mixer or rotary beater until smooth.

Return to trays and finish freezing.

Makes 8 servings.

MRS. RACHEL POWELL, *South English, Iowa;* MRS. C. A. GRAYBILL, *Martinsburg, Pa.*

## Orange Sherbet

| | |
|---|---|
| 1½ cups orange juice | 1 tablespoon grated orange rind |
| 1/3 cup lemon juice | 1 cup water |
| 1¼ cups sugar | 2 cups milk |

Combine sugar and water and cook until a syrup is formed.
Cool and add fruit juices and grated rind.
Slowly add milk and stir until well blended.
Pour into freezing trays and freeze at fast speed until firm.
Remove from tray and break into pieces with a wooden spoon.
Beat with electric mixer or rotary beater until smooth.
Return to refrigerator to complete freezing.
Makes 8 servings.

MRS. PAUL ROUPP, *Hesston, Kan.*

## Orange and Grapefruit Sherbet

| | |
|---|---|
| 1½ cups sugar | 2 cups orange and grapefruit juice |
| 2 cups top milk | blend (canned) |

Combine sugar and juice.
Add milk slowly and stir until well blended.
Pour into freezing trays and freeze at fast speed until firm.
Remove from tray and break into chunks with a wooden spoon.
Beat with electric mixer or rotary beater until smooth.
Return to trays and finish freezing.
Makes 8 servings.

MRS. HERMAN RINKENBERGER, *Bradford, Ill.*

## Pineapple Sherbet

| | |
|---|---|
| 1 can crushed pineapple (9 oz.) | 2 tablespoons hot water |
| 2 cups buttermilk | 1 egg white |
| 1 cup sugar | 1 teaspoon vanilla |
| 1½ teaspoons gelatin | |

Dissolve gelatin in hot water.
Combine sugar and pineapple.
Add buttermilk slowly and stir until well blended. Add vanilla.
Add dissolved gelatin and blend well into mixture.
Pour into freezing tray and freeze at high speed until firm.
Remove from tray and break into pieces with a wooden spoon.
Beat with electric mixer or rotary beater until smooth.
Add stiffly beaten egg white and return to refrigerator to finish freezing.
Makes 8 servings.

MRS. MAGGIE MARTIN, *Rittman, Ohio*

## Summer Delight

### *Frozen Fruit*

| | |
|---|---|
| 2 oranges | 2 cups water |
| 2 lemons | 2 cups sugar |
| 2 bananas | |

Squeeze oranges and lemons.

Mash bananas through a sieve.

Combine juices, banana pulp, sugar and water.

Stir until sugar is dissolved.

Pour into freezing tray and freeze at fast speed.

Stir 2 or 3 times during freezing.

Makes 6 servings.

MRS. C. R. EBERSOLE, *La Junta, Colo.;* MRS. MARVIN E. HOSTETLER, *Orrville, Ohio*

# GELATIN DESSERTS

## Apricot Delight

| | |
|---|---|
| 1 quart water | 1 package orange gelatin |
| 3 tablespoons tapioca | 1 cup boiling water |
| 1 cup sugar | 1/2 pound dried apricots |
| 1/2 teaspoon salt | |

Cook tapioca in 1 quart water until soft.

Cook dried apricots until tender and rub through a sieve.

Dissolve gelatin in hot water.

Combine all ingredients and pour into a mold.

Chill until set or firm.

Unmold and garnish with whipped cream.

Makes 6-8 servings.

MRS. MARK RHODES, *Columbiana, Ohio*

## Pineapple Bavarian Cream

| | |
|---|---|
| 1 1/2 tablespoons plain gelatin | 1 pint boiling water |
| 1/2 cup cold water | 1 cup whipping cream |
| 2 cups crushed pineapple | 2 tablespoons lemon juice |
| 1/4 teaspoon salt | 1 dozen marshmallows, chopped |
| 1/2 cup sugar | |

Dissolve gelatin in cold water and let stand 15 minutes.

Add boiling water and stir until smooth.

Add sugar, salt and pineapple with juice to gelatin mixture.

Add chopped marshmallows and blend ingredients together.

Pour mixture into mold and chill in refrigerator until it begins to congeal.

Whip the cream until thick and fold into congealed mixture.

Return to refrigerator until set.

Nuts may be added if desired.

Makes 8 servings.

MRS. N. D. MAST, *Fentress, Va.;* MRS. FRANK HERR, *Washingtonboro, Pa.*

## Creamy Delight

½ package lime gelatin
½ package strawberry gelatin
2 cups boiling water
I pint vanilla ice cream

Add 1 cup of boiling water to strawberry gelatin and stir until dissolved.

Add remaining cup of boiling water to lime gelatin and stir until dissolved.

Pour each into separate molds and chill in refrigerator until gelatin begins to congeal.

Whip 1 cup of ice cream into each.

Pile red and green gelatin lightly together in sherbet glasses.

A good dessert for Christmas or festive occasions or at the end of a heavy dinner.

Makes 6-8 servings.

MRS. ARTHUR H. CLABAUGH, *Hanover, Pa.*

## Delightful Dessert

I package strawberry gelatin
I cup hot water
½ cup minute tapioca
½ cup sugar
I quart water
½ pound marshmallows
½ cup pineapple tidbits
I cup whipping cream

Dissolve gelatin in hot water.

Pour into mold and chill until partially congealed.

Beat with a rotary egg beater and return to refrigerator.

Combine sugar and tapioca and add 1 quart of water.

Cook until tapioca is soft.

Chill and beat with rotary beater.

Add chopped marshmallows and pineapple bits to tapioca.

Whip cream until thick and fold into mixture.

Dip gelatin lightly into sherbet glasses and pile tapioca-marshmallow mixture on top.

Makes 6-8 servings.

DINA MOSER, *Canton, Ohio*

## Graham Cracker Fluff

| | |
|---|---|
| 2 egg yolks | I cup whipping cream |
| 1/2 cup sugar | I teaspoon vanilla |
| 2/3 cup milk | 3 tablespoons melted butter |
| I package gelatin (I tablespoon) | 3 tablespoons sugar |
| 1/2 cup cold water | 12 graham crackers |
| 2 egg whites | |

Beat egg yolks and add sugar and milk.

Cook in top of double boiler until slightly thickened.

Soak gelatin in the cold water.

Pour hot mixture over softened gelatin and stir until smooth.

Chill until slightly thickened.

Add stiffly beaten egg whites, vanilla and whipped cream to chilled mixture.

Combine melted butter, cracker crumbs and sugar to make crumbs.

Sprinkle half of crumbs in bottom of serving dish.

Add mixture and top with remaining crumbs.

Let chill in refrigerator until set.

Makes 6-8 servings.

MRS. M. J. EICHELBERGER, *Shickley, Neb.*; MRS. OREN YODER, *Parnell, Iowa*
MRS. SAMUEL LANDIS, *Souderton, Pa.*

## Lemon Bisque

| | |
|---|---|
| I package lemon gelatin | 1 1/2 cups evaporated milk |
| 1 1/4 cups boiling water | 2 1/2 cups vanilla wafer crumbs |
| Juice and rind of I lemon | I cup chopped nuts (optional) |
| 1/2 cup sugar | |

Dissolve gelatin in boiling water.

Add sugar, lemon juice, and grated rind.

Chill mixture until congealed.

Beat until fluffy.

Chill evaporated milk and whip it until stiff.

Add to mixture.

Add chopped nuts.

Spread ½ of crumbs in the bottom of a baking dish or oblong pan 7 x 9 inches.

Add mixture and top with remaining crumbs.

Let stand in refrigerator overnight.

Cut in squares when ready to serve.

Makes 8-10 servings.

MRS. SAMUEL JANZEN, *Greensburg, Kan.*

## Macaroon Pudding

| | |
|---|---|
| 2 cups milk | 1 tablespoon plain gelatin |
| 3 eggs, separated | 12 macaroons |
| 1 cup sugar | ½ cup whipping cream |

Heat milk in top of double boiler.
Beat egg yolks and add sugar.
Add ½ cup scalded milk to beaten yolks.
Then add eggs to milk.
Cook until custard coats a spoon (about 2 minutes).
Remove from heat and add gelatin.
Stir until it is dissolved.
Beat egg whites until stiff and fold into mixture.
Line serving dish with macaroons and add pudding.
Garnish with whipped cream.
Makes 6-8 servings.

MIRIAM SHAFFER, *Martinsburg, Pa.*

## Marshmallow Whip

| | |
|---|---|
| 1 package strawberry gelatin | 1 quart crushed peaches or pineapple |
| 1 cup hot water | ½ pound marshmallows |
| 1 cup cold water | 2 cups whipping cream |

Dissolve gelatin in hot water.
Add cold water and chill until partially congealed.
Whip gelatin until light and fluffy.
Add crushed fruit and marshmallows that have been cut in quarters.
Whip cream.
Fold whipped cream into mixture and return to refrigerator.
This can be made the day before it is to be served.
Makes 8 servings.

MRS. JOHN HERSHEY, *Rohrerstown, Pa.*

## Pineapple Snow

| | |
|---|---|
| 1 package orange gelatin | ½ cup sugar |
| 1 cup hot water | 1 cup crushed pineapple, drained |
| 1 cup pineapple juice and water | ½ cup whipping cream |

Dissolve gelatin in hot water.
Add pineapple juice and remaining water.
Chill until partially congealed.
Whip until fluffy.
Add drained pineapple.
Whip cream and add sugar.

Fold into mixture.
Serve plain or garnish with whipped cream.
Makes 6-8 servings.

MRS. ERBIE SAUDER, MRS. LYDIA ZIMMERMAN, *East Earl, Pa.*

## Rosy Vanilla Whip

| | |
|---|---|
| 1 package raspberry gelatin | 1 package vanilla pudding |
| 2 cups water | 2 cups milk |

Prepare gelatin and vanilla pudding as directed on package.
Chill gelatin until partially congealed and then beat until fluffy.
Add cooled pudding and beat until well blended.
Pour mixture into sherbet glasses or serving dish and chill until set.
Garnish with fresh fruit or whipped cream.
Makes 8 servings.

MRS. ALLEN GEHMAN, *Adamstown, Pa.*

## Strawberry Soufflé

| | |
|---|---|
| 1 tablespoon plain gelatin | 2 cups crushed strawberries |
| 6 tablespoons cold water | 1/2 cup sugar |
| 1/4 teaspoon salt | 1/2 cup whipping cream or |
| 3 eggs, separated | evaporated milk |

Separate eggs and beat yolks slightly.
Add 2 tablespoons water, salt and sugar.
Cook mixture in top of double boiler until it thickens, stirring constantly.
Remove from heat.
Put 4 tablespoons cold water in a bowl and sprinkle gelatin over top.
When gelatin has dissolved, add it to hot custard.
Stir until it is well blended through mixture.
Cool mixture and then add crushed strawberries, whipped cream and
   stiffly beaten egg whites.
Blend well into mixture.
Pour into a large mold or small individual molds that have been rinsed
   in cold water.
Chill in refrigerator until set.
Makes 8 servings.

MRS. ELI NUSSBAUM, *Apple Creek, Ohio*

Variation:

Replace water with pineapple juice and strawberries with 1 cup crushed
   pineapple.

MRS. SAMUEL EBY, *Clearspring, Md.*

## Spanish Cream

| | |
|---|---|
| 1 tablespoon plain gelatin | 3 eggs, separated |
| 3 cups milk | 1/4 teaspoon salt |
| 1/2 cup sugar | 1 teaspoon vanilla |

Soak gelatin in cold milk for 10 minutes.

Add sugar and salt and stir until it is dissolved.

Heat in top of double boiler until milk is scalded.

Beat egg yolks slightly and add ½ cup hot milk.

Stir mixture into remaining milk and cook until slightly thickened (about 4 minutes).

Stir constantly.

Remove from heat and cool slightly.

Fold in stiffly beaten egg whites and vanilla.

Turn into molds and chill until firm.

Makes 8 servings.

MARY HOSTETLER, *Iowa City, Iowa;* ERMA ERNST, *Kitchener, Ont., Can.*

# MISCELLANEOUS REFRIGERATOR DESSERTS

## Ambrosia

| | |
|---|---|
| 3 oranges | 1/4 cup shredded coconut |
| 3 bananas | Maraschino cherries |

Remove sections from oranges and cut in thirds.

Slice bananas.

Combine fruits and chill in refrigerator.

When serving, top with shredded coconut and cherries.

Makes 4 servings.

MARGARET LAMBERTSON, *Pocomoke City, Md.*

## Angel Food Cake Dessert

| | |
|---|---|
| 1 large angel food cake broken into small pieces | 4 eggs, separated |
| 6 ounces chocolate chips | 3 tablespoons powdered sugar |
| 2 tablespoons water | 1/2 cup whipping cream |

Put chocolate chips in top part of double boiler.

Add water and stir until chocolate is melted.

Beat egg yolks until light and then add sugar.

Add egg and sugar mixture to melted chips and stir until smooth. Cool.

When cool, add stiffly beaten egg whites and whipped cream.

Blend into mixture.

Place alternate layers of cake pieces and chocolate mixture in a greased
    loaf pan.
Have chocolate mixture on top.
Chill in refrigerator for at least 12 hours.
Makes 8 servings.

Mrs. Clarence Swartzendruber, *Kalona, Iowa*

## Apricot Pudding

| | |
|---|---|
| ½ pound dried apricots | 1 package orange gelatin |
| 4 cups water | ¼ teaspoon salt |
| 3 tablespoons tapioca | ½ cup whipping cream |
| 1 cup sugar | |

Cook apricots until tender. Add sugar.
Bring 4 cups water to the boiling point.
Add tapioca and cook until clear.
Add gelatin and salt and stir until gelatin is dissolved.
Remove from heat and add apricot pulp.
Chill thoroughly and garnish with whipped cream.
Makes 6 servings.

Mrs. Melvin Rohrer, *Wadsworth, Ohio*

## Chocolate Surprise

| | |
|---|---|
| 1 cup sugar | 3 eggs, beaten |
| 3 tablespoons cocoa | 3 tablespoons butter |
| 3 tablespoons cornstarch | 6 graham crackers |
| ¼ teaspoon salt | ½ teaspoon vanilla |
| 2 cups top milk (scalded) | ½ cup chopped walnuts |

Combine sugar, cocoa, cornstarch and salt; add scalded milk.
Add mixture to beaten eggs and mix thoroughly.
Cook until smooth and thickened, stirring constantly.
Remove from heat and add butter, vanilla, graham cracker crumbs, and
    chopped nuts.
Chill until firm.
Serve with whipped cream.
Makes 6 servings.

Mrs. Walter Weaver, *Christiana, Pa.*

## Lady Finger Chocolate Dessert

| | |
|---|---|
| 2 ounces sweet chocolate | 4 eggs, separated |
| 2 tablespoons sugar | 1½ dozen lady fingers |
| 2 tablespoons hot water | 1 teaspoon vanilla |
| ¼ teaspoon salt | |

Melt chocolate in top of double boiler.
Add sugar, salt, and hot water and stir until smooth.
Add beaten egg yolks and cook 2 minutes longer.
Remove from heat and cool. Add vanilla.
Add stiffly beaten egg whites and fold into mixture.
Arrange lady fingers in log cabin fashion in a serving dish.
Pour mixture over them and top with whipped cream.
Makes 6 servings.

MRS. JOHN DANFORD, *Dayton, Ohio*

## Lemon Pudding

| | |
|---|---|
| ¼ cup lemon juice | 3 eggs, separated |
| Grated rind of 1 lemon | 1 cup graham cracker or |
| ¾ cup sugar | vanilla wafer crumbs |
| ¼ teaspoon salt | 1 cup whipping cream |

Combine fruit juice and rind, sugar, salt and beaten egg yolks.
Cook mixture until thickened.
Cool slightly and fold in stiffly beaten egg whites.
Then add whipped cream and blend into mixture.
Grease refrigerator tray and line bottom with crumbs, reserving some
    crumbs for top.
Pour in filling and sprinkle remaining crumbs on top.
Freeze until set. Do not turn control higher.
Makes 6 servings.

MABEL STOLTZFUS, *Westover, Md.;* ANNIE AND EDNA WENGER, *Harrisonburg, Va.*

## Marshmallow Strawberry Delight

| | |
|---|---|
| 24 graham crackers | 1 cup whipping cream |
| 5 tablespoons melted butter | ½ cup chopped nuts |
| 1 cup milk | 1½ cups strawberries, drained |
| 1 cup chopped marshmallows | |

Crush graham crackers and add melted butter.
Mix thoroughly and then put ½ of crumbs in the bottom of a buttered
    mold.
Scald milk and add chopped marshmallows.
Stir for 2 minutes and then set aside until cold.
Add crushed fruit, nuts and whipped cream.
Cover with remaining crumbs and chill for 12 hours in refrigerator
    before serving.
Crushed pineapple may be used in place of strawberries.
Makes 6 servings.

WILMA TROYER, *Harper, Kan.*

## Peach Marlow

32 marshmallows
2 tablespoons water
1 tablespoon lemon juice

1 cup crushed peaches
(fresh or canned)
1 cup whipping cream

Chop marshmallows and add water.

Heat in a saucepan over low heat, folding over and over until marshmallows are almost melted.

Remove from heat and continue folding until mixture is smooth.

Cool and then fold in crushed peaches.

Add lemon juice and whipped cream.

Pour mixture in freezing tray and freeze until set but not hard.

Makes 6-8 servings.

MRS. C. N. STEINER, *Sterling, Ill.*

## Pineapple Fluff

2 cups crushed pineapple
1 cup sugar
2 cups water and pineapple juice

2 tablespoons cornstarch
3 eggs, separated
½ pound marshmallows

Drain juice from pineapple and add enough water to make 2 cups liquid.

Heat 1½ cups juice to boiling point.

Combine cornstarch and sugar, add remaining juice to make a smooth paste.

Add paste to hot liquid and cook until thickened, stirring constantly.

Add beaten egg yolks and cook 2 minutes longer.

Remove from heat and cool slightly.

Add beaten whites, crushed pineapple and chopped marshmallows.

Fold into mixture.

Chill thoroughly.

Makes 6-8 servings.

ELIZABETH GEHMAN, *Mohnton, Pa.;* MRS. EDITH MARTIN, *East Earl, Pa.*

## Pineapple Pudding

2 cups crushed graham crackers or
   vanilla wafers
1 cup crushed pineapple
1 cup chopped dates
½ cup chopped nuts

1/3 cup melted butter
2/3 cup powdered or granulated sugar
2 eggs, beaten
1 cup light cream

Combine crumbs, pineapple, chopped dates and nuts.

Press into square pan (8 inches).

Combine sugar, melted butter and beaten eggs.

Mix thoroughly and add cream.

Pour this mixture over crumbs and chill for 24 hours.
Cut in squares and garnish with whipped cream.
Makes 8 servings.

MRS. JENNIE A. L. GABLE, *York, Pa.*

## Pineapple Torte

| | |
|---|---|
| 3 eggs, separated | 2 tablespoons lemon juice |
| 1/4 teaspoon salt | 2 tablespoons sugar |
| 1/2 cup sugar | 1 cup whipping cream |
| 1 1/2 cups crushed pineapple | 2 cups vanilla wafer crumbs |

Beat egg yolks and add sugar and salt.
Drain juice from pineapple.
Add pineapple and lemon juice.
Cook in top of double boiler until mixture coats a spoon.
Stir constantly.
Remove from heat, add crushed pineapple and cool.
Beat egg whites until stiff.
Add 2 tablespoons sugar to make a meringue.
Fold whipped cream and custard into meringue.
Spread half of the crumbs over the bottom and sides of a greased
    refrigerator tray.
Add custard mixture and cover with remaining crumbs.
Freeze for 3 to 4 hours or until firm.
Makes 6-8 servings.

MRS. FRANCIS SMUCKER, *Orrville, Ohio*

## Pineapple Rice

| | |
|---|---|
| 1 cup cold boiled rice | 6 marshmallows |
| 1 cup whipping cream | 1 cup crushed pineapple |
| 1/2 cup sugar | 1/4 cup chopped nuts |

Whip cream.
Add sugar and rice and blend into cream.
Add diced marshmallows and chill.
Drain pineapple and chill thoroughly.
When ready to serve, add well-drained pineapple and chopped nuts
    and fold into mixture.
Pile lightly into sherbet glasses.
Fresh peaches or strawberries may be used in place of pineapple.
Makes 6 servings.

LUCILLE FAY MUMAW, *Dalton, Ohio*

## Vanilla Wafer Dessert

1 pound vanilla wafers
First filling:
  ½ cup butter
  ½ cup powdered sugar
  3 eggs, separated
  1 teaspoon vanilla

Second filling:
  5 tablespoons cocoa
  4 tablespoons boiling water
  1 cup powdered sugar
  3 eggs, separated

Roll wafers until fine and divide into 3 parts.

Line an oblong loaf pan with waxed paper.

Put ⅓ of the crumbs in bottom of pan.

Make first filling by creaming together sugar and butter.

Add beaten egg yolks and vanilla.

Fold in stiffly beaten whites.

Add this filling to crumbs in loaf pan.

Cover with second part of crumbs.

Add second filling made by rubbing sugar into cocoa, and adding boiling water and egg yolks to make a smooth paste.

Fold in stiffly beaten egg whites.

Add filling to second layer of crumbs.

Add third layer of crumbs.

Cover and set in refrigerator for 12 to 24 hours.

Cut in squares and serve with whipped cream.

Makes 16 servings.

MRS. JOHN DANFORD, *Dayton, Ohio*

# MISCELLANEOUS DESSERTS

## Knee Patches or Swiss Crumpets

3 eggs
1 cup cream

4 cups flour
½ teaspoon salt

Beat eggs and add cream.

Sift flour and salt together and stir into mixture to make a soft dough.

Take a piece of dough the size of a large marble and roll as thin as possible. (The Swiss used to cover the knee with a tea towel and then stretch dough over knee until very thin.)

Fry in deep fat 375° until a delicate brown.

Drain and dust with powdered or granulated sugar.

Makes 24-30 patches.

A popular treat at weddings and holiday feasts!

MRS. LEAH HOSTETTER, *Harper, Kan.;* MRS. AARON STEINER, *Dalton, Ohio*

## Plowlines or Funnel Cakes

3 eggs
2 cups milk
4 cups flour

¼ cup sugar (optional)
½ teaspoon salt
2 teaspoons baking powder

Beat eggs and add milk and sugar.

Sift flour, salt and baking powder together.

Add dry ingredients to egg and milk mixture.

Beat batter until smooth.

This batter should be thin enough to run through a small funnel.

Drop from funnel into hot deep fat 375°, holding finger over bottom of funnel to control amount of batter released.

Make into one of the following designs:

Start at center of pan, swirling batter outward in a gradually enlarging circle, being careful not to touch circles.

Or let batter run through funnel into hot fat into any shape you desire, crisscrossing to make an intricate design.

Fry until a golden brown and remove from fat and drain.

Makes about 30 cakes, depending on size.

MRS. ABRAM SHANK, *Clearspring, Md.*; MRS. JOHN HARNISH, *Lancaster, Pa.*

## Pond Lilies

2 eggs
1½ cups flour

¼ teaspoon salt
1 tablespoon shortening

Beat eggs.

Add flour and salt. Stir until a smooth dough.

Add melted shortening and work into dough.

Divide dough into small pieces the size of a large marble.

Roll as thin as possible in a circle 3 inches in diameter.

Make 8 cuts, starting from outer edge of circle and cutting toward center.

Leave center the size of a quarter.

Put a drop of water in the center and place another round (made similar to first one) on top.

Press centers together with finger.

Bake in deep hot fat 375°.

Hold centers down with end of a wooden spoon and let edges curl to resemble lilies.

Fry until golden brown and then remove from fat and drain.

Fill centers with whipped cream or crushed fruit in season.

Makes 8-12 cakes.

MRS. LILLIE WINGARD, *Boswell, Pa.*

## Tangle Cakes

| | |
|---|---|
| 2 eggs | Approximately 5 cups flour |
| 1½ cups sugar | 1 teaspoon soda |
| ¼ cup shortening | 1 cup sour milk |
| ½ teaspoon salt | ¼ teaspoon nutmeg (optional) |

Cream shortening and sugar.

Add eggs and beat again.

Sift dry ingredients together and add alternately with sour milk.

Beat thoroughly after each addition.

Roll dough in thin pieces and cut in strips ½ inch wide.

Tangle several strips together and fry in deep fat 375°.

Makes 30-36 cakes.

MRS. ABRAM SHANK, *Clearspring, Md.*

## Cream Puffs

| | |
|---|---|
| 1 cup flour | ½ cup butter |
| ¼ teaspoon salt | 4 eggs |
| 1 cup boiling water | |

Place butter and boiling water in saucepan.

Keep on low heat until butter is melted.

Sift flour and salt together and add all at one time to the boiling water and fat.

Stir vigorously until mixture leaves sides of pan and forms a ball.

Remove from heat and add unbeaten eggs, one at a time.

Beat thoroughly after the addition of each egg.

Drop by tablespoonfuls onto a greased baking sheet, placing about 2 inches apart.

Bake at 425° for 30 minutes or until beads of moisture no longer appear on surface.

Makes 12 to 15 cream puffs.

When cool, cut a slit in the side of each and fill with whipped cream or the following filling:

| | |
|---|---|
| 2 cups milk | 5 tablespoons flour |
| 2/3 cup sugar | ¼ teaspoon salt |
| 3 eggs, separated | 1 teaspoon vanilla |

Scald 1½ cups milk in top of double boiler.

Combine sugar, flour and salt.

Add remaining milk to dry ingredients to make a smooth paste.

Add paste to scalded milk and cook until thickened, stirring constantly.

Slowly add beaten egg yolks and cook 2 more minutes.

Remove from heat and add vanilla. Cool.
When cooled, add stiffly beaten egg whites and blend into mixture.

MRS. WARREN A. EICHER, *Milford, Neb.*; MRS. M. M. DEINER, *Versailles, Mo.*
EMMA KINSINGER, *Grantsville, Md.*

## Chocolate Puffs

| | |
|---|---|
| 2 squares unsweetened chocolate (2 oz.) | 5 egg whites |
| 1 cup sugar | ½ teaspoon salt |
| ½ cup milk | ¼ teaspoon cream of tartar |
| | 1 teaspoon vanilla |

Combine grated chocolate and sugar in top of double boiler.
When chocolate is melted, add milk and cook to soft ball stage.
Remove from fire and add vanilla.
Beat egg whites until foamy.
Add salt and cream of tartar.
Continue beating until whites are stiff.
Slowly fold hot syrup into beaten egg whites.
Pour into buttered baking dish or greased muffin tins and set in pan of hot water.
Bake until firm (about 35 minutes).
Serve with custard sauce (page 350).
Makes 6-8 servings.

DELPHIA AND INA RHODES, *Harrisonburg, Va.*

## Basket Ball Fluff

| | |
|---|---|
| 2 cups soft bread crumbs | 4 eggs, separated |
| 4 cups scalded milk | 3 tablespoons butter |
| ½ cup sugar | ½ cup raisins |
| 1 cup chopped marshmallows | 1 teaspoon vanilla or |
| ½ teaspoon salt | ¼ teaspoon nutmeg |

Scald milk.
Beat egg yolks, add sugar, salt and flavoring.
Combine crumbs, raisins and chopped marshmallows.
Pour hot milk slowly into egg mixture and mix thoroughly.
Pour this mixture over crumb mixture.
Pour into greased baking dish.
Beat egg whites until stiff.
Add 4 tablespoons sugar and pile lightly on top of mixture.
Bake at 325° until meringue is a golden brown.
Serves 8.

MRS. HAROLD H. LAHMAN, *Elkton, Va.*

## Lemon Meringue Blossoms

| | Filling: |
|---|---|
| 3 egg whites | ¾ cup sugar |
| ⅛ teaspoon salt | ⅛ teaspoon salt |
| ½ teaspoon vinegar | 3 tablespoons cornstarch |
| ¼ teaspoon vanilla | 1½ cups boiling water |
| 1 cup sugar | 3 egg yolks |
| | Juice of 2 lemons |
| | 2 tablespoons grated lemon rind |

Combine egg whites, salt, vinegar and vanilla.

Beat until partly stiff and then add sugar gradually.

Continue to beat until very stiff.

Shape in mounds, dropping from a large spoon onto a cookie sheet covered with plain, ungreased paper.

Shape into nests with back of spoon.

Bake at 300° for 45 minutes.

Remove from paper immediately and fill with lemon filling.

If difficult to remove, dip a spatula in water and lift them off paper.

To make filling:

Combine sugar, salt and cornstarch.

Add boiling water and cook in top of double boiler until thickened.

Add beaten egg yolks, juice and rind of lemon.

Cook 3 more minutes, stirring constantly.

Cool before filling meringues.

Makes 8 meringues.

STELLA HUBER STAUFFER, *Tofield, Alta., Can.*

## Supreme Delight

| | |
|---|---|
| ½ cup butter | ¼ cup chopped dates |
| 2 cups sugar | 1 tablespoon vinegar |
| 4 eggs, separated | ½ teaspoon salt |
| ¼ cup pecan nuts | Vanilla ice cream |

Cream butter and sugar together.

Add beaten egg yolks, chopped nuts, dates and vinegar.

Beat egg whites until frothy, add salt.

Continue to beat until stiff.

Fold stiffly beaten whites into first mixture.

Pour into a buttered baking dish and set in a pan of hot water.

Bake at 325° until mixture is set (about 40 minutes).

Top with vanilla ice cream when serving.

Makes 6-8 servings.

MRS. ANABEL SOMMERFELD. *Halstead, Kan.*

# SAUCES FOR DESSERTS

## Butterscotch Sauce

| | |
|---|---|
| 1 cup brown sugar | 2 tablespoons butter |
| 1 cup corn syrup | 1 teaspoon vanilla |
| 1 cup light cream | |

Combine sugar, syrup and cream and cook until syrup forms a soft ball when dropped in cold water (238°).

Remove from heat and add butter and vanilla.

Delicious when served on vanilla ice cream.

Makes 1½ cups.

MRS. FORD R. KREIDER, *Seville, Ohio*

## Cambridge Sauce

| | |
|---|---|
| 1/3 cup butter | 1½ tablespoons cold water |
| 1 cup powdered sugar | ½ cup boiling water |
| 2 teaspoons flour | |

Cream butter and sugar together.

Make a paste of flour and cold water.

Add hot water gradually and cook for 5 minutes.

Then pour hot mixture into creamed butter and sugar and stir until smooth and sugar is dissolved.

Delicious served on chocolate and other puddings.

Makes about 1 cup.

MRS. ALLEN GINGERICH, *Lowville, N. Y.*

## Chocolate Sauce

| | |
|---|---|
| 2 squares of unsweetened chocolate (2 oz.) or ½ cup cocoa | 1 tablespoon cornstarch |
| 1 cup sugar | 1 tablespoon butter |
| 1 cup hot water | ⅛ teaspoon salt |
| | 1 teaspoon vanilla |

Melt chocolate in top part of double boiler.

Gradually add hot water and stir until smooth.

Dissolve cornstarch in 2 tablespoons cold water and add to chocolate mixture.

Add sugar and salt and stir until dissolved.

Cook over boiling water until mixture is thick and smooth (about 8 to 10 minutes).

Stir frequently.

Remove from heat and add butter and vanilla.

Makes about 1½ cups.

MRS. G. P. SHOWALTER, *Broadway, Va.*; MRS. EPENTUS FETTEROLF, *Lansdale, Pa.*

## Custard Sauce

2 eggs
4 tablespoons sugar
1/8 teaspoon salt

1 1/2 cups scalded milk
1/2 teaspoon vanilla

Scald milk in top of double boiler.

Beat eggs and add sugar and salt.

Slowly add scalded milk to egg and sugar mixture.

Cook over hot water until mixture thickens slightly and coats a metal spoon (about 5 minutes).

Remove immediately from hot water and set pan in cold water to cool quickly.

Overcooking causes custard to curdle.

When cool, add vanilla.

Makes about 2 cups.

DELPHIA AND INA RHODES, *Harrisonburg, Va.*

## Fruit Juice Sauce

1/2 cup sugar
1 1/2 tablespoons cornstarch
1 tablespoon lemon juice

1 1/2 cups fruit juice (juice from any canned fruit may be used)
1 tablespoon butter

Mix sugar and cornstarch.

Add fruit juice and bring to a boil.

Cook for 3 minutes, stirring constantly.

Remove from heat and add lemon juice and butter.

Makes 1½ cups.

## Hard Sauce

1/4 cup butter
3/4 cup granulated sugar or
1 cup powdered sugar
1 teaspoon boiling water

1/8 teaspoon salt
1 teaspoon vanilla or
2/3 teaspoon lemon extract

Cream butter and sugar together thoroughly.

Add salt, boiling water and flavoring.

Beat until fluffy.

Allow to chill before serving.

Makes about 1 cup.

Delicious when served on steamed pudding and fruit desserts.

Variation:

Add 2 teaspoons of orange juice and grated orange rind instead of vanilla or lemon flavoring.

## Lemon Sauce

½ cup sugar
1½ tablespoons cornstarch
1½ cups boiling water

⅛ teaspoon salt
2 tablespoons butter
Grated rind and juice of 1 lemon

Combine sugar, salt, and cornstarch.
Add boiling water and stir until a smooth paste.
Cook slowly until thickened and clear.
Stir constantly.
Remove from heat and add lemon rind and juice and butter.
Stir until ingredients are well blended.
Makes about 1½ cups.

VIRGINIA PEBLEY, *Johnstown, Pa.*; MRS. OLIVER BAIR, *Hanover, Pa.*

## Maple Sauce

1 cup maple syrup
1 tablespoon butter
1 teaspoon flour

⅛ teaspoon salt
1 teaspoon vanilla

Melt butter and add flour and salt.
Cook 2 minutes and add syrup.
Cook 1 minute, stirring constantly.
Remove from heat and add vanilla.
Makes 1 cup.

MRS. ALVIN N. ROTH, *Wellesley, Ont., Can.*

## Maple Syrup

3 cups sugar
2 cups boiling water

1 teaspoon maple flavoring
¼ teaspoon vinegar

Dissolve sugar in boiling water. Cook together for 5 minutes. Cool.
Add maple flavoring and vinegar and blend into mixture.
Let stand 24 hours before using.
Makes about 1 quart.

MRS. SYLVESTER LEHMAN, *Apple Creek, Ohio*

## Orange Sauce

2/3 cup sugar
2 tablespoons cornstarch
Grated rind of 1 orange
Juice of 3 oranges

2 cups boiling water
⅛ teaspoon salt
1 tablespoon butter

Combine sugar and cornstarch.
Add orange juice and grated rind.

Add boiling water and cook until thickened.
Remove from heat and add butter.
Makes about 2 cups.

MRS. ABNER MUSSELMAN, *Elmira, Ont., Can.*

## Pear-Orange Bake

4 pears
½ cup sugar
¼ cup orange juice

¼ cup water
1½ teaspoons grated orange rind

Pare, halve and core fruit.
Combine sugar, orange juice, and water, and bring to boiling point.
Add pears and simmer in a covered pan until tender (about 20 minutes).
Remove fruit and add orange peel and simmer for 3 to 5 minutes longer.
Chill and serve as a topping for vanilla ice cream.
Enough to top 8 servings.

RUTH STRONG, *Mechanicsburg, Pa.*

## Strawberry Supreme

2 cups crushed strawberries

1 cup sugar

Crush strawberries thoroughly.
Add sugar and stir until it is dissolved.
Chill.
Delicious topping for ice cream or sponge cake.

LIZZA KNOPP, *Salem, Ohio*

# Pastry, Pies and Tarts

## Chapter XI

I HAVE ONLY A FAINT RECOLLECTION OF THE PIE SHELF HANGING IN Grandmother's springhouse. This shelf was suspended by wires attached to heavy joists in the ceiling. Although that shelf has always been empty in my time, it has spoken of days past when Grandmother was young and kept her larder full of goodies. On pie-baking day, which was usually Saturday morning, that swinging shelf fairly groaned with the weight of 16 to 18 pies. No wonder the hostess of long ago need not know ahead of time that guests were coming! She was always prepared!

The old-fashioned "safe" followed the shelf in the springhouse as an excellent storage place for pies. It was a cupboard much like any other set of shelves, except that the doors were made of tin. These were beautifully decorated with designs that looked as if they were made with a hammer and nail. These holes, although small enough that no fly could pass through, aided in ventilation.

Some of the favorite pies of those days are still favorites in Mennonite families today. A number of these are not to be found in modern cookbooks, however. Although we have no way of tracing their history, we are convinced that some of these recipes were brought by memory from the old country. Among the most popular ones are the crumb pies and open-faced sour cream fruit pies, including apple, peach and raisin. There are other types of crumb pies with a chewy layer underneath. Two more favorites are the buttermilk custard and the green tomato pies.

I can still recall how as a child I sat and watched my grandmother make pies. She kept a blue-and-white-spotted enamel container in the flour bin, and in that she always made her pastry. She would sift a large amount of flour in this and then add lard for shortening. She never thought of measuring her ingredients, for her experienced fingers knew just when she had enough fat or liquid. And what did it matter anyway, if she added a bit too much fat? She would just add a little more flour and thus have dough enough to make an extra "half-moon turnover" for the grandchildren. Her pastry was not quite so rich as ours today: thus she could work quickly, for it was more easily handled. As I remember those pies, however, they were certainly good.

Grandmother's troubles were not over when she had taken the last pie from the oven. Many of the old brick and stone houses, some of which are still to be found in Lancaster County, Pennsylvania, and Rockingham County, Virginia, had a back and a front stairway to the second floor. The back steps led to rooms above the kitchen and were occupied as bedrooms by the growing boys of the family. There was no connection between those rooms and the ones in the front of the house on the second floor, where the parents and the girls of the family had their rooms. When the house was quiet and all the family supposedly were asleep, what a temptation it was for Henry, Daniel, Jonas, and Abe to slip down the back stairs and relieve the pie shelf of one or more of its number.

# PIES

## Pastry (for a 9-inch double-crust pie)

| | |
|---|---|
| 2¼ cups flour | ½ teaspoon salt |
| 2/3 cup shortening | 1/3 cup cold water |

Combine flour and salt in a mixing bowl.

Cut shortening into flour with a pastry blender or two knives.

Do not overmix; these are sufficiently blended when particles are the size of peas.

Add water gradually, sprinkling 1 tablespoon at a time over mixture.

Toss lightly with a fork until all particles of flour have been dampened.

Use only enough water to hold the pastry together when it is pressed between the fingers. It should not feel wet.

Roll dough into a round ball, handling as little as possible.

Roll out on a lightly floured board into a circle ⅛ inch thick and 1 inch larger than the diameter of the top of the pan.

## To Make Pastry Shell

Roll dough as in preceding recipe.

Fit circle into a pie plate and trim edges with scissors or a sharp knife. Let ½ inch extend over rim.

Turn edge under and flute with fingers to make a standing rim.

Prick shell all over with a fork to prevent air bubbles.

Bake at 450° for 12 to 15 minutes or until a golden brown.

## Two-Crust Pies

Use pastry recipe on preceding page.

Divide dough into 2 equal portions.

Roll bottom crust as in preceding recipe.

Place filling in the shell.

Roll remaining dough for top crust. Decorate top with favorite design, leaving sufficient holes to allow steam to escape during cooking. Moisten edges of lower crust with cold water. Add top crust.

Press edges together tightly with tines of a fork or with fingers.

Bake as directed in recipe.

## Apple Pie

| | |
|---|---|
| 3 cups diced apples | 2 tablespoons rich milk |
| 2/3 cup sugar | 2 tablespoons butter (optional) |
| 1 tablespoon flour | Pastry for two 9 inch crusts |
| ½ teaspoon cinnamon or nutmeg | (page 354) |

Mix apples, sugar, flour and spice together until well blended.

Place mixture in unbaked crust.

Add rich milk and dots of butter over the top.

Place strips or top crust on pie as desired.

Fasten securely at edges.
Bake in hot oven, 400° for 50 minutes.
Makes 1 (9 inch) pie.

MRS. EDISON GERBER, *Walnut Creek, Ohio*

## Apple Crumb Pie

| | |
|---|---|
| 6 tart apples | ¾ cup flour |
| I cup sugar | I teaspoon cinnamon |
| 1/3 cup butter | Pastry for one 9 inch shell (page 354) |

Pare apples and cut into eighths.
Mix ½ cup sugar and cinnamon together and sprinkle over apples.
Put apple mixture into unbaked pastry shell.
Combine remaining sugar and flour. Add butter and rub together until crumbs are formed.
Sprinkle fine crumbs over apples.
Bake at 425° for 10 minutes and then reduce temperature to 350°.
Bake 35 minutes longer.
Reheat just before serving.
Delicious when served with cheese.

MRS. D. H. BENDER, *Palmyra, Mo.*

## Apple Custard Pie (I)

| | |
|---|---|
| 6 tart apples | I teaspoon cinnamon |
| I cup sugar | 1½ cups milk |
| I cup flour | Pastry for one 9 inch crust (page 354) |
| 2 tablespoons butter | |

Mix sugar and flour together and put in the bottom of a pastry shell.
Pare apples and cut quarters; fit tightly together in the shell.
Sprinkle apples with cinnamon and dot with butter.
Pour milk over the mixture.
Bake at 375° for approximately 50 minutes.
This makes 1 (9 inch) pie.

MRS. MINNIE HAMILTON, *Sheridan, Ore.*

## Apple Custard Pie (II)

| | |
|---|---|
| 2 cups applesauce | ¼ cup melted butter |
| ½ cup sugar | Pastry for one 9 inch crust (page 354) |
| 2 eggs, separated | |

Add sugar, melted butter and egg yolks to applesauce.
Mix well.
Beat egg whites until they stand up in peaks.

Fold beaten whites into apple mixture.
Pour into unbaked pie shell.
Bake at 375° for approximately 35 minutes.
Delicious!

MRS. MICHAEL WHETZEL, *Broadway, Va.*

## Candied Apple Pie

2 cups sliced apples
1½ cups brown sugar
½ cup butter

I cup flour
I cup whipped cream

Grease a 9 inch pie plate.
Cover bottom with layer of sliced pared apples.
Add ½ cup brown sugar.
Mix together butter, flour and remaining sugar.
Sprinkle mixture over apples and bake for 45 minutes at 375°.
Serve with whipped cream.
Serves 6.

MRS. ALLEN GINGERICH, *Lowville, N. Y.*

## Delicious Open-Faced Apple Pie

7 medium-sized apples
¾ cup sugar
2 tablespoons butter
1/3 cup flour

¼ cup water
2 tablespoons lemon juice
Pastry for I (9 inch) shell (page 354)

Mix butter, sugar and flour together thoroughly.
Sprinkle half of this mixture in the bottom of an unbaked pastry shell.
Place apple halves tightly together in crust with cut side down.
Cover with remainder of crumb mixture.
Mix water and lemon juice and pour over apples.
Bake at 425° for 15 minutes and then reduce temperature to 375°.
    Continue to bake 35 minutes.
May be served with whipped cream.

MAGGIE W. MOYER, *Waterloo, Ont., Can.*

Variation:
The water and lemon juice may be omitted and ⅔ cup cream added
    instead.
Sprinkle with cinnamon before baking.

MRS. DAVID A. HATHAWAY, *Philadelphia, Mo.*

## Deep-Dish or Old-Time Family Pie

| | |
|---|---|
| I quart sliced apples | 2 teaspoons cinnamon |
| 1½ cups sugar | ¼ cup water |
| 2 tablespoons butter | Pastry for 3 (9 inch) shells (page 354) |

Line the sides and bottom of a square or rectangular baking dish (7 x 10 inches) with pastry.

Add thinly sliced apples that have been mixed with sugar and cinnamon.

Dot butter over the top. Add water.

Fit a crust over the top. Make openings in top crust to allow steam to escape.

Bake at 425° for 20 minutes, reduce temperature to 375° and continue to bake 40 minutes.

Cut in squares and serve with warm, sweetened milk and cream.

Serves 8.

MRS. JOHN HORST, *Salem, Ohio*

## Dried Apple Custard Pie

| | |
|---|---|
| ½ cup dried apples | 1½ tablespoons flour |
| ½ cup sugar | I teaspoon grated orange rind |
| 2 eggs, separated | 1¼ cups milk |
| ½ teaspoon salt | Pastry for I (9 inch) crust (page 354) |

Soak dried apples in warm water for 1 hour.

Cook apples in water in which they have soaked. When soft, rub through a sieve or mash fine.

Add flour, salt, sugar, egg yolks and orange rind.

When thoroughly mixed, add milk.

Fold in stiffly beaten egg whites.

Pour mixture into unbaked pie shell.

Bake at 375° for 40 minutes.

MRS. AMOS KOLB, *Spring City, Pa.*

## Dried Snitz Pie

| | |
|---|---|
| 2 cups dried tart apples | ¼ teaspoon powdered cloves |
| 2/3 cup sugar | ½ teaspoon cinnamon |
| 1½ cups water | Pastry for 2 (9 inch) crusts (page 354) |

Soak apples in 1½ cups warm water.

Cook apples in water in which they were soaked.

When soft, rub apples through a colander.

Add sugar and spices.

Put mixture in an unbaked pie shell.

Cover pie with top crust. Fasten at edges.

Bake at 425° for 15 minutes, reduce temperature to 375° and continue
to bake for 35 minutes.

This makes 1 (9 inch) pie.

MRS. LEANDER GANTZ, *Marietta, Pa.*

## Dutch Apple Pie

3 cups sliced apples
1 cup brown sugar
4 tablespoons butter
3 tablespoons flour

1 teaspoon cinnamon
3 tablespoons top milk
Pastry for 1 (9 inch) crust (page 354)

Combine flour, sugar and cinnamon.

Cut in the butter with a pastry blender.

Place sliced apples in an unbaked pie shell.

Sprinkle crumb mixture over top.

Add milk.

Bake at 375° for 45 minutes or until apples are soft, and a rich syrup
has formed.

MRS. RALPH L. VOGT, *Hesston, Kan.*

## Fried Apple Turnovers (Very Old)

2 cups dried apples
½ cup sugar   .
2 tablespoons butter

1 teaspoon cinnamon
Pastry for 2 (9 inch) shells (page 354)

Soak dried apples in 1½ cups warm water.

Cook until tender.

Drain off most of the juice.

Add sugar, butter and cinnamon to apples.

Roll pastry as for pies, and cut into 4 to 5 inch squares or circles.

Place several spoonfuls of apples on one-half of square.

Moisten edges and then fold over other half of square.

Press edges together securely.

Fry in deep fat at 375° for approximately 4 minutes or until golden
brown on both sides. If baked in oven, bake at 375° for approximately 20 minutes.

MRS. AARON STOLTZFUS, *Premont, Texas*

## Apple Butter Pie

½ cup apple butter
2 eggs
½ cup sugar
1½ tablespoons cornstarch

1 teaspoon cinnamon
2 cups milk
Pastry for 2 (9 inch) crusts (page 354)

Add beaten eggs, sugar, cornstarch and cinnamon to apple butter. Mix well.

Add milk gradually to mixture and blend together.

Pour into an unbaked pastry shell.

Cut strips of dough ¼ inch wide and place on top of pie in lattice fashion.

Bake at 375° for 35 minutes.

Makes 1 (9 inch) pie.

MRS. EDNA LEHMAN, *Holsopple, Pa.*

## Banana Cream Pie

| | |
|---|---|
| ¾ cup sugar | 1 tablespoon butter |
| 3 tablespoons cornstarch | 1 teaspoon vanilla |
| ¼ teaspoon salt | 1 cup sliced bananas |
| 2 eggs, separated | Pastry for 1 (9 inch) crust (page 354) |
| 2 cups milk | |

Combine sugar, salt and cornstarch.

Add 1½ cups of milk.

Cook in a double boiler until thickened.

Beat yolks of eggs and add remaining milk.

Add egg mixture slowly to custard, and cook 2 more minutes.

Remove from heat and add butter and vanilla.

Slice bananas and place them in the bottom of a baked crust.

Add cream filling and cover with meringue.

Brown meringue in moderate oven (350°) until golden brown. This will require 12-15 minutes.

This makes 1 (9 inch) pie.

BERTHA DIENER, *Versailles, Mo.*

## Banbury Tarts

| | |
|---|---|
| ½ cup raisins | ½ cup nuts (walnuts) |
| ½ cup dates | 1 egg |
| 1 cup sugar | 2 tablespoons lemon juice |
| ¼ cup butter | Pastry for 1 (9 inch) crust (page 354) |

Chop raisins and dates.

Combine all ingredients except lemon juice, and cook slowly for 10 minutes.

Remove from heat, add lemon juice and cool.

Roll pastry and line tart or muffin tins or cut in 3 inch squares.

Place 2 spoonfuls of filling in each shell.

Cover with crust and pinch edges together.
Bake at 400° for 20 to 25 minutes.

MRS. LEWIS BENDER, *Wellman, Iowa*

For variety, the egg white may be separated and beaten for meringue.
Place meringue on top of tarts instead of top crust, and bake at 325°
until golden brown.

## Butter Tarts

1 cup brown sugar
1 egg
3 tablespoons butter

2 tablespoons corn syrup
1 teaspoon vanilla
Pastry for 1 (9 inch) crust (page 354)

Mix sugar and butter together.
Add egg, syrup, and vanilla and combine well.
Line 6 tart pans with pastry; place 2 large spoonfuls of mixture in each.
Bake at 400° for about 20 minutes, or until pastry is delicately browned.

MRS. MERVIN WEBER, *Kitchener, Ont., Can.*

## Fruit Tarts (Perischki)

2 cups dried peaches, apricots or
prunes
1/2 cup sugar

1 1/2 cups warm water
Pastry for 2 (9 inch) shells (page 354)

Soak dried fruit in warm water for 1 hour.
Cook until tender and add sugar.
Drain and cool.
Roll pastry and cut into 3 to 4 inch squares.
Put filling in center of square.
Moisten edges and bring corners up on top and press together.
Bake at 400° for 20 minutes or until golden brown.

HELEN LORENZ, *Mountain Lake, Minn.*

## Buttermilk Pie

1 cup sugar
2 cups buttermilk
2 eggs
2 tablespoons butter

2 tablespoons flour
1 teaspoon lemon flavoring
Pastry for 1 (9 inch) crust (page 354)

Combine sugar and flour.
Add beaten eggs, melted butter, milk and flavoring.
Pour into unbaked pie crust.
Bake at 400° for 10 minutes then to 350° for 30 minutes.
This makes 1 (9 inch) pie.

MRS. FREEDLEY SCHROCK, *Hesston, Kan.*

## Butter Raisin Tarts

| | |
|---|---|
| I cup brown sugar | ¾ cup water |
| I cup raisins | I teaspoon vanilla |
| 2 tablespoons butter, melted | Pastry for I (9 inch) crust (page 354) |
| I egg | |

Combine all ingredients and cook slowly for 7 minutes.

Line muffin or tart pans with pastry.

Put several spoonfuls of filling in each tart.

Bake at 400° for 20 to 25 minutes.

Makes 6-8 servings.

MRS. ALLEN SCHULTZ, *Milverton, Ont., Can.;* MRS. MAURICE ROES, *Lowville, N. Y.*

## Butterscotch Pie

| First Part: | Second Part: |
|---|---|
| ½ cup brown sugar | I egg yolk |
| 3 tablespoons boiling water | ½ cup flour |
| I tablespoon butter | ½ cup granulated sugar |
| ½ teaspoon salt | I½ cups boiling water or milk |
| ½ teaspoon vanilla | Pastry for I (9 inch) crust (page 354) |
| ⅛ teaspoon soda | |

Combine brown sugar, 3 tablespoons boiling water, butter and salt.

When mixture begins to boil, add soda.

Boil until syrup forms a hard ball in cold water.

Combine egg yolk, flour and granulated sugar, slowly add boiling water.

Add second mixture to first and bring to a boil.

Pour custard in a baked pie shell.

Top with meringue and bake at 350° for about 12 minutes or until
    meringue is golden brown.

This makes 1 (9 inch) pie.

MRS. RAYMOND TROYER, *Sugar Creek, Ohio*

## Cake Filled Pielets

| | |
|---|---|
| I 1/3 cups sifted flour | I egg, well beaten |
| ½ teaspoon soda | ¼ cup raisins |
| ¼ teaspoon salt | 1/3 cup milk |
| ½ teaspoon cinnamon | 1/3 cup molasses |
| ½ teaspoon nutmeg | Red, tart jelly |
| 1/3 cup shortening | Pastry (page 354) |
| ½ cup sugar | |

Sift flour, soda, salt and spices together.

Cream shortening and add sugar gradually.

Add egg and beat well.

Add dry ingredients alternately with milk and molasses.

Line muffin or tart pans with pastry.

Place 1 teaspoon tart jelly in each, then add mixture.

Bake at 400° for 20-25 minutes.

Makes 8 tarts.

MARY HURST, *Seville, Ohio*

## Caramel Pie

I cup brown sugar
1/3 cup flour
2 tablespoons butter
½ teaspoon salt

3 eggs, separated
2 cups milk
½ teaspoon vanilla
Pastry for I (9 inch) crust (page 354)

Heat 1½ cups milk in top of double boiler.

Combine flour, sugar and salt and make a paste with remaining ½ cup milk.

Add mixture to hot milk and cook until thickened.

Add beaten egg yolks and cook 2 minutes longer.

Pour custard in a 9 inch baked pie crust.

Cover with meringue and bake at 350° until golden brown.

MRS. J. EARLY SUTER, *Harrisonburg, Va.*

## Cottage Cheese Pie (I)

Crust:
I package zwieback, ground
(6 ounces)
I cup sugar
¼ cup melted butter
½ teaspoon cinnamon

Filling:
3 eggs, separated
I teaspoon salt
6 ounces cottage cheese
I cup sugar
2 tablespoons flour
I teaspoon vanilla
I cup cream
I cup milk

Mix together the zwieback crumbs, sugar, and cinnamon.

Add melted butter and pat mixture in a 9 inch pie tin.

To make filling, add egg yolks, salt, sugar and flour to cottage cheese.

Add milk, cream and vanilla; when thoroughly combined, add beaten egg whites.

Pour mixture into crust.

Reserve a few of the crumbs to sprinkle on top.

Bake at 350° for 1 hour.

This is delicious.

MRS. ARTHUR RUTH, *Chalfont, Pa.*

## Cottage Cheese Pie (II)

1½ cups cottage cheese
½ cup sugar
2 tablespoons flour
¼ teaspoon salt

2 eggs, separated
¼ teaspoon cinnamon or nutmeg
2 cups milk
Pastry for 1 (9 inch) crust (page 354)

Combine cottage cheese, sugar, flour, salt and spice.
Add beaten egg yolks and mix thoroughly.
Add milk gradually to make a smooth paste.
Fold in beaten egg whites.
Pour into unbaked pastry shell.
Bake at 350° for 1 hour.
Makes 1 (9 inch) pie.

Mrs. Willis D. Moyer, *Souderton, Pa.;* Mrs. Amos H. Bechtel, *Spring City, Pa.*

## German Cottage Cheese Cakes

2 cups cottage cheese
¼ teaspoon salt
2 eggs, separated

2 cups flour
Water
Pastry for 2 (9 inch) crusts (page 354)

Combine cottage cheese, egg yolks and salt.
Add egg whites to flour.
Add enough water to moisten flour, as for pastry.
Roll dough and cut in 6 inch circles.
Put 2 tablespoons of cheese mixture on half of the circle.
Fold over other side and fasten edges securely.
Drop half-moons in a large pan of boiling water.
When done, these will float on top of the water.
Remove from water and pour brown butter over top.
These are delicious.
Makes 6 to 8 cakes.

Mrs. Callie Burkholder Leitzel, *Hutchinson, Kan.*

## Cherry Pie

2½ cups sour cherries
1/3 cup cherry juice
1/3 cup brown sugar
1/3 cup granulated sugar

3 tablespoons minute tapioca
1 tablespoon butter
⅛ teaspoon almond extract
Pastry for 2 (9 inch) crusts (page 354)

Combine cherries, juice, sugars, flavoring and tapioca.
Let stand 15 minutes.
Pour into pastry-lined pie plate. Dot with butter.
Place crust or strips on top as preferred.

Bake at 425° for 10 minutes, then in moderate oven (375°) for 30
minutes.

Makes 1 (9 inch) pie.

MRS. FANNIE A. L. GABLE, *York, Pa.;* MRS. IRA EIGSTI, *Buda, Ill.*

## Chocolate Cream Pie

| | |
|---|---|
| 2 squares chocolate or | 3 tablespoons cornstarch or |
|    3 tablespoons cocoa |    4 tablespoons flour |
| 2 cups milk | 2 eggs, separated |
| 1 cup sugar | 1 teaspoon vanilla |
| 1 tablespoon butter | Pastry for 1 (9 inch) crust (page 354) |
| 1/2 teaspoon salt | |

Melt chocolate in top of double boiler.

Add 1½ cups milk and bring to boiling point.

Combine sugar, salt and cornstarch.

Add remaining milk to make a smooth paste.

Add paste to milk and cook until thickened.

Beat egg yolks.

Pour a small amount of hot mixture over yolks before adding them to
milk.

Cook 2 more minutes.

Remove from heat and add butter and vanilla.

Cool and pour into baked pie shell.

Cover with meringue and bake at 350° for about 12 minutes or until
meringue is a golden brown.

A SISTER, *Manheim, Pa.*

## Cinnamon Pie

| | |
|---|---|
| 2 cups soft bread crumbs | 2 cups milk |
| 1/2 cup brown sugar | 1 teaspoon cinnamon |
| 2 eggs | Pastry for 1 (9 inch) crust (page 354) |

Line pie plate with pastry.

Add bread crumbs.

Cover crumbs with brown sugar.

Beat eggs and add milk.

Pour mixture over crumbs.

Sprinkle with cinnamon.

Bake at 350° for 35 minutes.

Makes 1 (9 inch) pie.

MRS. HENRY A. MARTIN, *Kitchener, Ont., Can.*

## Old-Fashioned Coconut Pie

| | |
|---|---|
| 1 fresh coconut, grated | 3 egg whites |
| 1 cup sugar | Pastry for 2 (9 inch) crusts (page 354) |
| 3 cups milk | |

Combine grated coconut, sugar and milk.

Fold in stiffly beaten egg whites.

Pour mixture into unbaked pie shells.

Bake at 350° for 40 to 45 minutes.

This amount makes 2 (9 inch) pies.

SARAH K. BEAN, *Creamery, Pa.*

## Coconut Cream Pie

| | |
|---|---|
| 2 cups milk | 1/2 teaspoon salt |
| 1/2 cup sugar | 1 1/4 cups shredded coconut |
| 4 tablespoons cornstarch | 1 teaspoon vanilla |
| 2 eggs, separated | Pastry for 1 (9 inch) crust (page 354) |
| 1 tablespoon butter | |

Scald 1½ cups milk in top of double boiler.

Combine sugar, salt and cornstarch.

Add remaining milk.

Pour paste into hot milk and cook until thickened.

Beat egg yolks.

Pour small amount of hot mixture over yolks before adding them to milk.

Cook 2 minutes longer.

Remove from heat, add butter, vanilla and ¾ cup shredded coconut.

Cool and pour into baked shell.

Cover with meringue made by adding 4 tablespoons sugar to beaten egg white.

Sprinkle remaining coconut over top and bake at 350° until golden brown.

Makes 1 (9 inch) pie.

MRS. LAUREN SHANK, *North Lima, Ohio;* MRS. JOHN A. LEHMAN, *Boswell, Pa.*

## Damson Pie

| | |
|---|---|
| 1 cup damson preserves or | 1 cup milk |
| 2 cups fresh seeded damsons | 1/4 cup cream |
| 1 1/2 cups sugar if preserves not used | 1 tablespoon butter |
| 2 eggs | Pastry for 2 (9 inch) crusts (page 354) |

If fresh damsons are used, cook them until tender and rub through a colander.

Add eggs, sugar, milk and cream.

Pour into an unbaked crust. Dot with butter.

Cover with top crust.

Bake at 425° for 15 minutes, reduce heat to 375° and continue to bake for 30 minutes.

Makes 1 (9 inch) pie.

MRS. ETTER HEATWOLE, *Waynesboro, Va.*

## Elderberry Pie

2½ cups elderberries  
¾ cup sugar  
2 tablespoons flour  

⅛ teaspoon salt  
3 tablespoons lemon juice  
Pastry for 2 (9 inch) crusts (page 354)

Line a pie pan with pastry.

Stem and wash elderberries and fill pie shell.

Mix sugar, salt and flour and sprinkle over berries.

Cover with top crust and fasten edges securely.

Bake at 425° for 10 minutes, reduce temperature to 350° and bake 30 minutes longer.

Makes 1 (9 inch) pie.

MRS. ROY E. BLOSSER, *Orrville, Ohio*

For variation, crumbs may be sprinkled over top of elderberries instead of putting on top crust.

For crumbs, rub together:

4 tablespoons flour  
3 tablespoons sugar  

2 tablespoons melted butter

MRS. ELMER MACK, *Souderton, Pa.*

## Elderberry Custard Pie

1 cup elderberry juice  
¼ cup flour  
1 cup sugar  
¼ teaspoon salt  

1 egg, separated  
1 cup milk  
Pastry for 1 (9 inch) crust (page 354)

Bring elderberry juice to boiling point.

Combine sugar, flour and salt.

Add ¼ cup milk.

Add paste to juice and cook until thickened.

Remove from heat and add egg yolk and milk.

Fold in stiffly beaten egg white.

Pour mixture into unbaked shell and bake at 350° for 30 minutes.

Makes 1 (9 inch) pie.

MRS. ELMER MAUST, *Grantsville, Md.*

## Funny Cake Pie

Top Part:
- ½ cup sugar
- ¼ cup shortening
- 1 egg
- ½ cup milk
- 1 teaspoon baking powder
- 1 cup flour
- ½ teaspoon vanilla

Lower Part:
- ½ cup sugar
- ¼ cup cocoa
- 1/3 cup hot water
- ¼ teaspoon vanilla
- Pastry for 1 (9 inch) crust (page 354)

Mix top part like cake batter, creaming fat, and adding sugar and egg.
Add milk alternately with sifted dry ingredients.

For lower part, combine sugar and cocoa.

Add hot water and vanilla.

Line pie plate with pastry.

Add lower part first and then pour top part over it.

Bake at 375° for approximately 40 minutes.

Makes 1 (9 inch) pie.

BARBARA MOYER, *Telford, Pa.*

## Graham Cracker Pie

Crust:
- 16 graham crackers
- 6 tablespoons melted butter
- 1/3 cup sugar
- 1 teaspoon cinnamon
- 1 tablespoon flour

Filling:
- 2 cups milk
- 2 eggs, separated
- 1/3 cup sugar
- 2 tablespoons cornstarch
- ½ teaspoon salt
- ½ teaspoon vanilla

Combine ingredients for crust and press ¾ of it into pie plate.

Save remainder of crumbs to put on top.

Bake crust at 400° for 10 minutes.

Remove from oven and cool.

To make filling, combine sugar, salt, cornstarch and egg yolks.

Add a little milk to make a paste.

Heat milk in double boiler and add flour paste.

Cook until thickened. Add vanilla.

Pour filling into pie shell and top with meringue.

Sprinkle remaining crumbs on top and bake at 350° until a golden
brown.

Makes 1 (9 inch) pie.

GERALDINE GINGERICH, *Lowville, N. Y.;* CORA MARSH, *Salix, Pa*

For variation, use lemon filling made as follows:

- 1 cup condensed milk
- Juice of 2 lemons, grated rind of 1
- 2 egg yolks
- ¼ teaspoon salt

Combine ingredients.

Pour into graham cracker crust.

Beat egg whites until stiff, add 3 tablespoons sugar.

Spread meringue over top 'and sprinkle with crumbs.

Brown pie in 350° oven until golden brown.

Chill in refrigerator 6 hours before serving.

MRS. WILLIAM GOOD, *Spring City, Pa.*

## Grape Pie

| | |
|---|---|
| 3½ cups Concord grapes | 1½ tablespoons butter |
| 1 cup sugar | 1 tablespoon lemon juice |
| 4 tablespoons flour | Pastry for 2 (9 inch) crusts (page 354) |

Wash, drain and stem grapes.

Remove skins and simmer pulp for 5 minutes.

Do not add any water to pulp.

While hot, press pulp through a sieve to remove seeds.

Combine strained pulp with skins.

Combine sugar and flour and add to grapes.

Blend in lemon juice and melted butter.

Pour into pastry lined plate.

Cover with top crust or strips.

Bake at 425° for 10 minutes, then reduce heat to 350° for 30 minutes.

Makes 1 (9 inch) pie.

MRS. C. N. STEINER, *Sterling, Ill.;* MRS. JACOB HALLMAN, *Kitchener, Ont., Can.*

For variation, add crumbs instead of top crust.

To make crumbs rub together the following:

| | |
|---|---|
| ¾ cup flour | 1/3 cup melted butter |
| ½ cup sugar | |

Bake pie at 350° for 40 minutes.

MRS. B. L. BUCHER, *Dallastown, Pa.*

## Green Tomato Pie

| | |
|---|---|
| 3 cups green tomatoes, sliced | 2 tablespoons flour |
| ½ cup brown sugar | 1 teaspoon cinnamon |
| ½ cup molasses | ¼ teaspoon nutmeg |
| ½ cup water | Pastry for 2 (9 inch) crusts (page 354) |

Slice tomatoes in thin rings. Do not pare.

Cover with boiling water and let stand 10 minutes. Drain.

Put tomato slices in unbaked pastry shell.

Combine sugar, flour and spices.

Add molasses and water.

Pour mixture over tomatoes.

Cover with a top crust.

Bake at 425° for 15 minutes, reduce temperature to 375° and continue
to bake 30 minutes.

Makes 1 (9 inch) pie.

Mrs. S. E. Hostetter, Denbigh, Va.

## Ground Cherry Pie

2½ cups ripe ground cherries
½ cup brown sugar
1 tablespoon flour

2 tablespoons water
Pastry for 2 (9 inch) crusts (page 354)

Wash ground cherries and place in unbaked pie shell.

Mix sugar and flour and sprinkle over cherries.

Sprinkle water over top.

Cover with top crust. Seal edges securely.

Bake at 425° for 15 minutes, reduce temperature to 375° and continue
to bake for 25 minutes.

Makes 1 (8 inch) pie.

Mrs. Elam Wenger, Bareville, Pa.

For variation, crumbs may be used instead of top crust.

For crumbs rub together:

3 tablespoons flour
3 tablespoons sugar

2 tablespoons butter

Mrs. William D. Moyer, Telford, Pa.

## Old-Fashioned Lemon Cake Pie

Filling:
  Juice and rind of 1 lemon
  ½ cup brown sugar
  ½ cup molasses
  2 tablespoons cornstarch
  1 egg
  1 cup boiling water

Topping:
  ½ cup sugar
  ½ cup sour cream
  ½ teaspoon soda
  1¼ cups flour (approximately)
  Pastry for 1 (9 inch) crust (page 354)

For filling, combine sugar, cornstarch and molasses.

Add egg and juice and grated rind of lemon.

Gradually add boiling water.

Cook until thickened.

Pour filling into pastry-lined pie plate.

Make sweet dough topping and roll out ¼ inch thick.

Cut in strips and place over top of pie in lattice fashion.

Bake at 350° for 45 minutes.

Makes 1 (9 inch) pie.

MRS. S. D. ROHRER, *Wadsworth, Ohio;* MRS. SAMUEL M. LANDIS, *Perkasie, Pa.*
MRS. A. C. LOUX, *Souderton, Pa.*

## Old-Fashioned Lemon Custard

Juice and rind of 1 lemon
1 egg
1 cup sugar
2½ tablespoons flour

1½ cups boiling water
½ cup sour cream
Pastry for 2 (9 inch) crusts (page 354)

Combine sugar and flour.

Add egg, sour cream, and juice and rind of lemon. Beat thoroughly.

Gradually add boiling water and mix thoroughly.

Pour mixture into pastry lined pie plate.

Cover with top crust. Fasten securely.

Bake at 375° for 40-45 minutes.

Makes 1 (9 inch) pie.

GRANDMOTHER SHOWALTER

## Lemon Meringue Pie

1 lemon, juice and rind
2 cups water
1 cup sugar
¼ teaspoon salt

3 eggs, separated
4 tablespoons cornstarch
1 tablespoon butter
Pastry for 1 (9 inch) crust (page 354)

Combine ½ cup water and cornstarch to make a thin paste.

Combine sugar and remaining 1½ cups water.

Bring to boiling point over direct heat.

Add cornstarch paste and cook until mixture begins to thicken.

Put mixture in double boiler and cook for 15 minutes.

Pour over slightly beaten egg yolks and cook 1 minute longer.

Add grated lemon rind, juice and butter and blend well.

Cool and pour into baked pie shell.

Add 4 tablespoons sugar and 1 teaspoon lemon juice to stiffly beaten egg whites.

Pile meringue lightly on top of pie.

Bake at 350° until a golden brown.

Makes 1 (9 inch) pie.

MRS. FRANK RABER, *Detroit, Mich.;* JESSIE HAMILTON, *Sheridan, Ore.*
MRS. N. G. KEYSER, *Souderton, Pa.*

## Easy Lemon Meringue Pie

| | |
|---|---|
| 1 (15 ounce) can condensed milk | 2 eggs, separated |
| 1/2 cup lemon juice | 2 tablespoons sugar |
| Grated rind of 1 lemon | Pastry for 1 (9 inch) crust (page 354) |

Combine milk, lemon juice and rind, and egg yolks.

Pour mixture in baked pie shell.

Beat egg whites and add sugar.

Pile meringue lightly on top of filling.

Bake at 350° until a golden brown.

Makes 1 (9 inch) pie.

NAOMI DELP, *Souderton, Pa.*

## Lemon Sponge

| | |
|---|---|
| Juice and rind of 1 lemon | 1/2 teaspoon salt |
| 1 cup sugar | 2 tablespoons butter |
| 3 tablespoons flour | 1 1/2 cups hot water or milk |
| 3 eggs, separated | Pastry for 1 (9 inch) crust (page 354) |

Cream butter, add sugar and egg yolks. Beat well.

Add flour, salt, lemon juice, grated rind and water or milk.

Fold in stiffly beaten egg whites.

Pour in unbaked pie shell.

Bake at 350° for 40-45 minutes.

Makes 1 (9 inch) pie.

MRS. ALDUS BRACKBILL, *Harrisonburg, Va.;* MRS. ELMER GROSS, *Blooming Glen, Pa.*
MRS. OTTO SAYLOR, *Johnstown, Pa.*

## Mincemeat For Pie

| | |
|---|---|
| 1 1/2 pounds beef | 1/2 pound citron |
| 1 1/2 pounds pork | 2 quarts chopped apples |
| 1/2 pound suet | 1 cup molasses |
| 2 pounds seedless raisins | 2 teaspoons ground cloves |
| 2 pounds currants | 3 teaspoons each of cinnamon and |
| 2 pounds granulated sugar | ginger |
| 1 pound brown sugar | 1 teaspoon nutmeg |
| 2 oranges | 1 cup cider |
| 2 lemons | |

Cook beef, pork and suet until tender.

Mince fine or grind through food chopper.

Cook raisins and currants until soft.

Chop citron, apples, oranges and lemon very fine or grind through coarse blade of food chopper.

Add meat and other ingredients and simmer together for 12 minutes.
Put in jars and seal while hot.

Makes 7 quarts.

MRS. ABRAM GODSHALL, *Kulpsville, Pa.;* MRS. SAMUEL ROES, *Lowville, N. Y.*

To make mince pies:

Fill an unbaked pie shell with mincemeat (about 3 cups). Pastry for 2
(9 inch) crusts (page 354).

Cover with a top crust. Seal edges.

Bake at 425° for 15 minutes. Reduce temperature to 375° and continue
to bake for 35 minutes.

## Green Tomato Mincemeat

| | |
|---|---|
| 3 pounds green tomatoes | 2½ tablespoons cinnamon |
| 3½ pounds apples | 2 teaspoons ground cloves |
| 2 pounds brown sugar | 1 tablespoon nutmeg |
| 2 pounds seedless raisins | 1 tablespoon grated lemon rind |
| 1 cup ground suet | 3 tablespoons lemon juice |
| 1 tablespoon salt | 1¼ cups vinegar |

Mince tomatoes or grind them through food chopper.

Add salt and let stand 1 hour.

Drain tomatoes and add water enough to cover.

Bring to a boil and cook for 5 minutes. Drain.

Pare, core and chop apples very fine.

Add tomatoes and other ingredients. Mix thoroughly.

Bring to boiling point and simmer for 1 hour.

Stir frequently.

Fill hot, sterilized jars. Seal.

Makes 7 pints.

To make pies, follow directions in preceding recipe.

MRS. A. J. SCHROCK, *Sugar Creek, Ohio;* LIZZIE HORST, *Wadsworth, Ohio*

## Molasses Tarts

| | |
|---|---|
| ½ cup sugar | 1½ cups sour milk |
| ½ cup molasses | 2 tablespoons flour |
| 1 egg | ½ teaspoon soda |
| ½ cup sour cream | Pastry for 2 (9 inch) crusts (page 354) |

Combine sugar, flour and molasses.

Add beaten egg.

Add soda to sour milk and combine with sugar mixture.

Add sour cream and blend together.

Pour mixture into an unbaked pie shell or 6 tart shells.

Cover with strips of dough placed in lattice fashion.
Bake at 400° for 35-40 minutes. Bake 20 minutes if tart shells are used.
Makes 1 (9 inch) pie.

PHYANNA BAUMAN, *St. Jacobs, Ont., Can.*

## Montgomery Pie

Bottom Part:
- ½ cup molasses
- ½ cup sugar
- I egg
- I cup water
- 2 tablespoons flour
- Juice and rind of ½ lemon

Top Part:
- 2/3 cup sugar
- ¼ cup butter or margarine
- I egg, beaten
- ½ teaspoon soda
- ½ cup sour milk
- 1¼ cups flour

Combine ingredients for the bottom part of pie.
Pour into an unbaked pie shell.
For topping, combine butter and sugar.
Add egg and beat thoroughly.
Add milk and sifted dry ingredients alternately.
Spread topping over mixture in pie shell.
Bake at 375° for 35-40 minutes.
Makes 1 (9 inch) pie.

IDA M. GABLE, *York, Pa.*

## Grandmother's Old-Fashioned Crumb or Gravel Pie

- 2 cups flour
- ½ cup sugar
- 4 tablespoons butter

- I teaspoon soda
- ½ cup sour cream
- Pastry for I (9 inch) crust (page 354)

Combine sugar, flour and soda.
Cut in butter with knives or pastry blender.
Add sour cream.
Rub together into coarse crumbs.
Put crumbs loosely into an unbaked pie shell.
Bake at 375° for 35 minutes.
Makes 1 (8 inch) pie.
This pie is especially good when dunked in coffee.

MRS. PETE SWOPE, *Harrisonburg, Va.*

## Old-Fashioned Baked Custard Pie

- 3 cups milk
- 3 eggs
- 1/3 cup sugar
- ½ teaspoon salt

- 2 teaspoons flour
- ¼ teaspoon nutmeg
- Pastry for I (9 inch) crust (page 354)

Combine sugar and flour.

Add beaten eggs.

Bring milk to boiling point and add gradually to egg mixture.

Pour into an unbaked pie shell and sprinkle nutmeg over the top.

Bake at 350° for 40-45 minutes or until an inserted silver knife comes out clean.

Makes 1 (9 inch) pie.

ANNA B. SHOWALTER, *Broadway, Va.*

## Orange Pie

| | |
|---|---|
| 1 cup sugar | 1 cup water |
| 4 tablespoons flour | Juice of 1/2 lemon |
| 1/4 teaspoon salt | 2 tablespoons butter |
| 1/2 cup orange juice | 2 eggs, separated |
| Grated rind of 1 orange | Pastry for 1 (9 inch) crust (page 354) |

Combine sugar, salt and flour.

Add water and fruit juices.

Cook mixture until thickened.

Add beaten egg yolks and cook 2 minutes longer.

Remove from heat and add butter and grated rind.

Pour mixture in baked pie shell.

Beat egg whites for meringue, add 3 tablespoons of sugar and 1 teaspoon orange or lemon juice.

Bake at 350° for 12 minutes, or until meringue is a golden brown.

Makes 1 (9 inch) pie.

MRS. WILLIS MILLER, *Harrisonburg, Va.*

## Open-Face Peach Pie

| | |
|---|---|
| 14 fresh peach halves | 2 tablespoons butter |
| 3/4 cup sugar | 2 tablespoons lemon juice |
| 1/4 cup flour | Pastry for 1 (9 inch) crust (page 354) |
| 1/4 cup water or peach juice | |

Combine sugar, butter and flour to make crumbs.

Sprinkle half of this mixture in the bottom of an unbaked crust.

Place peach halves with cut side up on pie shell.

Cover with remaining crumb mixture.

Add fruit juices or water.

Bake at 375° for 40-45 minutes.

May be served with whipped cream.

Makes 1 (9 inch) pie.

MAGGIE W. MOYER, *Waterloo, Ont., Can.*

For variation, use strips of dough over the top instead of crumbs.

## Pecan Nut Pie

3 eggs
1 cup dark corn syrup
1/4 cup sugar
1/8 teaspoon salt
2 tablespoons butter, melted

1 tablespoon flour
1/4 cup water
3/4 cup pecan nut meats
Pastry for 1 (9 inch) crust (page 354)

Combine sugar, flour and salt.

Add beaten eggs.

Add water to molasses and combine with egg mixture.

Add melted butter and chopped nuts.

Pour mixture into an unbaked pie shell.

Bake at 425° for 10 minutes, then reduce temperature to 350° and bake
35 minutes longer.

Makes 1 (9 inch) pie.

MRS. J. D. GRABER, *Elkhart, Ind.;* MRS. JOHN MARTIN, *Waynesboro, Va.*

## Pineapple Cream Pie

2 cups milk
3/4 cup sugar
3 eggs, separated
1/4 teaspoon salt

1/3 cup flour
2 tablespoons butter
1 cup crushed pineapple
Pastry for 1 (9 inch) crust (page 354)

Scald milk.

Combine butter, sugar, salt, flour and egg yolks.

Add hot milk gradually, stirring constantly.

Cook in double boiler until thickened.

Add drained, crushed pineapple.

Cool and pour into a baked pie shell.

Top with meringue made by adding 4 tablespoons sugar to stiffly beaten
egg whites and bake at 350° for 12 minutes.

Makes 1 (9 inch) pie.

MRS. MILTON FALB, *Orrville, Ohio*

For variation, 1 cup shredded coconut may be added.

MRS. HERSHEY WEAVER, *Blue Ball, Pa.*

Another variation is made by adding whole eggs to mixture and then
top with whipped cream when serving.

MRS. JOHN R. VAN PELT, *Columbiana, Ohio*

## Pineapple Sponge Pie

1 cup sugar
3 eggs, separated
1 cup milk
1/8 teaspoon salt

2 tablespoons butter
1 1/2 tablespoons flour
3/4 cup drained pineapple
Pastry for 1 (9 inch) crust (page 354)

Cream butter and add beaten egg yolks.

Combine flour, sugar and salt.

Add dry ingredients to egg-sugar mixture.

Add pineapple and milk and blend thoroughly.

Fold in stiffly beaten egg whites.

Pour mixture in an unbaked crust and bake at 425° for 8 minutes, then reduce temperature to 325°, continue to bake 30-35 minutes longer.

Makes 1 (9 inch) pie.

MRS. ED BRUNNER, *Souderton, Pa.*

## Prune Custard Pie

2½ cups prunes, cooked and seeded
2 eggs
4 tablespoons sugar
1½ tablespoons flour
½ cup cream
½ cup prune juice
½ teaspoon cinnamon
Pastry for 1 (9 inch) crust (page 354)

Combine sugar and flour and sprinkle half of it in bottom of an unbaked pie shell.

Add beaten eggs, cream and prune juice to chopped prunes.

Put mixture in crust and add remaining sugar and flour mixture.

Sprinkle with cinnamon.

Bake at 425° for 10 minutes and then reduce heat to 350° and continue to bake about 30 minutes.

Makes 1 (9 inch) pie.

MRS. ALLEN H. ERB, *La Junta, Colo.*

## Pumpkin Pie

1½ cups cooked pumpkin
1 cup brown sugar
1½ cups milk, scalded
3 eggs, separated
½ teaspoon salt
1 tablespoon cornstarch
¼ teaspoon ginger
¼ teaspoon cloves
1 teaspoon cinnamon
Pastry for 1 (9 inch) crust (page 354)

Cook pumpkin and rub through a sieve.

Add beaten egg yolks, sugar, salt, cornstarch and spices.

Gradually add scalded milk and mix thoroughly.

Fold in stiffly beaten egg whites.

Pour mixture into an unbaked crust.

Bake at 425° for 10 minutes, then reduce heat to 350° and continue baking for 30 minutes.

Makes 1 (9 inch) pie.

MRS. LESTER HOSTETLER, *North Newton, Kan.*; SUSAN VEIL, *Scalp Level, Pa.*
MRS. ADOLF JOHNSON, *Sweet Home, Ore.*

Variation (I):

Add to preceding recipe:

2 tablespoons orange juice

1 teaspoon grated orange rind

½ cup nuts

MRS. ROBERT REIST, *Falfurris, Tex.*

Variation (II):

Reserve egg whites for meringue, to which the following may be added:

4 tablespoons sugar

10 marshmallows, cut fine

½ cup shredded coconut or finely chopped nuts

Bake at 325° for 12 minutes or until meringue is a golden brown.

## Quakertown Crumb Pie

Bottom Part:

½ cup brown sugar

½ cup molasses

1 egg

1½ cups water

1 tablespoon flour

1 teaspoon vanilla

Top Part:

1 cup flour

½ cup brown sugar

¼ cup shortening

½ teaspoon soda

Pastry for 1 (9 inch) crust (page 354)

Combine ingredients for bottom part and cook until thickened.

Combine flour and soda for top part.

Add sugar and melted fat.

Pour bottom mixture into an unbaked crust.

Sprinkle crumbs over top.

Bake at 375° for 35-40 minutes.

Makes 1 (9 inch) pie.

MRS. LIZZIE ANDERS, *Telford, Pa.;* MRS. IRA LANDIS, *Lititz, Pa.*

## Raisin Pie

1 cup raisins

2 cups water

½ cup sugar

1 egg

3½ tablespoons flour or minute tapioca

¼ teaspoon salt

1 tablespoon butter

2 tablespoons lemon juice

1 teaspoon grated lemon rind

Pastry for 1 (9 inch) crust (page 354)

Add warm water to raisins, cover and cook slowly for 20 minutes.

Drain and add enough water to juice to make 2 cups.

Combine flour or tapioca, sugar, salt and liquid.

Cook over direct heat until thickened, stirring constantly.

Pour small amount of hot mixture over beaten egg. Stir vigorously.

Return to saucepan and bring to a boil.

Remove from heat, add butter, lemon juice and rind.

Cool and pour into a baked pie shell.

Cover with whipped cream when serving.

Mrs. B. L. Bucher, *Dallastown, Pa.*

For variety add 2 eggs. Separate eggs and use whites for meringue on top. Bake at 325° until a golden brown.

Ola A. Brenneman, *Kalona, Iowa;* Mrs. Ralph Vogt, *Hesston, Kan.*

## Raspberry Tart

1 pint canned raspberries
1 cup sugar
1½ tablespoons flour
1 cup whipping cream

2 tablespoons powdered sugar
½ teaspoon vanilla
Pastry for 1 (9 inch) crust (page 354)

Rub canned or freshly cooked raspberries through a fine sieve to remove seeds.

Add sugar and bring to boiling point.

Add ¼ cup water to flour and make a smooth paste.

Stir flour paste into hot berries and cook until thickened.

Pour mixture into unbaked crust and bake at 400° until crust is browned (about 35 minutes).

Before serving, top with whipped cream to which powdered sugar and vanilla have been added.

Makes 1 (9 inch) pie.

Mrs. H. Landis, *Lancaster, Pa.*

## Rhubarb Pie

3 cups diced, pink rhubarb
1½ cups sugar
3 tablespoons flour
¼ teaspoon salt

1 tablespoon lemon or orange juice
2 eggs, separated
Pastry for 1 (9 inch) crust (page 354)

Cut rhubarb in pieces ¼ inch thick.

Arrange in an unbaked pie shell.

Combine sugar and flour, add egg yolks and lemon juice.

Stir until a smooth paste is formed.

Pour mixture over rhubarb.

Cover with meringue made with egg whites or with a top crust.

Bake at 425° for 10 minutes and then reduce heat to 325° and bake for 30 more minutes.

Mrs. P. A. Friesen, *Greensburg, Kan.;* Mrs. S. J. Bucher, *Harman, W. Va.*

Variation:

Do not cover pie, but fold in stiffly beaten egg whites just before pouring mixture into pastry shell.

> Mrs. Walter Whisler, *Hanover, Pa.*; Sarah K. Bean, *Creamery, Pa.*

## Shoo Fly Pie

**Bottom Part:**
- I cup dark mild molasses
- I egg, beaten
- ¾ cup boiling water
- ½ teaspoon soda

**Top Part:**
- 1¼ cups flour
- 2 tablespoons shortening
- ½ cup brown sugar
- Pastry for I (9 inch) crust (page 354)

Dissolve soda in hot water; add molasses and beaten egg.

Combine sugar and flour and rub in shortening to make crumbs.

Pour one-third of the liquid into an unbaked crust.

Add one-third of the crumb mixture.

Continue alternate layers, putting crumbs on top.

Bake at 375° for approximately 35 minutes.

Makes 1 (9 inch) pie.

> Mrs. Arthur Ruth, *Chalfont, Pa.*; Mrs. Roland Detweiler, *Souderton, Pa.*
> Mrs. C. R. Ebersole, *La Junta, Colo.*

## Sour Cream Apple Pie

- 3 cups tart apples, chopped
- ¾ cup sugar
- 3 tablespoons flour
- ⅛ teaspoon salt
- I cup sour cream
- I teaspoon cinnamon
- Pastry for I (9 inch) crust (page 354)

Combine sugar, salt and flour.

Add sour cream and beat until smooth.

Add chopped apples and mix thoroughly.

Pour mixture in an unbaked crust.

Mix 1½ tablespoons of sugar with cinnamon and sprinkle over top of pie.

Bake at 425° for 15 minutes, reduce heat and continue to bake for 35 minutes.

Makes 1 (9 inch) pie.

> Mrs. Joseph E. Hershberger, *Iowa City, Iowa*; Mrs. J. Paul Yoder, *Parnell, Iowa*

## Sour Cream Berry or Cherry Tart

- 2½ cups elderberries or blackberries
- I cup sugar
- 2 tablespoons flour
- I cup sour cream
- Pastry for I (9 inch) crust (page 354)

Wash berries or seeded cherries and place in an unbaked crust.

Combine sugar and flour.

Add sour cream and blend thoroughly.

Pour mixture over fruit.

Bake at 425° for 15 minutes, reduce heat and continue to bake for 30 minutes.

Makes 1 (9 inch) pie.

Rosa Kemp, *Loogootee, Ind.*

## Sour Cream Peach Tart

| | |
|---|---|
| 12 to 14 peach halves | 1 cup sour cream |
| 1 cup sugar | Pastry for 1 (9 inch) crust (page 354) |
| 2 eggs | |

Place peach halves tightly together in unbaked crust.

Beat eggs, add sugar and sour cream. Mix thoroughly.

Pour mixture over peaches and bake at 425° for 15 minutes. Reduce heat to 375° and continue to bake for 35 minutes.

Makes 1 (9 inch) pie.

Stella Huber Stauffer, *Tofield, Alta., Can.*

## Sour Cream Raisin Pie

| | |
|---|---|
| 1 cup raisins | 2 eggs, separated |
| 1/2 cup sugar | 1 cup sour cream |
| 1 1/2 tablespoons flour | 1 teaspoon cinnamon or lemon juice |
| 1/8 teaspoon salt | Pastry for 1 (9 inch) crust (page 354) |

Combine sugar, salt, flour and cinnamon.

Beat yolks thoroughly and add mixed dry ingredients.

Add finely chopped raisins and sour cream.

Cook mixture until thickened. Stir constantly.

Pour into a baked pastry shell.

Beat egg whites until they stand in peaks.

Add 4 tablespoons of sugar and spread on pie.

Brown meringue in a 350° oven for approximately 12 minutes, or until it is a golden brown.

Makes 1 (9 inch) pie.

Mrs. Ruth Stauffer, *Harrisonburg, Va.;* Mrs. Jessie Wenger, *Versailles, Mo.*

## Fresh Strawberry Tart

| | |
|---|---|
| 1 quart fresh or frozen strawberries | 1 1/4 cups cold water |
| 1 cup sugar | Few drops of red coloring |
| 4 tablespoons cornstarch | 1 cup whipping cream |
| 1/4 teaspoon salt | Pastry for 1 (9 inch) crust (page 354) |
| 1 tablespoon lemon juice | |

Dissolve sugar in ½ cup water and bring to a boil.

Add remaining water to cornstarch to make a smooth paste.

Add paste to mixture and cook until transparent. Remove from heat.

Add salt, lemon juice and enough coloring to make a light shade of red.

Reserve 1 cup berries for garnishing pie.

Cut remaining berries in 2 or 3 pieces.

Pour mixture over these berries and let cool.

Pour into baked pie shell.

Garnish with whipped cream and whole strawberries.

Makes 1 (9 inch) pie.

MRS. ELMER WAGLER, *Loogootee, Ind.;* MRS. PAUL L. SWOPE, *North Lima, Ohio*

## Vanilla Pie

Bottom Part:
- ½ cup brown sugar
- ½ cup dark molasses
- 1 tablespoon flour
- 1 egg
- 1 cup water
- 1 teaspoon vanilla

Top Part:
- 1 cup flour
- ½ cup brown sugar
- ¼ cup shortening
- ½ teaspoon soda
- ½ teaspoon baking powder
- Pastry for 1 (9 inch) crust (page 354)

Combine ingredients for lower part and cook until thickened.

Pour into unbaked pie shell.

Top with crumbs made by combining sugar, flour, soda, baking powder and melted shortening.

Bake at 375° for 40-45 minutes.

Makes 1 (9 inch) pie.

MRS. AMOS LEIS, *Wellesley, Ont., Can.*
MRS. NOAH HUNSBERGER, *St. Jacobs, Ont., Can.*
MRS. M. C. SHOWALTER, *Broadway, Va.*

## Walnut Custard Pie

- 1 cup brown sugar
- 2 eggs, separated
- 3 tablespoons flour
- 1 cup water
- ¾ cup molasses
- ¾ cup nuts, chopped
- Pastry for 1 (9 inch) crust (page 354)

Mix sugar and flour, add beaten eggs.

Add molasses, water and chopped nuts. Mix thoroughly.

Pour into unbaked pie shell and top with strips, or separate eggs, using whites for meringue to put on top.

If last method is used, pour cooked custard into baked shell and put in oven at 325° for 12 minutes.

Makes 1 (9 inch) pie.

MRS. ELMER N. KAUFFMAN, VERNA FRY, *Manheim, Pa.*

# Beverages

## Chapter XII

ON HOT SUMMER DAYS DURING BARLEY AND WHEAT HARVEST, Grandmother, in the absence of a thermos jug, would fill a kettle with a tight-fitting cover with cold mint tea. Little Peter, who was yet too young to help in the field, would run sometimes a half-mile to the back of the farm, in order that the drink would reach the thirsty harvesters before it should become warm.

Grandmother had her own way of serving a cool drink without using ice cubes from the electric refrigerator. The cool waters dipped from the depths of the spring or drawn by rope and bucket from the hand-dug well were always refreshing.

Favorite drinks of long ago were made from the teas that grew in beds along the fence of the old-fashioned garden. Among these were sage, catnip, hoarhound, horse mint, thyme and peppermint. That early family, which for the most part was a self-sustaining one, produced enough of these herbs for drinking and medicinal purposes.

Besides the many teas that grew in the garden or along the little stream that flowed from the spring, there were other possibilities for beverages. At the lower end of this old garden, numerous grapevines trailed along the fence or were supported by a frame. These yielded a variety of luscious grapes in early autumn. The smallest of these grapes were picked from the bunches and prepared by numerous methods as a tasty drink. This grape juice was stored in large stone jars and kept in the cellar to be used as desired.

The blackberry cordial often spoken of by great-grandmother was sometimes used as a beverage but more often taken for its medicinal properties. Blackberries of that day were not the cultivated varieties we have today. Instead, they were to be found growing wild on the hills and in the woods. When they ripened in July, it was not unusual that the whole family spend an entire day berrying.

There was nothing that "hit the spot" so well as a tin of cold pennyroyal tea or grape juice after one had been piling hay or tying sheaves of grain for half a day. Grandmother knew this; so on these busy days when the men of her family worked from sunup until long after sundown she often planned a party. She worked all afternoon preparing a delicious repast to take to the field for supper. When it was ready, she hitched the horse to the buggy and drove to the field. She selected a tree nearest to where the men were working, and there in its shade she spread a red and white checkered cloth. On it she lay a feast of cold roast ham, freshly baked bread and apple butter, cup cheese, fruit, shoo fly pie, ginger cakes and gallons of mint tea. While the men ate, she kept away the flies by shaking an old-time fly brush made by sewing strips of paper on a hollow stick. What a shame there was never an artist among them to paint for us this picture of bygone days!

## Appetizer

| | |
|---|---|
| 2 cups sugar | ¼ cup lemon juice |
| 4 cups water | Grated rind of 2 oranges |
| 2 cups orange juice | |

Dissolve sugar in water and cook 20 minutes.

Remove from heat and add orange juice and rind and lemon juice.

Pour in freezing tray of refrigerator and freeze in cubes.

When frozen, put 2 or 3 cubes in each glass and fill glass with ginger ale. This amount will fill 2 trays.

Mrs. Amos Kreider, *Lititz, Pa.*

## Blackberry or Currant Cordial

| | |
|---|---|
| 2 quarts blackberries or currants | 2 cups sugar to each pint of juice |
| 1 quart weak vinegar | |

Clean and wash berries or currants.
Drain and pour the vinegar over them.
Let stand 24 hours.
Strain through a sieve or colander.
Add sugar to juice and stir until dissolved.
Boil for 30 minutes and then pour in bottles and seal.
When serving as a drink, dilute to suit taste.
A very old recipe.

Fannie M. Weber, *Mohnton, Pa.*

## Hot Chocolate

| | |
|---|---|
| 2 squares unsweetened chocolate (2 ounces) | ⅛ teaspoon salt |
| 1/3 cup sugar | 1 quart milk |
| | ½ cup boiling water |

Grate chocolate in top of double boiler.
Add sugar, salt and boiling water and stir until a smooth paste.
Place pan over direct heat and cook syrup 3 minutes.
Add milk gradually and heat to boiling point.
Beat until frothy.
Add whipped cream or marshmallow to each cup.
Makes 6 servings.
If chocolate syrup is used, add 2 tablespoons for each cup of milk used.

## Cocoa

| | |
|---|---|
| 3 tablespoons cocoa | ⅛ teaspoon salt |
| 1/3 cup sugar | 6 marshmallows |
| ½ cup warm water | ½ teaspoon vanilla (optional) |
| 1 quart milk | |

Mix sugar, salt and cocoa together.
Add warm water and stir to a smooth paste.
Cook for 3 minutes.
Scald milk in top of a double boiler.
Add slowly to cocoa mixture and stir until well blended.

Add vanilla.

Beat with a rotary egg beater until frothy.

Top each cup with a marshmallow or whipped cream.

Makes 6 servings.

MRS. WILLIS LEDERACH, *Lederach, Pa.*

## To Make Coffee

There are many brands of coffee and just as many methods of making it, but here are a few general rules:

1. Measure water and coffee for good results each time.
2. The recommended proportion is 2 tablespoons coffee to each ¾ to 1 standard measuring cup.
3. To make 6 servings, use ½ to ¾ cup coffee to 4½ cups water.
4. Make coffee just before it is to be served.
5. Serve only freshly made coffee, as reheated coffee has a flat taste.
6. Keep coffee pot absolutely clean.

## Iced Coffee

Make coffee double strength and pour the hot coffee over plenty of ice in tall glasses.

As the ice melts, it will dilute the coffee.

Top the glass with whipped cream or vanilla ice cream.

## Eggnog

| | |
|---|---|
| 4 eggs | ½ cup cream |
| 4 cups milk | ⅛ teaspoon nutmeg |
| 4 tablespoons lemon juice or | ⅛ teaspoon salt |
|    diluted vinegar | 1/3 cup sugar |

Beat eggs until thick and lemon colored.

Add sugar, nutmeg, and lemon juice.

Add ice-cold milk and cream.

Beat with a rotary beater until frothy.

Makes 6 large glasses.

FANNIE M. WEBER, *Mohnton, Pa.*

## Elderberry Drink

| | |
|---|---|
| 4 quarts elderberries | 2 cups sugar to each quart of juice |
| Vinegar to cover | ¼ teaspoon oil of wintergreen |
| |    ( optional) |

Wash berries and cover with vinegar.

Let stand 24 hours.

Squeeze through a cloth bag and measure juice.

Add sugar and stir until dissolved.

Boil for 20 minutes.

Pour into bottles and seal.

Makes 2½ quarts.

MRS. WARREN BEAN, *Creamery, Pa.*

## Fruit Punch (With Tea Base)

| | |
|---|---|
| 1½ cups sugar | 1½ cups lemon juice |
| 1 cup water | 2 cups orange juice |
| ⅛ teaspoon salt | 1 quart ginger ale |
| 1½ cups strong tea infusion | Mint leaves |

Combine sugar and water and cook on low heat for 1 minute.

Cool the syrup and pour over ice.

To make tea infusion, add 3 teaspoons tea to 1½ cups water.

Add the fruit juices, tea and salt and mix well.

Add ginger ale just before serving.

Place a sprig of mint in each glass as it is served.

Serves 12.

MRS. LEWIS STRITE, *Harrisonburg, Va.*

## Spiced Punch

| | |
|---|---|
| 1½ cups sugar | 1 quart orange juice (canned or fresh) |
| 2 cups water | 2 cups lemon juice |
| 1 teaspoon whole cloves | 2 cups grapefruit juice |
| 1 stick cinnamon (4 inches) | 2 cups pineapple juice |

Simmer sugar, water and spices together for 10 minutes.

Strain and cool.

Add fruit juices.

Add ice when serving.

Serves 12.

MRS. LEWIS STRITE, *Harrisonburg, Va.*

## Grape Juice (I)

| | |
|---|---|
| 10 pounds grapes | 3 pounds sugar |
| 2 cups water | |

Wash grapes and put them in a large enamel pan.

Add water and cook until soft.

Drain through a cloth or jelly bag.

Add sugar and stir until dissolved.

Bring juice to boiling point.

Pour in bottles and seal. Process in hot-water bath for 20 minutes.

This amount makes 4 quarts of juice.

Mrs. Martin S. Good, *Manheim, Pa.*; Mrs. Bessie Souder, *Sellersville, Pa.*

## Grape Juice (II)

1 cup grapes
½ cup sugar

Boiling water

Wash grapes and put them in a sterile quart jar.

Add sugar and fill jar with boiling water.

Stir with a silver spoon to dissolve sugar. Seal. Process in hot-water bath for 20 minutes.

If silver spoon is placed in jar before boiling water is added, it will keep jar from cracking.

Mrs. Allen H. Erb, *La Junta, Colo.*

## Grape Juice (Uncooked)

2 gallons grapes
6 ounces tartaric acid

1 cup sugar to 2 cups juice

Wash grapes.

Mix acid and grapes and crush in earthenware container.

Let stand in cool place for 4 days.

Stir 2 times each day. Strain through a cloth.

Add sugar to liquid and stir until dissolved.

Let stand 4 more days, stirring twice each day.

Put in sterile bottles and seal. Process in hot-water bath for 20 minutes.

Makes 4 quarts.

Mrs. Lydia Wyse, *Archbold, Ohio*

## Lemonade

6 lemons
1½ cups sugar

2½ quarts water

Slice lemons in thin rings and place in porcelain or enamel container.

Add sugar and pound with a wooden mallet to extract juice.

Let stand 20 minutes and then add cold water and ice cubes.

Stir until well blended.

Makes 3 quarts.

To use rind along with pulp and juice adds flavor and is also an economy.

## Red Lemonade

1 cup white syrup
½ cup lemon juice
¼ cup red cherry juice

1 quart ice water
⅛ teaspoon red coloring

Combine syrup and fruit juices.
Stir until well blended.
Add ice water and red coloring.
Mix together.
Makes 1½ quarts.

MRS. ELLIS MACK, *Souderton, Pa.*

## Lemon Syrup Drink

1 dozen lemons
5 pints boiling water
6 pounds sugar

5 oranges
2 ounces citric acid
1 ounce tartaric acid

Squeeze lemons and oranges.
Cut skins of fruit in thin slices and cook for 3 minutes in the water.
Strain and add sugar and fruit juices.
Bring to a boil and stir until sugar dissolves.
Add acids and stir until they are melted.
Remove from heat and pour in sterile jars. Seal.
Makes 4 quarts of syrup.
When serving, add 1 tablespoon of syrup to each glass of cold water.

M. LOEWEN, *Altona, Man., Can.*

## Orange and Lemon Delight

9 oranges
4 lemons

3 cups sugar
2 cups water

Combine sugar and water and boil together 2 minutes. Cool.
Squeeze oranges and lemons and strain.
Add cooled sugar syrup and mix thoroughly.
Can be kept for some time in refrigerator and used as desired.
Dilute to suit taste.
Makes 2 quarts.

MRS. H. N. TROYER, *Hartville, Ohio*

## Raspberry Drink

9 quarts raspberries
Vinegar

1 cup sugar to each cup juice

Wash and crush raspberries.

Cover with vinegar and let stand 24 hours.

Strain through a cloth bag and measure juice.

Add sugar according to recipe.

Boil for 15 minutes. Pour into sterile bottles and seal.

This may be diluted when serving as a drink.

Makes 4 quarts.

MRS. SAMUEL ZEHR, *New Bremen, N. Y.*

## Spiced Cider

| | |
|---|---|
| 6 cups sweet cider | ½ teaspoon grated lemon rind |
| 20 whole cloves | ½ teaspoon grated orange rind |
| 3 sticks cinnamon | |

Combine spices and 3 cups cider and place over low heat.

Bring to boiling point and simmer 5 minutes.

Remove from heat and let stand 30 minutes.

Add remaining cider, orange and lemon rind. Chill.

When ready to serve, pour over ice cubes.

Garnish with orange or lemon slices.

Makes 8-10 servings.

MRS. SAMUEL S. SHANK, *Broadway, Va.*

## Tea

To make good tea, carry out the following rules:

1. Use freshly drawn water brought to a bubbling boil.
   Water that has boiled for some time has a flat taste.
2. Use an earthenware or nonmetal container for steeping the tea.
   Metal alters the flavor of the tea.
3. The teapot should be heated by allowing boiling water to stand in it
   several minutes before making the tea.
4. Allow 1 teaspoon tea leaves to each cup of water plus "one for the
   pot."
5. Pour boiling water over tea and allow to steep 3 to 5 minutes.
   Never allow tea to boil.
   To allow leaves to remain in tea too long develops a bitter flavor.
6. Serve hot or cold with sugar and lemon or cream as desired.

## To Make Clear Iced Tea

Pour the freshly made hot tea over plenty of ice cubes in tall glasses.

Serve with sprigs of mint or thin lemon slices.

## Tomato Juice

| | |
|---|---|
| 1 peck tomatoes | 2 stalks celery |
| 4 medium-sized peppers | 1½ cups sugar |
| 4 onions | 2 tablespoons salt |

Chop vegetables, add water to partially cover, and cook until soft.
Strain through a cloth bag or fruit press.
Add sugar and salt and bring to boiling point.
Pour into sterilized jars and seal.
Makes 4 quarts.

Mrs. Roy Zimmerman, *Ephrata, Pa.*; Mrs. D. R. Hostetter, *Harrisonburg, Va.*

## Vegetable or Potassium Broth

### An Appetizer

| | |
|---|---|
| 4 cups chopped celery | 1 cup parsley, chopped |
| 3 cups carrots, chopped | 2 quarts cold water |
| 2 cups spinach, chopped | 1 teaspoon salt |

Mix chopped vegetables and add water and salt.
Bring to boiling point and then remove from heat and let stand 30 minutes.
Strain and chill.
Serve as an appetizer.
Makes 2½ quarts.

Mrs. Ezra Long, *Sterling, Ill.*

## Vico

### Hot Drink for Children

| | |
|---|---|
| ½ cup cocoa | ⅛ teaspoon salt |
| 1 cup sugar | ¼ teaspoon vanilla |
| 2 cups water | |

Combine cocoa, sugar and salt.
Add water and stir until well blended.
Cook for 5 minutes. Cool and bottle.
Makes 3 cups syrup.
Add 2 tablespoons of syrup to each cup of scalded milk.

Mrs. F. Johnston, *Altona, Man., Can.*

# Pickles
## and
## Relishes

### Chapter XIII

A KIND LADY ONCE SAID TO "TILLIE THE MENNONITE MAID," "MY DEAR, don't you know that you should not eat so many pickles. Vinegar is not good for you; it will drain all the color from your cheeks." Tillie retorted somewhat saucily, so the story goes, "Who wants pink cheeks at the expense of pickles?" After all, Grandmother lived to be ninety, she thought, and she never missed a dinner without the proverbial "seven sours."

Our great-grandmothers' love for the sour things induced them to pickle about everything imaginable. Who still does not enjoy little seckel pears pickled whole, as Grandmother prepared them, with the stems attached? The spiced peaches, crab apples, sour cherries or grapes still taste delicious too. Then there are the long strips of watermelon rind and the yellow strips of spiced cantaloupe that are delicious accompaniments to any dinner.

Besides all the fruits, there were a host of vegetables that Grandmother pickled. One interesting old "receipt" book has a recipe for "Pickled Lily." This no doubt refers to piccalilli, having been spelled as granny thought the name sounded. Green tomato pickle in all its various forms was a favorite of the olden times. There was the type made by cooking slices of the vegetable in sweet vinegar solution. Another variety of this green tomato pickle called for raisins, and still another apples. Our own family favorite, known as "granddaddy's green tomato pickle," was still another type. This was made by placing in a crock alternate layers of raw sliced tomatoes and sliced onions. Salt and spices were added generously, and then a plate and heavy weight were placed on top. After several days the juice was drained off and vinegar and sugar added. It is a crisp, uncooked pickle, which my father still asks for each fall when the last of the green tomatoes are gathered. Beet pickle was and still is a favorite of many families. Another recipe sent in by a number of contributors and called "my mother's favorite pickle," is a relish made of shredded beets and cabbage.

Great-grandfather never allowed any of his brood to leave food on their plates at the table. Even the fat meat or "speck" had to be eaten. Great-grandma once more rallied to the need of filling her place as a "helpmeet," this time for her children. She made all kinds of sauces and relishes to pour over that fat meat, and thus helped it to slide down easily! Tomato and gooseberry catsup and chili sauce were favorites. In spring she had another sauce. She walked along the streams or old rail fence and dug roots from the horse-radish plant. These roots she grated and to them added salt and vinegar.

Great-grandma shall long be remembered, not only for her ability to get things done but for her ingenuity in finding the wherewithal to do them.

# PICKLES

## Beet Pickle

2 quarts diced or sliced beets, cooked
3 small onions
3 green peppers
1/2 cup grated horse-radish

2 cups vinegar
3 cups sugar
3 teaspoons salt

Dissolve sugar and salt in hot vinegar.

Add horse-radish and bring to a boil.

Add beets and chopped onion and simmer 20 minutes.

Place in 2 sterilized quart jars or keep in refrigerator.

MRS. KATIE THOMAS, *Johnstown, Pa.*

## Beet Pickle (Cold)

| | |
|---|---|
| 1 gallon beets, cooked | 2½ cups brown sugar |
| 1/3 cup prepared mustard | 3 cups vinegar |
| 1/3 cup salt | ½ cup cold water |

Cook beets until tender. Skin.

Slice and place in a stone crock or jar.

Mix mustard, sugar and salt and add vinegar and water.

Pour mixture over beets and keep in a cool place.

These are ready to use after 24 hours.

MRS. EARL BRENNEMAN, *Lima, Ohio*

## Best Ever Pickles

| | |
|---|---|
| 300 cucumbers, 2 inches long | ¼ cup salt |
| 2/3 cup salt | ¼ cup dry mustard |
| Boiling water to cover | ½ cup mixed pickle spices |
| 2 quarts vinegar | 3 pounds sugar |
| ¼ cup sugar | |

Wash pickles and place in a large stone jar.

Add ⅔ cup salt and cover with boiling water.

Let stand overnight and then drain and wipe dry.

Return to stone jar and cover with vinegar, ¼ cup sugar, salt and spices.

Reserve the 3 pounds of sugar, adding ½ cup each morning.

Stir with a wooden spoon after each addition.

When sugar is all used, they are ready to use.

MRS. HOWARD CARTER, *Sheldon, Wis.*

## Bread and Butter Pickle

| | |
|---|---|
| 30 medium-sized cucumbers, (1 gallon, sliced) | 3 cups sugar |
| 8 medium-sized onions | 3 cups vinegar |
| 2 large red or green peppers | 2 tablespoons mustard seed |
| ½ cup salt | 1 teaspoon turmeric |
| | 1 teaspoon whole cloves |

Slice cucumbers in thin rings. Do not pare.

Slice onions in thin rings.

Cut peppers in fine strips.

Dissolve salt in ice water and pour over sliced vegetables.

Let stand 3 hours and drain.

Combine vinegar, sugar and spices and bring to a boil.

Add drained vegetables and heat to boiling point. Do not boil.

Pack into sterilized jars and seal.

MRS. WILLIAM E. MARTIN, *Wellman, Iowa;* MRS. EDNA NEWCOMER, *Dallastown, Pa.*
MRS. AMOS LEIS, *Wellesley, Ont., Can.*

## Busy Sister
### Brine for Cold Pickle

| | |
|---|---|
| 1 gallon vinegar, plus 1 gallon water | 1 tablespoon powdered alum |
| 1 cup salt | 1 tablespoon ground allspice |
| 2 cups sugar | (optional) |
| ½ cup grated horse-radish | 1 tablespoon ground cloves |
| 1 tablespoon ground mustard | (optional) |

Dissolve salt, sugar, and alum in vinegar weakened with water.

Add grated horse-radish.

Tie spices in a cloth bag and place on top of pickles.

More cucumbers may be added as they are used.

MRS. LEWIS WENGER, *Harrisonburg, Va.*

## Raw Cabbage Pickle (Old)

| | |
|---|---|
| 1 large head cabbage | ½ cup sugar |
| 1½ tablespoons salt | ¾ cup vinegar |
| 1 teaspoon celery or mustard seed | |

Shred cabbage coarsely.

Add salt and sugar and work it well into the cabbage.

Add vinegar and spice and let stand 12 hours before serving.

MRS. AMOS K. MAST, *Cochranville, Pa.*

## Carrot and Cucumber Pickle

| | |
|---|---|
| 10 cups carrots, diced | 3 tablespoons salt |
| 10 cups cucumbers, chopped | 2 tablespoons celery seed |
| 5 red peppers | 4 tablespoons flour |
| 3 cups vinegar | 1 tablespoon dry mustard |
| 2 cups water | 1 tablespoon turmeric |
| 5 cups sugar | |

Dice carrots and cook until tender.

Add chopped cucumbers and red peppers.

Combine sugar, salt, flour, vinegar and spices.

Add vegetables to liquid and cook until slightly thick.

Put into hot jars and seal.

MRS. ABRAM G. METZ, *Telford, Pa.*

## Cassia Bud Pickles

75 pickles, about 3 inches long
I cup salt
Boiling water to cover
I tablespoon powdered alum

3 pints vinegar
1½ tablespoons cassia bud
I tablespoon celery seed
6 cups sugar

Dissolve salt in boiling water and pour over pickles.

Let stand for 1 week. Drain.

Dissolve alum in enough boiling water to cover pickles.

Let stand 24 hours and drain.

Cut pickles in halves or quarters lengthwise; cover with boiling water.

Let stand 24 hours and drain.

Combine vinegar, sugar and spices and bring to a boil.

Pour hot liquid over pickles and let stand for 3 days.

Reheat liquid each day.

Keep covered in a stone jar or seal in glass jars. Very good.

MRS. HOWARD D. SHOWALTER, *Broadway, Va.*

## Celery Pickle

3 quarts chopped celery
3 cups vinegar
I cup water
4 cups sugar

2 tablespoons salt
I tablespoon dry mustard
I teaspoon turmeric

Cut celery stems into 1 inch lengths.

Cook in salt water until tender but not soft. Drain.

Combine vinegar, sugar, water and spices. Bring to a boil.

Add celery and bring to boiling point.

Pack in jars and seal.

HELEN ERNST, *Kitchener, Ont., Can.*

## Chunk Pickle

I gallon cucumber chunks
½ cup salt
Boiling water to cover
3 cups sugar
3 cups vinegar
I cup water

I teaspoon allspice
I teaspoon dry mustard
I teaspoon mustard seed
I teaspoon celery seed
½ teaspoon turmeric

Cut medium-sized cucumbers into 1 inch chunks.

Add salt and cover with boiling water.

Let stand overnight and drain.

Combine sugar, vinegar, water and spices.

Bring to a boil and add pickles.

When the boiling point has been reached, can and seal.
Makes 4 quarts.

Mrs. Ira Newcomer, *Seville, Ohio*

## Corn Pickle or Salad

| | |
|---|---|
| 12 ears corn | 1 cup sugar |
| ½ head cabbage | 1 cup vinegar |
| 4 peppers, red or green | 1 cup water |
| 1 bunch celery | 1½ tablespoons dry mustard |
| 1½ tablespoons salt | |

Cook corn on the cob until tender. Cut off.

Chop cabbage, celery and peppers into small pieces and cook until
tender, but not soft. Drain.

Mix vegetables together and add sugar, salt, vinegar and mustard.

Bring to a boil and put in jars.

Seal.

An attractive, tasty accompaniment to any dinner.

Esther Rhodes, *Dayton, Va.*; Mrs. Noah Zimmerman, *Mechanicsburg, Pa.*

## Cucumber Sweet Pickle (Short Process)

| | |
|---|---|
| 1 gallon cucumbers | 1 cup water |
| 6 cups sugar | 1½ quarts vinegar |
| 1 cup salt | 2 tablespoons mixed spices |

Wash cucumbers and wipe them dry.

Dissolve salt in 1 gallon cold water and pour over cucumbers.

Let stand 24 hours and drain.

Puncture each cucumber 3 times with a needle.

Combine ½ of the sugar, vinegar, water and spices.

Simmer liquid for 30 minutes.

Add cucumbers to liquid and continue to simmer 15 minutes.

Let stand in a jar for 2 days.

Drain off the liquid and pack pickles in hot jars.

Add remaining sugar to liquid and boil for 5 minutes.

Pour over pickles and seal.

Mrs. Roy E. Blosser, *Orrville, Ohio*

## Cucumber and Pepper Pickle

| | |
|---|---|
| 3 quarts cucumbers, sliced | 2½ cups sugar |
| 3 green peppers, sliced | 1 quart vinegar |
| 6 medium-sized onions, sliced | 1 tablespoon mustard seed |
| 2 tablespoons salt | ¼ teaspoon alum |

Pare cucumbers and slice in thin rings.

Slice onions and peppers and mix vegetables together.

Add salt and let stand 3 hours.

Drain liquid off vegetables and add sugar, alum, vinegar and mustard seed.

Bring to a boil and pack in jars. Seal.

MRS. FRANCES SHENK, *Sheridan, Ore.*

## Curry Powder Pickles

| | |
|---|---|
| ½ peck cucumbers, 2 inches long | 1 tablespoon celery seed |
| ½ cup salt | ¼ cup ground mustard or |
| Water to cover | 2 tablespoons mustard seed |
| 1 quart vinegar | 2 teaspoons curry powder |
| 3 cups sugar | ½ teaspoon powdered alum |

Wash cucumbers and cover with salt water.

Let stand 3 hours and then drain.

Combine vinegar, sugar, alum and spices.

Bring to a boil and add cucumbers.

When the boiling point has been reached again, pack pickles in hot jars and seal.

MRS. PAUL WELDY, *Montgomery, Ind.*

## Dill Tomatoes

| | |
|---|---|
| 2 quarts small green tomatoes | 2 cups vinegar |
| 2 small onions or cloves of garlic | 2 cups water |
| 2 stems celery | ¼ cup salt |
| ½ green pepper | 1 bunch dill |

Wash small green tomatoes and pack in jar.

Add small onion, diced pepper and chopped celery.

Place dill on top of jar.

Combine water, vinegar, and salt and boil for 5 minutes.

Pour hot liquid over tomatoes and seal.

These are ready to serve in 6 weeks.

MRS. D. H. BENDER, *Palmyra, Mo.*

## Dutch Lunch Pickles

| | |
|---|---|
| 1 gallon cucumbers, quartered lengthwise | 4 cups vinegar |
| 4 cloves garlic | 1 cup water |
| 4 small onions | ¼ cup salt |
| 4 pieces dill or 4 grape leaves | 2 cups sugar |
| | 1 tablespoon mixed spices |

Cut medium-sized cucumbers into quarters lengthwise.

Place in cold salt water overnight.

In the morning, drain and pack in jars.

Add 1 clove garlic, 1 sliced onion and 1 piece of dill or a grape leaf to each jar.

Combine vinegar, water, sugar and spices and bring to a boil.

Pour over pickles and seal or keep in refrigerator or cellar in a stone jar.

These are ready to eat in 1 week.

MRS. DEWEY WOLFER, *Sheridan, Ore.*

## Eight-Day Pickles

| | |
|---|---|
| 4 gallons medium-sized pickles | 1½ tablespoons mustard seed |
| Horse-radish leaves | 3 quarts vinegar |
| 2 tablespoons powdered alum | 10 cups sugar |
| 1½ tablespoons celery seed | 2 ounces cinnamon bark |

Make a salt solution, using 1 cup salt to each gallon of water.

Pour over cucumbers, enough to cover, and allow to stand 6 days.

Drain and pour boiling water over them.

Allow to stand overnight and then drain.

Cut pickles into 1 inch chunks.

Cover with horse-radish leaves and powdered alum and pour boiling water over them.

Let stand 1 day and night, drain and cover again with boiling water.

Let stand 1 hour and drain.

Combine vinegar, sugar and spices.

Bring to a boil and pour over pickles.

Pack in jars and seal.

MRS. WALTER WEAVER, *Christiana, Pa.*

## End of the Garden Pickle

| | |
|---|---|
| 2 cups sliced cucumbers | 1 cup diced onion |
| 2 cups chopped red or green peppers | 2 tablespoons celery seed |
| 2 cups chopped cabbage | 4 tablespoons mustard seed |
| 2 cups chopped green tomatoes | 4 cups vinegar |
| 2 cups green string beans | 4 cups sugar |
| 2 cups diced carrots | 2 tablespoons turmeric |
| 2 cups chopped celery | |

Slice cucumbers. Chop cabbage, tomatoes and peppers.

Soak overnight in salt water, using ½ cup salt to 2 quarts water.

In the morning, cut string beans and chop carrots and celery.

Cook until tender, but not soft.

Drain vegetables which soaked overnight and combine with cooked vegetables.

Combine vinegar, sugar and spices and bring to a boil.

Add vegetables and simmer together for 10 minutes.

Pack into jars and seal.

MRS. MILDRED SCHROCK, *Sheridan, Ore.*

## Fourteen-Day Sweet Pickles

| | |
|---|---|
| 15 pounds medium-large cucumbers | 2 quarts vinegar |
| 1 cup salt | 2½ pounds brown sugar |
| Water to cover | 1 tablespoon celery seed |
| 1 tablespoon powdered alum | 1 ounce stick cinnamon |
| Horse-radish leaves | |

Wash cucumbers and place in salt brine to cover, using 1 cup salt to 1 gallon water.

Let stand 7 days in a stone jar. Drain.

Arrange alternate layers of cucumbers and horse-radish leaves in the jar.

Cover with boiling water and let stand until next day.

On the ninth day, remove horse-radish leaves and drain.

Dissolve alum in boiling water and pour over cucumbers enough water to cover.

On the tenth day, drain off liquid and bring it to a boil.

Allow to remain on the cucumbers until the twelfth day.

Drain and cut pickles in 1 inch chunks.

Combine sugar, vinegar and spices and bring to a boil.

Pour hot liquid over cucumber pieces.

The next day, drain liquid and bring to a boil.

Pour over pickles.

On the fourteenth day, pack pickles in jars.

Bring liquid to a boil, fill jars and seal.

MRS. FRANK VAN PELT, *Columbiana, Ohio*

## French Tomato Pickle (Old)

| | |
|---|---|
| 1 peck green tomatoes, sliced | 2 tablespoons curry |
| 6 onions, sliced | 2 tablespoons turmeric |
| 1 cup salt | 2 teaspoons cinnamon |
| 2 quarts vinegar | 2 teaspoons cloves |
| 1 pound sugar | 2 teaspoons allspice |
| 2 teaspoons powdered mustard | |

Slice the green tomatoes and onions.

Mix 1 cup salt through them and let stand overnight.

In the morning, drain and allow to stand 15 minutes in a weak vinegar
    solution.

Drain.

Combine vinegar, sugar and spices and bring to a boil.

Add vegetables and simmer slowly for 3 minutes.

Pack in jars and seal.

This is a rich pickle

Mrs. Menno M. Brubacker, Waterloo, Ont., Can.

## Granddaddy's Green Tomato Pickle

| | |
|---|---|
| 1 gallon green tomatoes, sliced | 3 cups vinegar, plus ½ cup water |
| 8 medium-sized onions | ¼ cup salt |
| 1 tablespoon mustard seed | 1 cup sugar |

Slice tomatoes in thin slices, do not peel.

Slice onions in thin rings.

Place alternate layers of sliced tomato and onion in a crock.

Sprinkle with mustard seed and salt. Let stand overnight. Drain. Salt
    should not be added to vinegar.

Combine sugar and vinegar and pour over tomatoes.

Cover with a plate and let stand 24 hours before using.

This is a cold, crisp pickle. Very tasty.

Mrs. H. D. H. Showalter, Broadway, Va.

## Green Tomato and Apple Pickle

| | |
|---|---|
| 1½ gallons green tomatoes, chopped | 2 teaspoons mustard seed |
| 1/3 cup salt | 1 teaspoon each of cinnamon, cloves |
| 1 large onion | and allspice |
| 2 quarts chopped apples | 2 pounds sugar |
| 1 bunch celery, chopped | 1 quart vinegar |

Sprinkle the salt over the chopped tomatoes and let stand overnight.

In the morning, drain and add chopped onion, celery and apples.

Mix spices with the sugar and add vinegar.

Add liquid to pickle mixture and simmer slowly for 1 hour.

Pack into hot jars and seal.

Mrs. J. E. Kauffman, Tofield, Alta., Can.

## Green Tomato and Raisin Sweet Pickle

| | |
|---|---|
| 1 gallon green tomatoes, chopped | 1 pint vinegar |
| 4 pounds sugar | 1 teaspoon each of mace, cloves |
| ½ cup salt | and allspice |
| 1 pound seedless raisins | 3 sticks cinnamon bark |
| ½ cup water | |

Place chopped tomatoes in a stone jar.
Mix salt through them well.
Let stand 12 hours and drain.
Combine sugar, spices, vinegar and water and bring to a boil.
Then add raisins and cook until they are plump.
Add well-drained tomatoes and cook until tender.
Place in hot jars and seal.
This is an old recipe and a delicious pickle.

MRS. ANNA KAUFFMAN, *Nampa, Idaho*

## Sweet Tomato Pickle

| | |
|---|---|
| 1 gallon green tomatoes, sliced | 1 tablespoon whole cloves |
| 1 quart vinegar | 4 sticks cinnamon |
| 3 pounds brown sugar | 3 tablespoons salt |

Wash tomatoes and slice in thin rings. Do not peel.
Cook in salt water until tender, but not soft. Drain.
Combine vinegar, sugar and spices and boil for 15 minutes.
Pour hot syrup over drained tomatoes and let stand for 4 days.
Drain off syrup and cook until it thickens.
Add tomatoes and bring to a boil.
Put into jars and seal.

MRS. JESS GOOD, *Lima, Ohio*

## Green String Bean Pickle

| | |
|---|---|
| 3 quarts string beans | 1 teaspoon ground mustard |
| 2 tablespoons salt | 1 teaspoon celery seed |
| 3 cups sugar | 2 teaspoons turmeric |
| 3 pints vinegar | 1/4 cup flour |

Cut beans into 1 inch pieces.
Cook in salt water until tender, but not soft.
Combine sugar, salt, flour and spices with the vinegar.
Cook together until slightly thickened.
Add beans and bring to a boil.
Put into hot jars and seal.

MRS. JESSE SHORT, *Archbold, Ohio*

## Mixed Vegetable Pickle

| | |
|---|---|
| 1 large head cauliflower | 1 quart carrots, cut in inch pieces |
| 1 quart small cucumbers | 1 quart Lima beans |
| 1 quart small onions, whole | 1 quart vinegar |
| 1 quart celery, diced | 2 cups sugar |
| 2 red sweet peppers, chopped | 2 tablespoons salt |
| 2 green peppers, chopped | 4 tablespoons dry mustard |

Break cauliflower into flowerlets. Cut peppers and carrots into bite-size
  pieces.
Cook each vegetable separately in salt water until tender, but not soft.
Mix cooked vegetables lightly.
Combine sugar, vinegar, salt and mustard and bring to a boil.
Add mixed vegetables and heat again to the boiling point.
Put into hot jars and seal.

MRS. MATTIE WYSE, *Archbold, Ohio*

## Mother's Favorite Pickle

| | |
|---|---|
| 1 quart cabbage, chopped | ½ teaspoon black pepper |
| 1 quart beets, cooked | 1 cup grated horse-radish |
| 1 tablespoon salt | 3 cups vinegar |
| 2 cups sugar | |

Put cabbage through coarse blade of food chopper.
Dice beets and mix with cabbage.
Combine salt, sugar, vinegar, horse-radish and pepper.
Pour over vegetables and mix well.
Pack into jars and seal or place in a crock and keep in a cool place.

MRS. GEORGE S. BAST, *Wellesley, Ont., Can.*

## Open Jar Pickle

| | |
|---|---|
| 9 pounds medium-sized cucumbers | 3 pounds sugar |
| 1 tablespoon alum | 6 cups vinegar |
| 1 pint vinegar | 1 ounce stick cinnamon |
| 1 pint water | ½ ounce whole allspice |

Make salt brine to cover cucumbers, using 1 cup salt to 1 gallon water.
Let stand for 3 days and then drain.
Soak cucumbers in cold water for the next 3 days; changing the water
  each day.
Drain and cut pickles crosswise into 2 or 3 pieces.
Mix 1 pint vinegar with 1 pint water, add alum and allow pickles to
  simmer in this solution for 2 hours.
For a greener appearance, a little green coloring may be added.
Drain and pack in earthen or glass jar.
Combine sugar, vinegar and spices and let boil 5 minutes.
Pour hot syrup over pickles.
These pickles need not be sealed and will keep indefinitely.
They are crisp and delicious.

MRS. GEORGE F. MILLER, *Sterling, Ill.*

## Sweet Peach Pickle

| | |
|---|---|
| 7 pounds peaches, whole | 1 ounce stick cinnamon |
| 3½ pounds sugar | 1 ounce whole cloves |
| 1 pint vinegar | |

Select ripe but rather firm peaches. Cling peaches may be used.

Dip peaches in hot water and peel. Leave whole.

Bring sugar and vinegar to a boil.

Add peaches.

Add cinnamon bark and whole cloves that have been tied in a bag.

Simmer until peaches are tender but not soft.

Place peaches in jars and continue boiling the syrup until it is slightly thick.

Pour syrup over peaches and seal.

To prevent peaches from shriveling, the syrup may be removed from the peaches next day and allowed to boil until it thickens again. Seal.

MRS. LESTER WYSE, *Chief, Mich.*

## Pickled Crab Apples

| | |
|---|---|
| 8 pounds fruit | 4 sticks cinnamon |
| 9 cups sugar | 1 tablespoon whole cloves |
| 2 quarts vinegar | |

Select firm, ripe crab apples.

Do not pare. Leave stems attached.

Combine vinegar, sugar and spices. Boil 5 minutes.

Add fruit and cook slowly until tender.

Let fruit stand in syrup overnight.

In the morning drain off syrup and cook until the consistency of honey.

Pack fruit in hot jars and cover with hot syrup. Seal.

MRS. ALVA SWARTZENTRUBER, *Hydro, Okla.*

## Pickled Cherries

| | |
|---|---|
| 6 pounds sour cherries, seeded | 1 quart vinegar |
| 6 pounds sugar | |

Seed the cherries and place in a stone crock.

Cover with vinegar and let stand overnight.

In the morning, drain off liquid.

Add sugar to the cherries and mix together.

Let stand 7 days, stirring well each day.

These keep without sealing and are excellent when used in salads or as an appetizer.

MRS. LIZZIE KNOPP, *Salem, Ohio;* MRS. FRANK GOOD, *Bareville, Pa.*

## Pickled Seckel Pears

7 pounds seckel pears
3½ pounds sugar
1 pint vinegar

1 cup water
3 sticks cinnamon
1 tablespoon cloves

Wash and pare the pears, leaving stems attached.
Tie spices in a bag and add to sugar, vinegar and water mixture.
Boil 5 minutes.
Add pears and cook slowly until tender and transparent.
Place fruit in hot jars and pour hot syrup over it. Seal.

MRS. RUDY BRENNEMAN, *Lima, Ohio*

## Pickled Watermelon Rind

5 pounds watermelon rind
2½ pounds sugar
2 cups vinegar

2 cups water
½ teaspoon oil of cloves
½ teaspoon oil of cinnamon

Pare the watermelon and cut rind in 2 inch pieces.
Mix ½ cup salt with 2 quarts water and soak rind overnight.
Drain and rinse with clear water. Drain again.
Cook in fresh water until tender. Drain.
Combine sugar, vinegar, water and spices.
Bring the syrup to a boil and pour it over the rind.
Let stand overnight.
In the morning, drain off the syrup and cook it several minutes.
Repeat for 3 days.
On the third day, cook rind and syrup together for 3 minutes.
The fruit remains clear if the oil of spices are used.
Makes 6 pints.

MRS. B. L. BUCHER, *Dallastown, Pa.;* MRS. RALPH HEATWOLE, *Dayton, Va.*

## Pickled Watermelon (Russian)

5 pounds watermelon rind
3 tablespoons salt
1 large bunch dill

3 cups water
¼ cup vinegar

Pare watermelon and slice; sprinkle each slice on both sides with salt.
Let stand for 3 hours.
Pack rind in jars or crocks and place a bunch of dill on top of each.
Combine water and vinegar and pour over brine.
Let stand at least 3 days before serving.

MRS. GEORGE P. EITZER, *Mountain Lake, Minn.*

## Spiced Cantaloupe

| | |
|---|---|
| 6 pounds cantaloupe | 4 sticks cinnamon or |
| 1 tablespoon alum | ½ teaspoon oil of cinnamon |
| 4 quarts water | 1 tablespoon whole cloves or |
| 3 pounds sugar | ½ teaspoon oil of cloves |
| 1 quart vinegar | |

Pare cantaloupe and cut in strips 2 x 1 x ⅛ inches.
Dissolve alum in 4 quarts water and bring to a boil.
Add fruit and cook 15 minutes. Drain.
Combine vinegar, sugar and spice.
Add fruit and simmer slowly until fruit is clear (about 20 minutes).

MRS. SAMUEL DILLER, *Paramount, Md.*

## Spiced Gooseberries (Old)

| | |
|---|---|
| 5 pounds gooseberries | 2 tablespoons cinnamon |
| 3 pounds brown sugar | 1 tablespoon ground cloves |
| 1 pint vinegar | |

Wash gooseberries and remove stems.
Combine sugar and vinegar.
Tie spices in a bag and add to syrup.
Bring liquid to a boil and add berries.
Cook for 20-30 minutes.
Pack into hot jars and seal.

LUELLA MOSHEIR, *Lowville, N. Y.*

## Spiced Grapes

| | |
|---|---|
| 4 pounds grapes | 1 pint vinegar |
| 4 pounds sugar | 1 teaspoon whole cloves |

Wash grapes.
Combine sugar, vinegar and cloves.
Bring to a boil.
Add grapes and cook 20 minutes.
Pack into jars and seal.
Delicious when served with roast pork.

MRS. BRUCE MOWERY, *Chambersburg, Pa.*

## Spiced Plums

| | |
|---|---|
| 4 quarts plums | 6 drops oil of cloves |
| 3½ cups sugar | 6 cups vinegar |
| 6 drops oil of cinnamon | |

Wash plums and leave whole.
Combine sugar, vinegar and spices.
Bring to a boil and cook for 5 minutes.
Prick plums with a fork and pack them into jars.
Pour boiling syrup over them and let stand for 3 days.
Drain off syrup and cook again until it thickens.
Add plums and bring to a boil.
Pack in jars and seal.

VERNA NAFZIGER, *Archbold, Ohio*

## Seven-Day Sweet Pickles

| | |
|---|---|
| 7 pounds medium-sized cucumbers | 8 cups sugar |
| Water to cover | 2 tablespoons salt |
| 1 quart vinegar | 2 tablespoons mixed pickle spices |

Wash cucumbers and cover them with boiling water.
Let stand 24 hours and drain.
Repeat each day for 4 days, using fresh water each time.
On the fifth day, cut cucumbers in ¼ inch rings.
Combine vinegar, sugar, salt and spices.
Bring liquid to a boil and pour over sliced cucumbers.
Let stand 24 hours.
Drain syrup and bring to a boil.
Pour over cucumbers.
Repeat on the sixth day.
On the last day, drain off the syrup again and bring it to a boil.
Add cucumber slices and bring to the boiling point.
Pack into hot jars and seal.
These are very crisp and delicious pickles.

MRS. SAMUEL NAFZIGER, *Kalona, Iowa*

## Thickened Mustard Pickle

| | |
|---|---|
| 2 gallons cucumbers, sliced | 5 pounds sugar |
| ½ cup salt | 4 teaspoons mustard seed |
| 2 quarts onions, sliced | 5 tablespoons flour |
| 2 red sweet peppers | 2 teaspoons turmeric |
| 2 quarts vinegar | |

Slice cucumbers in thin rings and sprinkle with salt.
Let stand until morning and drain.
Slice onions and chop peppers.
Mix vegetables together.
Combine sugar, spices, flour and turmeric, add vinegar.

Bring to a boil and cook until slightly thickened.
Add mixed vegetables and bring to boiling point.
Pack in jars and seal.

MRS. MOSE HOFFMAN, *Goshen, Ind.*

## Winter Dill Pickles

| | |
|---|---|
| 100 medium-sized cucumbers | 10 quarts water |
| ½ cup salt | 1 quart vinegar |
| 4 quarts water | 2 cups salt |
| Cherry or grape leaves | Garlic |
| Dill | 4 small hot peppers |

Wash cucumbers and leave whole.
Make a brine by adding ½ cup salt to each 4 quarts water.
Cover cucumbers with brine and soak overnight.
Combine vinegar, water and salt and bring to a boil.
Let liquid stand overnight.
In the morning, drain the cucumbers and pack them in stone or glass
  jars between layers of grape or cherry leaves.
Add dill, garlic and a hot pepper to each jar.
These may be kept indefinitely without sealing them.

MRS. SAM J. GOERING, *North Newton, Kan.*

# RELISHES

## Apple Chow Chow

| | |
|---|---|
| 4 tart apples, chopped | 2 red peppers, chopped |
| 4 cups celery, chopped | 2 cups sugar |
| 4 cups carrots, chopped | 2 cups vinegar |
| 2 green peppers, chopped | 1 teaspoon celery seed |

Chop celery and carrots fine.
Cook until almost tender and then add chopped peppers and apples.
Combine sugar, vinegar and celery seed.
Pour liquid over mixture and bring to a boil.
Pack in jars and seal.

MRS. JOHN W. KOLB, *Phoenixville, Pa.*

## Apple Chutney

| | |
|---|---|
| 12 tart apples | 2 cups sugar |
| 1 red pepper | 2 cups vinegar |
| 2 green peppers | Juice of 4 lemons |
| 1 pound raisins | 1 tablespoon ginger |
| 1 cup celery, chopped | 1 tablespoon salt |

Wash and chop apples. Do not pare them.

Add chopped peppers, celery and raisins.

Combine sugar, salt and ginger; add vinegar and lemon juice.

Pour liquid over mixture and simmer until thick.

Pour into hot jars and seal.

MRS. DANIEL MARTIN, Sheldon, Wis.

## Barbecue or Hot Dog Relish

| | |
|---|---|
| 1 peck green tomatoes | 1 cup salt |
| 1 medium-sized head cabbage | 3 pints vinegar |
| 6 red sweet peppers | 8 cups sugar |
| 6 medium-sized onions | 2 tablespoons mixed pickle spices |

Grind tomatoes in food grinder. Add salt and let stand overnight.

Drain and add ground peppers and onions and finely chopped cabbage.

Combine sugar, vinegar and spices that have been tied in a bag.

Add liquid to mixed vegetables and simmer for 30 minutes.

Pack into hot jars and seal.

MRS. ELMER J. HERR, Hanover, Pa.

## Barbecue Relish

| | |
|---|---|
| 8 ripe tomatoes | 1 pint vinegar |
| 6 green peppers | 2 cups sugar |
| 6 onions | 1/2 teaspoon cloves |
| 8 tart apples | 1 teaspoon cinnamon |
| 6 red peppers | 1 tablespoon salt |

Grind vegetables and apples through coarse blade of food grinder.

Combine sugar, salt, spices and vinegar.

Pour liquid over mixture and cook slowly for 20 minutes.

Pack into jars and seal.

MRS. W. L. WILT, Johnstown, Pa.

## Beet Relish

| | |
|---|---|
| 1 quart beets, cooked | 1 quart vinegar |
| 1/2 cup grated horse-radish | 1 teaspoon salt |
| 1 cup sugar | |

Chop beets very fine.

Combine sugar, salt, vinegar and horse-radish.

Mix with beets.

This may be brought to a boil and then canned, or it may be kept in a
cool place indefinitely.

Chopped onions and green peppers may be added to this relish.

ESTHER HERSHBERGER, Kalona, Iowa

## Beet Relish with Cabbage

| | |
|---|---|
| 1 quart chopped beets | 1 tablespoon salt |
| 1 quart cabbage, chopped | 1 teaspoon pepper |
| 1 cup grated horse-radish | 1 quart vinegar |
| 1 cup sugar | |

Chop beets and cabbage very fine.

Add sugar, salt, vinegar, horse-radish and pepper.

Mix cold and seal tightly.

This is an old recipe and a very good relish.

ELSIE YODER, *North Lima, Ohio*

## Carrot Relish

| | |
|---|---|
| 10 cups carrots | 3 cups vinegar |
| 10 cups cucumbers | 4 tablespoons flour |
| 5 cups red and green peppers | 2 tablespoons salt |
| 2 cups onions | 2 tablespoons celery seed |
| 3½ cups sugar | 1 tablespoon dry mustard |
| 2 cups water | 1 teaspoon turmeric |

Chop all the vegetables into small pieces.

Cook carrots until almost tender and add the other vegetables.

Combine sugar, salt, spices and vinegar and pour over vegetables.

Simmer slowly for several minutes and then add flour, mustard and turmeric.

Cook 5 minutes longer.

Pour into hot jars. Seal.

MRS. HENRY BECHTEL, *Spring City, Pa.;* IRMA ALDERFER, *Souderton, Pa.*

## Catsup (Tomato)

| | |
|---|---|
| ½ bushel ripe tomatoes | 2 tablespoons salt |
| 2 large onions | 2 teaspoons celery seed |
| 6 peppers, red or green | 2 teaspoons ground mustard |
| 1 bunch celery, chopped | 1 teaspoon paprika |
| 4 sticks cinnamon bark | 2 cups sugar |
| 1 tablespoon whole cloves | 3 cups vinegar |

Cut the tomatoes into quarters. Do not peel.

Crush only enough to remove a small portion of juice.

Bring to a boil and cook for 3 minutes.

Pour through a sieve and let drain without crushing.

Cook onions, celery and peppers until tender and press through a sieve.

Mix tomato pulp with other strained vegetables.

Combine sugar, salt and vinegar.

Tie spices in a bag and add to liquid.

Boil liquid for 5 minutes, add vegetable pulp and simmer for 30 minutes.

Pour into hot jars and seal.

Makes approximately 14 quarts.

Mrs. M. J. Gingerich, *Hartville, Ohio*

## Catsup (Corn)

| | |
|---|---|
| 2 quarts corn | 2 tablespoons salt |
| 2 quarts cabbage | 1 teaspoon pepper |
| 2 cups sugar | 3 tablespoons dry mustard |
| 1 quart vinegar | 1 tablespoon turmeric |
| 1 pint water | |

Cut kernels of corn from the ears.

Chop cabbage in fine pieces.

Combine sugar, salt, pepper, water and vinegar.

Bring liquid to a boil and add cabbage.

Cook for 3 minutes and then add the corn.

Add turmeric and mustard and cook for 20 minutes.

Mrs. Allen Schultz, *Milverton, Ont., Can.*

## Catsup (Gooseberry)

| | |
|---|---|
| 4 pounds gooseberries | 1 tablespoon cinnamon bark |
| 2 pounds sugar | 1 tablespoon whole cloves |
| 1 cup vinegar | 1 teaspoon pepper |
| 1 teaspoon salt | |

Combine sugar, salt, pepper and vinegar.

Tie spices in a bag and add to liquid.

Bring to a boil.

When hot, add the gooseberries.

Cook until thick.

Pour into jars and seal.

This is delicious when served with cold meat.

Mrs. A. E. Reesor, *Wellesley, Ont., Can.*

## Corn Relish

| | |
|---|---|
| 1 quart corn | 1 quart vinegar |
| 1 quart cabbage, chopped | 1 quart sugar |
| 1 quart onions | 1 teaspoon celery seed |
| 1 quart cucumbers | 1 tablespoon salt |
| 1 quart ripe tomatoes | ½ teaspoon turmeric |

Chop the vegetables and mix together.

Combine sugar, salt, spices and vinegar.

Add liquid to mixed vegetables and cook slowly for 15 minutes.

Put into jars and seal.

Mrs. E. S. Garber, Nampa, Idaho

## Chow Chow

| | |
|---|---|
| 1 quart cucumbers, diced | 1 pint red peppers |
| 1 quart string beans | 1 cup small onions |
| 1 quart Lima beans | 1 tablespoon dry mustard |
| 1 quart corn | 2 cups sugar |
| 1 pint celery | 1 quart vinegar |
| 1 pint green peppers | |

Chop vegetables the desired size and cook separately.

Cook until tender, not soft.

Drain cooked vegetables and mix together.

Combine sugar, mustard and vinegar.

Bring to a boil.

Add mixed vegetables to hot liquid and bring to boiling point.

Put into hot jars and seal.

Mrs. Olive Bergey, Souderton, Pa.

## Chili Sauce

| | |
|---|---|
| 1 peck ripe tomatoes | 2 cups sugar |
| 6 green peppers | 2 cups vinegar |
| 6 red peppers | 3 tablespoons salt |
| 10 medium-sized onions | 1/4 teaspoon oil of cloves |
| 1 bunch celery | 1/4 teaspoon oil of cinnamon |

Chop onions, peppers and celery.

Wash tomatoes, dip in boiling water and slip off skins.

Chop tomatoes and add to other vegetables.

Combine sugar, salt, vinegar and spices.

Add liquid to chopped vegetables and cook slowly for 1½ to 2 hours.
Stir frequently.

Pour into hot jars and seal.

Katie Leatherman, La Junta, Colo.; Mrs. Gilbert Lind, Nampa, Idaho

## Christmas Relish

| | |
|---|---|
| 4 red peppers | 1 bunch celery |
| 4 yellow peppers | 1 tablespoon salt |
| 4 green peppers | 2 cups sugar |
| 8 onions | 2 cups vinegar |

Cut peppers, celery and onions in long strips.
Sprinkle salt over mixed vegetables and let stand 30 minutes.
Combine sugar and vinegar and add to mixture.
Cook slowly for 15 minutes.
Pour into jars and seal.

MRS. CLETUS KING, *Belleville, Pa.*

## Cold Vegetable Relish

| | |
|---|---|
| 1 peck ripe tomatoes | 1/3 cup salt |
| 1½ cups celery, chopped | 1½ quarts vinegar |
| 4 peppers, red or green | 2 pounds brown sugar |
| 6 large onions | ¼ cup mustard seed |

Chop celery, peppers, onions and tomatoes in small pieces.
Combine sugar, salt, vinegar and mustard seed.
Mix liquid with vegetables and put in a stone or glass jar.
Stir at 2 hour intervals during the first day.
This may be sealed in jars or kept in an open jar indefinitely.

MRS. DEWEY WOLFER, *Sheridan, Ore.*

## Cranberry Relish

| | |
|---|---|
| 1 pound raw cranberries | 1 cup crushed pineapple (optional) |
| 3 raw apples | 2 cups sugar |
| 2 oranges | ½ cup nuts (optional) |

Grind cranberries, apples and oranges through coarse blade of food
   grinder.
Use peeling of 1 orange.
Add sugar and let stand 6 to 8 hours in refrigerator.
Add nuts just before serving.
Serves 8.

MRS. CLIFFORD CRESSMAN, *Kitchener, Ont., Can.;* LIZZIE K. GROFF, *Lancaster, Pa.*

## Cucumber Relish

| | |
|---|---|
| 1 peck large cucumbers | 1 tablespoon celery seed |
| 6 large onions | 2 tablespoons mustard seed |
| 3 cups sugar | 3 cups vinegar |
| 1/3 cup salt | |

Pare and grind cucumbers and onions.
Sprinkle salt over mixture and let stand 1 hour. Drain.
Combine sugar, spices and vinegar and pour over vegetables.
Cook slowly for 25 minutes.
Pour into jars and seal.

MRS. JACOB NEUENSCHWANDER, *Apple Creek, Ohio*

## Dixie Relish

| | |
|---|---|
| 1 quart cabbage, chopped | 1/2 cup sugar |
| 1 pint green pepper | 1 quart vinegar |
| 1 pint red sweet pepper | 2 tablespoons celery seed |
| 1 pint onions | 4 tablespoons mustard seed |
| 1/3 cup salt | 2 hot red peppers |

Chop vegetables in small pieces or grind through coarse blade of food chopper.

Mix together and add salt and enough water to cover.

Let stand in a large jar or enamel pan overnight.

In the morning, drain and add spices, sugar and vinegar.

Cook slowly for 15 to 20 minutes.

Pack in jars and seal.

MRS. I. K. METZLER, *Accident, Md.*

## Fruit Relish

| | |
|---|---|
| 8 pears | 2 tablespoons salt |
| 8 peaches | 4 cups sugar |
| 20 ripe tomatoes | 1 quart vinegar |
| 2 red sweet peppers | 2 tablespoons mixed pickling spices |
| 6 small onions | |

Pare the fruit and vegetables and chop rather coarsely.

Mix together and add sugar, salt, vinegar and spices that have been tied in a bag.

Cook slowly for 2 hours.

Pour into jars and seal.

MRS. ADELINE MARTIN, *Conestoga, Ont., Can.*

## Golden Relish

| | |
|---|---|
| 4 cups carrots | 2 cups sugar |
| 4 cups celery | 2 cups vinegar |
| 2 green peppers | 2 tablespoons salt |
| 4 tart apples | 2 tablespoons celery seed |
| 2 red sweet peppers | |

Clean and chop the vegetables and apples.

Mix together and add sugar, salt, vinegar and spices.

Cook slowly for 20 minutes.

Pour into jars and seal.

MRS. SUSIE HOUGH, *Colorado Springs, Colo.*

## Health Relish

12 peppers, red or green
6 pounds cabbage
6 medium-sized carrots
6 medium-sized onions
1 cup salt

3 pints vinegar
2 pounds sugar
1 tablespoon celery seed
1 tablespoon mustard seed

Grind the cabbage and add salt.

Let stand 3 hours.

Then squeeze the cabbage from the brine.

Grind peppers, carrots and onions and mix with the cabbage.

Add the sugar, vinegar and spices.

This is a cold relish and keeps indefinitely when packed in jars and sealed, or it may be kept in a cool place in a large jar.

MRS. CHARLES H. BENNER, *Souderton, Pa.*

## Mustard Piccalilli

3 heads cauliflower
2 bunches celery
1 quart small onions
2 quarts green beans
3 quarts corn
2 dozen large cucumbers
1 quart carrots

2 quarts Lima beans
1 quart prepared mustard
3 pounds sugar
1 cup salt
2 quarts vinegar
1 tablespoon turmeric
3 tablespoons flour

Cut vegetables in desired size and cook each one separately until tender.

Mix together and add sugar, salt, mustard and vinegar.

Bring to a boil and add flour and turmeric that have been mixed with ½ cup water.

Bring to a boil again and when slightly thickened pack into jars.

MRS. RACHEL NISLY, *McMinnville, Ore.*

## Pepper Relish

12 green peppers
12 red sweet peppers
12 onions
12 green tomatoes

3 tablespoons salt
3 cups sugar
3 cups vinegar

Grind peppers and onions together through coarse blade of chopper or chop very fine.

Grind tomatoes separately.

Pour enough boiling water over ground peppers and onions to cover.

Let stand 5 minutes and drain.

Bring vinegar, sugar and salt to a boil and add ground vegetables.
Cook together for 10 minutes and then pack into hot jars and seal.

MINERVA JOHNSON, *Scottdale, Pa.*; MRS. PAUL STIERLY, *Chester Springs, Pa.*
MRS. REBECCA BLOUGH, *Davidsville, Pa.*

## Red Pepper Relish

| | |
|---|---|
| 12 large red peppers | 1½ tablespoons salt |
| 3 cups sugar | 2 cups vinegar |

Grind peppers through coarse blade of food chopper.
Add sugar, salt and vinegar.
Simmer for about 1 hour or until relish is thickened.
Pack into hot jars and put paraffin on top.

GRACE E. ZOOK, *Belleville, Pa.*

## Tomato Relish

| | |
|---|---|
| 1 quart green tomatoes | 2 cups brown sugar |
| 5 small onions | 1 quart vinegar |
| 2 red sweet peppers | 1 tablespoon mustard seed |
| 1 quart cabbage, chopped | 2 teaspoons turmeric |
| 3 tablespoons salt | |

Chop vegetables very fine and mix together.
Add sugar, salt, spices and vinegar.
Cook slowly for 30 minutes.
Pack into hot jars and seal.

MRS. H. N. TROYER, *Hartville, Ohio*

## Sandwich Spread (I)

| | |
|---|---|
| 6 cups cucumbers, ground | ½ cup butter |
| 4 cups onions, ground | 1 pint vinegar |
| 3 red sweet peppers | 3 tablespoons flour |
| 3 green peppers | 4 eggs, beaten |
| ½ cup salt | 1 teaspoon mustard seed |
| 3 cups sugar | 1 teaspoon celery seed |
| 1 cup cream | |

Grind the vegetables through coarse blade of food chopper.
Add salt and mix together well.
Let stand 2 hours.
Cover with vinegar, bring to a boil, then drain and press dry.
Combine butter, sugar, flour, eggs, spices and 1 pint vinegar.
Add to vegetable mixture and cook 5 minutes.
Add cream and bring to a boil.
Pack into hot jars and seal.

MRS. NOAH HILTY, *Marshallville, Ohio*

## Sandwich Spread (II)

4 quarts green tomatoes
6 red sweet peppers
6 green peppers
6 yellow peppers
3 bunches celery
1 pint cucumbers, ground
1 large head cabbage

1 cup salt
2 quarts vinegar
4 cups sugar
1½ cups flour
1 tablespoon turmeric
½ cup prepared mustard

Grind all the vegetables through the coarse blade of food chopper.
Add salt and let stand overnight.
In the morning, drain and add 1½ quarts vinegar.
Bring to a boil, and cook 10 minutes.
Combine sugar, flour, turmeric and mustard.
Add remaining vinegar to make a paste; add thickening to hot mixture.
Cook for 3 minutes, and pack into hot jars and seal.

MRS OSCAR HOSTETLER, *Topeka, Ind.*

## Sandwich Spread (III)

24 peppers, green or red
12 green tomatoes
3 large onions
1 pint prepared mustard
3 cups sugar

1 quart vinegar
3 teaspoons celery seed
4 tablespoons flour
⅓ cup salt
1 quart salad dressing

Grind the vegetables and sprinkle with salt.
Let stand overnight; in the morning, drain well.
Add mustard, sugar, flour, vinegar and celery seed.
Cook slowly for 15 minutes, stirring frequently.
Remove from stove and add salad dressing.
Pour into jars and seal with paraffin.
Ground meat may be added when this spread is used.

MRS. DAVID KORNHAUS, MRS. ALLEN AMSTUTZ, *Orrville, Ohio*

## Pickled Baby Ears of Corn

Pick 2 qts. of baby ears of corn 2 to 3 inches long. These tiny ears are formed before the tassel begins to show. Use field corn rather than garden varieties.

Husk cobs and parboil 3 to 5 minutes. Pack into hot sterilized jars and add a few strips of red sweet pepper to each jar. Cover with a hot syrup made from:

1 cup water
1 cup granulated sugar
2 cups white vinegar

2 teaspoons salt
1 tablespoon pickling spice
(tied in bag)

Seal jars. These pickles are found mainly among the Mennonites of Ontario, Canada.

MRS. ARCHIE KINSIE. *Breslau. Ontario*

# Jellies,
## Jams, Preserves

### Chapter XIV

My GRANDMOTHER'S JELLY CUPBOARD WAS AS PICTURESQUE AS A COLOR book! I used to get a peep inside when I spent a week with her occasionally as a child. My interest in her jellies was never apparent when she passed them at the table as an accompaniment to one of her meals, but I always weakened when she decided to interrupt my play by calling time out for an afternoon snack. On those occasions she would lead me to the cupboard and inquire which of the many jars I would like to have her open. At first I chose only for the brightest colors, as I was too small to have any idea which would be the most delicious. Then one day she chanced to spread my bread with ground-cherry preserves and from that time on it was my favorite. These little yellow berries grew on

418

vines close to the ground and were about the size of a cherry. The little round fruit was covered with a thin, lacy shell that would pop open when it was ripe.

Because of Great-grandpa's "sweet tooth" and the many foods with which he ate "spreading," Great-grandma had to make a lot of jelly and preserves. There were numerous ones among her favorites that we seldom see today. The quince tree, which was numbered among the trees in her back yard, bore a hard fruit with a fuzzy skin. When pared and ground, these made a most delicious quince honey. Watermelon preserves had an excellent flavor when they were fresh. The tiny little red cubes of melon had a tendency to become sugary, however.

There were also the clear, transparent pear preserves, with a close rival in the sour cherry preserves. The delicate pink rhubarb conserve was pretty, and so were the yellow tomato preserves. For jellies, clear, red crab apple and the deeper red currant were hard to beat.

There were all kinds of fruit butters too, some of which have had their day. Among these were pear, plum, grape and elderberry butter. Apple butter has always been a favorite. It is delicious when served with scrapple, fried mush or cottage cheese.

Many interesting stories are handed down from the "apple snitzing" days of long ago. The night before the apple butter was to be made some of the young folks from the neighborhood would come in to help pare apples. Between chatter, sweet cider, and pop corn, the required bushel and a half of apple snitz were soon prepared. The following evening Grandma watched the men lift the thirty-gallon kettle of butter from the fire. How happy she was if, when the last crock had been filled, there was enough left to send gifts to each of her neighbors!

## Apple Butter (Small Amount)

2 quarts apple cider  
4 quarts apples  
2 cups sugar  

2 cups dark corn syrup  
1 teaspoon powdered cinnamon or  
¼ teaspoon oil of cinnamon  

Boil the cider until it is reduced to 1 quart.

Pare apples, core and slice in thin pieces.

Add apples to cider and cook slowly until the mixture begins to thicken. Stir frequently.

Then add sugar, syrup and cinnamon.

Continue to cook until a little of the butter, when cooled on a plate, is of a good consistency to spread.

Yield 5 to 6 pints.

STELLA HUBER STAUFFER, *Tofield, Alta., Can.*

## Apple Butter (Large Amount)

| | |
|---|---|
| 20 gallons sweet cider | 15 pounds sugar |
| 8 gallons apples | 1 tablespoon oil of cinnamon |

Use a large 30 to 40 gallon copper kettle.

Heat cider to boiling and let cook until reduced to about half the former amount.

Pare and slice apples into eighths.

Add ½ the apples and cook until they are soft.

Add the remaining apples and cook until they are soft, stirring frequently.

Add sugar and stir constantly to prevent burning.

When a little of the butter that has cooled is of a good consistency to spread, remove butter from fire.

Add oil of cinnamon and mix thoroughly.

This makes approximately 12 gallons.

MRS. SUSIE HOCHSTETLER, *Shanesville, Ohio*

## Apple Butter (Oven Method)

| | |
|---|---|
| 7 pounds apples (16 cups sauce) | 2 tablespoons powdered cinnamon |
| 3 pounds brown sugar | or |
| 1 cup vinegar or cider | 1 cup of crushed pineapple |

Cook apples until soft and press through a sieve.

Add remaining ingredients and put in the oven.

Bake 3 hours at 350°.

Stir occasionally.

Pour into jars and seal.

Makes 5 quarts.

MRS. M. E. WEAVER, *Annville, Pa.*

## Apricot Jam

| | |
|---|---|
| 1 pound dried apricots | 1 No. 2 can crushed pineapple or |
| 1 quart water | 2 oranges and 1 lemon |
| 6 cups sugar | |

Soak apricots 3 hours in warm water.

Grind through medium-fine blade of food chopper.

If oranges are used, grind one orange with rind.

To the apricot pulp add pineapple or orange and lemon juice.

Add sugar and cook rapidly until thick.

Stir frequently.

Pour into jars and seal.

MRS. ELMER MACK, *Souderton, Pa.*

## Blackberry Jelly

2 quarts blackberries    Sugar
3 cups water

Wash blackberries, add water and bring to boiling point.

Cook until berries are soft.

Remove from heat and strain through cloth bag; do not squeeze the bag
if you want jelly that is clear and sparkling.

Measure liquid and bring to a boil.

Add gradually same amount of sugar as liquid.

Cook rapidly until jelly begins to thicken.

Pour into glasses. When cool, cover with paraffin.

## Carrot Marmalade

2 pounds carrots    4 lemons
3 pounds sugar    ¾ cup chopped nuts

Steam or cook carrots until tender.

Add sugar and the juice of 4 lemons.

Add the rind of 2 lemons.

Cook 20 minutes, stirring occasionally.

Add nuts just before removing from stove.

Pour into jars and seal.

MAXINE MUMAW, *Dalton, Ohio*

## Cherry Preserves

3 pounds red cherries    3 pounds sugar

Stem and seed cherries.

Bring to boiling point, stirring frequently.

Add sugar gradually, stirring to keep from sticking.

Cook preserves 20 minutes.

Add a few drops of red coloring.

If they are not as thick as desired, drain liquid and cook to desired
thickness.

Combine cherries and thickened syrup.

Pour into a crock or bowl and let stand 12 hours.

Put into jars and cover with paraffin.

MRS. CARL G. SHOWALTER, *Broadway, Va.*

## Citron Preserves

3 pounds citron    Juice of 1 lemon
2 pounds sugar

Slice citron very thin and cut in small pieces.
Add sugar and mix thoroughly.
Let stand overnight.
Cook until the citron is clear and transparent.
Add lemon juice and cook 2 more minutes.
Pour into jars and seal.

Mrs. Bertha Landis, *Sterling, Ill.*

## Crab Apple Jelly

4 cups crab apple juice                3 cups sugar

Wash apples and cut into quarters.
Do not pare.
Put apples in a saucepan.
Add enough water until it can be seen through pieces of fruit.
Cover and cook slowly until apples are soft.
Pour into a bag and suspend over a bowl; let hang until juice no longer
    drips; do not squeeze bag.
Measure juice and bring it to a boil.
Add sugar gradually and cook rapidly until it begins to thicken.
When the last 2 drops on the spoon run together and "sheet off," remove
    jelly from stove.
Pour into hot jelly glasses and cover with paraffin.

Stella Huber Stauffer, *Tofield, Alta., Can.*

## Cranberry Jam

1 quart raw cranberries                2½ cups sugar
2 cups boiling water

Wash and clean cranberries.
Add boiling water and cook for 20 minutes.
Rub fruit through a sieve.
Add sugar and bring to a boil.
Cook quickly until thick.
Pour into jars or molds.

Mrs. L. S. Kreider, *Wadsworth, Ohio*

## Cranberry Conserves

1 pound cranberries (4 cups)           2 cups hot water
2 oranges                              4 cups sugar
1 cup chopped raisins                  1 cup chopped nuts

Grind raw cranberries and oranges through a food chopper.
Add hot water and bring to a boil.

Cook quickly until fruit is soft.

Add raisins, sugar and hot water.

Cook over moderate heat, stirring occasionally until thickened.

Remove from heat and add nuts.

Pour into hot jars and seal.

MRS. FANNIE WOUGHT, *Cullom, Ill.*

## Elderberry Jelly

2 cups elderberry juice
2 cups apple juice (thick)

3 cups sugar

Cook elderberries until soft and then strain.

Cook apples, which have not been pared, in a moderate amount of water.

When tender, strain through bag; do not squeeze.

Combine the juices and bring to a boil.

Add sugar gradually and cook rapidly.

Cook until the jelly stage has been reached.

Pour into hot jars and cover with paraffin.

MRS. ELMER MAUST, *Grantsville, Md.*

## Grape Conserve

6 pounds grapes (stemmed)
6 pounds sugar
1 pound raisins

3 oranges
1 cup chopped nuts

Remove hulls and cook pulp until tender.

Rub through a sieve to remove seeds.

Combine pulp and hulls.

Add sugar, raisins, juice and grated rind of oranges.

Cook until thick.

Add nuts and remove from heat.

Pour into hot glasses and seal with paraffin.

MRS. PERRY E. SHANK, *Broadway, Va.*

## Grape Jam

4 cups grape pulp
6 cups sugar

½ cup water

Wash and stem grapes.

Add water and cook until soft.

Rub through a sieve to remove seeds and skins.

Return to stove and add sugar.

Cook until thick, stirring constantly to prevent burning.
Pour into jelly glasses and cover with paraffin.

BERTHA FAST, *Mountain Lake, Minn.*

## Green Tomato Jam

| | |
|---|---|
| 8 cups green tomatoes | ¼ cup vinegar |
| 4 cups sugar | 1 tablespoon powdered cinnamon or |
| 2 lemons | 1 teaspoon ginger |

Wash the tomatoes and remove any spots.
Cover with boiling water and let stand 5 minutes.
Drain and slice into thin pieces.
Add layers of sliced lemon and sugar.
Add vinegar and sprinkle with spice.
Let mixture stand overnight.
In the morning, cook rapidly until the tomatoes are clear and the liquid
   is like syrup.
Pour into hot jars and seal.

MRS. JOHN N. STOLTZFUS, *Parkesburg, Pa.*

## Mixed Fruit Preserves

| | |
|---|---|
| 3 cups sour cherries | 2 cups red raspberries or strawberries |
| 3 cups fresh apricots | 7 cups sugar |

Wash and seed cherries.
Plunge apricots into boiling water and remove skins and seeds.
Cut into quarters.
Wash the berries and cap them.
Mix the fruits and sugar together and cook rapidly.
Cook until fruits are clear and tender.
Pour into hot jars and seal

MRS. SUSIE DOUGH, *Colorado Springs, Colo.*

## Muskmelon Conserve

| | |
|---|---|
| 1 pound diced muskmelon or cantaloupe | 2 lemons |
| 1 pound sugar | ¼ teaspoon powdered alum |
| | ¾ cup chopped nuts |

Pare the melon and dice into small pieces.
Add sugar and thinly sliced lemon.
Cook rapidly until thick.
Add alum and cook 2 minutes longer.

Remove from stove.

Add nuts.

Pour into clean glasses and seal with paraffin.

Mrs. Alvin N. Roth, *Wellesley, Ont., Can.*

## Orange Marmalade (I)

| | |
|---|---|
| 1 dozen oranges | 1 pint water |
| 1½ pounds sugar | 1 lemon |

Wash oranges and lemon and cut them into thin slices.

Cover with cold water and let stand overnight.

Bring to a boil and cook slowly until the rind can be pierced easily.

Add sugar and cook rapidly until thick.

Pour into jars and seal with paraffin.

Mrs. Verna Wymer, *Canton, Ohio*

## Orange Marmalade (II)

| | |
|---|---|
| 3 large or 6 small oranges | 3 quarts water |
| 1 lemon | 4 pounds sugar |

Wash oranges and lemon and squeeze to remove the juice.

Grind the rinds, and mix juice and rind together.

Add the water and let stand overnight.

In the morning, bring to a boil and cook 1 hour.

Add the sugar; when it has dissolved, cook rapidly until thick.

Pour into jars and seal.

Mrs. E. S. Hallman, *Tuleta, Texas*

## Peach Honey

| | |
|---|---|
| 3 cups soft peaches, crushed | 3½ pounds sugar |
| 2 cups water | 1 teaspoon powdered alum |

Add water to crushed peaches and cook until peaches are soft.

Add sugar; when it has dissolved, cook rapidly until thick.

Add alum and cook 1 minute longer.

Let stand until cooled.

Pour into jars and seal with paraffin.

Marie Blosser, *Harrisonburg, Va.*

## Peach Marmalade

| | |
|---|---|
| 2 quarts sliced peaches | 1 small bottle maraschino cherries |
| 3 oranges | Sugar |

Wash peaches and remove skins and seeds.
Remove juice from oranges.
Grind peaches, rind of 1 orange and cherries.
Mix fruit together and measure.
Add as much sugar as you have fruit.
Bring to a boil and cook rapidly until thick.
Pour into jars and seal.

GRACE E. ZOOK, *Belleville, Pa.*

## Peach and Pineapple Marmalade

| | |
|---|---|
| 1 gallon peach slices | 2 oranges |
| 1 cup crushed pineapple | Sugar |

Remove skins and seeds from peaches. Cut into thin slices.
Squeeze juice from oranges, and slice rind of 1 orange in thin strips.
Mix fruit together and bring to a boil.
Add sugar, ¾ pound for each pound of fruit.
When it is dissolved, cook rapidly until thick.
Pour into hot jars and seal.

MRS. CLARENCE WHISSEN, *Broadway, Va.*

## Peach Preserves

| | |
|---|---|
| 6 pounds peaches, sliced | ½ cup water |
| 6 pounds sugar | |

Remove skins and seeds from peaches. Cut into thin slices.
Add water to sliced peaches and bring to a boil.
Add sugar.
When it has dissolved, cook rapidly until fruit is clear and syrup is thickened.
Pour into jars and seal.

MRS. ABNER WEAVER, *Waynesboro, Va.*

## Pear Butter

| | |
|---|---|
| 2 quarts pear pulp | 2 pounds sugar |

Wash pears and remove core and peeling.
Cut into quarters and add a little water.
Cook until tender.
To the pulp add sugar and mix together well.
Place in a 350° oven for 3 hours.
Stir occasionally.
Pour into jars and seal.

MRS. C. A. GRAYBILL, *Martinsburg, Pa.*

## Pear Honey

8 pounds pears (Keiffer preferred)    2 cups crushed pineapple
8 pounds sugar

Remove peeling and core from pears.
Grind pears in food chopper.
Add crushed pineapple and then add sugar gradually.
Bring to a boil and cook until thick (about 20 minutes).
Stir frequently to prevent it from burning.

Mrs. Lydia Zimmerman, *East Earl, Pa.;* Mrs. Maynard Brenneman, *Kalona, Iowa*

## Pear Marmalade

4 pounds sliced pears    3 oranges
4 pounds sugar

Remove peeling and core from pears.
Wash oranges and remove seeds.
Grind pears and oranges through food chopper.
Bring fruit to a boil and add sugar.
Cook until thick.
Pour into jars and seal.

Mrs. Ralph Diller, *Sheldon, Wis.*

## Pear Preserves

4 pounds sliced pears    2 cups crushed pineapple
6 cups sugar

Peel and core pears.
Slice pears into thin pieces.
Bring to a boil and add the sugar.
When the pears are soft, add the crushed pineapple, and cook until fruit
    is clear and syrup is thickened (about 20 minutes).
Pour into jars and seal.

Mrs. Sallie Musser, *Adamstown, Pa.;* Mrs. Glen Burkholder, *Kalona, Iowa*

## Pear and Apricot Jam

5 pounds pears, ground    1 cup water
1 pound dried apricots    4½ pounds sugar

Peel and core pears.
Grind raw pears and dried apricots through food chopper.
Add water and bring to a boil.
Add sugar gradually until all has been dissolved.

Cook until fruit is clear and syrup is thickened.
Pour into jars and seal.

MRS. DANIEL STONER, *Columbia, Pa.*; MRS. ILA WEAVER, *Millersburg, Pa.*

## Pineapple Preserves

4 cups fresh pineapple          4 cups water
4 cups sugar

Pare the pineapple and remove eyes.
Cut fruit into small pieces or cubes.
Add water to pineapple and cook in a covered pan until tender.
Add sugar and cook until fruit is clear and syrup is thickened.
Pour into jars and seal.

MRS. AMOS HORST, *Hagerstown, Md.*

## Pineapple and Apricot Jam

1 pound dried apricots          1 cup sugar to each cup fruit
1 medium-sized fresh pineapple

Soak apricots in water until soft.
Pare the pineapple and remove eyes.
Grind the drained apricots and pineapple. Measure.
Bring fruit to a boil and add sugar gradually (the same amount as fruit
    pulp).
Cook until fruit is clear and jam is thick.
Pour into jars and seal.

MRS. PAUL MARTIN, *Campbell, Ohio*

## Plum Conserve

2½ cups damson plums           ½ lemon
½ cup seedless raisins          1 orange
2½ cups sugar                  1 cup English walnuts (chopped)

Wash and stem plums.
Cut in quarters and remove seeds.
Add ½ cup water and bring to a boil.
Add raisins, sugar, orange and lemon juice.
Add lemon peel and a little orange peel cut very fine.
Cook until fruit is clear and syrup is thickened.
Remove from heat and add chopped nuts.
Pour into jars and seal.

MRS. ARLAND E. LONGACRE, *Bally, Pa.*

## Pumpkin Marmalade

3 quarts pumpkins, diced      1 lemon
8 cups sugar      1 orange

Pare the pumpkin, remove seeds and grind through food chopper.
Add sugar, mix together and let stand overnight.
Remove seeds from orange and lemon and grind pulp and rind.
Add to pumpkin and cook until fruit becomes clear.
Pour into jars and seal.

MRS. A. H. ERB, *La Junta, Colo.*

## Quince Honey

2 cups grated quince      1 pint water
2 cups grated apples      4 pounds sugar

Wash and pare quinces and apples. Core and cut into quarters.
Grate or grind both fruits and mix together.
Add water to fruit and bring to a boil.
Add sugar gradually and stir until all has been dissolved.
Cook slowly until fruit is clear and mixture is thick (about 20 minutes).
Pour into jars and seal.

MRS. M. H. GODSHALL, MRS. HARVEY L. ALDERFER, *Souderton, Pa.*

## Red Pepper Jam

12 large red sweet peppers      2 cups vinegar
1 tablespoon salt      3 cups sugar

Wash peppers and remove seeds.
Grind through the medium blade of food chopper.
Sprinkle ground peppers with salt and let stand 3½ hours.
Drain and add sugar and vinegar.
Cook on moderate heat until thick (about 1 hour).
Pour into hot jars and cover with paraffin.

MRS. MARK STAUFFER, *Harrisonburg, Va.*

## Red Raspberry Preserves

1 quart red raspberries      4 pounds sugar
2 cups tart apples      2 cups water

Wash and cap berries.
Cook sugar and water together until it spins a thread.
While it is cooking, pare and core apples.
Grind through food chopper.
Add ground apples to syrup and cook 4 minutes.

Then add the capped berries and cook 9 minutes longer.
Pour into hot jars and seal.

Mrs. D. C. Hostetler, *Orrville, Ohio*

## Rhubarb Conserve

| | |
|---|---|
| 10 cups diced rhubarb | 1 lemon |
| 8 cups sugar | 1 cup chopped nuts |
| 3 oranges | 1½ cups seedless raisins (optional) |

Wash and clean rhubarb.

Cut into small pieces.

Add sugar, orange and lemon juice.

Grind rind of lemon and 1 orange and add.

Cook slowly, stirring occasionally.

When thick, add chopped nuts and remove from heat.

Pour into glasses and seal.

Makes 6 pints.

Lydia Driver, *Versailles, Mo.*

## Strawberry Honey

| | |
|---|---|
| 2½ cups crushed strawberries | 1 1/3 cups water |
| 3 pounds sugar | 1 teaspoon powdered alum |

Cook water and sugar together for 7 minutes.

Add crushed berries and boil for 5 minutes.

Add powdered alum and remove from heat.

Pour into jars and seal.

Cora Mason, *Harrisonburg, Va.;* Mrs. Mabel Mowery, *Chambersburg, Pa.*

## Strawberry Marmalade

| | |
|---|---|
| 2 quarts strawberries | 2 oranges |
| 1 medium-sized fresh pineapple | 6 cups sugar |

Wash and cap the strawberries.

Pare the pineapple and remove eyes.

Cut into fine pieces.

Remove the juice of both oranges.

Grind the rind of 1 orange.

Mix fruit together and bring to a boil.

Add sugar and cook until fruit is clear and syrup is thickened.

Pour into jars and seal.

Mrs. Willis Miller, *Harrisonburg, Va.*

## Strawberry Preserves

3 cups fresh strawberries               3 cups sugar

Wash and cap strawberries.
Put in a large kettle and pour sugar into a cone-shaped pile in the center
    of the berries.
Do not stir.
Place on low heat and cook slowly until the juice is extracted.
Increase the heat and boil rapidly for approximately 20 minutes.
Remove from heat and let stand for 24 hours, stirring occasionally.
Pour into jars and seal.

MRS. B. L. BUCHER, *Dallastown, Pa.*

## Watermelon Preserves

4 cups diced watermelon rind       ½ lemon
3 cups sugar                    ½ cup crushed pineapple (optional)

Use the white part of the rind and a thin strip of the pink melon for
    color.
Cut into ¼ inch cubes.
Add sugar to the melon and slowly bring to a boil.
Slice the lemon into thin strips and add along with crushed pineapple.
Cook faster after the sugar is dissolved.
Cook until the fruit is clear and the syrup is thickened.
Pour into jars and seal.

GRANDMOTHER SHOWALTER

## Yellow Tomato Preserves

1 pound yellow tomatoes peeled     ¾ pound sugar
   and sliced                      ½ lemon

Peel tomatoes and cut into thin pieces.
Add sugar and let stand 1 hour.
Add thinly sliced lemon and rind.
Cook until the tomatoes are clear and the syrup is thickened.
Pour into jars and seal.

STELLA HUBER STAUFFER, *Tofield, Alta., Can.*

# Candies
## and
# Confections

### Chapter XV

GREAT-GRANDMA WATCHED THAT OLD SUGAR BARREL IN THE PANTRY with misgivings. The canning season and jelly making of the summer months had drained heavily upon the family's supply. It was some months yet until Great-grandpa would be traveling to a distant city for his annual wagon load of supplies. Pies were a necessity for the happiness of the family during the week. And Sunday dare not come around without a cake, for fear unexpected company would arrive for dinner. The children liked candy too, but it was not a "have to be," for it was considered a luxury.

"Just wait a few more weeks, Susan," Grandpa would say. "That cane patch is about ready and that will help solve our problems." On a clear,

432

crisp day in late autumn they made a fire under that big kettle and boiled sorghum molasses. With gallons of this molasses, the young folks could now have their candy in the form of a taffy pull. Many of their friends were invited in for the evening. While Grandma boiled the taffy they sang and played games. What fun they had pulling taffy, and what blisters!

I asked an older lady not long ago what kind of confections they made when she was a girl. She told me that they seldom had candy except at Christmas, and then they had only taffy and crackerjack.

There were a few hard candies made during those early days in case the sugar barrel did hold out. Vinegar candy was always good, especially when Grandma rolled it into little round balls while it was still warm. Then it had all the selling features of our lolly pops, except for the stick. Hard hoarhound candies were good if you liked their flavor. Grandpa and Grandma carried them in their pockets to church to pass around to the children, or to use in warding off a coughing spell.

The young folks of olden times no doubt had a number of "goodies" we do not know about today. We feel, however, that they missed a lot never to have tasted our creamy fudges, caramels and chocolates!

## Butter Jets

| | |
|---|---|
| I pound confectioner's sugar | I teaspoon vanilla |
| ¼ pound butter | I brick dipping chocolate (8 oz.) |
| I tablespoon milk | |

Rub soft butter into sifted sugar.

Add milk and vanilla.

Mix thoroughly and roll in desired shapes.

To melt chocolate, cut it in small pieces and melt slowly in the top of a double boiler.

Coat candies with melted chocolate and allow to harden.

MRS. LEROY WENTLING, *Lititz, Pa.*

## Butterscotch Caramels

| | |
|---|---|
| 3 cups brown sugar | I teaspoon lemon juice or vanilla |
| ¼ pound butter | ½ cup water |

Combine ingredients except flavoring in a heavy saucepan. Place over low heat and stir until sugar is dissolved.

Increase heat and stir constantly.

Cook until candy forms a firm ball when dropped into cold water (246°).

Add flavoring and pour into flat, greased pan.
Cool slightly and mark into 1 inch squares.

MRS. WILLIAM F. GEISER, *Apple Creek, Ohio*

## Candy Crispies

| | |
|---|---|
| 1 cup sugar | ½ package Rice Krispies (3½ oz.) |
| 1 cup corn syrup | 1 cup shredded coconut |
| 1 cup thin cream | 1 cup salted peanuts |
| ½ package of corn flakes (4 oz.) | |

Cook sugar, syrup and cream together until it forms a soft ball in cold
water (236°).
Stir only until sugar is dissolved.
Crush corn flakes coarsely and mix with Krispies, coconut and peanuts.
Pour hot syrup over mixture and blend together.
Press into a flat, buttered pan.
Cut into squares when almost cold.

MRS. JOHN Y. SWARTZENDRUBER, *Kalona, Iowa*
MRS. CHARLES VAN PELT, *Columbiana, Ohio*
MRS. RAY MAST, *Sugar Creek, Ohio*

## Candy Loaf

| | |
|---|---|
| 6 cups sugar | 1 cup chopped nuts |
| 2 cups thin cream | 1 cup shredded coconut |
| 1 cup white syrup | 2 ounces unsweetened chocolate |

Cook the sugar, syrup and cream together until it forms a soft ball when
a small amount is dropped in cold water (236°).
Remove from heat and beat until creamy.
Divide into 3 parts.
Add the nuts to one, the coconut to another and the melted chocolate to
the third.
Knead each part until it is smooth and free from lumps.
Place 1 layer above the other in a flat, greased pan.
Sprinkle with chopped nuts.
This can be sliced as desired. It improves with age.

MRS. ELMER J. KING, *West Liberty, Ohio*

## Candied Grapefruit Rind

| | |
|---|---|
| 1 pound grapefruit rind | 1 pound sugar |

Cut grapefruit rind in strips ½ inch wide.
Partially cover with water.
Bring to a boil and cook for 20 minutes. Drain.

Add clear water and cook again.

Repeat this procedure until the rind is tender.

Add sugar after last cooking and cook until rind is clear.

Drain and roll in sugar.

RUTH ANN SHARP, *Greenwood, Del.*

## Caramel Candy

| | |
|---|---|
| 2 cups sugar | 1 can evaporated milk (15 oz.) |
| 2 cups syrup | 1 teaspoon vanilla |
| ½ cup butter | 1 cup chopped nuts |
| ⅛ teaspoon salt | |

Bring sugar and syrup to a boil.

Add butter and salt.

When the boiling point has been reached again, add the milk slowly in a fine stream.

Keep bubbling, but do not cook rapidly.

Stir constantly to prevent scorching.

Cook syrup to 244° or until it makes a firm ball when dropped in cold water.

Remove from heat and add vanilla and chopped nuts.

Set in a pan of cold water to stop the cooking.

When slightly cooled, pour into a buttered pan 5 x 10 inches.

Mark with a heavy knife while slightly warm into 1 inch squares.

Let stand overnight and then wrap in waxed paper.

Care must be taken to prevent scorching while cooking.

MRS. SIMON GINGERICH, *Goshen, Ind.*

## Chocolate Fudge

| | |
|---|---|
| 2 cups sugar | 2 tablespoons butter |
| 2 tablespoons corn syrup | 1 teaspoon vanilla |
| ¾ cup milk | 1 cup chopped nuts |
| 2 squares chocolate | |

Cook sugar, syrup, milk and chocolate together until it forms a soft ball when dropped in cold water (236°).

Remove from heat and add butter.

Cool until you can hold your hand on the bottom of the pan (112°).

Add vanilla and nuts and beat until creamy.

Pour into buttered pan 4 x 8 inches.

Mark into squares and cool.

This is a creamy, moist and delicious fudge.

MRS. H. D. ALDERFER, MRS. NATHAN KEYSER, *Souderton, Pa.*
MRS. SAMUEL NAFZIGER, *Kalona, Iowa*

## Jiffy Chocolate Fudge (Uncooked)

| | |
|---|---|
| 15 oz. can condensed milk | 1 teaspoon vanilla |
| 2 (7 oz.) packages semisweet chocolate | 1 cup chopped nuts |
| 1/8 teaspoon salt | |

Melt the chocolate in the top of double boiler. Add salt.

Add condensed milk and stir until well blended.

Remove from heat and add vanilla and nuts.

Pour into a flat, buttered pan 5 x 10 inches.

Chill for 2 to 3 hours. When firm, cut into squares.

Makes approximately 2 pounds.

MRS. FRANK H. HERSHEY, *Kinzers, Pa.;* KATIE RUTT, *New Holland, Pa.*

## Chocolate Fudge Roll

| | |
|---|---|
| 2 cups sugar | 2 tablespoons flour |
| 3 tablespoons butter | 1 cup water |
| 4 tablespoons cocoa | 1 teaspoon vanilla |
| 1/8 teaspoon salt | |

Combine sugar, cocoa, salt and flour.

Add water and cook until syrup forms a soft ball when dropped in cold water (236°).

Remove from heat and add butter and vanilla.

Pour into a greased pan and cool without stirring until it is lukewarm (112°).

Beat until stiff and then knead until soft and creamy.

Shape into a roll and store in refrigerator.

Slice as desired.

MRS. DON KREIDER, *Wadsworth, Ohio*

## Chocolate Pineapple Fudge

| | |
|---|---|
| 2 cups granulated sugar | 1 cup rich milk |
| 2 cups brown sugar | 1/2 cup chopped nuts |
| 1/2 cup pineapple juice | |

Cook sugar, pineapple juice and milk together until it forms a soft ball when dropped in cold water (236°).

Remove from heat and add chopped nuts.

Cool to lukewarm and beat until creamy.

Put in a flat, buttered pan.

When cold, cut in squares.

MRS. FLOYD NEWCOMER, *Seville, Ohio*

## Chocolate Caramels

| | |
|---|---|
| 1 cup granulated sugar | 5 tablespoons cocoa or |
| 1 cup brown sugar | 2 squares chocolate |
| 1 cup milk | ½ cup sifted flour |
| 1 cup molasses | 1 teaspoon vanilla |
| 1½ tablespoons butter | |

Mix together the sugar, molasses and milk.

Cook on medium heat for 10 minutes and add cocoa or chocolate and flour.

Continue cooking until syrup forms a firm ball when dropped in cold water (246°).

Stir constantly to prevent scorching.

Pour into flat, buttered pan; when cool cut into squares.

Roll in confectioner's sugar if desired.

ANNA LONGACRE, *Spring City, Pa.;* GRANDMOTHER SENSENIG, *Oley, Pa.*

## Chocolate Graham Fudge

| | |
|---|---|
| 2 squares chocolate | 1¾ cups graham cracker crumbs |
| 14 oz. can sweetened condensed milk | 1 cup chopped nuts |
| ½ teaspoon vanilla | |

Melt chocolate in top of double boiler.

Add condensed milk slowly and bring to a boil.

Stir constantly, cooking until mixture thickens.

Remove from heat.

Add vanilla, crumbs and one-half of nuts.

Spread one-half of remaining nuts in the bottom of a buttered pan.

Spread fudge on top of nuts and sprinkle with remaining nuts.

Let stand overnight and cut in squares.

MRS. PAUL FETROW, *Camp Hill, Pa.*

## Chocolate Drop Candies

| | |
|---|---|
| ½ cup riced or mashed potatoes | ½ cup shredded coconut |
| 3 cups powdered sugar | ½ cup walnuts |
| ½ cup seedless raisins, chopped | 1 teaspoon vanilla |
| ½ cup chopped dates | 1 brick dipping chocolate (8 oz.) |

Mix all the ingredients and shape into small balls.

Melt the dipping chocolate by placing it in the top of a double boiler.

Dip the balls into the melted chocolate and drop on waxed paper.

VILLINA CRESSMAN, *Waterloo, Ont., Can.*

## Coconut Candy

1½ cups brown sugar
3 cups granulated sugar
1 1/3 cups milk

1 teaspoon butter
1 small coconut, grated or ground
1 teaspoon vanilla

Grind or grate the fresh coconut.
Mix sugar, milk and butter together.
Stir until sugar is dissolved.
When the mixture comes to a boil, add coconut.
Cook until a soft ball forms when dropped in cold water (236°).
Remove from heat and add vanilla.
Pour into a flat, buttered pan.
Cut into squares when cold.

## Coconut Fudge Roll or Patties

2 cups granulated sugar
2 cups brown sugar
1 1/3 cups thin cream
4 tablespoons light syrup
2 teaspoons vanilla

1½ squares chocolate, melted
1 tablespoon butter
1½ cups grated coconut
1 cup chopped nuts

Combine sugar, syrup, cream and melted chocolate.
Cook until it forms a soft ball when dropped in cold water (236°).
Remove from heat and add butter.
Let cool until lukewarm, add coconut, nuts and vanilla.
Beat until creamy.
Drop on waxed paper or shape into rolls.
Roll in coconut and chill.
Slice with a sharp knife.

MRS. NOAH J. ROTH, *Canby, Ore.*; MRS. ADOLF JOHNSON, *Sweet Home, Ore.*

## Coconut-Potato Fudge (Uncooked)

2 medium-sized potatoes
4 tablespoons melted butter
½ pound shredded coconut

2 pounds confectioner's sugar
2 teaspoons vanilla
4 squares sweet chocolate (4 ounces)

Cook potatoes until soft and rub through sieve or ricer.
Add melted butter and confectioner's sugar.
Mix together well and then add coconut and vanilla.
Beat until creamy.
Pour into a flat, buttered tin.
When set, pour over it the melted chocolate.
Let stand 2 hours. Cut into squares.

ANNA MARY STALTER, *Elida, Ohio*

## Cracker Jack

| | |
|---|---|
| 1 cup sorghum molasses | 1 tablespoon butter |
| 1 cup sugar | 1/4 teaspoon soda |
| 1 teaspoon vinegar | 5 quarts popped corn |
| 2 tablespoons water | 1 cup peanuts |

Mix sugar, molasses, butter, water and vinegar together.

Cook until it makes a hard ball when dropped in cold water (265°).

Stir frequently during last part of cooking to prevent scorching.

Remove from heat and add soda.

Stir lightly. While it still foams, pour over the popcorn mix.

Pour into a flat, buttered pan. When cool, crumble into small pieces.

MRS. WILLIAM F. GEISER, *Apple Creek, Ohio*
MRS. NORMAN M. YODER, *Stuarts Draft, Va.*

## Date Loaf Candy

| | |
|---|---|
| 3 cups sugar | 1 1/2 cups chopped dates |
| 1 cup milk | 1 cup walnuts or pecans, chopped |
| 1 tablespoon butter | 1 teaspoon vanilla |

Cook sugar, milk and butter together until syrup forms a very soft ball when dropped in cold water (236°).

Add chopped dates and cook for 3 minutes longer.

Remove from heat and cool to lukewarm temperature.

Add nuts and vanilla. Beat until creamy.

Turn out on a damp cloth and roll.

Slice when cold.

MRS. OTTO SAYLOR, *Holsopple, Pa.;* MRS. WALTER BURKHOLDER, *Harrisonburg, Va.*

## Divinity Candy

| | |
|---|---|
| 3 cups sugar | 3 egg whites |
| 1 cup white syrup | 1 cup chopped nuts |
| 1/2 cup hot water | 1 teaspoon vanilla |

Cook sugar, syrup and water together until syrup forms a hard ball when dropped in cold water (265°). Do not stir after sugar is dissolved.

Pour syrup slowly over the stiffly beaten egg whites.

Beat until creamy, add chopped nuts and vanilla.

Pour in buttered pans and cut into squares or drop from spoon onto waxed paper.

MARIE BRUNK, *Delphos, Ohio;* MRS. ELSIE MISHLER, *Sheridan, Ore.*

## English Toffee

| | |
|---|---|
| 1¼ cups brown sugar | ¾ cup chopped nuts |
| 1 cup butter | 1 cup Hershey's sweet chocolate bar, chopped |

Combine sugar and butter and cook until a hard ball is formed when syrup is dropped in cold water (265°).

Place finely chopped nuts in bottom of greased pan.

Pour syrup over nuts, making a layer ¼ inch thick.

While hot, add Hershey bar broken in small pieces.

Spread with knife and sprinkle with chopped nuts.

Chill and break into desired shapes.

Mrs. R. J. Rich, *Washington, Ill.*

## Fondant

| | |
|---|---|
| 2 cups sugar | 2 tablespoons white syrup |
| 2/3 cup water | 4 tablespoons marshmallow crème |
| ⅛ teaspoon salt | 1 teaspoon vanilla |

Combine sugar, salt and water. Add syrup.

Stir only until sugar is dissolved.

Be careful not to get any sugar crystals from sides of the pan into syrup as it cooks.

Keep cover on pan part time so steam will keep crystals from forming.

Cook until syrup forms a soft ball when dropped in cold water (236°).

Pour on a greased platter and do not disturb until you can hold your hand on the bottom of the plate (112°).

Add vanilla and stir.

Place marshmallow crème in mixing bowl and pour cooled syrup over it.

Stir or knead until fondant becomes perfectly smooth.

Work into a ball, wrap in wax paper and allow to ripen in a tightly covered jar for at least 24 hours.

This may be used as filling for chocolate creams, or a base for nuts and fruits, or as mint patties.

Mrs. Jacob Stoltzfus, *Belleville, Pa.*

## Fruit Candy (I)

| | |
|---|---|
| 1 pound dates | 1 pound confectioner's sugar |
| 1 pound raisins | ½ pound dipping chocolate |
| ½ pound peanuts | |

Chop or grind dates, raisins and peanuts.

Mix with powdered sugar and press with hands into a buttered pan.

Cover with melted chocolate and cut in squares.

MRS. MILTON FALB, *Orrville, Ohio*

## Fruit Candy (II)

| | |
|---|---|
| 3 cups sugar | 1½ cups nuts |
| 1 cup thin cream | 1 pound figs |
| 1 tablespoon butter | 1 pound dates |
| 1 pound raisins | 1 pound coconut |
| 1 teaspoon vanilla | |

Cook sugar, cream and butter together until syrup forms a soft ball
   when dropped in cold water.

Remove from heat and beat until creamy.

Mix finely chopped fruits and nuts and add to candy.

Work together and shape into rolls.

Wrap in a damp cloth and let ripen 2 weeks before using.

MRS. SUSIE KNOPP, *Salem, Ohio*

## Hoarhound Candy (I)

| | |
|---|---|
| 3½ pounds brown sugar | 3 ounces hoarhound |
| 3 cups hot water | |

Add hoarhound to hot water and cook about 20 minutes. Strain.

Add sugar and cook until syrup forms a hard ball when dropped in cold
   water (265°).

Pour into a greased pan.

When cool, form into small balls or cut into squares.

MRS. WILLIAM F. GEISER, *Apple Creek, Ohio*

## Hoarhound Candy (II)

| | |
|---|---|
| 2 cups sugar | 1 cup boiling water |
| ½ cup syrup | 1 teaspoon hoarhound tea leaves |
| ¼ cup honey | 1 tablespoon vinegar |
| 1 tablespoon butter | |

Mix sugar, syrup and honey together.

Pour boiling water over tea leaves and let steep 5 minutes.

Strain tea and add to sugar mixture.

Cook until syrup forms a hard ball when dropped in cold water (265°).

Add vinegar and butter and pour on buttered plates to cool.

While slightly warm, mark in squares with the back of a knife.

MRS. LYDIA GREISER, *Archbold, Ohio*

## Ice Cream Candy

2 cups sugar  
1 cup water  
1 teaspoon cream of tartar  

1 teaspoon vanilla  
1 tablespoon butter  

Combine sugar and water and bring to a boil.

Dissolve cream of tartar in a little water and add.

Cook until syrup forms a hard ball when dropped in cold water (265°).

Remove from heat and add vanilla.

When cooled, pull like taffy until snowy white.

MRS. ETHEL LAHMAN, *Harrisonburg, Va.*

## January Goodies

½ cup sugar  
1/3 cup molasses  

1/3 cup water  
1/3 cup butter  

Combine ingredients and cook until syrup forms a hard ball when dropped in cold water (265°).

Pour on buttered plates and cut in squares.

MRS. WILLIAM F. GEISER, *Apple Creek, Ohio*

## Marshmallow Candy

3 tablespoons plain gelatin  
½ cup cold water  
⅛ teaspoon salt  

3 cups sugar  
1 cup water  
1 teaspoon vanilla  

Soak gelatin in ½ cup cold water for 20 minutes.

Combine sugar with 1 cup water and bring to a boil (236°).

Cook syrup until it forms a soft ball in cold water.

Remove from heat and add to gelatin.

Beat for 20 minutes.

Add vanilla and salt.

Pour on buttered tins, making a layer ⅜ inch thick.

When cold, cut in squares and roll in confectioner's sugar or shredded coconut.

MRS. JOSEPH D. HEATWOLE, *Bridgewater, Va.*  
MRS. FRANK VAN PELT, *Columbiana, Ohio*

## Maple Candy

3 cups brown sugar or maple sugar  
1 cup cream  

1 teaspoon maple flavoring  
1 cup nuts, chopped  

Combine sugar and cream and cook until it forms a soft ball in cold water (236°).

Cool to lukewarm and beat until creamy.
Add nuts and flavoring.
Turn into buttered pans and mark in squares.

SYLVIA LEHMAN, *Orrville, Ohio*

## Mashed Potato Candy

½ cup mashed potatoes          ½ cup peanut butter
I pound confectioner's sugar

Mix warm mashed potatoes with sifted sugar.
Roll out in an oblong shape and spread with peanut butter.
Roll up like a jelly roll and cut in slices.

MRS. EDGAR CLINE, *Broadway, Va.*

## Mexican Orange Candy

3 cups sugar                   Grated rind of 2 oranges
1½ cups top milk               I cup nuts
½ cup butter

Melt 1 cup sugar in a heavy pan and let turn a golden brown. Stir
    constantly.
Scald milk and add the caramelized sugar.
Stir until sugar is melted.
Add remaining sugar and cook until syrup forms a firm ball (not hard)
    when dropped in cold water (246°).
Add grated orange rind, salt, butter and nuts.
Beat until creamy.
Pour into buttered pans and mark in squares.

MARY VAN PELT, *Columbiana, Ohio*

## Nut-Coated Marshmallows

3 cups chopped nuts            2/3 cup water
2 cups brown sugar             1½ pounds fresh marshmallows
½ teaspoon salt

Chop nuts very fine and mix with salt.
Boil sugar and water together until it forms a soft ball when dropped in
    cold water (236°).
Remove from heat and set in a large pan of hot water.
Brush loose powder from marshmallows and drop one at a time into
    hot syrup.
When coated on all sides, lift out and drain.

Roll in chopped nuts and place on waxed paper.
If syrup becomes too thick, reheat but do not boil.

MRS. CLARENCE WHISSEN, *Broadway, Va.*

## Old-Fashioned Molasses Nut Candy

| | |
|---|---|
| 2 cups brown sugar | I cup chopped nuts |
| I cup molasses | I tablespoon vinegar |
| I tablespoon butter | 1/8 teaspoon soda |

Combine ingredients (except nuts) and cook until syrup forms a hard
ball when dropped in cold water (265°).
Remove from heat and add soda. Stir well.
Add nuts and pour into buttered pans.
Mark into squares.

MRS. HARRY A. DERSTINE, *Souderton, Pa.*

## Old-Fashioned Taffy

| | |
|---|---|
| I cup molasses | 2 tablespoons butter |
| I cup sugar | I teaspoon soda |
| I cup thin cream | I cup finely chopped nuts (optional) |

Combine molasses, sugar and cream and bring to a boil.
Cook until it forms a firm ball when dropped in cold water (252° F).
Remove from heat and add butter and soda.
Add chopped nuts. Stir well.
Pour onto buttered plates and cool until it can be cut into small
squares about ⅓ inch in diameter. This taffy is not pulled.

MRS. RUTH STAUFFER, *Harrisonburg, Va.*

## Old-Fashioned Slap Jack

| | |
|---|---|
| I quart sorghum molasses | I tablespoon butter |
| 2 pounds white sugar | |

Combine ingredients and cook until syrup forms a hard ball when
dropped in cold water (265°).
Pour into buttered pans and let cool until it can be pulled.
Butter hands slightly and rub with wintergreen flavoring.
Pull until stiff. Shape as desired and cut into suitable lengths with
scissors.

MRS. HARRY A. DERSTINE, *Souderton, Pa.*

## Peanut Brittle

| | |
|---|---|
| 2 cups sugar | 1 teaspoon butter, melted |
| 1 cup white syrup | 1 teaspoon soda |
| ½ cup water | 1 teaspoon vanilla |
| 3 cups raw peanuts | |

Combine sugar, syrup and water.

Cook to the soft-ball stage (236°).

Add peanuts and melted butter and continue cooking until syrup is a golden brown (290°). Stir during last few minutes of cooking.

Remove from heat and add soda and vanilla.

Stir until mixture thickens.

Pour into buttered tins and break into pieces when cold.

If roasted peanuts are used, add to syrup before removing from heat.

Mrs. M. T. Brackbill, *Harrisonburg, Va.*; Mrs. Paul Maust, *Montgomery, Ind.*

## Peanut Butter Fudge (Uncooked)

| | |
|---|---|
| ½ cup peanut butter | ¼ cup chopped nuts |
| 2/3 cup condensed milk | 2 squares baking chocolate (2 ounces) |
| 1¾ cup confectioner's sugar | |

Mix peanut butter, milk and melted chocolate.

Add sugar and nuts.

Knead with hands and shape into a roll 1 inch in diameter.

Wrap in wax paper and store in refrigerator 4 to 5 days.

Slice in rings and serve.

Mrs. Kent Shank, *Harrisonburg, Va.*

## Peanut Butter Candy

| | |
|---|---|
| ¾ cup thin cream | 3 tablespoons peanut butter |
| 2 cups brown sugar | 1 teaspoon vanilla |

Combine ingredients and cook until it forms a soft ball when dropped in cold water (236°).

Remove from heat, cool to lukewarm and beat until creamy.

Pour into buttered pans and cut in squares.

Mrs. Jacob D. Showalter, *Broadway, Va.*

## Popcorn Balls

| | |
|---|---|
| 5 quarts popped corn | 1/3 teaspoon salt |
| 2 cups sugar | 1 teaspoon vanilla |
| 1½ cups water | 1 tablespoon vinegar |
| ½ cup white corn syrup | |

Pop the corn and remove the hard kernels.

Combine sugar, syrup and water. Bring to a boil, stirring only until sugar is dissolved.

Cook until it forms a hard ball when dropped in cold water (270°).

Add vinegar, salt and vanilla and blend into mixture.

Pour hot syrup slowly over the corn, stirring so that each kernel may be evenly coated.

Shape into balls and let stand in a cool place.

Each ball may be wrapped in wax paper if desired.

Peanuts may be added.

MARGARET LAMBERTSON, *Pocomoke City, Md.;* MRS. BYARD EARLY, *Dayton, Va.*

### Chocolate Popcorn Balls

| | |
|---|---|
| 1½ cups sugar | 1/3 cup sorghum molasses |
| ½ cup corn syrup | 3 tablespoons butter |
| 2/3 cup water | 3 squares chocolate (3 ounces) |
| 1 teaspoon vanilla | 4 quarts popped corn, slightly salted |

Combine sugar, syrup and water.

Cook to hard-ball stage (270°).

Add molasses and butter and cook until brittle stage is reached (280°).

Remove from heat and add melted chocolate and vanilla.

Pour over popped corn and mix together well.

Shape into balls.

MRS. HENRY E. YODER, *Grantsville, Md.*

### Sugared Popcorn

| | |
|---|---|
| 2 cups sugar | 2 tablespoons butter |
| 1 cup water | 5 quarts popped corn |

Combine sugar, water, and butter.

Cook until syrup forms a hard ball when dropped in cold water (265°).

Pour over popped corn and stir until each kernel is coated evenly with syrup.

Coloring and flavoring may be added if desired.

FRANCES AMSTUTZ, *Dalton, Ohio*

### Puffed Rice Balls

| | |
|---|---|
| ½ cup corn syrup | 2 tablespoons vinegar |
| ½ cup molasses | 6 cups puffed rice |
| 2 tablespoons butter | 1 cup nuts, chopped |

Mix nuts and puffed rice together.

Combine syrup, molasses, butter and vinegar.

Cook to hard-ball stage.

Pour over puffed rice and mix together.

Shape into balls and let cool.

Mrs. Alvin Witmer, Hartville, Ohio

## Puffed Rice Candy

2 cups sugar
1 cup water
4 tablespoons molasses

2 teaspoons vinegar
2 tablespoons butter
1 small package puffed rice (3½ oz.)

Combine sugar, water, molasses, vinegar and butter and bring to a boil.

Cook syrup until it forms a hard ball when dropped in cold water (265°).

Add puffed rice and mix together.

Pour onto buttered platters and cool. Cut in squares.

Mrs. Raymond Nace, Souderton, Pa.; Mary L. Guntz, Phoenixville, Pa.

## Sea Foam Candy

2 cups brown sugar
½ cup water

2 egg whites
¼ cup English walnut halves

Combine water and sugar and cook until syrup forms a hard ball when dropped in cold water (265°).

Remove from heat and add stiffly beaten egg whites.

Beat until thick and creamy.

Drop from a spoon on greased plates or wax paper. Do not scrape bottom of pan.

Press a half of English walnut on each piece.

Mrs. Emma K. Hursh, Parkesburg, Pa.

## Taffy

1 cup sugar
1 cup honey or syrup

⅛ teaspoon salt
1 tablespoon butter

Combine ingredients and cook until syrup forms a hard ball when dropped in cold water (265°).

Pour onto buttered plates and cool until it can be pulled.

Butter hands slightly and pull until stiff. Cut in desired shapes.

Mrs. Alice Hartman, Elida, Ohio

## Salt Water Taffy

1 cup corn syrup
2 cups sugar
¾ cup water

1 tablespoon cornstarch
1 tablespoon butter
1 teaspoon salt

Combine ingredients and cook until syrup forms a hard ball when dropped in cold water.

Remove from heat and pour onto buttered plates.

When cool enough to handle, pull until a golden brown.

Cut in desired shapes.

MRS. SIMON MARTIN, *Kitchener, Ont., Can.*

## Spearmint Candy

2 cups sugar
½ cup white syrup
½ cup water

I egg white
½ teaspoon spearmint extract

Combine ingredients, except egg white, and cook until syrup forms a hard ball when dropped in cold water (265°).

Remove from heat and add gradually to beaten egg white. Add flavoring.

Beat until creamy.

Drop from a spoon on waxed paper.

KATIE RUTT, *New Holland, Pa.*

## Stuffed Dates

2 cups seeded dates

½ cup almonds, pecans or walnuts

Chop nuts very fine.

Stuff each date with nuts.

Roll in confectioner's sugar.

MARGARET LAMBERTSON, *Pocomoke City, Md.*

## Turkish Delight

3 tablespoons gelatin
½ cup cold water
2 cups sugar
½ cup hot water

Grated rind and juice of I lemon
Grated rind and juice of I orange
I cup nuts (optional)
Red or green food coloring

Soften gelatin in cold water.

Combine sugar and hot water and heat to boiling.

Cook for 10 minutes and add gelatin.

Simmer slowly for another 10 minutes.

Add fruit juice and rind and red or green coloring as desired.

Strain into a loaf pan, large enough that the depth of the mixture will be approximately 1 inch.

Add chopped nuts if desired.

Chill until firm and cut into squares.
Roll in confectioner's sugar.

ADA ALDERFER, *Souderton, Pa.*

## Vinegar Candy

2 cups sugar 2 tablespoons butter
½ cup vinegar

Combine ingredients and cook until mixture is brittle when dropped in
  cold water (270°).
Pour onto buttered plates.
Mark into squares while warm or roll into small balls.
This is an excellent hard candy.
An old family favorite.

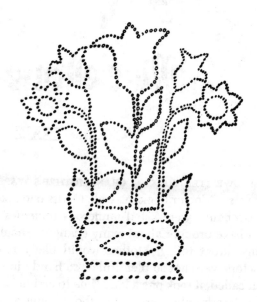

# Miscellaneous

## Chapter XVI

THAT OLD HANDWRITTEN BOOK OF GRANDMOTHER'S WAS MORE THAN A recipe book; it was a "doctor book" as well. On its back pages under the heading of "miscellany" were listed numerous remedies for many ills. Again the years have brought about many changes. Should Junior get a fish bone in his throat today, Mother would likely rush him to the doctor. But doctors were not so plentiful or so handy in Grandmother's time, and when called, it took one a long time to arrive in the horse-and-buggy days. So Grandmother resorted to those home remedies listed in the back of her book. The lodged fish bone in Benny's throat was simple enough to remove by her remedy; he merely had to swallow a raw egg!

Along with these remedies were many helpful suggestions to use on the farm or in the house. It was no doubt very helpful for Grandpa to "know how to get at the weight of cattle" in the absence of scales. An old book said, "If the animal girths five feet, it will weigh between 700 and 750 pounds." It must have helped Grandma, too, in dyeing rags for rugs, to know how many ounces of cochineal to add to oxalic acid, in order to make them red. Since we buy most of our dyes and medicines today, these old recipes hold little more than historical value.

It is difficult, however, to plan a cookbook without having a chapter for miscellaneous recipes. As in Grandma's book, so in the back of this one you will find some oft-used recipes that do not rightfully belong in any of the preceding chapters. Many of our farm families make home-made soap, using their collection of meat scraps and fats. Some families do not have access to lockers and still enjoy dried and canned corn. There are also folks who will appreciate knowing how to clean wall-paper and to make simple hand lotions. These recipes, along with others, are to be found in this chapter.

## Homemade Grape Nuts

3½ cups graham flour  
1 cup brown sugar or  
  ¾ cup syrup  
2 cups buttermilk or sour milk  
1 teaspoon salt  
1 teaspoon soda  

Sift flour.  
Measure and add soda and salt.  
Sift again.  
Add sugar to flour and mix thoroughly.  
Add buttermilk to dry ingredients.  
Beat until smooth.  
Spread dough ¼ inch thick on flat, greased pans.  
Bake at 375° for approximately 15 minutes or until crisp and a golden brown.  
Let cool thoroughly and grind through a food chopper.  
Crisp in oven just before serving.

Mrs. J. M. Brenneman, *Elida, Ohio;* Mrs. Alva Swartzentruber, *Hydro, Okla.*

## To Dry Sweet Corn (I)

3 quarts fresh corn  
½ cup sugar  
¼ cup salt (scant)  
2 tablespoons flour  
½ cup cream  

Cut fresh corn off the cobs.  
Combine sugar, salt and flour and mix thoroughly.  
Add dry ingredients to corn and blend together.

Add cream and mix thoroughly.

Spread corn in thin layers and dry in a slow oven (250°).

Stir frequently.

When corn is thoroughly dried, store in tight containers.

Mrs. Paul Maust, *Montgomery, Ind.*

## To Dry Sweet Corn (II)

Cook corn on cob for 3 minutes.

Cut off and spread on flat pans to dry.

Dry in slow oven (250°), stirring frequently.

When thoroughly dry, place in sterilized jars and seal.

Corn prepared in this way keeps well.

Mrs. H. D. H. Showalter, *Broadway, Va.*

## To Dry Hay Beans

Wash and string green beans.

Hull kernels from older beans.

Break or cut green beans in 1 inch lengths.

Cook beans for 20-30 minutes or until green color disappears.

Spread beans in thin layers in flat pans.

Dry in the sun or in a slow oven (250°) until thoroughly dry.

Place dried beans in a cloth bag and tie to rafters as Grandmother did or store in sealed cans.

Beans may also be dried without preliminary cooking.

Place in pans and dry in sun or in attic.

These require a longer drying period.

From Grandmother's Book

## To Hull Corn for Hominy

| | |
|---|---|
| 1 quart shelled corn | 2 tablespoons soda |
| 2 quarts cold water | |

Wash corn thoroughly.

Add soda and water and soak overnight.

In the morning, bring to a boil in the same water in which corn has soaked.

Cook for 3 hours or until hulls loosen.

Add more water as necessary during the cooking process.

Drain off water and wash corn in clear water, rubbing vigorously until all the hulls are removed.

Bring to a boil again in clear water and drain off water.

Repeat this again. Drain.

Add salt, 1 teaspoon to each quart of hominy.

Use an enamel kettle for cooking hominy; do not use aluminum.

MRS. ELLA ROHRER, *Wadsworth, Ohio*

## Liquor for Canning Stuffed Sausage

| | |
|---|---|
| 1 gallon boiling water | ½ cup sugar |
| ¾ cup salt | 1 clove garlic |

Dissolve sugar and salt in boiling water and bring to boiling point.

Add sausage and garlic and cook for 30 minutes.

Pack sausage in sterilized jars and cover with boiling liquid.

This is enough liquid to cover 10 quarts of sausage.

MRS. SAMUEL NAFZIGER, *Kalona, Iowa*

## How to Keep Raisins from Getting Sugary

Wash raisins in hot water 2 or 3 times.

Drain thoroughly.

Place a cloth on baking sheet and spread raisins on cloth.

Let stand 2 days and then remove cloth.

Put in a slow oven (250°) to dry for one hour.

Pack in sterilized jars and seal tightly.

Raisins prepared in this way will keep for years.

MRS. JESSE J. SHORT, *Archbold, Ohio*

## Homemade Hand Lotion

| | |
|---|---|
| ½ gill glycerin | ¼ ounce gum tragacanth |
| ½ gill alcohol | ½ gill cologne |

Dissolve gum in 1 cup lukewarm water.

Soft water should be used.

Let stand 24 hours or until it gels, and add other ingredients.

Shake well and dilute with warm soft water until the desired consistency is obtained.

MRS. GEORGE S. BAST, *Wellesley, Ont., Can.;* MRS. IRA EIGSTI, *Buda, Ill.*

## A Good Remedy for Worms on Cabbage

Use a gallon tin can with tight-fitting lid.

Punch bottom of can full of holes with a nail.

Fill can ¾ full with slaked lime.

Add 2 cups of sifted ashes and mix thoroughly.

Dust cabbage late in the evening or early morning when leaves are
   damp with dew.

Repeat as often as worms appear.

A very inexpensive method that is effective.

MAGGIE DRIVER, *Versailles, Mo.*

## To Clean Silverware

Fill a gallon aluminum kettle ¾ full of water.

Add 3 tablespoons of Ivory or Lux soap flakes.

Bring to boiling point and add silverware.

Cook for 10 minutes.

Remove from water and rinse in hot water.

Rub thoroughly with a soft, dry towel.

This is especially good for pieces of silver difficult to clean.

MRS. LYDIA HESS, *Marion, Pa.*

## Homemade Laundry Soap

| | |
|---|---|
| 16 pounds meat scraps | 7½ gallons water |
| 3 pounds caustic soda or lye | 2 pints salt |

Dissolve caustic soda in water in an iron kettle.

Remove 1¼ gallons of solution in a stone jar.

Add meat scraps to remaining solution and bring to boiling point.

Cook until scraps are dissolved, approximately 2 hours.

Add the 1¼ gallons of solution during cooking period.

Add 2 pints of salt and blend into mixture.

Dip mixture into another kettle to cool or allow to cool in kettle in
   which soap cooked.

When cold and hard, cut in blocks of desired shape and size.

MRS. ALVA SWARTZENTRUBER, *Hydro, Okla.*
MRS. FRANK F. SCHMIDT, *Greensburg, Kan.*

## Cold Laundry Soap

| | |
|---|---|
| 2 quarts strained grease | ½ cup ammonia |
| I can lye (I pound) | 2 tablespoons borax dissolved in |
| I quart water | ½ cup water |

Combine lye and water in a stone jar or earthenware vessel.

Stir until lye is dissolved.

Let lye solution cool and then pour over cooled melted grease.

Stir until lye and grease are thoroughly combined.

Add ammonia and dissolved borax and stir until quite thick (about the
   consistency of honey).

Pour into a granite or earthenware mold.
Let stand several hours, but cut before hard.
Put pieces of soap in a dry place to harden.

MRS. P. L. FREY, *Archbold, Ohio;* MRS. WALTER WEAVER, *Christiana, Pa.*

## Food for a Barn Raising

This bit of information was found in a quaint, old handwritten recipe book from Great-grandmother's day. It is included here mainly for the purpose of giving us a peep into the past. As many of us know, a "barn raising" was quite an event during those early years. When a new barn was built, all the friends and neighbors came on the specified day to help put up the framework of the barn. This policy is still carried out in some communities where neighbors are neighborly. Homemakers of our day will no doubt be astounded at all the food consumed in one day. What is more difficult to believe is that it was all made in Great-grandmother's kitchen.

Here is the list as I found it:

        115 lemon pies
        500 fat cakes (doughnuts)
         15 large cakes
          3 gallons applesauce
          3 gallons rice pudding
          3 gallons cornstarch pudding
         16 chickens
          3 hams
         50 pounds roast beef
        300 light rolls
         16 loaves bread
            Red beet pickle and pickled eggs
            Cucumber pickle
          6 pounds dried prunes, stewed
          1 large crock stewed raisins
          5 gallon stone jar white potatoes and the same amount of sweet potatoes

Enough food for 175 men.

# HOUSEHOLD HINTS

*For the Kitchen*

Dry green celery or parsley leaves until crumbly. Store in covered jars to use as seasoning in soups and fillings.

After rice has been cooked and drained, place a slice of dry bread on top of the rice and cover. The bread will absorb the moisture and the rice will be dry and fluffy.

Before melting chocolate, rub the inside of the pan it is to be melted in with butter. The chocolate will not stick to the pan.

When washing pans and baking dishes to which food has adhered during cooking, turn the pan upside down in steaming, sudsy water. Food will loosen in a very short time.

When cookie dough is soft and difficult to handle, place it between pieces of waxed paper that have been floured. Roll to desired thickness, remove top paper and cut cookies.

To gel fruit juices that are difficult to gel, such as peach juice, add 1½ teaspoons plain gelatin to each cup of juice. Soften gelatin in 3 teaspoons juice and add to remaining hot juice. Add 1 teaspoon lemon juice to each quart of fruit juice.

Before discarding the empty catsup bottle, pour some vinegar into the bottle and use in making French dressing.

Pour melted paraffin on the cut end of cheeses or dried beef to keep them from molding or drying out.

To improve the flavor of green string beans, place 1 or 2 small onions in kettle before adding beans.

Singe chicken or other fowl by holding over burner of oil or gas stove.

When baking whole fish, wrap in well-oiled cheesecloth. When fish is done, it can be lifted from baking pan without falling to pieces. To remove cloth, slip a spatula under fish and slide cloth out after fish is on platter.

When pork or beef liver is tough, run it through a food chopper. Season and drop by spoonfuls into hot frying pan.

Wash fresh pineapples thoroughly before paring. Cover parings with water and cook until soft. Use strained juice for making jelly.

To keep muffins from burning around the edges, fill one section with water instead of batter.

Stick 2 or 3 pieces of macaroni in the center of the top of a double crust pie. The juice bubbles up these sticks and prevents pie from running over.

Do not beat egg whites for cakes or meringue until ready to use. If allowed to stand, some of the white will return to liquid.

To prevent onions from burning your eyes, hold them under water when peeling or slicing them.

## Miscellaneous

To make yellowed piano keys white again, rub them with a cloth dipped in cologne water. Be careful not to touch the black keys.

Add 1 teaspoon of castor oil or 2 tablespoons of olive oil to the roots of your fern every 3 or 4 months to promote their growth.

To prevent clothes from sticking to line on a cold winter day, wipe the line with a cloth moistened with vinegar.

When making a rolled hem, put a row of machine stitching near edge to be rolled. This prevents stretching and aids in speeding up the job.

When watering house plants, use warm water rather than cold. The cold water shocks some plants to the extent that the roots are damaged and growth is retarded.

Do not wring out corduroy after laundering. Hang it up dripping wet, and it will be fluffy after it dries.

When wrapping a package for mailing, dip cord in water to moisten. The cord will shrink as it dries and will make a tighter package.

Do not discard empty pint-size ice cream containers. Clean them thoroughly and paint in bright colors and use them for house plants. These add a decorative note to your windows.

For dusting out corners and crevices, use a new soft paint brush. This is also good for dusting books and bric-a-brac.

Remove chewing gum from chair bottoms or table linens by massaging with an ice cube. Pick off hard gum in small pieces.

To keep scatter rugs from slipping on polished hardwood floors, place old rubber jar rings under each corner; fasten them with adhesive tape.

Place pieces of cloth moistened in camphor in your silverware drawer to help prevent tarnishing.

Remove white marks on your furniture by rubbing them with boiled linseed oil.

If your needle is rusty, push it into a piece of soap several times, and it will come out smooth.

When wooden knitting needles or crochet hooks get rough, paint them with clear nail polish.

Save the empty adhesive tape spool to wind your tape measure on. This will save trying moments caused by a jumbled sewing basket.

Apply a coat of paraffin to the bottom of your flowerpots to prevent them from scratching your table or other pieces of furniture.

To remove paraffin from the tops of jelly glasses, lay a piece of string across the top of glass just long enough to hang over edges and pour hot paraffin over it. When removing paraffin, lift by the ends of the string.

Another way to remove paraffin is to place the top of a milk bottle on the jelly. Leave the pull-up tab raised before pouring paraffin over it. When ready to use, pull by tab and the paraffin can be removed easily.

A cracked flower vase may be sealed so that it is water-tight to cold water by melting paraffin and filling up the cracks.

Remove stubborn sink stains by adding 3 tablespoons of liquid washing compound to 1 quart water. Pour on spots and let stand for several minutes.

To remove starch from an electric iron, heat it to "Rayon" and rub over sheets of waxed paper.

If your basement is dark, paint the bottom basement step with white paint. This will prevent accidents.

To remove a spot from the oven caused by a pie or casserole dish running over, first let the oven cool, then place a cloth on the spot and saturate it with household ammonia. Let soak 2 hours, then rinse.

To give new life and body to a rayon dress that has been laundered a number of times, add 1 teaspoon of plain gelatin to 1 quart of water in the last rinse.

Boiled rice water makes an excellent starch for dainty collars, cuffs and baby dresses.

A small brush with stiff bristles should be kept with your laundry equipment. Use this to brush shirt collars and other soiled pieces of clothing.

When drying chenille bedspreads, turn tufts inside. These will rub together while flapping in the breeze and will become soft and fluffy.

An interesting way to serve a meal to a convalescing child is to use a bright muffin pan. In a 6 compartment pan there is 1 place for a glass of milk, 4 places for food and another compartment for flowers.

# INDEX